The
Uses and Abuses
of
Weaponized
Interdependence

The
Uses and Abuses
of
Weaponized
Interdependence

Edited by
DANIEL W. DREZNER
HENRY FARRELL
ABRAHAM L. NEWMAN

BROOKINGS INSTITUTION PRESS
Washington, D.C.

The Brookings Institution is a private nonprofit organization devoted to research, education, and publication on important issues of domestic and foreign policy. Its principal purpose is to bring the highest quality independent
research and analysis to bear on current and emerging policy problems. Interpretations or conclusions in Brookings publications should be understood to be
solely those of the authors.

Library of Congress Control Number: 2020948886
ISBN 9780815738374 (pbk)
ISBN 9780815738381 (ebook)

9 8 7 6 5 4 3 2 1

Typeset in Sabon

Composition by Elliott Beard

Contents

II
FINANCE

III
TECH

IV
ENERGY

V
STATE-OWNED NETWORKS

VI
RESPONSES TO WEAPONIZED INTERDEPENDENCE

1

Introduction

The Uses and Abuses of Weaponized Interdependence

DANIEL W. DREZNER

Weaponized interdependence (WI) is defined as a condition under which an actor can exploit its position in an embedded network to gain a bargaining advantage over others in a contained system. In their 2019 *International Security* paper, Henry Farrell and Abraham Newman argue that WI challenges long-standing ways that international relations experts think about globalization.[1] States with political authority over central economic nodes "can weaponize networks to gather information or choke off economic and information flows, discover and exploit vulnerabilities, compel policy change, and deter unwanted actions."[2] This formulation compels scholars and practitioners alike to think differently about foreign economic policy, national security, and grand strategy for the twenty-first century.

To understand the ways in which weaponized interdependence affects U.S. foreign policy, let's start with TikTok.

TikTok is a mobile phone app that allows users to share short, mostly amusing videos to social media platforms. According to its website, TikTok's mission "is to inspire creativity and bring joy." Less than three years after its 2016 launch, it was one of the most downloaded apps in the United States, achieving a faster adoption rate than Instagram.

TikTok also attracted the attention of CFIUS, the Committee on Foreign Investment in the United States. Why was CFIUS, an inter-agency body tasked with defending the national security interests of the United States in foreign acquisitions of U.S. firms, interested in a video app? One reason is that a Chinese social media company named ByteDance created it. In 2017, ByteDance acquired Musical.ly, a U.S. firm with millions of users for its music app. ByteDance rebranded the app as TikTok and used Muscial.ly's subscriber base to expand rapidly into the U.S. market. That takeover triggered CFIUS's inter-est. Over the past five years, CFIUS has paid increasing attention to foreign purchases of tech and data firms. A prior CFIUS investigation forced Chinese owners to divest the purchase of app companies like Grindr.[3]

Why would CFIUS care about foreign ownership of Grindr or TikTok? While there were allegations that TikTok censored content critical of China, that was not CFIUS's motivation.[4] The commit-tee was interested because social media firms affect national security through the trove of personal data that their subscribers provide to use the service. Policymakers are concerned about whether the Chinese government would ever compel ByteDance into sharing that data. A coauthor of the 2018 law expanding CFIUS's powers explained, "It's about the underlying distrust of the Chinese government and what, theoretically, they could do with this data."[5]

TikTok's owners and managers repeatedly denied that they would hand over any data to the Chinese government.[6] This did not as-suage the concerns of U.S. policymakers. In the fall of 2019, Senators Chuck Schumer and Tom Cotton jointly requested that U.S. intelli-gence officials investigate whether TikTok posed a national security threat, saying in a letter, "With over 110 million downloads in the U.S. alone, TikTok is a potential counterintelligence threat we cannot ignore."[7] By the summer of 2020, President Trump had announced his intention to ban TikTok unless ByteDance sold the firm to a U.S. corporation. That the Chinese government could exploit TikTok as a panopticon to harvest information about the United States proved to be a rare source of bipartisan concern.

The parable of TikTok is emblematic of mounting U.S. concerns that great power rivals such as China and Russia are weaponizing rising levels of economic interdependence. In the case of Russia, the concern comes from Moscow's control over Eurasian energy infrastructure, particularly gas pipelines. As far back as the 1990s, the Russian Federation exploited its control over the pipelines to coerce other post-Soviet states into policy concessions.[8] Russia continued to use gas cutoffs as a means of influencing its vulnerable neighbors into the 2000s.[9] Gazprom, the Russian state natural gas company, has spent the past decade expanding its network, constructing the Nord Stream 2 and TurkStream pipelines to boost exports to Western and Southern Europe.[10] As a result, U.S. officials have expressed concerns that energy dependence on Russia will increase Europe's vulnerability to economic pressure.[11]

Fears of China are even more outsized, with U.S. officials worrying that China's Belt and Road Initiative (BRI) could create path-dependent financial and transit networks in which recipient countries are at the mercy of China's largesse. The Center for Global Development dubbed this "debt-trap diplomacy."[12] A bipartisan 2018 letter from fifteen U.S. senators asserted, "The goal for BRI is the creation of an economic world order ultimately dominated by China." That same year the secretary of the navy warned that China was "weaponizing capital" with BRI.[13]

The United States has also attempted to block Chinese telecom firms Huawei and ZTE from dominating the global network standard for 5G, the next generation of cellular network technology offering broadband access. The Trump administration has claimed that the Chinese government will exploit Huawei and ZTE's role in any 5G network to gain covert access to confidential or sensitive data, compromising national security. Beginning in 2018, the federal government imposed a series of import controls and law enforcement measures designed to restrict these firms' access to the U.S. market. The administration also threatened allies that the United States might halt cooperation on intelligence sharing unless they restrict the role of Chinese firms in crafting their 5G networks.[14] Secretary of State Mike Pompeo warned in December 2019, "Thanks to the way 5G networks are built, it's impossible to separate any one part of the network from another. . . . . It's critical that [allies] not give control of their critical infrastructure to Chinese tech giants like Huawei, or ZTE."[15] The success of these efforts has been mixed, however, in no small part because Huawei has already embedded itself so deeply in these networks.[16]

It would seem U.S. policymakers are confronting weaponized interdependence for the first time. Setting the proper context reveals two important facts, however. First, the United States has been weaponizing interdependence since the dawn of this century. The structural power of the United States over financial and cyber networks has enabled successive administrations to enhance America's coercive tools of statecraft. The centrality of the dollar to global capital markets has empowered the United States to ramp up its use of financial sanctions. Control over internet protocols facilitated the U.S. intelligence community's surveillance capacities. As Emily Meierding discusses in her chapter, in 2017 the Trump administration announced an intention to shift from "energy independence" to "energy dominance." The United States has exploited weaponized interdependence far more frequently than it has been targeted by it.

Second, just because U.S. officials claim that weaponized interdependence exists does not make it so. Russian efforts to exploit its transit network to extract concessions from neighboring states have yielded uneven efforts at best. The scope of China's debt-trap diplomacy remains contested, as Thomas Cavanna notes in his chapter. Concerns during the COVID-19 pandemic that China would exploit its centrality in medical supply chains proved to be exaggerated.[17] Even in the rare instances in which China appears to have successfully exploited its leverage—as when it withheld rare-earth exports to coerce Japan in a 2010 dispute—the long-term effect was to weaken China's coercive capabilities.[18]

Weaponized interdependence is real, but how real remains a matter of serious debate. The purpose of this edited volume is to define the scope of that debate and understand the dynamics at play. *Uses and Abuses of Weaponized Interdependence* details two levels at which WI can be used and abused. The first level concerns statecraft. Great powers, smaller states, and non-state actors are increasingly interested in weaponizing key economic and social networks.

While these actors have been eager to exploit WI, they also seem quite prone to abusing it as well. The Trump's administration's efforts at weaponized interdependence threatened to bankrupt Russia's Rusal aluminum company and China's ZTE, outcomes the administration neither anticipated nor intended. The administration's overall record on coercive statecraft suggests a paltry return while eviscerating U.S. soft power.[19] Actors run the risk of abusing their role as central hubs, putting their network centrality at risk for the future.

The second level concerns scholarship, where WI offers an opportunity for scholars to bridge multiple gaps. Weaponized interdependence provides an opportunity for scholars to weigh in on policy. It straddles the intersection of security studies and international political economy. At the same time, the "abuses" portion also applies to analysts. There is a clear danger of conceptual stretching. If one were to judge WI based solely on public commentary, anything and everything has been weaponized.[20] It is all too easy for analysts to deploy the term *weaponized* to describe situations that have little to do with WI, using the label to attract attention and inflate threats. As several of the chapters in this volume make clear, weaponized interdependence does not exist in every sphere of international relations.

This volume strives to establish the rough boundaries of the policy problem. What areas of the global political economy are most likely to be vulnerable to choke-point effects and panopticon effects? How sustainable is the continued use of weaponized interdependence? What are the possible responses from targeted actors? How sustainable is the open global economy if weaponized interdependence becomes a regular tool of statecraft?

These questions matter for policymakers as well as scholars. Either explicitly or implicitly, the U.S. government has been operating on the principle that weaponized interdependence is a pervasive fact of twenty-first century international relations. The Trump administration has exploited network centrality in finance to apply "maximum pressure" campaigns on a variety of U.S. adversaries.[21] The administration's strategy documents and policy actions imply that it views relations with China as a situation rife with WI possibilities. Furthermore, as the examples above suggest, these moves have robust bipartisan support. If the United States is exaggerating the pervasiveness of weaponized interdependence, the risk of sabotaging Sino-American relations and permanently disrupting the liberal international order is high. A better appreciation of WI's scope is an absolute necessity.

A Brief Historiography of Interdependence

The concept of weaponized interdependence is new;[22] the idea that interdependence affects international relations is not. As Farrell and Newman correctly observe, the liberal approach to international politics largely viewed the development of interdependence through a benign lens. This was for three reasons. First, economic interdependence was theorized as constraining the likelihood of violent conflict. Liberals have long argued that economic interdependence has a pacifying effect on world politics. From Kant's *Perpetual Peace* to Norman Angell's *Great Illusion* to Robert Keohane and Joseph Nye's *Power and Interdependence*, the causal logic was clear: economic interdependence raises the costs of disruption to that exchange. This incentivizes the relevant actors to continue to cooperate, reducing the likelihood of defection.

The second reason was that complex interdependence was viewed through the lens of globalization, which was presumed to have a leveling effect in world politics. The first generation of political science research on this topic painted networks as flattening hierarchies and fragmenting state power, an idea that seeped into public discourse. According to Thomas Friedman, for example, the internet was a "sudden revolution in connectivity [that] constituted a major flattening force."[23] This perception persisted into the current decade; until recently, entities like WikiLeaks were put forward as examples of how networked non-state actors could challenge the great powers.[24] If interdependence empowered domestic actors within great powers and enriched rising powers and non-state actors on the global stage, the likelihood of deeper globalization increased. The ability of any one actor to exploit the vagaries of complex interdependence would be reduced.

The final reason was that, to the extent that interdependence disproportionately empowered any actor, the true beneficiary was the

United States. Interdependence scholars were fully cognizant that asymmetric dependence and networked power were possible outcomes of greater globalization. During the late Cold War and post–Cold War eras in which the interdependence literature flourished, however, the United States was the unparalleled economic hegemon. International relations theory has often followed shifts in the distribution of power.[25] To the extent that the United States was viewed as the beneficiary of asymmetries in interdependence, observers were largely sanguine about the outcome. Anne-Marie Slaughter argued that in a networked world, "The state with the most connections will be the central player, able to set the global agenda and unlock innovation and sustainable growth. Here, the United States has a clear and sustainable edge."[26] It is only as the United States has faced rising great powers that policymakers and analysts have recognized the possible downsides of weaponized interdependence.[27]

While the benign view of economic interdependence was the dominant one, there were always dissenting voices. Realists have long argued that interdependence was more likely to breed conflict than cooperation, because the multiplicity of interactions would also increase the number of possible frictions in an anarchic world.[28] Scholars working in the "capitalist peace" tradition argued that while mutual interdependence did reduce interstate conflict, asymmetric trade ties undermined the pacific effects of commerce."[29] These criticisms are noteworthy but rely on different causal logics than weaponized interdependence. They primarily operate at the relational level between dyads rather than the systemic level.

Over the past decade, a few other scholars have argued that the networked structure of global economic flows has long facilitated WI. Economic historians noted that British policymakers were well aware of their financial network power in the run-up to the First World War.[30] Thomas Wright warned in 2013 about the "potentially destabilizing vulnerabilities" that existed in a globalized economy, specifically referencing the dangers posed by Huawei and ZTE.[31] In 2016 the World Economic Forum released a white paper warning that "all of the infrastructure of globalization risks being weaponized: the financial sector, supply chains, the energy sector and the global trading regime."[32] Mark Leonard, of the European Council on Foreign Relations, similarly warned that rising levels of connectivity meant that "interdependence, once heralded as a barrier to conflict, has turned into a currency of power."[33]

Two other strands of research also laid the foundations for an appreciation of weaponized interdependence. Networked-based explanations for international relations took root over the past two decades.[34] Global political economy scholars observed that financial flows in particular displayed a "hub-and-spoke" network, in which the United States became even more central to capital markets after the 2008 financial crisis.[35] As Farrell and Newman note, there are significant spheres of the global economy in which a network analysis reveals winner-take-all dynamics. In contrast to the popular vision of networks as flat, decentralized systems, global economic networks reveal a hierarchy and the structural concentration of power.[36]

Finally, the literature on economic coercion began to observe the ways in which the United States exploited its network centrality in finance to impose punishing sanctions on allies and adversaries alike. This innovation in financial statecraft began with the anti–money laundering initiative of the late 1990s.[37] Changes in post-9/11 domestic institutions accelerated the pace, as did the recognition by U.S. authorities that these kinds of sanctions imposed significantly greater costs on targeted states.[38] The rising costs of military statecraft also made financial sanctions more attractive as a policy option. Sanctions scholars observed the myriad ways that sanctions exploiting U.S. centrality in financial networks were more difficult to evade and more likely to harm target economies.[39]

Farrell and Newman's paper draws on much of this work while extending the WI argument in multiple ways. First, they clarify how this phenomenon is different from asymmetric dependence, a phenomenon that has been researched since the days of Albert Hirschman.[40] Dyadic patterns of asymmetric dependence can be changed more easily than patterns of dependence that rely on networked structures. There are more exit options from dyads than system-wide networks, and the elasticity of relationships are likely to be greater as well. Second, consistent with their prior research, they note the necessary condition of developing domestic institutions capable of exploiting network centrality.[41] Third, in elaborating on the choke-point and panopticon effects, they clarify the causal mechanisms through which actors can exploit weaponized interdependence.

What We Know about Weaponized Interdependence

To use the argot of social science, the contributors to this volume are interested in weaponized interdependence as an independent and dependent variable. Farrell and Newman point out the role that domestic institutions play in the ability to exploit weaponized interdependence. Additional factors are likely to matter as well. What are the conditions under which a network is ripe for weaponized interdependence? Why would potentially vulnerable actors agree to join a network that exposed them to panopticon and/or choke-point effects? If weaponized interdependence is observed, how successful are efforts to exploit it? How are actors able to resist weaponized interdependence? Is there a coercive point after which actors are willing to absorb the costs necessary to disrupt an economic network?

A few themes run through the chapters in this volume. The first is that the network externalities of any structure powerfully affect the likelihood of weaponized interdependence being present and exploitable. These externalities exist when the utility derived from using a network is a function of the number of other actors using the same network. With common pool resources, network externalities are negative—the greater the use, the less utility derived by each actor. When they are positive, however—as has been the case with networks as variegated as the Society for Worldwide Interbank Financial Telecommunications (SWIFT) and TikTok—they spread quickly and stick around. Some positive network externalities are more powerful than others. Social media, for example, generate greater network externalities than search engines. The rapidity of network diffusion makes the emergence of WI possible despite the wariness of actors operating in an anarchic world. The increasing utility of scale raise the barriers for any actor to exit from that network, facilitating the opportunities for successful surveillance and coercion.

Beyond network externality properties, there appear to be two other factors that facilitate the emergence of weaponized interdependence. The first, paradoxically, is the failure of centrally located actors to comprehend the possibility of WI. A recurring theme in this volume is that embedded networks existed for some time before actors comprehended how to weaponize them.[42] For instance, U.S. centrality in global capital markets existed long before the federal government embraced financial sanctions. Indeed, even as the first tentative steps toward sanctioning began, U.S. Treasury Department officials resisted such actions, believing them to be counterproductive.[43] These same officials were surprised by the potency of U.S. financial statecraft over time.[44] As Michael Mastanduno notes in his chapter, the opportunity and willingness to exploit WI are not always in synch.

A lack of awareness by possible sanctioners could be a necessary condition for WI to emerge, because the lack of strategic awareness puts potential targets at ease. Furthermore, the longer a central power does not exploit such a network, the more reassuring regardless of whether WI emerges or not. The logic of habit might be viewed by less powerful actors as sufficiently potent to permit further interdependence—which, ironically, increases the probability of future exploitation attempts.[45]

A related driver for the emergence of WI is the prominence of non-state actors. For example, in capital markets and cyberspace, firms and nonprofits—many of which are not headquartered in the United States—have created and/or fostered key networks. Non-state actors are less likely to trigger wariness from smaller or weaker states than a state-owned enterprise (such as Gazprom) or a national government (like China) erecting similar structures. On the other hand, the low degree of successful WI in the energy and transportation sectors is noticeable. In those areas, the heavier hand of the state has made possible network entrants warier of joining. This, in turn, reduces the likelihood of weaponized interdependence ever emerging.

The hypotheses for the use and success of weaponized interdependence are more straightforward. As previously noted, both domestic institutions and the network externality properties of the sector itself play important roles. Beyond that, the kinds of technology that undergird the relevant network also play a role. The more vulnerable the sector in question is to disruptive innovation, the more fragile the system that enables WI in the first place. This makes possible coercers more reluctant to risk exploiting WI. It also encourages targets to find work-arounds to avoid making concessions. Technologies that require massive fixed-cost investments are generally less vulnerable to disruption.

Comparing and contrasting weaponized interdependence with more conventional instances of economic sanctions also yields useful insights. The traditional playbook on sanctions is well known within the scholarly and policymaking communities.[46] Sanctions are more likely to work when the demands are clear, when there is multilateral cooperation supporting the sanctions, when no "black knights" are willing to step in and economically support the target, and when expectations of future conflict between the target and sender are muted. Low conflict expectations also act as a barrier restraining sanctioners from threatening coercion in the first place. The paradox of economic coercion has long been that states are most eager to sanction targets that they will be the least likely to coerce.

The existence of weaponized interdependence alters the calculus of traditional economic statecraft by easing the necessary conditions for coercion. Multilateral cooperation is no longer necessary, since network centrality endows critical actors with sufficient leverage to coerce unilaterally. Similarly, concerns about black knights are also reduced. It is extremely difficult for rival powers to erect competing networks from scratch. In the case of the dollar, for example, Russian, Chinese, and European efforts to shift away from the current global reserve currency have been fitful at best and feeble at worst. Compared to its rivals, the dollar looks stronger now than it did a decade ago during the depths of the Great Recession. Finally, because weaponized interdependence imposes lower costs on the sanctioner, the threshold conditions for coercing allies is significantly reduced. Simply put, it is easy for actors to deploy weaponized interdependence on allies as well as adversaries.

Stepping back, three things become immediately apparent about the use of weaponized interdependence as a tool of coercion compared to more conventional sanctions. The first is that the use of WI is far likelier. All of the threshold conditions for weaponizing interdependence are lower than for trade sanctions. Less multilateral support is needed, more targets can be considered, and WI sanctions are also likely to be more potent. Second, the factors governing sanctions success remain largely unchanged. The Trump administration's financial sanctions against Iran or Venezuela have not led to concessions, although the secondary sanctions have worked against U.S. allies in Europe. These outcomes are consistent with prior research on economic coercion. Weaponized interdependence does not guarantee successful statecraft; it merely increases the probability of coercion being attempted.[47] Third, even when WI is weak or nonexistent, the shadow it casts on world politics is long. As many of the subsequent chapters note, many WI attempts have failed because possible targets anticipate such threats and take actions to ward them off. Both the increase in coercion and the defense against such attempts, however, also affect the contours of the global political economy.

The Rest of This Volume

The rest of this edited volume is broken into six sections. The first section considers the theory of weaponized interdependence. The next chapter is a reprinting of Farrell and Newman's groundbreaking 2019 paper. Michael Mastanduno then considers the conditions under which the United States is likely to exploit WI, and Stacie Goddard discusses how revisionist actors may or may not exploit WI to advance their interests.

The next four sections examine different empirical domains to measure the relative potency of the WI phenomenon. Harold James and Thomas Oatley explore the ways in which weaponized interdependence exists in global financial networks. For cyberspace, Natasha Tusikov considers how the structure of the internet makes it fertile ground for WI; Adam Segal examines the battles between China and the United States over the development of 5G networks. On energy, Emily Meierding considers whether WI can aid the United States in its quest for "energy dominance." Mikhail Krutikhin examines Russia's ineffective use of Gazprom to foster WI in Europe. Florian Bodamer and Kaija Schilde examine state-run networks in the developed world for the creation of fighter aircraft. Thomas Cavanna looks at one state-run network—China's Belt and Road Initiative—to see if WI is present.

The final section of the book examines how actors are responding to the WI phenomenon. Bruce Jentleson considers the implications of weaponized interdependence on U.S. grand strategy. Sarah Bauerle Danzman explains why CFIUS is an imperfect tool for the United States to ward off WI. Charli Carpenter applies WI to the ideational network of human rights and notes the ways in which great powers in that domain are vulnerable to "reverse panopticon" effects. Amrita Narlikar looks at how the global south will cope with greater uses and abuses of weaponized interdependence. Finally, Farrell and Newman extend and refine their argument in response to the rest of the contributors.

Notes

1. Henry Farrell and Abraham L. Newman, "Weaponized Interdependence: How Global Economic Networks Shape State Coercion," *International Security* 44 (Summer 2019), pp. 42–79.

2. Ibid., p. 45.

3. Geoffrey Gertz, "Is TikTok a Threat to National Security?" *Washington Post*, November 11, 2019. See also Sarah Bauerle Danzman, "Investment Screening in the Shadow of Weaponized Interdependence," chapter 14 in this volume.

4. On those concerns, see Drew Harwell and Tony Room, "TikTok's Beijing Roots Fuel Censorship Suspicion as It Builds a Huge U.S. Audience," *Washington Post*, September 15, 2019; Alex Hern, "Revealed: How TikTok Censors Videos That Do Not Please Beijing," *The Guardian*, September 25, 2019.

5. Quoted in Raymond Zhong, "TikTok's Chief Is on a Mission to Prove It's Not a Menace," *New York Times*, November 18, 2019.

6. Ibid. See also TikTok's October 24, 2019, statement on their website: https://newsroom.tiktok.com/en-us/statement-on-tiktoks-content -moderation-and-data-security-practices.

7. Tony Romm and Drew Harwell, "TikTok Raises National Security Concerns in Congress as Schumer, Cotton Ask for Federal Review," *Washington Post*, October 24, 2019.

8. Daniel W. Drezner, *The Sanctions Paradox: Economic Statecraft and International Relations* (Cambridge University Press, 1999), chapters 5–7.

9. Mikael Wigell and Antto Vihma, "Geopolitics versus Geoeconomics: The Case of Russia's Geostrategy and Its Effects on the EU," *International*

Affairs 92 (May 2016), 605–27.

10. Dimitar Bechev, "Russia's Pipe Dreams Are Europe's Nightmare," *Foreign Policy*, March 12, 2019; Bechev, *Rival Power: Russia in Southern Europe* (Yale University Press, 2017).

11. Anna Shiryaevskaya and Dina Khrennikova, "Why the World Worries about Russia's Natural Gas Pipeline," Bloomberg, November 10, 2019.

12. John Hurley, Scott Morris, and Gailyn Portelance, "Examining the Debt Implications of the Belt and Road Initiative from a Policy Perspective," Center for Global Development Policy Paper 121, March 2018.

13. The senators' letter can be accessed at www.grassley.senate.gov/news/ news-releases/grassley-senators-express-concerns-over-china-s-debt-trap -diplomacy-developing. Navy secretary quoted in Geoff Ziezulewicz, "Top Navy and Marine Corps Officials Pan China's Expansion plans," *Military Times*, March 7, 2018.

14. Elias Groll, "Washington Tries a Softer Approach in Anti-Huawei Campaign," *Foreign Policy*, April 11, 2019; Laurens Cerulus, Tim Starks, and Eric Geller, "Trump's Huawei Ban Spooks Allies, Industry," *Politico*, May 20, 2019.

15. Michael R. Pompeo, "Europe Must Put Security First with 5G," *Politico*, December 2, 2019.

16. David Sanger, "Trump Wants to Wall Off Huawei, but the Digital World Bridles at Barriers," *New York Times*, May 27, 2019; Michele Savini Zangrandi, "Disentangling Huawei from the U.S. Has Proven Harder than Anticipated," Peterson Institute for International Economics, December 4, 2019, www.piie.com/blogs/realtime-economic-issues-watch/disentangling -huawei-us-has-proven-harder-anticipated.

17. See, for example, Congressional Research Service, "COVID-19: China Medical Supply Chains and Broader Trade Issues," April 6, 2020.

18. Eugene Gholz and Llewelyn Hughes, "Market Structure and Economic Sanctions: The 2010 Rare Earth Elements Episode as a Pathway Case of Market Adjustment," *Review of International Political Economy*, forthcoming.

19. Daniel W. Drezner, "Economic Statecraft in the Age of Trump," *Washington Quarterly* 42 (Fall 2019), 7–24.

20. See, for example, Parag Khanna, *Connectography* (New York: Random House, 2016); Simon Clark, "The New Kind of Warfare Reshaping Global Politics," *Washington Monthly*, December 6, 2019; and Quin Hillyer, "Ben Sasse Warns of Major Chinese Threat," *Washington Examiner*, November 20, 2019.

21. Drezner, "Economic Statecraft in the Age of Trump."

22. The practice of WI is not new at all, as shown in Harold James, "Weaponized Interdependence and International Monetary Systems," chapter 5 in this volume.

23. Thomas Friedman, *The World is Flat* (New York: Farrar, Strauss and Giroux, 2005), p. 59.

24. See, for example, Moisés Naim, *The End of Power* (New York: Basic Books, 2013).

25. Ido Oren, *Our Enemies and U.S.: America's Rivalries and the Making of Political Science* (Cornell University Press, 2002).

26. Anne-Marie Slaughter, "America's Edge: Power in the Networked Century," *Foreign Affairs* 88 (January/February 2009), p. 95.

27. Relatedly, it is only as the Trump administration accelerated and broadened the use of weaponized interdependence that U.S. allies focused on the phenomenon.

28. Kenneth Waltz, *Theory of International Politics* (Boston: Addison-Wesley, 1979); Joanne Gowa, *Allies, Adversaries, and International Trade* (Princeton University Press, 1994).

29. Erik Gartzke and Oliver Westerwinter, "The Complex Structure of Commercial Peace Contrasting Trade Interdependence, Asymmetry, and Multipolarity," *Journal of Peace Research* 53 (May 2016), pp. 325–43.

30. Nicholas Lambert, *Planning Armageddon: British Economic Warfare and the First World War* (Harvard University Press, 2012).

31. Thomas Wright, "Sifting through Interdependence," *Washington Quarterly* 36 (Fall 2013), p. 7.

32. World Economic Forum, "The Age of Economic Coercion," white paper, January 2016.

33. Mark Leonard, ed., *Connectivity Wars* (London: European Council on Foreign Relations, 2016), p. 15

34. David Grewal, *Network Power: The Social Dynamics of Globalization* (Yale University Press, 2008); Emilie M. Hafner-Burton, Miles Kahler, and Alexander H. Montgomery, "Network Analysis for International Relations," *International Organization* 63 (Summer 2009), pp. 559–92.

35. Thomas Oatley and others, "The Political economy of Global Finance: A Network Model," *Perspectives on Politics* 11 (March 2013), pp. 133–53; Oatley, "Toward a Political Economy of ComplexInterdependence," *European Journal of International Relations* 25 (December 2019), 957–78.

36. Grewal, *Network Power*.

37. Beth Simmons, "The International Politics of Harmonization: The Case of Capital Market Regulation," *International Organization* 55 (Summer 2001): 589-620.

38. Juan Zarate, *Treasury's War* (New York: PublicAffairs, 2013).

39. Daniel W. Drezner, "Targeted Sanctions in a World of Global Finance." *International Interactions* 41 (Summer 2015), pp. 755–64; Dursun Peksen and Byunghwan Son, "Economic Coercion and Currency Crises in Target Countries," *Journal of Peace Research* 52 (July 2015), pp. 448–62; Peter Harrell and Elizabeth Rosenberg, *Economic Dominance, Financial*

Technology, and the Future of U.S. Economic Coercion (Washington: Center for New American Security, 2019).

40. Albert Hirschman, *National Power and the Structure of Foreign Trade* (University of California Press, 1945).

41. Nikhil Kalyanpur and Abraham Newman, "Mobilizing Market Power: Jurisdictional Expansion as Economic Statecraft," *International Organization* 73 (Winter 2019), pp. 1–34; Henry Farrell and Abraham L. Newman, *Of Privacy and Power* (Princeton University Press, 2019).

42. This mirrors the ways in which even private-sector actors fail to anticipate which innovations catch on. Amazon, for example, did not realize the revolution it ushered in when it introduced cloud computing. The company merely believed it had found a use for server space that was idle beyond holiday seasons. See Scott Malcolmson, "The Real Fight for the Future of 5G," *Foreign Affairs*, November 14, 2019. Also akin to state actors, Amazon has learned to use its coercive capacities over time. See Daisuke Wakabayashi, "Prime Leverage: How Amazon Wields Power in the Technology World," *New York Times*, December 15, 2019.

43. Benn Steil and Robert Litan, *Financial Statecraft: The Role of Financial Markets in American Foreign Policy* (Yale University Press, 2006).

44. Zarate, *Treasury's War.*

45. On habit, see Ted Hopf, "The Logic of Habit in International Relations," *European Journal of International Relations* 16 (December 2010), pp. 539–61.

46. R. Harrison Wagner, "Economic Interdependence, Bargaining Power, and Political Influence," *International Organization* 42 (Summer 1988), pp. 461–83; Drezner, *The Sanctions Paradox.*

47. One possible exception is that the panopticon effect enables more focused efforts at statecraft.

I

THEORY

2

Weaponized Interdependence

How Global Economic Networks Shape State Coercion

HENRY FARRELL
ABRAHAM L. NEWMAN

In May 2018, Donald Trump announced that the United States was pulling out of the Joint Comprehensive Plan of Action agreement on Iran's nuclear program and reimposing sanctions. Most notably, many of these penalties apply not to U.S. firms, but to foreign firms that may have no presence in the United States. The sanctions are consequential in large part because of U.S. importance to the global financial network.[1] This unilateral action led to protest among the United States' European allies: France's finance minister, Bruno Le Maire, for example, tartly noted that the United States was not the "economic policeman of the planet."[2]

The reimposition of sanctions on Iran is just one recent example of how the United States is using global economic networks to achieve its strategic aims.[3] While security scholars have long recognized the crucial importance of energy markets in shaping geostrategic outcomes,[4] financial and information markets are rapidly coming to play similarly important roles. In Rosa Brooks's evocative description, globalization has created a world in which everything became war.[5] Flows of finance, information, and physical goods across borders create both new risks for states and new tools to alternatively exploit or mitigate those risks. The result, as Thomas Wright describes it, is a world where unprecedented levels of interdependence are combined with continued jockeying for power, so that states that are unwilling to engage in direct conflict may still employ all measures short of war.[6]

Global economic networks have security consequences, because they increase interdependence between states that were previously relatively autonomous. Yet, existing theory provides few guideposts as to how states may leverage network structures as a coercive tool and under what circumstances. It has focused instead on trade relations between dyadic pairs and the vulnerabilities generated by those interactions.[7] Similarly, work on economic sanctions has yet to fully grasp the consequences of economic networks and how they are being weaponized. Rather, that literature primarily looks to explain the success or failure of direct sanctions (i.e., sanctions that involve states denying outside access to their own markets individually or as an alliance).[8] Power and vulnerability are characterized as the consequences of aggregate market size or bilateral interdependencies. In addition, accounts that examine more diffuse or secondary sanctions have focused more on comparative effectiveness than on theory building.[9]

In this article, we develop a different understanding of state power, which highlights the structural aspects of interdependence. Specifically, we show how the topography of the economic networks of interdependence intersects with domestic institutions and norms to shape coercive authority. Our account places networks such as financial communications, supply chains, and the internet, which have been largely neglected by international relations scholars, at the heart of a compelling new understanding of globalization and power.[10] Globalization has transformed the liberal order, by moving the action away from multilateral interstate negotiations and toward networks of private actors.[11] This transformation has had crucial consequences for where state power is located in international politics, and how it is exercised.

We contrast our argument with standard liberal accounts of complex interdependence. The initial liberal account of interdependence paid some attention to power, but emphasized bilateral relationships. Subsequent liberal accounts have tended either to avoid the question of power, focusing on mutual cooperative gains, to suggest that apparently lopsided global networks obscure more fundamental patterns of mutual dependence, or to posit a networked global order in which liberal states such as the United States can exercise "power with" (the power to work together constructively with allies) to achieve liberal objectives.[12]

Our alternative account makes a starkly different assumption, providing a structural explanation of interdependence in which network topography generates enduring power imbalances among states. Here we draw on sociological and computational research on large-scale networks, which demonstrates the tendency of complex systems to produce asymmetric network structures, in which some nodes are "hubs," and are far more connected than others.[13]

Asymmetric network structures create the potential for "weaponized interdependence," in which some states are able to leverage interdependent relations to coerce others. Specifically, states with political authority over the central nodes in the international networked structures through which money, goods, and information travel are uniquely positioned to impose costs on others. If they have appropriate domestic institutions, they can weaponize networks to gather information or choke off economic and information flows, discover and exploit vulnerabilities, compel policy change, and deter unwanted actions. We identify and explain variation in two strategies through which states can gain powerful advantages from weaponizing interdependence; they respectively rely on the panopticon and chokepoint effects of networks. In the former, advantaged states use their network position to extract informational advantages vis-à-vis adversaries, whereas in the latter, they can cut adversaries off from network flows.

To test the plausibility of our argument, we present detailed analytic narratives of two substantive areas: financial messaging and internet communications.[14] We selected these areas as they are significant to a range of critical security issues including rogue-state nonproliferation, counterterrorism, and great power competition.

Moreover, global finance and the internet are often depicted as being at the vanguard of decentralized economic networks. As such, they offer an important test of our argument and a contrast to the more common liberal perspective on global market interactions.

At the same time, financial messaging and internet communication see important variation in the level and kind of control that they offer to influential states. In the former, the United States, in combination with its allies, has sufficient jurisdictional grasp and appropriate domestic institutions to oblige hub actors to provide it with information and to cut off other actors and states. In internet communications, the United States solely has appropriate jurisdictional grasp and appropriate institutions to oblige hub actors to provide it with information, but does not have domestic institutions that would allow it to demand that other states be cut out of the network. This would lead us to expect that in the case of financial messaging, the United States and its allies will be able to exercise both the panopticon and chokepoint effects—so long as they agree. In contrast, in internet communications, the United States will be able to exercise the panopticon effect even without the consent of its allies, but will not be able to exercise the chokepoint effect. This variation allows us to demonstrate the limits of these network strategies and also show that they are not simply coterminous with United States market size or military power. Empirically, the cases draw on extensive readings of the primary and secondary literature as well as interviews with key policymakers.

Our argument has significant implications for scholars interested in thinking about the future of conflict in a world of global economic and information networks. For those steeped in the liberal tradition, we demonstrate that institutions designed to generate market efficiencies and reduce transaction costs can be deployed for coercive ends. Focal points of cooperation have become sites of control. For those researchers interested in conflict studies and power, we show the critical role that economic relations play in coercion. Rather than rehashing more conventional debates on trade and conflict, we underscore how relatively new forms of economic interaction—financial and information flows—shape strategic opportunities, stressing in particular how the topography of global networks structures coercion.

Here, we use basic insights from network theory to rethink structural power, linking the literatures on economic and security relations to show how coercive economic power can stem from structural characteristics of the global economy. Finally, the article begins to map the deep empirical connections between economic networks—for example, financial messaging, dollar clearing, global supply chains, and internet communication—and a series of pressing real-world issues—including counterterrorism, cybersecurity, rogue states, and great power competition.

We begin by explaining how global networks play a structural role in the world economy. Next, we describe how these networks, together with domestic institutions and norms, shape the strategic options available to actors, focusing on what we describe as the panopticon and chokepoint effects. We provide detailed parallel histories of how networks in financial communication and internet communication developed and were weaponized by the United States. We conclude by considering the policy implications of clashes between states such as the United States that have weaponized interdependence and other states looking to counter these influences.

Statecraft and Structure: The Role of Global Networks

As globalization has advanced, it has fostered new networks of exchange—whether economic, informational, or physical—that have remade domestic economies, densely and intimately interconnecting them in ways that are nearly impossible to unravel.[15] The financial sector depends on international messaging networks, which have become the key means through which domestic banks and financial institutions arrange transfers and communicate with each other. Informational networks such as the internet are notoriously internationalized: a single web page can stitch together content and advertisements from myriad independent servers, perhaps located in different countries. Physical manufacture depends on vast tangled supply chains that extend globally, greatly complicating trade wars, since high tariffs on importers are likely to damage the interests of domestic suppliers.

Such networks have typically been depicted by liberals as a form of "complex interdependence," a fragmented polity in which "there were multiple actors (rather than just states), multiple issues that were not necessarily hierarchically ordered, and force and the threat of force were not valuable tools of policy."[16] Such arguments allowed some space for the exercise of bilateral power, showing how states that depended on imports from other states, and had no ready substitutes, were vulnerable to outside pressure. However, liberal scholars stressed the power resources of actors rather than structural factors, in particular the dispersion of power across such networks, and often emphasized how interdependence generated reciprocal rather than one-sided vulnerabilities.

As globalization progressed, liberals have continued to argue that global networks result in reciprocal dependence, which tends to make coercive strategies less effective. Thus, for example, Robert Keohane and Joseph Nye describe globalization as involving the development of "networks of interdependence." Although they accept that, as a "first approximation," the United States appears to be a hub in these networks, they also argue that it would be a "mistake to envisage contemporary networks of globalism simply in terms of a hub and spokes of an American empire that creates dependency for smaller countries."[17] Instead, Keohane and Nye suggest that there are multiple different possible hubs, reducing the dominance of great powers such as the United States. Furthermore, they argue that asymmetries are likely to diminish over time as "structural holes" are filled in.[18] More recently, Nye has argued that "entanglement" between states' economic and information systems can have important pacifying benefits for cybersecurity: precisely because states are interdependent, they are less liable to launch attacks that may damage themselves as well as their adversaries.[19]

Other liberal scholars, such as Anne-Marie Slaughter, claim that globalization creates decentralized networks that generate new opportunities for cooperative diplomacy.[20] Slaughter's guiding metaphor for globalization is a web connecting a network of points rather than a "chessboard." An arbitrarily large number of paths may connect two or several of these points together, suggesting that globalization is best understood as a nonhierarchical network in which the new arts of diplomacy consist in identifying the right relationships among the multitudes of possibilities to accomplish a given task. In such a network, liberals such as Slaughter argue, power is "power with," rather than "power over."[21]

Like these liberal accounts, our approach takes networks seriously. However, it starts from different premises about their genesis and consequences. First, we argue that networks are structures in the sociological sense of the term, which is to say that they shape what actors can or cannot do. An important body of emerging scholarship in international political economy, which we dub the "new structuralism," looks to understand the consequences of globally emergent phenomena for states and other actors.[22] In the longer term, such networks may change, but in the short to medium term, they are self-reinforcing and resistant to efforts to disrupt them.

Second, network structures can have important consequences for the distribution of power. In contradistinction to liberal claims, they do not produce a flat or fragmented world of diffuse power relations and ready cooperation, nor do they tend to become less asymmetric over time. Instead, they result in a specific, tangible, and enduring configuration of power imbalance. Key global economic networks—like many other complex phenomena—tend to generate ever more asymmetric topologies in which exchange becomes centralized, flowing through a few specific intermediaries.[23] Contrary to Keohane and Nye's predictions, key global economic networks have converged towards "hub and spoke" systems, with important consequences for power relations.[24]

Networks can be described more formally. Network theory starts from the basis that networks involve two elements: the "nodes," each representing a specific actor or location within the network; and the "ties" (sometimes called edges), or connections between nodes, which channel information, resources, or other forms of influence. In simple representations, these ties are assumed to carry resources or influence in both directions. The "degree" of a node is the number of ties that connect it to other nodes; the higher the degree, the more connections it enjoys. Empirically, these nodes may be specific physical entities such as the computers that run internet exchanges or institutions such as a particular bank. The pattern of nodes and links between them is the topography (or what international relations scholars might call the "structure") of the network.

In our account, as in other structural accounts such as neorealism, network structures are the consequence of the accumulated actions of myriad actors, which aggregate to produce structures that influence their behavior. Specifically, the market-focused strategies of business actors lead, inadvertently or otherwise, to highly centralized global networks of communication, exchange, and physical production. Asymmetric growth means that globalization—like other networked forms of human activity[25]—generates networks with stark inequality of influence.[26] The distribution of degree (i.e., of links across nodes) may approximate to a power law, or a log normal distribution, or a stretched exponential depending on particulars.[27] For the purposes of our argument, the exact statistical classification of the distributions is irrelevant; what is important is that social networks tend to be highly unequal.

Such inequalities may arise in a number of plausible ways. Simple models of preferential attachment suggest that as networks grow, new nodes are slightly more likely to attach to nodes that already have many ties than to nodes that have fewer such ties. As a result, sharply unequal distributions are likely to emerge over time.[28] Network effects, in which the value of a service to its users increases as a function of the number of users already using it, may lead actors to converge on networks that already have many participants, while efficiency concerns lead the network providers to create hub-and-spoke systems of communication. Finally, innovation research suggests that there are important learning-by-doing effects, in which central nodes in networks have access to more information and relationships than other members of the network, causing others to link to them preferentially to maintain access to learning processes.[29]

These mechanisms and others may generate strong rich-get-richer effects over the short to medium term, in which certain nodes in the network become more central in the network than others. The networks they generate are structural in the precise yet limited sense that, after they have emerged, they are highly resistant to the efforts of individual economic actors to change them; once networks become established, individual actors will experience lock-in effects.[30] Furthermore, under reasonable models of network growth, these topologies are self-reinforcing; as the pattern starts to become established, new nodes become overwhelmingly likely to reinforce rather than to undermine the existing unequal pattern of distribution.

Nor are these just abstract theoretical claims. They appear to describe many global economic networks.[31] Even when global networks largely came into being through entirely decentralized processes, they have come to display high skewness in the distribution of degree.[32] More plainly put, some nodes in these networks are far better connected than others. Studies of trade and banking show that the United States and the United Kingdom are exceptionally highly connected nodes in global financial networks.[33] It is increasingly difficult to map the network relations of the internet for technical reasons, yet there is good reason to believe that the internet displays a similar skew toward nodes in advanced industrial democracies such as the United States and (to a lesser extent) the United Kingdom.[34]

This activity is often driven by an economic logic. In a networked world, businesses often operate in a context where there are increasing returns to scale, network effects, or some combination thereof. These effects push markets toward winner-take-all equilibria in which only one or a few businesses have the lion's share of relationships with end users and, hence, profits and power. Even where networks are run by nonprofit actors, there are strong imperatives toward network structures in which most or even nearly all market actors work through a specific organization, allowing them to take advantage of the lower transaction costs associated with centralized communications architectures.

Once established, these centralized network structures are hard for outsiders to challenge, not least because they have focal power; challengers not only have to demonstrate that they have a better approach, but need to coordinate a significant number of actors to defect from the existing model or organization and converge toward a different one.

For example, Facebook's business model is centered on monetizing individuals' social networks through targeted advertisement and other means. It has been able to resist challengers with ostensibly better or less privacy-invasive products, because it is relatively costly for an individual, or even a medium-sized group, to move to a different service unless they know that everyone else is doing the same thing. Google similarly leverages the benefits of search and advertising data.[35] Large international financial institutions such as Citibank, security settlement systems such as Euroclear, consumer credit payment systems such as Visa/Mastercard, financial clearing houses such as the Clearing House Interbank Payments System, and financial messaging services such as the Society for Worldwide Interbank Financial Telecommunication (SWIFT) have become crucial intermediaries in global financial networks, acting as middlemen across an enormous number and variety of specific transactions. All these actors play key roles in their various architectures, coordinating and brokering numerous specific relationships, benefiting from efficiencies of scale and, in some cases, from the unique access to information that their brokerage position supplies.[36]

Notably, the most central nodes are not randomly distributed across the world, but are typically territorially concentrated in the advanced industrial economies, and the United States in particular. This distribution reflects a combination of the rich-get-richer effects common in network analysis and the particular timing of the most recent wave of globalization, which coincided with United States and Western domination of relevant innovation cycles.

In short, globalization has generated a new set of structural forces. Economic actors' myriad activities create self-reinforcing network topologies, in which some economic intermediaries—nodes— are centrally located with very high degree, and most other nodes are dependent on them. Once these topologies become established, it is difficult for economic actors to change or substantially displace them.

New Forms of Network Power: Panopticons and Chokepoints

The asymmetric networks that make up much of the structure of a globalized world were not constructed as tools of statecraft. They typically reflect the incentives of businesses to create monopolies or semi-monopolies, increasing returns to scale in certain markets, rich-get-richer mechanisms of network attachment, and the efficiencies available to more centralized communications networks. By building centralized networks, market actors inadvertently provide states, which are concerned with political as well as economic considerations, with the necessary levers to extend their influence across borders. Thus, structures that were generated by market actors in pursuit of efficiency and market power can be put to quite different purposes by states.

Here, we differentiate our account of power from two related but distinct sources of power that may result from economic interdependence. The first is market power. Although often underspecified, research on market power emphasizes the aggregate economic potential (measured in a variety of different ways ranging from the domestic consumer-base to aggregate gross domestic product) of a country. States with large economic markets can leverage market access for strategic ends. National economic capabilities, then, produce power resources.[37] The second source of power, which dates back to the pioneering work of Keohane and Nye and has been most thoroughly examined in the case of trade, involves bilateral dependence. States that rely on a particular good from another state and lack a substitute supplier may be sensitive to shocks or manipulation.[38]

Market size and bilateral economic interactions are important, but they are far from exhaustive of the structural transformations wreaked by globalization. Global economic networks have distinct consequences that go far beyond states' unilateral decisions either to allow or deny market access, or to impose bilateral pressure. They allow some states to weaponize interdependence on the level of the network itself. Specifically, they enable two forms of weaponization. The first weaponizes the ability to glean critical knowledge from information flows, which we label the "panopticon effect." Jeremy Bentham's conception of the Panopticon was precisely an architectural arrangement in which one or a few central actors could readily observe the activities of others. States that have physical access to or jurisdiction over hub nodes can use this influence to obtain information passing through the hubs. Because hubs are crucial intermediaries in decentralized communications structures, it becomes difficult—or even effectively impossible—for other actors to avoid these hubs while communicating.

This phenomenon existed in earlier periods of globalization as well. As Harold James describes it, "In the first era of globalization, expanding trade, capital and labour flows all tied economies together in what appeared to be an increasing and probably irreversible network," centered on the "commercial infrastructure provided by Britain," and in particular the financial infrastructure of the City of London.[39] As James notes, "the fact that Britain was the hub of trade finance and insurance gave its military planners, and its political-decision makers, a unique insight into how and where global flows of strategic goods went, and how those flows might be interrupted."[40]

As technology has developed, the ability of states to glean information about the activities of their adversaries (or third parties on whom their adversaries depend) has correspondingly become more sophisticated. The reliance of financial institutions on readily searchable archives of records converts bank branches and internet terminals into valuable sources of information. New technologies such as cell phones become active sensors. Under the panopticon effect, states' direct surveillance abilities may be radically outstripped by their capacity to tap into the information-gathering and information-generating activities of networks of private actors.

Such information offers privileged states a key window into the activity of adversaries, partly compensating for the weak information environment that is otherwise characteristic of global politics. States with access to the panopticon effect have an informational advantage in understanding adversaries' intentions and tactics. This information offers those states with access to the hub a strategic advantage in their effort to counter the specific moves of their targets, conduct negotiations, or create political frames.

The second channel works through what we label the "chokepoint effect," and involves privileged states' capacity to limit or penalize use of hubs by third parties (e.g., other states or private actors). Because hubs offer extraordinary efficiency benefits, and because it is extremely difficult to circumvent them, states that can control hubs have considerable coercive power, and states or other actors that are denied access to hubs can suffer substantial consequences. Again, there is some historical precedent for this phenomenon. Nicholas Lambert describes how the United Kingdom enjoyed a near monopoly over the communications infrastructure associated with international trade in the period before World War I, and developed extensive plans to use this monopoly to disrupt the economies of their adversaries, weaponizing the global trading system.[41] As Heidi Tworek argues, Germany responded to the UK stranglehold on submarine communication cables by trying to develop new wireless technologies.[42]

States may use a range of tools to achieve chokepoint effects, including those described in the existing literature on how statecraft, credibility, the ability to involve allies, and other such factors shape the relative success or failure of extraterritorial coercive policies.[43] In some cases, states have sole jurisdiction over the key hub or hubs, which offers them the legal authority to regulate issues of market use. In others, the hubs may be scattered across two or more jurisdictions, obliging states to work together to exploit the benefits of coercion. Our account emphasizes the crucial importance of the economic network structures within which all of these coercive efforts take place. Where there are one or a few hubs, it becomes far easier for actors in control of these nodes to block or hamper access to the entire network.

We explain variation in state strategies as a function of the structural topography of the network combined with domestic institutions and norms of the states attempting to make use of the network structures. First, only those states that have physical or legal jurisdiction over hub nodes will be able to exploit the benefits of weaponized interdependence. As we have already noted, the network hubs of globalization are not scattered at random across the world. Instead, they are disproportionally located in the advanced industrial countries, in particular the United States, which has led technological and market innovation in the most recent round of economic globalization. This geographic skew effectively means that only the United States and a couple of other key states and statelike entities (most notably, the European Union [EU] and, increasingly, China) enjoy the benefits of weaponized interdependence, although others may still be able to play a disruptive role.

Second, there will be variation across the national institutional structures associated with different issue areas. If states are to exploit hubs, they require appropriate legal and regulatory institutions.

Depending on domestic configurations of power and state-society relations, they may lack coercive capacity; alternatively, they may be able to prosecute strategies based only on panopticon effects and not on chokepoints, or vice versa. The literature on regulatory capacity, for example, demonstrates that the United States is not uniformly positioned to control market access.[44] In some areas, it has weak or decentralized regulatory institutions, or would face powerful domestic pushback. In such cases, states may find themselves structurally positioned to shape hub behavior but lack the institutional resources to exploit either or both the panopticon or chokepoint effects.

In other domains, national laws and norms constrain states from engaging in certain kinds of weaponization. Privacy laws in the EU, for example, limit the amount of data that may be collected or stored by commercial internet providers.[45] These institutions, which were adopted just as decentralized market processes generated new commercial networks of data exchange, mean that it is more difficult for many European governments to directly exploit panopticon effects. As history demonstrates, domestic institutions may change in response to new perceived external threats, but they may also be sticky, because domestic actors may fear that the new capacities will be turned against them as well as foreign adversaries.[46] Domestic institutions are usually themselves the product of intense internal political battles, so that they cannot costlessly be transformed to confront new international challenges.

The central expectation of our argument is that states' variable ability to employ these forms of coercion will depend on the combination of the structure of the underlying network and the domestic institutions of the states attempting to use them. States that have jurisdictional control over network hubs and enjoy sufficient institutional capacity will be able to deploy both panopticon and chokepoint effects. Variation in domestic institutions in terms of capacity and key norms may limit their ability to use these coercive tools even when they have territorial or jurisdictional claims over hubs. Where control over key hubs is spread across a small number of states, these states may need to coordinate with one another to exploit weaponized interdependence. States that lack access to, or control over, network hubs will not be able to exert such forms of coercion.

In the succeeding sections, we provide a plausibility probe for our argument. We present two analytic narratives covering different core policy domains of globalization—financial and international data flows. In each domain, we demonstrate how a similar structural logic developed, as highly asymmetric networks emerged, in which a few hubs played a key role. In contrast to liberal approaches, we show how states—most particularly, the United States—were able to take advantage of these network structures, to exploit panopticon effects or chokepoint effects. Importantly, our cases offer variation in the ability of the United States to deploy these strategies, distinguishing our argument from more conventional market power or bilateral vulnerability accounts.

The Rise of Network Inequality

Although globalization is often characterized as involving complexity and fragmentation, this section demonstrates how strong systematic inequalities have emerged in two issue areas—finance and information. In particular, these narratives demonstrate how market actors created institutions and technologies to overcome the transaction costs associated with decentralized markets and, in doing so, generated potential sites of control.

Global Finance and SWIFT's Centrality

To manage billions of daily transactions and trades, global finance relies on a much smaller set of backroom arrangements to facilitate capital flows—so-called payment systems. Businesses and banks depend on these payment systems to move funds from one entity to another. A key component of the payment system is reliable and secure communication between financial institutions regarding the multitude of transactions that occur globally on any given day.

Since the 1970s, interbank communication has been provided by SWIFT.[47] For much of the post–World War II period, only a few transnational banks engaged in cross-border transactions. Those that did had to rely on the public telegram and telex systems, which were operated by national telecommunications providers. These systems proved both slow and insecure. These inefficiencies led financial actors to create a number of competing platforms for interbank communication in the 1970s. Most notably, the First National City Bank of New York (FNCB, later renamed Citibank) developed a proprietary system known as Machine Readable Telegraphic Input (MARTI), which the company hoped to disseminate and profit from.

This system gave a big push to European banks and U.S. competitors of FNCB, which worried about what might happen if they became dependent on MARTI. The result was that a small group of European and U.S. banks cooperated in building a messaging system that could replace the public providers and speed up the payment process. SWIFT opened its doors in 1973 and sent its first message in 1977.

The main objective of the organization was to create a system for transferring payment instructions between entities engaged in a financial transaction including banks, settlement institutions, and even central banks. SWIFT plays a critical role in authorizing transactions, authenticating parties, and recording exchanges. It is a cooperative run by representatives from th financial institutions involved. SWIFT's headquarters were established near Brussels, Belgium, to sidestep the emerging rivalry between New York and London as the hubs of global banking.

For much of the 1970s, it was unclear if SWIFT would succeed. The organization had to develop a new secure messaging system that could efficiently transfer tremendous amounts of data and beat competitors such as MARTI. In 1977, it was used in 22 countries by roughly 500 firms with an annual traffic of approximately 3,000 messages. By 2016, it had become the dominant provider, serving more than 200 countries and some 11,000 financial institutions and carrying over 6.5 billion messages annually. As Susan Scott and Markos Zachariadis note, "Founded to create efficiencies by replacing telegram and telex (or 'wires') for international payments, SWIFT now forms a core part of the financial services infrastructure."[48] This network effect was an accidental rather than an intended outcome. Those involved in the original SWIFT project during the 1970s were focused on "creating an entity, a closed society, to bind members together in an organizational form that would employ standards designed to create efficiencies on transactions between the member banks."[49]

Eventually, the organization's dominance over financial messaging led to monopoly regulation by the Commission of the European Union. La Poste (the deregulated Postes, Télégraphes et Téléphones of France) sought access to the SWIFT network as part of its banking operations, and SWIFT denied the request on the grounds that La Poste was not a traditional banking institution. The European Commission's ruling in 1997 that SWIFT "holds a monopolistic position in the market for international payment message transfer" meant that it was a quasi utility and had to follow an open access model.[50] As a result, even more financial institutions began to use and become dependent on the SWIFT system. The more banks that used SWIFT, the more it created measurable network benefits for its members, and the less likely member banks were to defect.[51] By the turn of the millennium, nearly all major global financial institutions used the SWIFT system to process their transactions (see figure 2-1).

FIGURE 2-1
Annual SWIFT Messages in Millions

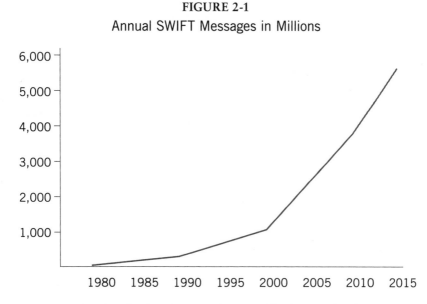

Note: SWIFT stands for Society for Worldwide Interbank Financial Telecommunications.

The Internet—All Roads Lead through Northern Virginia

When the internet came to public prominence in the early 1990s, it initially seemed as though it might provide a technology that was innately resistant to centralization. Authorities and political actors, including U.S. President Bill Clinton, believed that it was effectively invulnerable to central control.[52] In contrast to "centralized" networks such as the then-existing phone system, where different phones connected through a central switchboard, the internet was conceived as a "distributed" network, where there was a multiplicity of ties between different nodes, and no node was innately more important than any other.[53] The Transmission Control Protocol/Internet Protocol allowed servers to speedily identify blockages in the system and find alternative routes for information. In such a system, government control seemed difficult; as the prominent activist John Gilmore put it, the "Net interprets censorship as damage, and routes around it."[54] This resistance to blockages led some online libertarians to forecast the withering of the state and a new age of human freedom.[55]

Contradicting these heady prognoses, the underlying architecture of the internet became increasingly centralized over time.[56] Some hubs and interconnections between these hubs became far more important than others. States increasingly were able to impose controls on traffic entering and leaving their country, while censoring or controlling many ordinary uses of the internet.[57] The most important infrastructural elements of the internet are the fiber optic cables that provide service between the continents. These cables are far more efficient than competing channels such as satellite or legacy telephone wires. They are also geographically fixed. Ninety-seven percent of intercontinental internet traffic travels across roughly 300 cables.[58] The importance of these central communication nodes became painfully clear in 2008, when a ship's anchor severed two such cables (FLAG Europe Asia and SEA-ME-WE-4) off the cost of Egypt and shut down much of the internet in the Middle East and South Asia. The recurrence of such problems has led to concerns about vulnerability to sabotage.[59]

The increasing complexity and size of the modern internet threatens to slow connection speeds. In response, internet exchange points have emerged, which facilitate communication across service providers and infrastructure backbones.[60] These internet exchanges are often located in major cities and channel the majority of domestic internet traffic in the United States and Europe; they also support peer linkages between the different global networks that allow the internet to function. Once again, this means that a substantial amount of traffic travels through a few key nodes.

Network economies have similarly led to a centralization of the e-commerce economy, as both network effects and new kinds of increasing returns to scale cemented the global dominance of a small number of e-commerce companies. This dominance is in part thanks to U.S. government policy. The United States believed that, to the greatest extent possible, data governance should involve the free flow of content across borders (except, of course, where this interfered with the intellectual property or other vital interests of U.S. corporations). It should furthermore be based primarily on self-regulation, looking to business cooperation and market structures to regulate their business relations with consumers.[61]

This emphasis on self-regulation and individual choice gave private firms a great deal of freedom to set their own rules. In the 1990s, Clinton administration officials, led by Ira Magaziner, crafted a "Framework for Global Electronic Commerce" that was intended to shape the emerging international debate so as to push back against government regulation and, instead, favor self-regulatory approaches.[62] The U.S. government scotched plans by Jon Postel, an early technological leader in internet communications, to set up a global institution to regulate the internet with the help of the Internet Society and the UN's International Telecommunications Union, threatening him with criminal sanctions if he did not back down.[63]

Instead, it handed authority over domain names to a private nonprofit corporation under Californian law, the Internet Corporation for Assigned Names and Numbers (ICANN), which would work with for-profit entities to manage the technical aspects of coordination.[64] ICANN's ultimate authority stemmed from a contract with the Department of Commerce, which provided the U.S. government with a controversial implicit veto. Importantly, however, ICANN was designed according to a "stakeholder" model, under which private actors would take the lead in shaping its deliberations. The U.S. veto was primarily intended as a backstop against other states or international organizations wresting ICANN away from the private sector, rather than a calibrated tool for institutional interference.

Self-regulation and individual choice were also the organizing principles for U.S. domestic regulations. These principles were laid out in legislation including, most importantly, Section 230 of the 1996 Communications Decency Act, which protected e-commerce firms from "intermediary liability" for content put up by others.[65] This section was intended for a specific and relatively narrow purpose—to provide businesses with safe harbor against legal actions aimed at content posted by users. It ended up inadvertently supporting a new business model, in which e-commerce firms, rather than providing content themselves, would rely on their users to provide the content for them. They could then make their profits by acting as an intermediary between those users, analyzing their behavior, and offering targeted advertising services to their actual customers, people who wanted to sell products to the users leaving data trails behind them.

Section 230, together with network effects, led to the rapid domination of a small number of e-commerce and online firms. Companies such as Facebook and YouTube (owned by Google and then by Alphabet) were able to use the lack of intermediary liability to rapidly scale up, allowing enormous numbers of users to share content, without any need for companies to edit or inspect that content, except when they were informed of intellectual property violations. The result was a business model based on algorithms rather than employees.[66] Google could similarly take advantage of the lack of intermediary liability, while expanding into new services. It reaped the benefits of a feedback loop in which its users passively provided data, which could be categorized using machine learning techniques both to sell space to advertisers and to further improve Google services. Amazon, too, swiftly branched out, selling not only physical products, but cloud services, and acting as an intermediary across a wide variety of markets.

All these firms built themselves effective near monopolies. Facebook—once it had become established—was more or less impossible for competitors to displace, because its users had little incentive to migrate to a new system, and Facebook could buy and integrate potential new competitors long before they could become real threats. Google's data dominance provided the company with a nearly impregnable position, while Amazon's relentless growth into new marketplaces provided it with irresistible economies of scale.[67]

Although China has excluded these companies and developed domestic competitors, it has done so only by leveraging state power in ways that are far harder for small states and liberal democracies. As a result, a huge fraction of global data traffic is channeled through the servers of a handful of companies, which sit in the United States. Key aspects of the domain name system are run by ICANN, which provided some privileged actors with levers for achieving political outcomes.[68] As ever more online services move to cloud architectures, which store customer data and processing power in online data centers, cloud providers have emerged as central hubs.[69] One estimate, for example, suggests that 70 percent of global web traffic goes through Amazon Web Services in Northern Virginia (which had become established as a hub location decades earlier thanks to America Online).[70] Transcontinental fiber optic cables, internet exchanges, monopoly service providers and geographically concentrated data centers have all helped build a grossly asymmetric network, in which communications, rather than being broadly distributed, travel through key hubs, which are differentially concentrated in the United States, and channel the most global data exchanges.

Weaponizing the Hubs

With the rise of these central hubs across financial messaging and online communication, states (in particular the United States and members of the European Union) began to understand that they could exploit network properties to weaponize interdependence. In what follows, we use case evidence to demonstrate the two forms of network power—panopticon and chokepoint effects—and explain variation in their use. In particular, the case of financial messaging underscores the importance of institutional capacity and differences between the United States and Europe in their ability to employ these strategies. The case of the internet underscores how domestic institutions and norms constrain the behavior of the United States even when it has physical and legal jurisdiction over key hubs.

SWIFT, Counterterrorism, and Nonproliferation

SWIFT demonstrates how both the panopticon and chokepoint effects can work in global networks. Because SWIFT is central to the international payment system, it provides data about most global financial transactions and allows these transactions to take place. For the last twenty-five years, key states—most importantly the United States—have gradually transformed the repository into a surveillance asset and financial sector dependence into a tool of asymmetric interdependence.

Although the terrorist attacks of September 11, 2001, were a crucial moment in global surveillance politics, governments began considering SWIFT's potential much earlier. The Financial Action Task Force (FATF), a core global governance body focused on anti–money laundering, approached SWIFT in 1992.[71] FATF hoped to gain access to SWIFT records so as to track down illicit activity. At this point, SWIFT realized the peril of the economic efficiencies that it itself had created. As Lenny Schrank, a former chief officer of SWIFT, later reflected, "This was when we first began to think the unthinkable: that maybe we have some data that authorities would want, that SWIFT data would be revealed . . . and what to do about it . . . no one thought about terrorism at that time."[72] SWIFT refused the request, claiming that it could not provide information to public authorities and that such requests had to be directed to banks and other financial institutions engaged in the transaction. The organization claimed that SWIFT was a communications carrier much like a telephone operator rather than a data processor and thus should be immune to government monitoring.

SWIFT resisted government pressure for much of the 1990s, but succumbed after the September 11 attacks.[73] In the wake of the attacks, the U.S. Treasury began to examine ways to use the global financial system to curtail terrorist financing, targeting the terrorist money supply, and concluded that it could lawfully issue enforceable subpoenas against SWIFT to compel it to provide financial data. The Treasury initiative became known as the Terrorist Finance Tracking Program (TFTP) and targeted SWIFT as a key source of data. It was especially hard for SWIFT to resist Treasury demands, because the organization maintained a mirror data center containing its records in Virginia. In the years that followed, SWIFT secretly served as a global eye for the U.S. fight against terrorism, with the Treasury using the SWIFT system to monitor and investigate illicit activity.[74] As Juan Zarate, a former Treasury Department official, explained: "Access to SWIFT data would give the U.S. government a method of uncovering never-before-seen financial links, information that could unlock important clues to the next plot or allow an entire support network to be exposed and disrupted."[75]

The SWIFT data became the Rosetta stone for U.S. counterterrorism operations, as it shed light on the complex networks of terrorist financing.[76] The government used the data as a key forensic tool to identify terrorist operations, co-conspirators, and planning. This effort became so central to U.S. and European counterterrorism operations that when it was challenged by European actors worried about civil liberties, the U.S. government employed top officials including Secretary of State Hillary Clinton and Secretary of the Treasury Timothy Geithner to defend and demand the continuation of the program.[77] As one EU foreign minister concluded, "They pulled out all the moral and political stops."[78] After a joint review of the program, the European Commission argued: "The Commission is of the view that the TFTP remains an important and efficient instrument contributing to the fight against terrorism and its financing in the United States, the EU and elsewhere."[79] Despite initial public protests, the dominant coalition in EU politics quietly approved of the U.S. use of SWIFT to create a financial data panopticon, so long as the United States was prepared to share the proceeds.[80]

U.S. and EU efforts to weaponize SWIFT were not limited to the panopticon effect. As Joanna Caytas notes, "The most vulnerable element of financial infrastructure is its payments system, both at a national (macro) level and on an institutional (micro) plane."[81] Caytas furthermore argues that "disconnection from SWIFT access is, by any standard, the financial market equivalent of crossing the nuclear threshold, due to the vital importance of the embargoed services and near-complete lack of alternatives with comparable efficiency."[82]

As an example of the power of chokepoints, U.S. and European policymakers used SWIFT to reinforce the sanctions regime against Iran. A group of prominent U.S. policymakers, led by Ambassadors Richard Holbrook and Dennis Ross, started a private campaign, known as United Against Nuclear Iran (UANI) in the 2000s, to ratchet up pressure on the Iranian regime. The group targeted SWIFT as complicit in assisting the Iranian regime and contributing to its economic health.[83] As per SWIFT's 2010 annual report, some nineteen Iranian banks as well as another twenty-five institutions relied on the messaging system.[84] In January 2012, UANI sent a letter to SWIFT arguing that "the global SWIFT system is used by Iran to finance its nuclear weapons program, to finance terrorist activities and to provide the financial support necessary to brutally repress its own people."[85]

This campaign had consequences in both the United States and Europe. On February 2, 2012, the U.S. Senate Banking Committee adopted language that would have allowed the U.S. government to sanction SWIFT if it continued to allow Iranian financial institutions to use the SWIFT system, pushing the administration to adopt a more proactive stance.[86] The EU followed up on this threat in March, motivated both by both U.S. pressure and its own worries about Iran's nuclear program, and passed regulations that prohibited financial messaging services (e.g., SWIFT) from providing services to targeted institutions.[87]

The combination of EU and U.S. sanctions required SWIFT to cut Iranian banks out of its system. In 2012, the EU's Council banned the provision of financial messaging services to Iran.[88] As Lazaro Campos, a former chief executive officer of SWIFT, concluded, "This EU decision forces SWIFT to take action. Disconnecting banks is an extraordinary and unprecedented step for SWIFT. It is a direct result of international and multilateral action to intensify financial sanctions against Iran."[89]

The Iranian regime quickly felt the consequences, as its major financial institutions, including its central bank, found themselves locked out from the international payment system. As explained by a

EU official at the time, "It is a very efficient measure. . . . It can seriously cripple the banking sector in Iran."[90]

Unwinding the SWIFT measures became a key bargaining point in the negotiations over Iran's nuclear program.[91] During the negotiations with the United Nations Security Council's five permanent members, plus Germany, Iranian Foreign Minister Javad Zarif, made it clear that lifting the SWIFT ban was a top priority. "The deal will be made or broken," he said during an interview in July 2015, "[depending] on whether the United States wants to lift the sanctions or keep them."[92] Accordingly, lifting of the SWIFT measures was a key part of the eventual Iran deal.

Notably, the SWIFT measures were a result of joint pressure from both of the jurisdictions to which it was substantially exposed to. Had the United States not imposed pressure, it is unlikely that the European Union would have been able to act on its own; as Caytas notes, the EU's fragmented internal decision-making structures and lack of supple institutions undermines its ability to weaponize finance.[93] Equally, the United States might have had difficulties in acting unilaterally in the face of concerted EU opposition, given SWIFT's primary location in Europe.

In 2018, the politics of the SWIFT chokepoint became more complex. As the United States backed out of the Iran deal, it threatened to reimpose SWIFT restrictions on Iran, while the EU resisted the re-weaponization of SWIFT.[94] SWIFT responded to the threat of U.S. sanctions by delisting key Iranian institutions, while publicly maintaining that it was doing so to maintain the stability of the overall financial system. U.S. pressure has led European politicians such as German Foreign Minister Heiko Maas to begin discussing whether the EU needs to start building its own international financial payment channels, providing it with an alternative hub that is less vulnerable to U.S. pressure.[95] It is unclear, whether the EU is capable of building the necessary institutions to challenge the United States, given both internal political battles and external U.S. pressure against individual EU member states.[96]

The weaponization of SWIFT runs counter to the expectations of liberal accounts of globalization. It demonstrates how globalized networks can indeed be used to exercise "power over," both by gathering enormous amounts of data that can then be employed for security purposes and by systematically excluding states from participation in the world financial system. Exactly because the SWIFT organization was a crucial hub in global economic exchange, it allowed those states that had jurisdictional sway over it to employ the panopticon and chokepoint effects, just as our framework expects. Furthermore, the topology and existence of the global financial network provided the United States (and the EU) with extraordinary strategic resources. Without this network structure, both powers would not have been able to access data (e.g., on strategically important financial flows between third countries). In a counterfactual world, where the United States and the EU could only have unilaterally denied access to their own markets, or invoked bilateral dependencies to squeeze their adversaries, their efforts would have been far less effective, because adversary states could readily have turned to other financial partners.

The National Security Agency, PRISM, and Counter-terrorism

The United States enjoyed similar—and arguably even greater— dominance over information networks and e-commerce firms, thanks to asymmetric network structures. It was far less eager to deploy the chokepoint effect, however. This reflected strategic calculation of benefits; the United States believed that a general diffusion of communication technology and the global dominance of U.S. e-commerce firms was in its interests. It also reflected domestic institutional constraints. The United States had effectively precommitted to keeping e-commerce free from government control, except for truly compelling problems such as child pornography. This commitment meant that it had relatively few tools to oblige technology companies to do its bidding, and even where it did have such means, its commitment to openness imposed difficult trade-offs. Thus, for example, the U.S. sanctions regime applied to technology companies as well as other commercial actors, but the United States created specific (if dubiously beneficial) carve-outs (specific exceptions to the sanctions) intended to allow technology companies to support openness in Iran and other regimes subject to U.S. sanctions.[97]

The United States, under the Bill Clinton, George W. Bush, and

Barack Obama administrations, saw the spread of internet openness as linked to the spread of democracy, and thus strategically beneficial for the United States, as well as reflecting U.S. values.[98] In a much remarked upon speech, Secretary of State Clinton depicted the internet as a "network that magnifies the power and potential of all others," warning of the risks of censorship and celebrating the "freedom to connect" to "the internet, to websites, or to each other."[99] If the United States was to convince other states to refrain from controlling the internet, it also had to restrain itself, and moreover needed to ensure that the internet was not seen by other countries as a tool of direct U.S. influence. Thus, the United States largely refrained from putting overt pressure on e-commerce firms to help it achieve specific political outcomes. In one exceptional instance, a U.S. official asked Twitter officials to delay a temporary technical shutdown in the middle of the 2009 protests in Iran, in the belief that Twitter was playing an important part in helping organize the protests.[100] The action was controversial and was not publicly repeated. The United States also saw substantial commercial advantage in an open internet, warning that if states lapsed into "digital protectionism," then "global scalability—and thus the fate of American digital entrepreneurialism—will falter."[101]

Finally, the U.S. government sought to protect ICANN from a series of rearguard actions in the United Nations and other forums. When it appeared in 2005 that the EU might align itself with nondemocratic countries to move authority over domain names to a more conventional international organization, the United States pushed back forcefully.[102] Renewed pressure in 2012 combined with the Snowden revelations (the release of documents by Edward Snowden, a former National Security Agency [NSA] contractor, in 2013) to put the United States in a more awkward position: it finally accepted that ICANN needed to be separated from the U.S. government, and did so in the closing days of the Obama administration.[103]

Even while the United States declined to use chokepoints and promoted the cause of an open internet, it took enormous advantage of the panopticon effect. The concentration of network hubs and e-commerce firms within the United States offered extraordinary benefits for information gathering, which the United States was swift to take advantage of, especially after the September 11 attacks. After the attacks, the U.S. government quickly moved to leverage this advantage through the STELLARWIND program, which caused internal consternation within the Bush administration, and was eventually found by the Office of Legal Counsel to be illegal. It was soon replaced, however, by a variety of other programs designed to take advantage of the United States' unparalleled location at the heart of global networks of information exchange. In the blunt description of a former NSA director, Michael Hayden: "This is a home game for us. Are we not going to take advantage that so much of it goes through Redmond, Washington? Why would we not turn the most powerful telecommunications and computing management structure on the planet to our use?"[104] Redmond, Washington is the home city of Microsoft, but Hayden was likely referring more generally to the U.S. technology sector.

In some cases, the U.S. government was able to conduct surveillance through undisclosed direct relations with technology companies. Michael Hirsch describes how technology companies were worried about being seen as "instruments of government" but were willing to recognize that they needed to cooperate with the government on key issues.[105] Under the PRISM program, the U.S. government had substantial legal authority to compel the production of records and information regarding non-U.S. individuals from technology companies.

In addition, the U.S. government demanded the cooperation of telecommunications companies in carrying out "upstream collection" of large amounts of data from U.S. companies such as AT&T that help run the internet backbone. In the description of Ryan Gallagher and Marcy Wheeler, "According to the NSA's documents, it values AT&T not only because it 'has access to information that transits the nation,' but also because it maintains unique relationships with other phone and internet providers. The NSA exploits these relationships for surveillance purposes, commandeering AT&T's massive infrastructure and using it as a platform to covertly tap into communications processed by other companies."[106]

The United States can copy data in bulk and mine it later for valuable information, while superficially complying with U.S. laws that distinguish between the data of U.S. and non-U.S. citizens ("incidental collection" of data on U.S. citizens is permissible).[107] It has gathered data from internet exchange points and from the cable landing stations where undersea cables reach dry land. This data provided it with an alternative source of information to PRISM, and gave it direct reach into the internal data of U.S. e-commerce firms without their knowledge and consent, tapping, for example, into the communication flows through which Google reconciled data in different countries.

The Snowden revelations provoked political uproar, in both the United States and elsewhere. The result was a series of legal reforms that partly limited U.S. government access to the data of U.S. citizens, as well as policy measures including a presidential policy directive intended to reassure allies that the United States would not use their citizens' information in unduly invasive ways.

Other states certainly engaged in surveillance activities, including members of the EU (European privacy law does not currently prevent external surveillance for espionage, including European countries spying on each other, although it does restrict the ability of states to retain data on their own citizens). However, they lacked the "home advantage" of network centrality that Hayden described, and were correspondingly less able to gather useful information, so that the United States' European allies relied heavily on U.S. willingness to share surveillance data for their own security.[108]

Summary

The internet has regularly been depicted, both in the scholarly literature and in U.S. political debate, as a fundamentally liberal space characterized by open exchange and cooperation. This rhetoric serves to conceal the power dynamics that shape the relationship between the United States and online communications networks. For sure, the United States has not directly leveraged its dominance to create chokepoints, both because it lacks the domestic institutional capacity, and because several administrations have believed that its strategic and business interests are better served by open networks than the overt use of *force majeure*.[109] Yet the United States has also systematically exploited the panopticon effect to great benefit and has been able to do so even when its allies have formally objected. This degree of information-gathering power would be unthinkable either in a world where network forces did not tend to lead to grossly asymmetric outcomes benefiting states such as the United States or where states were limited to employing the tools of national markets and bilateral pressure.

Conclusion

There is a common trope in the literature on globalization, which suggests that greater economic exchange has fragmented and decentralized power relations. We, in contrast, argue that these economic interactions generate new structural conditions of power. Complex interdependence, like many other complex systems, may generate enduring power asymmetries.

This observation allows us to bring the literature on security, which has paid deep and sustained attention to the systemic and structural aspects of power, into direct debate with the literature on global markets, which has largely neglected it.[110] Theoretically, our account shows how the topography of networks shapes power relations, generating systematic differences in the ability of some states—and not others—to gather information and deny access to adversaries. Empirically, we show how decentralized patterns of economic exchange have led to centralized global networks such as SWIFT and the internet. As we discuss further in unpublished research, similar patterns prevail in other global networks such as the dollar clearing system and some globalized supply chains. Bringing these findings together, our article provides a historically detailed account of (1) how the new network structures that shape power and statecraft have come into being and (2) how these structures have been used to weaponize interdependence by privileged actors (who possess both leverage over network hubs and the appropriate domestic institutions that allow them to exercise this leverage).

Our research has far-reaching implications for the study of international affairs. Our argument brings scholars of economic interdependence and security studies into closer dialogue with one another, generating important new insights for both. On the one hand, we press scholars of international political economy to grapple with the fact that institutions, which may serve to drive efficiency gains and reduce transaction costs, may also serve as sites of control. On the other hand, we push scholars of international security to consider how economic globalization creates its own set of international structures—global networks—and thus generates new forms of state power.[111] More generally, our findings further suggest that international relations scholars need to pay far more attention to the practical workings of networks than they do at present.

Our evidence from the cases of financial and digital communication furthermore offer important support for our theoretical claims. States need both leverage over network hubs and appropriate institutions if they are to take advantage of the panopticon and chokepoint effects. States and jurisdictions that have potential leverage over network hubs, but do not have the appropriate institutions, cannot make good use of weaponized interdependence. Thus, the EU has fragmented instruments of financial regulation, which means that it has not been able to exercise control over SWIFT, except when its member states have agreed unanimously on formal sanctions under prodding from the United States. Lacking a regulator like the Treasury Department's Office of Foreign Assets Control, or legal instruments like those that the United States introduced after September 11, 2001, it has not been able to deploy market control to influence non-EU banks in the same ways that the United States has. However, although we do not discuss it here, other research indicates that the EU is perfectly capable of leveraging such control in domains where it has both influence over key hubs and well-developed institutions (e.g., in the area of privacy).[112]

U.S. capacity to weaponize interdependence similarly depends on domestic institutions as well as the topology of global networks. Thus, for example, the existing institutional capacity of the NSA and new laws introduced after the September 11 attacks allowed the United States to deploy the panopticon effect to enormous advantage, gathering vast quantities of strategic information. However, it lacked the appropriate institutions to oblige U.S. e-commerce companies to regulate other businesses and individuals or cut them out of the network, in the same way as it could use the U.S. correspondent banking system to regulate global networks.

Our framework also suggests that there are broader limits to weaponized interdependence. Not all markets rest directly on asymmetric networks. For example, international oil markets are sufficiently diversified that they are relatively liquid, and thus present no single point of control.[113] Where there are no network asymmetries, it will be difficult to weaponize interdependence. Moreover, not all sectors have been internationalized or rest heavily on networks of exchange. Finally, states that are less well integrated into the international economy are correspondingly less likely to be vulnerable to information gathering, while their vulnerability to the threatened or actual use of chokepoints will depend on the degree of autarky they have achieved.

We have now entered into a new stage of network politics, in which other states have begun to respond to such efforts. When interdependence is used by privileged states for strategic ends, other states are likely to start considering economic networks in strategic terms too. Targeted states—or states that fear they will be targeted—may attempt to isolate themselves from networks, look to turn network effects back on their more powerful adversaries, and even, under some circumstances, reshape networks so as to minimize their vulnerabilities or increase the vulnerabilities of others.[114] Hence, the more that privileged states look to take advantage of their privilege, the more that other states and nonstate actors will take action that might potentially weaken or even undermine the interdependent features of the preexisting system.[115] The ability of states to resist weaponized interdependence will reflect, in part, their degree of autonomy from those economic interests that seek to maintain the benefits of centralized exchanges even in the face of greater constraints on state authority.

The United States and its allies find themselves in a new and uncertain world, where rival powers and adversaries are seeking to insulate themselves from global networks, and perhaps over the longer run to displace these networks. Our arguments do not provide precise predictions as to the strategies that rivals and adversaries will deploy, although they do suggest how these strategies will be shaped by rival states' own national institutions and network positions. They highlight the importance of enduring, but not immutable network structures. States are locked into existing network structures only up to that point where the costs of remaining in them are lower than the benefits: should this change, one may see transitions to new arrangements.

Thus, for example, the initial U.S. decision to exclude the Chinese firm ZTE from global supply chains appears to have precipitated a major reconsideration by the Chinese government of China's reliance on foreign chip manufacturers and of the need for China to create its own domestic manufacturing capacities to mitigate its economic vulnerabilities.[116] This policy reorientation surely involves efforts to mitigate bilateral asymmetric vulnerabilities of the kind emphasized in traditional liberal accounts. However, it may also require the reconfiguration of entire networks of interlocking supply chains with global consequences. Similar concerns led to initial U.S. suspicion of Huawei and ZTE and to fears that their telecommunications equipment may have built-in vulnerabilities to assist Chinese surveillance. As interdependence becomes increasingly weaponized, global supply chains may unravel.

Western threats to weaponize SWIFT against Russia in the wake of the Ukraine crisis produced similar responses.[117] Then Prime Minister Dimitry Medvedev threatened that "our economic reaction and generally any other reaction will be without limits," while the chief executive of VTB, a major Russian bank, said it would mean that "the countries are on the verge of war, or they are definitely in a cold war."[118] In a major foreign policy speech, President Vladimir Putin warned that "politically motivated sanctions have only strengthened the trend towards seeking to bolster economic and financial sovereignty and countries' or their regional groups' desire to find ways of protecting themselves from the risks of outside pressure. We already see that more and more countries are looking for ways to become less dependent on the dollar and are setting up alternative financial and payments systems and reserve currencies. I think that our American friends are quite simply cutting the branch they are sitting on."[119]

This may help explain Russia's apparent reported interest in creating a blockchain-based payment system for the Eurasian Economic Union and other states interested in signing up.[120] Blockchain systems are designed to use "proof of work" or "proof of stake" and provable guarantees (systems based on mathematically secure theorems) to avoid any need for central authority (and hence any possibility of that authority being leveraged for political or other purposes).[121] In this way, a blockchain ledger for financial transactions could mute chokepoint strategies. That said, blockchain systems impose their own, sometimes quite unattractive risks and restrictions for state authorities.

Piecemeal worries over adversaries and resulting actions may erode global networks over the long term. More rapid change may occur if U.S. actions lead allies to seriously reconsider their exposure to global networks that they rely on far more heavily than China and Russia, but have not to this point seen as a threat vector. As Daniel Drezner has argued, the most plausible path to such a transition would involve the defection of U.S. allies, if they decided that the United States was abusing weaponized interdependence in ways that conflicted with their core interests.[122] Our account helps explain why this is so: it is the United States' West European allies that are most likely to have control or potential control over key nodes in global networks, or to be credibly able to set up their own alternatives.

European states have been willing to accept U.S. extraterritorial pressure, because of "shared democratic values and indeed economic interests."[123] Currently, they benefit more than they suffer from the U.S. exercise of network hegemony. However, this acquiescence "implies that [the equilibrium of transatlantic relations] should not be disturbed by the abuse of that which certain people perceive as a form of imperium in the domain of law."[124] Policymakers in Europe have started to explore financing options that are isolated from the U.S. financial system. While the practical effect of these specific initiatives may be limited in the short term, they put in motion a potential decoupling. This sanitization process may possibly fall victim to infighting within and among allies, but might also generate its own internal self-reinforcing dynamics.[125] If the current war of words between Europe and the United States over secondary sanctions devolves into clashing standards and competing financial instruments, the United States may face the slow erosion of its ability to weaponize key economic networks, constraining its ability to project power globally.

Notes

The authors are grateful to Miles Evers, Llewellyn Hughes, Woojeong Jang, Erik Jones, Miles Kahler, Nikhil Kalyanpur, Matthias Matthijs, Kathleen Mc-Namara, Daniel Nexon, Gideon Rose, Mark Schwartz, and William Wine-coff, as well as the anonymous reviewers for comments and criticism. Charles Glaser provided especially detailed and helpful comments on an early draft. Previous versions of this article were presented at the International Studies Association annual meeting in 2018, and at the Johns Hopkins University School of Advanced International Studies Research Seminar in Politics and Political Economy on April 17, 2018. The authors are also grateful to the participants and audience at both events for feedback. We thank International Security and MIT University Press for permission to rerelease the article in this volume.

1. The legal principles through which exposure is determined are complex. For a useful introduction, see Serena B. Wille, "Anti-Money-Laundering and OFAC Sanctions Issues," *CFA Institute Conference Proceedings Quarterly*, vol. 29 (2011), pp. 59–64.

2. Anne-Sylvaine Chassany, Michael Peel and Tobias Buck, "EU to Seek Exemptions from New US Sanctions on Iran," *Financial Times*, May 9, 2018 (www.ft.com/content/d26ddea6-5375-11e8-b24e-cad6aa67e23e).

3. Henry Foy, "EN+ President Steps Down in Move to Win US Sanctions Waiver," *Financial Times*, June 4, 2018 (www.ft.com/content/8c1ac0a6-67be -11e8-8cf3-0c230fa67aec.rusal).

4. Llewelyn Hughes and Austin Long, "Is There an Oil Weapon? Security Implications of Changes in the Structure of the International Oil Market," *International Security*, vol. 39 (Winter 2014/2015), pp. 152–189; Jeff D. Colgan, "Fueling the Fire: Pathways from Oil to War," *International Security*, vol. 38 (Fall 2013), pp. 147–180; Charles L. Glaser, "How Oil Influences U.S. National Security: Reframing Energy Security," *International* Security, vol. 38 (Fall 2013), pp. 112–146; Llewelyn Hughes and Phillip Y. Lipscy, "The Politics of Energy," *Annual Review of Political Science*, vol. 16 (May 2013), pp. 449–469.

5. Rosa Brooks, *How Everything Became War and the Military Became Everything* (New York: Simon and Schuster, 2017).

6. Thomas J. Wright, *All Measures Short of War: The Contest for the Twenty-First Century and the Future of American Power* (New Haven: Yale University Press, 2017).

7. Joanne Gowa, "Bipolarity, Multipolarity, and Free Trade," *American Political Science Review*, vol. 83 (December 1989), pp. 1245–1256; Brian M. Pollins, "Does Trade Still Follow the Flag?," *American Political Science Review*, vol. 83 (June 1989), pp. 465–480; John R. Oneal and others, "The Liberal Peace: Interdependence, Democracy, and International Conflict, 1950–85," *Journal of Peace Research*, vol. 33 (February 1996), pp. 11–28; Dale C. Copeland, *Economic Interdependence and War* (Princeton: Princeton University Press, 2014).

8. Robert A. Pape, "Why Economic Sanctions Do Not Work," *International Security*, vol. 22 (Fall 1997), pp. 90–136; Kimberly Ann Elliott, "The Sanctions Glass: Half Full or Completely Empty?" *International Security*, vol. 23 (Summer 1998), pp. 50–65; Daniel W. Drezner. *The Sanctions Paradox: Economic Statecraft and International Relations* (New York: Cambridge University Press, 1999); David A. Baldwin, "The Sanctions Debate and the Logic of Choice," *International Security*, vol. 24 (Winter 2000), pp. 80–107; Jonathan Kirshner, "Economic Sanctions: The State of the Art," *Security Studies*, vol. 11 (Summer 2002), pp. 160–179; Fiona McGillivray and Allan C. Stam, "Political Institutions, Coercive Diplomacy, and the Duration of Economic Sanctions," *Journal of Conflict Resolution*, vol. 48 (April 2004), pp. 154–172; Daniel W. Drezner, "Outside the Box: Explaining Sanctions in Pursuit of Foreign Economic Goals," *International Interactions*, vol. 26 (2001), pp. 379–410, which does consider secondary sanctions, as does the policy literature we discuss below.

9. See Peter D. Feaver and Eric B. Lorber, *Coercive Diplomacy and the New Financial Levers: Evaluating the Intended and Unintended Consequences of Financial Sanctions* (London: Legatum Institute, 2010); Orde F. Kittrie, "New Sanctions for a New Century: Treasury's Innovative Use of Financial Sanctions," *University of Pennsylvania Journal of International Law*, vol. 30 (Spring 2009), pp. 789–822; and Daniel W. Drezner, "Targeted Sanctions in a World of Global Finance," *International Interactions*, vol. 41 (2015), pp. 755–764. Secondary sanctions coexist with other tools to control international financial flows. For a useful recent overview, see Miles Kahler and others, *Global Governance to Combat Illicit Financial Flows: Measurement, Evaluation, Innovation* (Washington: Council on Foreign Relations, 2018).

10. Of course, there is a burgeoning scholarship on cybersecurity, which is relevant to the internet. See Sarah E. Kreps and Jacquelyn Schneider, *Escalation Firebreaks in the Cyber, Conventional and Nuclear Domains: Moving Beyond Effects-Based Logics* (Cornell University and U.S. Naval War College, 2018); Joseph S. Nye Jr., "Deterrence and Dissuasion in Cyberspace," *International Security*, vol. 41 (Winter 2016/17), pp. 44–71; Rebecca Slayton, "What is the Cyber Offense-Defense Balance? Conceptions, Causes and Assessment," *International Security*, vol. 41 (Winter 2016/17), pp. 72–109;

Henry Farrell and Charles L. Glaser, "The Role of Effects, Saliencies and Norms in U.S. Cyberwar Doctrine," *Journal of Cybersecurity*, vol. 3 (March 2017), pp. 7–17; and Jon R. Lindsay, "The Impact of China on Cybersecurity: Fiction and Friction," *International Security*, vol. 39 (Winter 2014/15), pp. 7–47. This literature, however, largely fails to address the network characteristics of the internet, focusing instead on variation in traditional metrics such as the offense-defense balance, the ability to deter or compel, and the treatment of the network characteristics of the internet either as a constant, or a straightforward determinant of state-level vulnerability or strength (so that technologically advanced states such as the United States will have a different set of strengths and vulnerabilities than states that rely less on technology). An earlier proto-literature on "netwar" examines how leaderless networks are becoming more important in world politics, but is primarily descriptive in nature. See John Arquilla and David Ronfeldt, *The Advent of Netwar* (Santa Monica: RAND Corporation, 1996). There is a technical literature that discusses networks, but it tends not to discuss the strategic aspects we focus on below. For an important exception, see Réka Albert, Hawoong Jeong, and Albert-László Barabási, "Error and Attack Tolerance of Complex Networks," *Nature*, vol. 406 (July 2000), pp. 378–382.

11. Kathryn Judge, "Intermediary Influence," *University of Chicago Law Review*, vol. 82 (Spring 2015), pp. 573–642.

12. See Robert O. Keohane and Joseph S. Nye Jr., *Power and Interdependence*, 4th ed. (New York: Longman, 2012); Kal Raustiala," The Architecture of International Cooperation: Transgovernmental Networks and the Future of International Law," *Virginia Journal of International Law*, vol. 43 (Fall 2002), pp. 1–92; Anne-Marie Slaughter, "Global Government Networks, Global Information Agencies, and Disaggregated Democracy," *Michigan Journal of International Law*, vol. 24 (Summer 2003), pp. 1044–1075; Anne-Marie Slaughter, *A New World Order* (Princeton: Princeton University Press, 2004); and Anne-Marie Slaughter, *The Chessboard and the Web: Strategies of Connection in a Networked World* (New Haven: Yale University Press, 2017). The classic critique of liberalism's emphasis on mutual gains from cooperation is Stephen D. Krasner, "Global Communications and National Power: Life on the Pareto Frontier," *World Politics*, vol. 43 (1991), pp. 336–366.

13. Albert-László Barabási and Réka Albert, "Emergence of Scaling in Random Networks," *Science*, vol. 286 (October 1999), pp. 509–512; M. E. J. Newman and Juyong Park, "Why Social Networks are Different from Other Types of Networks," *Physical Review E*, vol. 68 (September 2003), pp. 1–8; Aaron Clauset, Cosma Rohilla Shalizi, and M. E. J. Newman. "Power-Law Distributions in Empirical Data," *SIAM Review*, vol. 51 (December 2009), pp. 661–703; Emilie M. Hafner-Burton, Miles Kahler, and Alexander H. Montgomery. "Network Analysis for International Relations," *International*

Organization, vol. 63 (Summer 2009), pp. 559–592; and Stacie E. Goddard, "Embedded Revisionism: Networks, Institutions, and Challenges to World Order," *International Organization*, vol. 72 (Fall 2018), pp. 763–797.

14. Anecdotal evidence suggests similar processes are at work in a number of other areas, including dollar clearing and global supply chains. See, for example, Cheng Ting-Fang and Lauly Li, "'Huawei Freeze' chills global supply chain," *Nikki Asian Review*, December 8, 2018.

15. Recent scholarship in international political economy has begun to focus more explicitly on the relationship between structure and statecraft. For a network-based critique of state level reductionism similar to ours, see Thomas Oatley, "The Reductionist Gamble: Open Economy Politics in the Global Economy," *International Organization*, vol. 65 (April 2011), pp. 311–341.

16. Robert O. Keohane, "The Old IPE and the New," *Review of International Political Economy*, vol. 16 (February 2009), pp. 34–46, at pp. 36–37.

17. Keohane and Nye, *Power and Interdependence*, p. 253.

18. Ibid.

19. Nye, "Deterrence and Dissuasion in Cyberspace."

20. Raustiala, "The Architecture of International Cooperation"; Slaughter, *A New World Order*; and Slaughter, *The Chessboard and the Web*.

21. Slaughter, *The Chessboard and the Web*, p. 163.

22. See, in particular, Stacie E. Goddard, and Daniel H. Nexon, "The Dynamics of Global Power Politics: A Framework for Analysis," *Journal of Global Security Studies*, vol. 1 (February 2016), pp. 4–18; Mark Blyth and Matthias Matthijs, "Black Swans, Lame Ducks and the Mystery of IPE's Missing Macroeconomy," *Review of International Political Economy*, vol. 24 (April 2017), pp. 203–31; Seva Gunitsky, "Complexity and Theories of Change in International Politics," *International Theory*, vol. 5 (March 2013), pp. 35–63; and Thomas Oatley, "Towards a Political Economy of Complex Interdependence," *European Journal of International Relations* (forthcoming).

23. John F. Padgett and Christopher K. Ansell, "Robust Action and the Rise of the Medici, 1400–1434," *American Journal of* Sociology, vol. 98 (May 1993), pp. 1259–1319; and Judge, "Intermediary Influence."

24. Our argument builds on Susan Strange's notion of "structural power." See, for example, Susan Strange, *The Retreat of the State: The Diffusion of Power in the World Economy* (New York: Cambridge University Press, 1996). See also Susan K. Sell, "Ahead of Her Time? Susan Strange and Global Governance," in *Susan Strange and the Future of Global Political Economy*, in *Susan Strange and the Future of Global Political Economy: Power, Control, and Transformation*, edited by Randall Germain (London: Routledge, 2016). For different accounts, see Philip G. Cerny, *Rethinking World Politics: A Theory of Transnational Neopluralism* (New York: Oxford University Press, 2010); and Louis W. Pauly, "The Anarchical Society and a Global

Political Economy," in *The Anarchical Society at 40: Contemporary Challenges and Prospects*, edited by Hidemi Suganami, Madeline Carr and Adam Humphreys (New York: Oxford University Press, 2017). On network power, political theory, and international relations more generally, see David Singh Grewal, *Network Power: The Social Dynamics of Globalization* (New York: Oxford University Press, 2009).

25. Newman and Park, "Why Social Networks are Different from Other Types of Networks." An important literature in statistical physics and related disciplines studies the topology of large-scale networks, and how topology shapes, for example, processes of contagion. See Duncan J. Watts, "The 'New' Science of Networks," *Annual Review of Sociology*, vol. 30 (2004), pp. 243–270; and, for a useful overview, Mark Newman, Albert-László Barabási, and Duncan J. Watts (eds.), *The Structure and Dynamics of Networks* (Princeton: Princeton University Press, 2011). This literature has been underused by political scientists. For recent exceptions, see Hafner-Burton, Kahler, and Montgomery, "Network Analysis for International Relations"; Goddard, "Embedded Revisionism"; Miles Kahler ed., *Network Politics: Agency, Power, and Governance* (Ithaca: Cornell University Press, 2009); Thomas Oatley, *A Political Economy of American Hegemony: Buildups, Booms, and Busts* (New York: Cambridge University Press, 2015); and Brandon J. Kinne, "Defense Cooperation Agreements and the Emergence of a Global Security Network," *International Organization*, vol. 72 (Fall 2018), pp. 799–837.

26. Of course, some forms of international exchange are not networks in this sense—market transfers of commodities with a significant number of suppliers and no need for network infrastructure are unlikely to be subject to the dynamics we discuss here. We return to this point in the conclusion.

27. See Clauset, Shalizi, and Newman, "Power-Law Distributions in Empirical Data." For applications to security, see Aaron Clauset, Maxwell Young and Kristian Skrede Gleditsch, "On the Frequency of Severe Terrorist Events," *Journal of Conflict Resolution*, vol. 51 (February 2007), pp. 58–88; and Aaron Clauset, "Trends and Fluctuations in the Severity of Interstate Wars," *Science Advances*, vol. 4 (February 2018), pp. 1–9.

28. See Herbert A. Simon, "On a Class of Skew Distribution Functions," *Biometrika*, vol. 42 (December 1955), pp. 425–440; and Barabási and Albert, "Emergence of Scaling in Random Networks."

29. Ranjay Gulati, "Network Location and Learning: The Influence of Network Resources and Firm Capabilities on Alliance Formation," *Strategic Management Journal*, vol. 20 (May 1999), pp. 397–420; and Stephen P. Borgatti and Rob Cross, "A Relational View of Information Seeking and Learning in social networks," *Management Science*, vol. 49 (April 2003), pp. 432–445.

30. W. Brian Arthur, "Competing Technologies, Increasing Returns, and Lock-In by Historical Events," *The Economic Journal*, vol. 99 (March 1989),

pp. 116–131; and Paul A. David, "Clio and the Economics of QWERTY," *The American Economic Review*, vol. 75 (May 1985), pp. 332–337.

31. Thomas Oatley and others, "The Political Economy of Global Finance: A Network Model," *Perspectives on Politics*, vol. 11 (March 2013), pp. 133–153; and Oatley, *A Political Economy of American Hegemony*.

32. Réka Albert, Hawoong Jeong, and Albert-László Barabási. "Internet: Diameter of the World-Wide Web," *Nature*, vol. 401 (September 1999), pp. 130–131; Stefania Vitali, James B. Glattfelder, and Stefano Battiston, "The Network of Global Corporate Control," *PloS One*, vol. 6 (October 2011), pp. 1–6; and Camelia Miniou and Javier A. Reyes, "A Network Analysis of Global Banking: 1978–2010," *Journal of Financial Stability*, vol. 9 (June 2013), pp. 168–184.

33. On trade, see Giorgio Fagiolo, Javier Reyes, and Stefano Schiavo, "World-Trade Web: Topological Properties, Dynamics, and Evolution," *Physical Review E,* vol. 79 (March 2009), pp. 1–19; and Luca De Benedictis and Lucia Tajoli, "The World Trade Network," *The World Economy*, vol. 34 (August 2011), pp. 1417–1454; On finance, see Thomas Oatley and others., "The Political Economy of Global Finance"; and William Kindred Winecoff, "Structural Power and the Global Financial Crisis: A Network Analytical Approach," *Business and Politics*, vol. 17 (October 2015), pp. 495–525.

34. Soon-Hyung Yook, Hawoong Jeong, and Albert-László Barabási, "Modeling the Internet's Large-Scale Topology," *Proceedings of the National Academy of Sciences*, vol. 99 (October 2002), pp. 13382–13386.

35. On power relations in the platform economy, see Lina M. Khan, "The Ideological Roots of America's Market Power Problem," *Yale Law Journal Forum*, vol. 126 (June 2018), pp. 960–979 (www.yalelawjournal.org/pdf/Khan_xktx9xrh.pdf); and Lina M. Khan, "Amazon's Anti-Trust Paradox," *Yale Law Journal*, vol. 126 (January 2017), pp. 710–805.

36. Judge, "Intermediary Influence"; and Natasha Tusikov, *Chokepoints: Global Private Regulation on the Internet* (Berkeley: University of California Press, 2016).

37. George E. Shambaugh IV, "Dominance, Dependence, and Political Power: Tethering Technology in the 1980s and Today," *International Studies Quarterly*, vol. 40 (December 1996), pp. 559–588; Beth A. Simmons, "The International Politics of Harmonization: The Case of Capital Market Regulation," *International Organization*, vol. 55 (Summer 2001), pp. 589–620; Daniel W. Drezner, *All Politics is Global: Explaining International Regulatory Regimes* (Princeton: Princeton University Press, 2007); and Nikhil Kalyanpur and Abraham L. Newman, "Mobilizing Market Power: Jurisdictional Expansion as Economic Statecraft," *International Organization*, vol. 73 (Winter 2019), pp. 1–34.

38. Keohane and Nye, *Power and Interdependence*; Gowa, "Bipolarity, Multipolarity, and Free Trade"; Pollins, "Does Trade Still Follow the Flag?";

Oneal and others, "The Liberal Peace: Interdependence, Democracy, and International Conflict, 1950–85"; and Copeland, *Economic Interdependence and War.*

39. Harold James, "Cosmos, Chaos: Finance, Power and Conflict," *International Affairs*, vol. 90 (January 2014), pp. 37–57, at p. 43.

40. Ibid., p. 54.

41. Nicholas A. Lambert, *Planning Armageddon: British Economic Warfare and the First World War* (Cambridge: Harvard University Press, 2012).

42. Heidi J. S. Tworek, *News from Germany: The Competition to Control World Communications, 1900–1945* (Cambridge: Harvard University Press, 2019).

43. Sarah C. Kaczmarek and Abraham L. Newman, "The Long Arm of the law: Extraterritoriality and the National Implementation of Foreign Bribery Legislation," *International Organization*, vol. 65 (Fall 2011), pp. 745–770; Kal Raustiala, *Does the Constitution Follow the Flag? The Evolution of Territoriality in American Law* (New York: Oxford University Press, 2011); Tonya L Putnam, *Courts Without Borders: Law, Politics, and U.S. Extraterritoriality* (New York: Cambridge University Press, 2016).

44. David Bach and Abraham L. Newman, "The European Regulatory State and Global Public Policy: Micro-Institutions, Macro-Influence," *Journal of European Public Policy*, vol. 14 (September 2007), pp. 827–846; Elliot Posner, "Making Rules for Global Finance: Transatlantic Regulatory Cooperation at the Turn of the Millennium," *International Organization*, vol. 63 (October 2009), pp. 665–699; Tim Büthe and Walter Mattli, *The New Global Rulers: The Privatization of Regulation in the World Economy* (Princeton: Princeton University Press, 2011); and Kalyanpur and Newman, "Mobilizing Market Power."

45. Abraham L. Newman, *Protectors of Privacy: Regulating Personal Information in the Global Economy* (Ithaca: Cornell University Press, 2008).

46. Henry Farrell and Abraham L. Newman, "Making Global Markets: Historical Institutionalism in International Political Economy," *Review of International Political Economy*, vol. 17 (October 2010), pp. 609–638; Henry Farrell and Abraham L. Newman, "Domestic Institutions Beyond the Nation-State: Charting the New Interdependence Approach," *World Politics*, vol. 66 (April 2014), pp. 331–363.

47. Our history of SWIFT draws from Susan V. Scott and Markos Zachariadis, *The Society for Worldwide Interbank Financial Telecommunication (SWIFT): Cooperative Governance for Network Innovation, Standards, and Community* (London: Routledge, 2014). SWIFT is remarkably understudied by international security scholars, considering its empirical importance to sanctions. For a key exception, see Erik Jones and Andrew Whitworth, "The Unintended Consequences of European Sanctions on Russia," *Survival*, vol. 56 (October/November 2014), pp. 21–30. For discussions of SWIFT in

the EU-US relationship, see Marieke De Goede, "The SWIFT Affair and the Global Politics of European Security," *Journal of Common Market Studies*, vol. 50 (March 2012), pp. 214–230; and Henry Farrell and Abraham Newman, "The New Politics of Interdependence: Cross-National Layering in Trans-Atlantic Regulatory Disputes," *Comparative Political Studies*, vol. 48 (March 2015), pp. 497–526.

48. Scott and Zachariadis, *The Society for Worldwide Interbank Financial Telecommunication (SWIFT)*, p. 1.

49. Ibid., p. 107.

50. European Commission, "Following an Undertaking by S.W.I.F.T. to Change Its Membership Rules, the European Commission Suspends Its Action for Breach of Competition Rules," press release IP/97/870 (Brussels: European Commission, October 13, 1997), p. 2.

51. Susan V. Scott, John Van Reenen and Markos Zachariadis, *The Long-Term Effect of Digital Innovation on Bank Performance: An Empirical Study of SWIFT Adoption in Financial Services*, CPEP Discussion Paper No. 992 (London: London School of Economics Center for Economic Performance, 2017), (http://eprints.lse.ac.uk/id/eprint/83641).

52. William J. Clinton, remarks at the Paul H. Nitze School of Advanced International Studies, Johns Hopkins University, Washington D.C., March 8, 2000 (www.presidency.ucsb.edu/ws/?pid=87714).

53. On the theory of distributed networks, see Paul Baran, "On Distributed Communications Networks," *IEEE Transactions on Communications Systems*, vol. 12 (March 1964), pp. 1–9.

54. Philip Elmer-Dewitt, "First Nation in Cyberspace," *Time*, December 6, 1993 (http://content.time.com/time/magazine/article/0,9171,979768,00.html).

55. John Perry Barlow, "A Declaration of the Independence of Cyberspace," *Humanist*, vol. 56 (May/June 1996), p 18.

56. Albert, Jeong, and Barabási, "Diameter of the World-Wide Web."

57. Jack Goldsmith and Tim Wu, *Who Controls the Internet? Illusions of a Borderless World* (New York: Oxford University Press, 2006); Ronald Deibert and others, *Access Denied: The Practice and Policy of Global Internet Filtering* (Cambridge: MIT Press, 2008); Adam Segal, *The Hacked World Order: How Nations Fight, Trade, Maneuver, and Manipulate in the Digital Age* (New York: PublicAffairs, 2017); and Joshua A. Tucker and others, "From Liberation to Turmoil: Social Media and Democracy," *Journal of Democracy*, vol. 28 (October 2017), pp. 46–59.

58. Asia-Pacific Economic Cooperation Secretariat, "Economic Impact of Submarine Cable Disruptions" (Singapore: APEC Policy Support Unit, February 2013).

59. Ibid.

60. See Patrick S. Ryan and Jason Gerson, "A Primer on Internet Exchange Points for Policymakers and Non-Engineers" (Rochester: Social Science

Research Network, August 2012) (https://papers.ssrn.com/sol3/papers.cfm?abstract_id=2128103); Kuai Xu and others, "On Properties of Internet Exchange Points and Their impact on AS Topology and Relationship," in *Networking 2004: Networking Technologies, Services, and Protocols; Performance of Computer and Communication Networks; Mobile and Wireless Communications*, edited by Nikolas Mitrou (Berlin: Springer-Verlag, 2004), pp. 284–295.

61. Henry Farrell, interview with Ira Magaziner, New York City, New York, September 21, 2000.

62. White House, "A Framework for Global Electronic Commerce" (Washington: White House, 1997).

63. Milton L. Mueller, *Ruling the Root: Internet Governance and the Taming of Cyberspace* (Cambridge: MIT Press, 2009).

64. Ibid.

65. Jack M. Balkin, "The Future of Free Expression in a Digital Age," *Pepperdine Law Review*, vol. 36 (2008), pp. 427–444.

66. See, more generally, Frank Pasquale, *The Black Box Society: The Secret Algorithms That Control Money and Information* (Cambridge: Harvard University Press, 2015).

67. Khan, "Amazon's Anti-Trust Paradox."

68. See Laura DeNardis, "Hidden Levers of Internet Control: An Infrastructure-Based Theory of Internet Governance," *Information, Communication & Society*, vol. 15 (June 2012), pp. 720–738; and Tusikov, *Chokepoints*.

69. Bruce Schneier, "Censorship in the Age of Large Cloud Providers," *Lawfare*, June 7, 2018 (https://lawfareblog.com/censorship-age-large-cloud-providers).

70. Benjamin Freed, "70 Percent of the World's Web Traffic Flows through Loudoun County," *Washingtonian*, September 14, 2016 (www.washingtonian.com/2016/09/14/70-percentworlds-web-traffic-flows-loudoun-county).

71. On FATF, see Julia Morse, "Blacklists, Market Enforcement, and the Global Regime to Combat Terrorist Financing," *International Organization* (forthcoming); Eleni Tsingou, "Global Financial Governance and the Developing Anti-Money Laundering Regime: What Lessons for International Political Economy?" *International Politics*, vol. 47 (November 2010), pp. 617–637; and Anne L. Clunan, "The Fight Against Terrorist Financing," *Political Science Quarterly*, vol. 121 (Winter 2006/07), pp. 569–596.

72. Scott and Zachariadis, *The Society for Worldwide Interbank Financial Telecommunication (SWIFT)*, p. 128.

73. For an excellent overview of both SWIFT and the dollar clearing system, see Joanna Diane Caytas, "Weaponizing Finance: U.S. and European Options, Tools, and Policies," *Columbia Journal of International Law*, vol. 23 (Spring 2017), pp. 441–475.

74. Eric Lichtblau and James Risen, "Bank Data is Sifted by US in Secret

to Block Terror," *New York Times*, June 23, 2006 (www.nytimes.com/2006 /06/23/washington/23intel.html).

75. Juan C. Zarate, *Treasury's War: The Unleashing of a New Era of Financial Warfare* (London: Hachette, 2013), p. 50.

76. Lichtblau and Risen, "Bank Data is Sifted by U.S. in Secret to Block Terror."

77. For a detailed discussion, see Henry Farrell and Abraham Newman, *Of Privacy and Power: The Transatlantic Struggle over Freedom and Security* (Princeton: Princeton University Press, 2019).

78. Hans-Jürgen Schlamp, "EU to Allow US Access to Bank Transaction Data," *Spiegel Online*, November 27, 2009 (www.spiegel.de/international/ europe/spying-on-terrorist-cash-flows-eu-to-allow-us-access-to-bank -transaction-data-a-663846.html).

79. European Commission, "Joint Review Report of the implementation of the Agreement between the European Union and the United States of America on the processing and transfer of Financial Messaging Data from the European Union to the United States for the purposes of the Terrorist Finance Tracking Program" (Brussels: European Commission, 2017), p. 7.

80. Farrell and Newman, "The New Politics of Interdependence."

81. Caytas, "Weaponizing Finance," p. 449.

82. Ibid., p. 451.

83. United Against Nuclear Iran (UANI), "SWIFT Campaign," 2012 (www.unitedagainstnucleariran.com/index.php/swift).

84. SWIFT, "Annual Review, 2010: Common Challenges, Unique Solutions" (Brussels: SWIFT, 2010).

85. Ambassador Mark D. Wallace, "letter re: SWIFT and Iran to Yawar Shah" (Washington: UANI, January 30, 2012) (t/files/IBR%20Correspon dence/UANI_Letter_to_SWIFT_013012.pdf); and Jay Solomon and Adam Entous, "Banking Hub Adds to Pressure on Iran," *Wall Street Journal*, February 4, 2012 (www.wsj.com/articles/SB1000142405297020388990457 7201330206741436); and Jay Solomon and Adam Entous, "Banking Hub adds to Pressure on Iran," *Wall Street Journal*, February 4, 2012 (www.wsj.com/ articles/SB10001424052970203889904577201330206741436).

86. Jay Solomon, *The Iran Wars: Spy Games, Bank Battles, and the Secret Deals that Reshaped the Middle East* (New York: Random House, 2016).

87. "US presses EU to close SWIFT network to Iran," *Agence France -Presse*, February 16, 2012; and Samuel Rubenfeld, "SWIFT to Comply with EU Ban on Blacklisted Entities," *Wall Street Journal*, March 15, 2018 (https:// blogs.wsj.com/corruption-currents/2012/03/15/swift-to-comply-with-eu-ban -on-blacklisted-entities).

88. Aaron Arnold, "The True Cost of Financial Sanctions," *Survival*, vol. 58 (June/July 2016), pp. 77–100; and "Iran cut off from Global Financial System," *Associated Press*, March 15, 2012.

89. UANI, "UANI Issues Statement Following SWIFT's Announcement to Discontinue Services to EU-Sanctioned Iranian Financial Institutions," press release (Washington: UANI, March 15, 2012) (www.unitedagainstnucleariran.com/index.php/swift).

90. Rick Gladstone and Stephen Castle, "Global Network Expels as Many as 30 of Iran's Banks in Move to Isolate its Economy," *New York Times*, March 15, 2012 (www.nytimes.com/2012/03/16/world/middleeast/crucial-communication-network-expelling-iranian-banks.html).

91. Zarate, *Treasury's War*.

92. Arnold, "The True Costs of Financial Sanctions," p. 85.

93. Caytas, "Weaponizing Finance."

94. Sam Fleming, Philip Stafford and Jim Brunsden, "US and EU Head for Showdown over Shutting Iran off from Finance," *Financial Times*, May 17, 2018; and Richard Goldberg and Mark Dubowitz, "To Help Iran, Angela Merkel Tries to Pull a Fast one with SWIFT," *Wall Street Journal*, June 20, 2018.

95. Heiko Maas, "Wir lassen Nicht zu, dass die USA uber unsere kopfe hinweg handeln," *Handelsblatt,* August 28, 2018 (www.handelsblatt.com/meinung/gastbeitraege/gastkommentar-wir-lassen-nicht-zu-dass-die-usa-ueber-unsere-koepfe-hinweg-handeln/22933006.html).

96. Adam Tooze and Christian Odendahl, *Can the Euro Rival the Dollar* (London: Center for European Reform, 2018).

97. See Daniel Kehl, "US Government Clarifies Tech Authorizations under Iranian Sanctions," *Open Technology Institute Blog New America*, February 12, 2014 (www.newamerica.org/oti/blog/us-government-clarifes-tech-authorizations-under-iranian-sanctions).

98. Rebecca MacKinnon, *Consent of the Networked: The Worldwide Struggle for Internet Freedom* (New York: Basic Books, 2012); Daniel R. McCarthy, "Open Networks and the Open Door: American Foreign Policy and the Narration of the Internet," *Foreign Policy Analysis*, vol. 7 (January 2011), pp. 89–111; and Ryan David Kiggins, "Open for Expansion: U.S. Policy and the Purpose for the Internet in the Post-Cold War Era," *International Studies Perspectives*, vol. 16 (February 2015), pp. 86–105.

99. Hillary Rodham Clinton, "Remarks on Internet Freedom," speech given at the Newseum, Washington, D.C., January 21, 2010 (https://2009-2017.state.gov/secretary/20092013clinton/rm/2010/01/135519.htm).

100. Mark Landler and Brian Stelter, "Washington Taps into a Potent New Force in Diplomacy," *New York Times,* June 16, 2009 (www.nytimes.com/2009/06/17/world/middleeast/17media.html?_r=1&scp=2&sq=Twitter&st=cse).

101. Deputy US Trade Representative Robert Holleyman, "The Trans-Pacific Partnership and The Digital Economy," remarks at the Commonwealth Club of San Francisco, March 30, 2016 (https://ustr.gov/about-us/policy

-offices/press-office/speechestranscripts/2016/march/Remarks-Deputy-USTR
-Holleyman-Commonwealth-Club-TPP-Digital-Economy).

102. Segal, *The Hacked World Order.*

103. Edward Moyer, "US Hands Internet Control to ICANN," *CNET,*
October 1, 2016 (www.cnet.com/news/us-internet-control-ted-cruz-free-speech
-russia-china-internet-corporation-assigned-names-numbers/). Ted Cruz and
other Republicans claimed that the United States was giving away the internet.

104. Quoted in Michael Hirsch, "How America's Top Companies Created
the Surveillance State," *National Journal,* July 25, 2013 (www.nextgov.com/
cio-briefing/2013/07/analysis-how-americas-top-tech-companies-created
-surveillance-state/67490/).

105. Ibid.

106. Ryan Gallagher and Henrik Moltke, "The Wiretap Rooms: The
NSA's Hidden Hubs in Eight US Cities," *Intercept,* June 25, 2018 (https://
theintercept.com/2018/06/25/att-internet-nsa-spy-hubs/). See also Marcy
Wheeler, "Verizon Gets Out of the Upstream Surveillance Business," *Empty-
wheel,* May 6, 2017 (www.emptywheel.net/2017/05/06/verizon-gets-out-of
the-upstream-business).

107. For comprehensive descriptions of the various U.S. electronic surveillance programs, see Laura K. Donohue, *The Future of Foreign Intelligence:
Privacy and Surveillance in a Digital Age* (New York: Oxford University
Press, 2016); and Jennifer Stisa Granick, *American Spies: Modern Surveillance, Why You Should Care, and What to Do About It* (New York: Cambridge University Press, 2017). Many of the legal interpretations that allow
U.S. surveillance are still unknown, as are the details of key programs.

108. Maik Baumgärtner and others, "Der unheimliche dienst," *Der
Spiegel,* May 2, 2015 (www.spiegel.de/spiegel/print/d-134762481.html).

109. McCarthy, "Open Networks"; and Kiggins, "Open for Expansion."

110. For a prescient exception, see Thomas Wright, "Sifting through Interdependence," *Washington Quarterly,* vol. 36 (Fall 2013), pp. 7–23 (doi.or
g/10.1080/0163660X.2013.861706).

111. By examining such structures, scholars could speak better to other
scholarship examining the role of networks in international security. See God-
dard, "Embedded Revisionism"; Alexander Cooley and Daniel H. Nexon,
"'The Empire Will Compensate You': The Structural Dynamics of the U.S.
Overseas Basing Network," *Perspectives on Politics,* vol. 11 (December
2013), pp. 1034–1050; Daniel H. Nexon and Thomas Wright, "What's at
Stake in the American Empire Debate," *American Political Science Review,*
vol. 101 (May 2007), pp. 253–271; and Yonatan Lupu and Brian Greenhill,
"The Networked Peace: Intergovernmental Organizations and International
Conflict," *Journal of Peace Research,* vol. 54 (November 2017), pp. 833–848.

112. Farrell and Newman, *Of Privacy and Power;* and Kalyanpur and
Newman, "Mobilizing Market Power."

113. Hughes and Long, "Is There an Oil Weapon?" There may be more complex strategic questions and knock-on consequences. See Caitlin Talmadge, "Closing Time: Assessing the Iranian Threat to the Strait of Hormuz," *International Security*, vol. 33 (Summer 2008), pp. 82–117.

114. Henry Farrell and Abraham Newman, "The Janus Face of the Liberal Information Order," paper presented at the IO@75 Conference, Madison, Wisconsin, September 7–8, 2018; and Henry Farrell and Bruce Schneier, "Common-Knowledge Attacks on Democracy" (Cambridge: Berkman-Klein Center for Internet and Society, Harvard University, October 2018) (https:// cyber.harvard.edu/story/2018-10/common-knowledge-attacks-democracy).

115. Commercial actors too may look to disentangle themselves when the costs of state control start to exceed the benefits of network economies.

116. Jones and Whitworth, "The Unintended Consequences of European Sanctions on Russia"; and Edward White, "China Seeks Semiconductor Security in Wake of ZTE Ban," *Financial Times*, June 18, 2018 (www.ft.com/content/a1a5f0fa-63f7-11e8-90c2-9563a0613e56).

117. Gideon Rachman, "The Swift way to Get Putin to Scale Back His Ambitions," *Financial Times*, May 12, 2014 (www.ft.com/content/d6ded902-d9be-11e3-920f-00144feabdc0); "Too smart by Half? Effective Sanctions Have Always Been Hard to Craft," *Economist*, September 6, 2014 (www.economist.com/briefing/2014/09/06/too-smart-by-half); and "The Pros and Cons of a SWIFT Response," *Economist*, November 20, 2014 (www.econ omist.com/international/2014/11/20/the-pros-and-cons-of-a-swift-response).

118. "Russia to Respond to Possible Disconnection from SWIFT," *TASS*, January 27, 2015 (http://tass.com/russia/773628); and Gillian Tett and Jack Farchy, "Russian Banker Warns West over Swift," *Financial Times*, January 23, 2015.

119. Vladimir Putin, speech to Meeting of the Valdai International Discussion Club, *Valdai Discussion Club*, October 24, 2014 (http://en.kremlin .ru/events/president/news/46860).

120. "Bank of Russia Suggests FinTech's Ethereum Blockchain as Single System for EAEU," *TASS*, April 03, 2018 (http://tass.com/economy/997474).

121. For a tolerably accessible overview of the underlying technical issues, see Arvind Narayanan and others, *Bitcoin and Cryptocurrency Technologies: A Comprehensive Introduction* (Princeton: Princeton University Press, 2016). Popular accounts tend to underestimate the vulnerabilities of blockchain technologies.

122. Daniel W. Drezner, "Could Walking Away from the Iran Deal Threaten the Dollar?" *Washington Post*, August 12, 2015 (www.washing tonpost.com/posteverything/wp/2015/08/12/could-walking-away-from-the -iran-deal-threaten-the-dollar).

123. Authors' translation of Karen Berger (rapporteur), "Rapport d'Information Déposé en application de l'article 145 du Règlement par la Commis-

sion des Affaires Étrangeres et la Commission des Finances, en Conclusion des Travaux d'une Mission d'Information Constituée le 3 février 2016 sur l'Extra-territorialité de la Législation Américaine" (Paris: French General Assembly, October 5, 2016) (www.assemblee-nationale.fr/14/rap-info/i4082.asp).

124. Ibid.

125. Robin Emmott, "EU Considers Iran Central Bank Transfers to Beat U.S. sanctions," Reuters, May 18, 2018.

3

Hegemony and Fear

The National Security Determinants of Weaponized Interdependence

MICHAEL MASTANDUNO

Economic statecraft is the use of economic measures by state actors to achieve foreign policy goals.[1] Economic influence attempts may be blunt and comprehensive, as in many cases of postwar economic sanctions, or surgical and precise, as in more recent instances of "smart sanctions."[2] As conceived by Henry Farrell and Abraham L. Newman, weaponized interdependence is a distinctive form of economic statecraft. Like economic statecraft generally, it involves intervention by state actors in private markets to achieve public policy objectives. Like smart sanctions, weaponized interdependence is a precision instrument; states employ it by exploiting bottlenecks or choke points in existing networks that coordinate commercial, financial, or technological transactions. The critical distinction is that weaponized interdependence exploits regional or global network power, while economic influence attempts typically rely less on networks and more on the dependence of a target on the sending state's home market or sources of supply.

Only the strongest states enjoy the opportunity to weaponize interdependence. Relatively few states exercise effective control over economic networks deemed critical by state and private actors. Farrell and Newman note three public actors with adequate potential—the United States, the European Union (EU), and China.[3] Of the three, the United States is uniquely positioned. It enjoyed first-mover advantages in establishing the postwar liberal world economy, and notwithstanding the fact that economic capabilities have diffused to other states over time, U.S. structural power in finance and technology has persisted and arguably deepened as globalization has progressed since the Cold War.

For the United States, the foreign policy benefits of exploiting structural economic power are potentially massive. Albert Hirschman recognized long ago that asymmetries in interdependence offer sources of foreign policy influence to dominant states.[4] Building on that insight, Robert Keohane and Joseph Nye distinguish sensitivity from vulnerability interdependence, with the latter more consequential since weaker actors in that predicament find it costly to adjust or extricate themselves and thus are highly susceptible to coercion attempts.[5] The network power of the Unites States places other states, and private actors operating within those states, in extreme conditions of vulnerability interdependence. Thus, network power offers the U.S. government ideal opportunities to shape the behavior of friends, and weaken the capabilities of and compel policy changes from adversaries.

Yet, the potential costs to the United States of weaponizing interdependence are equally significant. The postwar economic order essentially has been America's order, and the underlying logic has been that deeper and wider interdependence serves American's strategic, economic, and ideological interests. Weaponizing interdependence disrupts an order that rests on interdependence. It compromises the profit-making activities of U.S.-based firms and banks that have made themselves, and their trade and financial partners, dependent on the efficient operation of financial networks and commercial supply chains. In terms of diplomacy, while each episode of weaponized interdependence may not be the functional equivalent of "going nuclear," the extreme dependence of other states and their firms on U.S.-controlled networks suggests that routine U.S. weaponization would be perceived as a significant escalation of economic conflict. Even if this weapon is mostly directed against "bad actors" (for example, Iran and North Korea), it necessarily imposes collateral damage against others in the form of secondary sanctions. U.S. trading partners, including long-standing U.S. allies, reasonably fear they might become direct targets as well. Finally, routine weaponization threatens to undermine the structural power on which those influence attempts are based by motivating vulnerable actors to bypass or ultimately replace U.S.-controlled networks.

To weaponize interdependence is a policy choice. The anticipated coercive benefits compete with other economic, diplomatic, and security priorities. State leaders, even if implicitly, must weigh the possible gains against short-term costs and long-term risks. Given that policy dilemma, the central question of this chapter is under what circumstances is the United States, the country best positioned to exploit this coercive tool, likely to weaponize interdependence?

In their seminal work on weaponized interdependence, Farrell and Newman address this question only indirectly. Their major contributions include accentuating network-based explanations for international outcomes, demonstrating that globalization and networks concentrate rather than diffuse national power, and spelling out mechanisms (panopticon and choke-point effects) through which network power is exercised.[6] Regarding the circumstances under which state actors are likely to weaponize interdependence, Farrell and Newman highlight two key factors: the structure of a given network (that is, which states have physical control or legal jurisdiction over it) and the state's domestic institutions or norms. They observe that "depending on domestic configurations of power and state-society relations, [states] may lack [or possess] coercive capacity."[7] In emphasizing network control and whether domestic institutions are accommodating, Farrell and Newman identify enabling conditions rather than put forth behavioral expectations. They help us understand whether states have the capacity to weaponize interdependence, but not whether they will weaponize.

This chapter extends Farrell and Newman's analysis by directly addressing conditions under which the United States is likely to weaponize international economic relationships. In the spirit of their call for bringing political economy and security studies into closer dialogue, I locate the answer in the security realm.[8] Specifically, two variables—the extent to which the international security environment appears threatening or nonthreatening, and the commitment of the United States to manage and sustain a liberal international political and economic order—are most important. The combined values of fear and hegemony offer a useful first cut for understanding how likely U.S. policymakers are to bear costs hoping to reap the benefits of employing this provocative tool.

The first section explores the role that fear and hegemony play in calculations to weaponize interdependence. The second section briefly illustrates the argument by examining three postwar episodes: the technology embargo adopted early in the Cold War, variation in the use of weaponization before and after September 11, 2001, and the experience of the Donald Trump administration. The third section considers the consequences of U.S. weaponization, focusing on how crises enhance domestic capacity to weaponize, how weaponization creates offense-defense spirals, and the risks of weaponization for U.S. structural power. The concluding section argues that weaponization will likely remain a routine instrument of U.S. economic statecraft.

Hegemony and Fear

Hegemony has multiple meanings, but in this context refers to a foreign policy strategy available to dominant states. States committed to hegemony pursue order-building strategies, regionally or globally, that rest on both asymmetric power and social consent. Hegemonic orders are hierarchical; however, they are based not simply on coercion, but on a meaningful degree of "buy-in" from secondary states that accept the leadership position of the dominant state as legitimate and are also willing to accept the order the state creates, and the rules and values embedded within it, in exchange for benefits.[9]

Postwar U.S. leaders consistently committed to some form of hegemonic projects. During the Cold War, the Unites States pursued a balance-of-power strategy against the Soviet Union but a hegemonic strategy toward allied states in Western Europe and East Asia. After the Cold War, U.S. leaders sought to enlarge their hegemonic order and integrate former adversaries, Russia and China, within it.[10] Promoting economic interdependence within the rules and norms of a liberal world economy was a critical component of U.S. hegemony across both periods. Although domestic opposition to hegemony, particularly its economic component, has built gradually over time, the Trump administration has been the first to openly question the desirability of the U.S. hegemonic strategy and to abandon core elements of it.[11]

The second key variable—fear—is among the most salient motivators of state behavior in world politics. In Thucydides's famous account of the Great Peloponnesian War, Spartan fear of rising Athenian power is cited as the war's central cause. More generally, theories on balance of power and balance of threat are premised on the motivating power of fear.[12] States fear threats to their survival, territorial integrity, and foreign policy autonomy. Over the long term, states value power and plenty, or both security and prosperity. Yet, in the short term, even liberal states find it necessary to sacrifice the economic gains of interdependence in response to security fears. Economic blockades during wartime are obvious examples of this calculation.[13] As the COVID-19 crisis of 2020 demonstrates, state leaders are willing to make extreme economic sacrifices in the face of fear and uncertainty, even if they are generated by an invisible virus rather than an adversarial state.

The extent to which U.S. leaders perceive the international environment as threatening, while difficult to measure precisely, clearly varies over time. For instance, U.S. policymakers were more fearful in the uncertain context of the early Cold War—they believed the Korean War was the first salvo of a coming world war—than they were once the Cold War normalized into a predictable pattern of competition and especially during the détente of the 1970s.[14] While U.S. officials perceived the international environment as relatively benign during the roaring 1990s, fear increased dramatically in the aftermath of September 2001.

In identifying conditions likely to lead to weaponized interdependence, the key point is that hegemony and fear cut against each other. A commitment to hegemony discourages leaders from weaponizing interdependence. Leaders need followers; hegemonic order requires that followers feel they have both political voice and material stake in the existing order, and are not simply subject to the coercive whims of the dominant power. In conditions of fear, on the other hand, state leaders are encouraged to weaponize interdependence in pursuit of urgent national security objectives. Even nineteenth-century Great Britain, the quintessential liberal leader, ultimately succumbed to the pressing security incentive on the eve of World War I and developed a plan to weaponize the global economic networks it controlled to gain advantage over Germany.[15] When hegemonic commitment is strongest, state leaders are reluctant to rock the boat; in conditions of extreme fear, they reach for whatever weapons are at their disposal.

Variations in the combination of fear and hegemony lead to different behavioral expectations in terms of weaponized interdependence. When the U.S. commitment to hegemony is strong and the international environment generally nonthreatening, there is little inclination to resort to this provocative, coercive tool. Conversely, when the international environment is threatening and the commitment to hegemony is weak, there is increased likelihood of weaponized interdependence. With both hegemonic commitment and a threatening environment, the result is modified use—a willingness to weaponize interdependence to meet security threats, coupled with efforts to minimize the damage to allied relationships and the open world economy upon which the hegemonic project rests. Finally, the combination of a nonthreatening environment without a hegemonic commitment generates no clear behavioral expectation. The absence of a security threat discourages weaponization, while the lack of hegemonic commitment may tempt policymakers to use formidable economic power to achieve other objectives. Figure 3-1 summarizes the possibilities.

Weaponizing Interdependence: Three Episodes

The evidence below is not intended to engage in rigorous theory testing but to establish the plausibility of this framework for understanding the U.S. likelihood to weaponize interdependence. The examples span different eras of postwar U.S. policy and highlight combinations of threat perception and hegemonic commitment.

FIGURE 3-1
Likelihood of Resort to Weaponized Interdependence

		Hegemonic Commitment	
		Strong	Weak
Perception of Security Environment	Benign	*Minimal use*	*Stochastic use*
	Threatening	*Modified use*	*Routine use*

Modified Weaponization: The Cold War Technology Embargo

Early in the postwar era, the United States committed both to containing the security threat posed by the Soviet Union and to building a hegemonic order founded upon economic interdependence with allied states in Europe and Asia. These two projects complemented each other in that a prosperous and cohesive alliance would be more capable of meeting the Soviet threat. But there was also a potential conflict. As the West prospered, continued trade between West and East could bolster Soviet military capability and threaten Western security. The U.S. solution was a modified weaponization of interdependence. The United States crafted a selective technological embargo against the Soviet Union while insulating Western interdependence from its effects.

Postwar trade in "dual-use" civilian and military technologies constituted an interdependent commercial network among private actors in finished goods (for example, computers) and the incorporation of components (such as integrated circuits). The United States was the central hub in this network, but allied states mattered because they could transship U.S.-origin technology and products to the Soviet bloc. As allies gradually recovered in the years after the war, they could serve as additional hubs as well. The Soviets, saddled with a technologically inferior economic system, had strong incentives to acquire Western technology.[16] They wanted access to the network, while the United States wanted to keep them out for security reasons.

The U.S. mechanism was a multilaterally coordinated embargo, CoCom (the Coordinating Committee for Multilateral Export Controls).[17] In deference to allied preferences for maintaining general East-West trade, CoCom exploited the choke-point effect: it focused selectively on restricting a subset of civilian technologies that alliance officials believed would contribute most significantly to Soviet military capability. Firms based in member countries were prohibited from exporting list items to Eastern destinations without an exception license. Exception requests helped U.S. officials exploit the panopticon effect by offering information on Soviet military needs. The United States was the enforcer of the embargo, responsible for keeping member states in line and for negotiating side deals with neutral states such as Sweden, Finland, and Austria, who were forced to cooperate secretly with the embargo in exchange for in-network access to U.S.-origin technology.

Secondary sanctions were the principal enforcement instrument. U.S. policymakers employed reexport controls—prohibitions against reexporting U.S.-origin components, products, or technologies without U.S. permission—to deter embargo violations. States with lax enforcement or foreign firms that violated CoCom rules jeopardized their network privilege of access to U.S. technology or even the U.S. domestic market. Allied governments chafed under what they viewed as the extraterritorial and coercive imposition of U.S. economic power.[18] Yet, they also knew that if CoCom cooperation remained robust, the United States would minimize the use of secondary sanctions and thereby achieve its dual objective of restricting militarily sensitive Western trade with the East while allowing the free flow of technology within the interdependent West.

The CoCom episode demonstrates, first, that although weaponized interdependence may be exercised unilaterally, in some cases effectiveness requires multilateral support.[19] Even at the peak of its technological dominance, the United States could not prevent technology from reaching the Soviet Union by itself unless it was prepared to deny technology to its allies as well. Second, both fear and hegemony help to account for the modified weaponization of the technology embargo. Without the Soviet threat, there would be no need for CoCom restrictions and the secondary sanctions to enforce them. Without its commitment to hegemony and Western interdependence, U.S. officials would have been tempted to take a "better safe than sorry" approach to the Soviet threat and restrict technology exports both to the Eastern bloc and to Western states determined to continue East-West trade.

Before and After September 11, 2001

The inclination of U.S. policymakers to weaponize interdependence differed sharply before and after September 11, 2001. Threat perception is the key variable accounting for this disparity.

Most U.S. leaders perceived a benign international environment during the 1990s. With the Cold War over, the United States faced neither an existential security threat nor great power competitors. Its foreign policy debates centered on whether to engage in peacekeeping and humanitarian intervention. The Bill Clinton team focused on hegemonic enlargement; it promoted democracy and expansion of the U.S.-led liberal international economic order.

Nevertheless, there were opportunities to weaponize. The impetus came from Congress, which sought to extend U.S. embargoes extraterritorially by imposing secondary sanctions against states trading with Iran, Libya, and Cuba.[20] The Iran and Libya Sanctions Act (ILSA) of 1996 directed the executive branch to exploit U.S. financial network power (for example, deny access to the U.S. banking system or to U.S. Export-Import Bank support) to compel foreign firms to forego participation in Iranian and Libyan energy projects. The Libertad Act of 1996 (Helms-Burton Act) did not specify financial network leverage, but, in the spirit of weaponized interdependence, it authorized U.S. claimants to extract compensation from foreigners who "trafficked" in Cuban property confiscated from U.S. sources. Since U.S. firms and individuals essentially monopolized ownership of Cuba's pre-Castro economy, authorizing compensation was a potent weapon available only to the U.S. government.

The Clinton administration rejected these weaponization opportunities. In keeping with its pursuit of hegemony, it sought to placate Congress but minimize disruptions to economic interdependence and diplomatic friction with partner governments. On Cuba, the administration perpetually delayed the right (every six months, after review) of U.S. claimants to sue in exchange for a vague U.S.-EU "common position" on the importance of supporting democracy in Cuba. Similarly, the administration chose not to enforce ILSA financial sanctions even in the face of blatant violations by European and Asian energy companies. Secretary of State Madeleine Albright defended the refusal to sanction as "by far the most effective way to serve *overall* U.S. interests" (emphasis added).[21]

Perception of the security environment changed drastically after the September 2001 attacks on U.S. soil. The country's leaders shifted abruptly from seeing a benign world moving in America's preferred direction to a frightening one posing urgent security threats based on the interplay of terrorism, rogue states, and weapons of mass destruction.[22] Suddenly U.S. foreign policy moved from "don't rock the boat" risk aversion to "time is no longer on our side" risk acceptance. With considerable public support, the George W. Bush administration launched simultaneous and risky military interventions almost unthinkable during the quiescent 1990s.

Incentives to weaponize changed as well. Determined to use all tools at their disposal, U.S. officials decided that financial intervention was critical to tracking and disrupting terrorist networks. The officials sought access to the treasure trove of private bank information controlled by the Society for Worldwide Interbank Financial Telecommunications (SWIFT). As Farrell and Newman note, U.S. officials sought access to SWIFT's data several times during the 1990s, to disrupt drug trafficking and money laundering.[23] However, the society's representatives said no, citing privacy concerns. But in the aftermath of September 11, 2001, with elevated security stakes, U.S. officials proved unwilling to take no for an answer. A combination of legal threats and the risk of public shaming in the face of possible future attacks forced SWIFT to reluctantly cooperate.[24]

Some analysts, citing U.S. willingness to initiate war in Iraq without UN or full NATO support, view the United States as having unilaterally abandoned its hegemonic commitments soon after September 11.[25] In weaponizing financial networks, however, hegemony remained a priority, with U.S. officials exercising restraint in exploiting the SWIFT network. Rather than demanding general access to network data, U.S. Treasury officials agreed to make specific, circumscribed requests and took great pains, confidentially, to demonstrate to SWIFT the national security payoff of the selective data gathered.[26] The Treasury Department wished to simultaneously extract network value for national security reasons and protect the integrity of SWIFT, which was critical to the effective functioning of the global financial system. Diplomatic relations mattered as well; top Federal Reserve officials made it a priority to reassure foreign central banks that the United States would protect the integrity of global financial networks, while State Department officials sought to reassure European governments that U.S. weaponization would be sensitive to privacy concerns and civil liberties. In a threatening security environment the United States was determined to employ a formidable weapon while seeking to reduce collateral damage to the supporting structures of its hegemonic power.

Trump: Weaponization without Hegemony

The Trump administration has earned a well-deserved reputation for the extraordinary exercise of U.S. economic power. It has shattered postwar norms by raising tariffs against allies and adversaries for a variety of domestic and foreign policy reasons. It has resorted to economic sanctions more than prior administrations and has weaponized network interdependence by deploying U.S. financial power against foreign firms trading with Iran, Russia, Venezuela, and Cuba, among others.[27] Prior administrations used sanctions regularly, secondary sanctions selectively, and rarely politicized tariffs unilaterally. The Trump administration has showcased all three routinely.

Perceptions of the security environment offer one plausible explanation. As the urgency of the war on terrorism gradually dissipated, both Barack Obama and Trump sought to extricate the United States from "endless" wars in Iraq and Afghanistan. But Trump officials have emphasized a new threat—after twenty-five years of unipolarity, the return of great power competition.[28] Not surprisingly, they have maintained sanctions against Russia and have made China the primary target of tariffs. Trump officials have also dusted off the CoCom playbook and introduced choke-point technology restrictions to slow the growth of Chinese military capabilities.[29] Trump's economic weaponization, however, goes well beyond the usual suspects of reemerging peer competitors. It has been used against an array of regional actors, including NATO allies such as Turkey.[30] Intensified great power competition alone cannot account for it.

The abandonment of hegemonic commitments is a more decisive shift that sets Trump apart from postwar presidents, each of whom pursued hegemony either enthusiastically or reluctantly. Trump has rejected hegemony publicly and as a matter of principle, viewing it as a series of "bad deals" for America. His greatest defiance of the postwar tradition has focused on the U.S. role as the promoter and manager of a liberal world economy.[31]

By abandoning hegemony, the Trump administration has liberated itself to use economic power in ways prior administrations resisted in deference to core diplomatic and economic priorities.[32] Prior administrations usually weaponized interdependence (for example, Nixon's unilateral closing of the gold window or Reagan's secondary sanctions during the pipeline crisis) to get their allies' attention and force a revised multilateral deal. The Trump administration weaponizes neither with apology nor with subsequent efforts to make amends or strike new bargains. It views U.S. structural power not as an asset to be nurtured and conserved, but as a set of off-the-shelf tools to satisfy domestic and foreign policy interests, large or small. As *The Economist* editorialized in 2019, "the world can now see the awesome force that a superpower can project when it is unconstrained by rules or allies."[33]

Consequences of U.S. Weaponization

There are three primary consequences of weaponization.

First, weaponization breeds the domestic capacity for further weaponization. Farrell and Newman argue convincingly that domestic legal authority and institutional latitude either constrain or facilitate the state's ability to weaponize.[34] That causal arrow works in reverse as well: resorting to weaponization, particularly when prompted by security threats and crises, expands state capacity and makes it easier to weaponize after the crisis.[35] The Export Control Act, passed in

1949 to enable economic warfare against the Soviet Union, gave the U.S. executive unprecedented authority in peacetime to restrict any type of trade to any destination. For private firms, what had been a right to export was abruptly transformed into a privilege to be granted by the state.[36] Over the course of the Cold War, U.S. officials applied that authority to many targets and extended it extraterritorially to cover not only reexports but also the overseas activities of U.S.-based multinationals. Similarly, to follow the money of terrorists after September 11, 2001, the Bush administration claimed new authority to disrupt financial networks and used the Patriot Act to expand anti-money laundering authority beyond banks to new entities like insurance companies and commodities brokers. The Treasury Department, a relative newcomer to the anti-terrorism game, developed its capacity and became a major player. The appetite of U.S. officials grew with the eating. The first time they weaponized SWIFT was an extraordinary step to achieve a specific crisis objective; subsequently it became more routine, an off-the-shelf tool used against other targets for other purposes. Many U.S. firms have long complained that their government developed an unhealthy "sanctions habit" during the Cold War. One of the cheerleaders of Treasury's financial network interventions similarly worried in retrospect that the United States might have become a little too comfortable with its new choke-point weapon.[37]

Second, routine weaponization prompts offensive-defensive spirals across borders. Actual or potential targets have incentives to insulate themselves or prepare retaliation. To the weaponizing state those steps only confirm the initial assessment and offer further reasons to weaponize. For example, China has long witnessed the reality of U.S. financial domination, even in the aftermath of a financial crisis triggered by the United States itself. China has watched the United States weaponize finance against states viewed as adversaries just as U.S. officials have become comfortable depicting China as an adversary. To Chinese leaders, efforts to develop alternatives to the U.S.-dominated SWIFT system or to promote the use of the yuan in China-sponsored infrastructure projects thus appear prudent and defensive.[38] To the U.S. foreign policy establishment, these steps further confirm that America is dealing with a country engaged in state-led, geoeconomic competition.[39] As Adam Segal notes, a similar dynamic has played out in the U.S.-China struggle over Huawei and control of 5G telecommunications networks.[40]

Third, routine weaponization may carry seeds of its own destruction by undermining the structural power on which it is based. Farrell and Newman are surely correct in arguing it is hard but not impossible for actors to overcome dependence once network domination reaches a critical stage.[41] Habitual U.S. weaponization, however, gives other actors incentives to try despite the difficulty. The difference between states that are not threatened, and thus tolerant residing in situations of structural dependence, and those that are sufficiently threatened to explore ways to break out, even if they have not yet developed the necessary tools, is significant. Effective hegemonic strategies nudge states into the first category, while routine weaponization pushes them into the second with incentives to chip away at the restraints that are binding them. China, for example, may not be positioned to challenge dollar dominance globally, but over time it can do so regionally.[42] The enduring paradox of structural power is that it is most effective when it is not explicitly used.

Facing the Future

The steady accumulation of structural power—in finance, technology, trade, and cyberspace—has been a signal achievement of postwar U.S. foreign policy. This power has offered U.S. policymakers opportunities to craft an international order that reflects U.S. values and interests. It has enabled U.S.-based firms to expand profitably at home and abroad. Structural power has granted successive administrations the extraordinary privilege to run the U.S. economy without facing the constraints and trade-offs of ordinary countries with ordinary currencies. It has continually reinforced the United States as the hub of global politics and economics. Like the fire extinguisher encased in glass so that it will not be used except in an emergency, weaponization of structural power should be reserved for extraordinary and easily justifiable circumstances such as national security crises.

Yet, if the argument of this chapter is correct, the United States is more likely to use weaponization regularly rather than exceptionally. To U.S. officials, the security environment will become more threatening as the comfort of a one-power world gives way to the sobering reality of great power competition and regional or global power transitions. The biggest constraint on weaponization, the U.S. commitment to hegemony, was under stress before Trump; his administration has openly defied it and mobilized a political coalition resistant to U.S. foreign policy establishment efforts to reassert it. The domestic capacity for weaponization has expanded with its use, while its perceived success in punishing adversaries and subjugating allies tempts U.S. officials to reach for weaponization to solve foreign policy problems. Finally, the intrinsic durability of structural power breeds complacency about the costs of using it. At least in the short term, the United States is unlikely to pay a high price for routinely breaking the glass.

Notes

1. David Baldwin, *Economic Statecraft* (Princeton University Press, 1985).

2. Arne Tostenson and Beate Bull, "Are Smart Sanctions Feasible?" *World Politics* 54 (April 2002), pp. 373–403.

3. Henry Farrell and Abraham L. Newman, "Weaponized Interdependence: How Global Economic Networks Shape State Coercion," *International Security* 44 (Summer 2019), p. 57.

4. Albert Hirschman, *National Power and the Structure of Foreign Trade* (University of California Press, [1945] 2018).

5. Robert Keohane and Joseph Nye, *Power and Interdependence: World Politics in Transition* (Boston: Little, Brown, 1977), pp. 11–18.

6. Farrell and Newman, "Weaponized Interdependence," pp. 49–55.

7. Ibid., p. 56.

8. Ibid., p. 75.

9. Ian Clark, *Hegemony in International Society* (Oxford University Press, 2011); and David Lake, *Hierarchy in International Relations* (Cornell University Press, 2009).

10. Michael Mastanduno, "Partner Politics: Russia, China, and the Challenge of Extending U.S. Hegemony after the Cold War," *Security Studies* 28 (July 2019), pp. 479–504.

11. Robert Jervis and others, eds., *Chaos in the Liberal Order: The Trump Presidency and International Politics in the Twenty-First Century* (Columbia University Press, 2018).

12. Stephen Walt, *The Origins of Alliances* (Cornell University Press, 1987).

13. W.M. Medlicott, *The Economic Blockade*, 2 vols. (London: HMSO, 1952–1959).

14. Robert Osgood, *NATO: The Entangling Alliance* (University of Chicago Press, 1962), pp. 68–69.

15. Nicholas Lambert, *Planning Armageddon: British Economic Warfare and the First World War* (Harvard University Press, 2012).

16. Philip Hanson, *Trade and Technology in Soviet-Western Relations* (Columbia University Press, 1982).

17. Michael Mastanduno, *Economic Containment: CoCom and the Politics of East-West Trade* (Cornell University Press, 1992).

18. The pipeline crisis of 1982 was the most salient example. Bruce W. Jentleson, *Pipeline Politics: The Complex Political Economy of East-West Energy Trade* (Cornell University Press, 1986).

19. As Farrell and Newman point out, "hubs may be scattered across jurisdictions, obliging states to work together to exploit the benefits of coercion." See "Weaponized Interdependence," p. 56.

20. Michael Mastanduno, "Extraterritorial Sanctions: Managing Hyper-Unilateralism in U.S. Foreign Policy," in *Multilateralism and U.S. Foreign Policy: Ambivalent Engagement*, edited by Stewart Patrick and Shepherd Forman (Boulder, CO: Lynne Rienner, 2002), pp. 295–322, at 305–17.

21. Mastanduno, "Extraterritorial Sanctions," p. 316.

22. White House, *The National Security Strategy of the United States of America*, September 2002.

23. Farrell and Newman, "Weaponized Interdependence," pp. 65–66.

24. Juan Zarate, *Treasury's War: The Unleashing of a New Era of Financial Warfare* (New York: PublicAffairs, 2013), pp. 49–53.

25. Ivo Daadler and James Lindsay, *America Unbound: The Bush Revolution in Foreign Policy* (Brookings Institution Press, 2003).

26. Zarate, *Treasury's War*, pp. 54–60.

27. Gibson Dunn, "2019 Year-End Sanctions Update," January 23, 2020, www.gibsondunn.com/2019-year-end-sanctions-update.

28. White House, *The National Security Strategy of the United States of America*, December 2017.

29. Noah Barkin, "Export Controls and the US-China Tech War," *China Monitor*, March 18, 2020.

30. Florian Bodamer and Kaija Schilde, "Weaponized Weapons: The U.S. F-35 and European Eurofighter Networks," chapter 11 in this volume.

31. Michael Mastanduno, "Trump's Trade Revolution," *The Forum* 17 (March 2020), pp. 523–48.

32. The Clinton administration, for example, was reluctant to weaponize ILSA; it feared the EU would bring a complaint to the World Tarde Organization (WTO) and did not wish to test the credibility of the new governance structure the United States worked hard to create. The Trump administration,

with no core commitment, has abused the WTO national security exception clause and attacked the WTO itself. Rachel Brewster, "The Trump Administration and the Future of the WTO," *Yale Journal of International Law Online* 44 (2018), pp. 1–10.

33. "Weapons of Mass Disruption," *Economist*, June 8, 2019, p. 13.

34. Farrell and Newman, "Weaponized Interdependence," pp. 57–58.

35. The U.S. capacity expanded most dramatically in the context of world wars. See Bruce W. Jentleson, "Weaponized Interdependence, the Dynamics of Twenty-first Century Power, and U.S. Grand Strategy," chapter 13 in this volume.

36. Mastanduno, *Economic Containment*, p. 27.

37. Zarate, *Treasury's War*, pp. 423–26.

38. Rush Doshi, "China's Role in Reshaping the International Financial Architecture: Blunting U.S. Power and Building Regional Order," in *China's Expanding Strategic Ambitions*, edited by Ashley Tellis and others (Seattle, WA: National Bureau of Asian Research, 2019), pp. 279–308.

39. Robert Blackwill and Jennifer Harris, *War by Other Means: Geo-economics and Statecraft* (Harvard University Press, 2016).

40. Adam Segal, "Huawei, 5G, and Weaponized Interdependence," chapter 8 in this volume.

41. They conclude that network structures are "enduring but not immutable." See "Weaponized Interdependence," p. 77.

42. Doshi, "China's Role in Reshaping the International Financial Architecture," pp. 296–99.

4

The Road to Revisionism

How Interdependence Gives Revisionists Weapons for Change

STACIE E. GODDARD

As globalization advanced throughout the twentieth century, states became enmeshed in new exchange networks. Economic, diplomatic, military, and communication networks embedded states in a series of complex, overlapping ties. For some commentators, this increasing interdependence promised a more peaceful world, transitioning states away from traditional "power politics." With their economic fates tied together, states were now more inclined to cooperate for mutual gain. Mutually vulnerable, states were more likely to eschew military force and war. And in a networked global order, states—especially liberal ones—were more likely to exercise "power with" (the power to work together constructively with allies) rather than "power over" one another.[1]

In their pathbreaking article, Farrell and Newman argue that, far from eliminating power politics, these global networks have instead become tools of power politics. Interdependence, they argue, creates asymmetric advantages for certain states, which occupy "hub" positions in exchange networks. The United States, in particular, has proven willing to weaponize interdependence, exploiting its position at the hub of global financial and communication networks to coerce others to do its bidding. While Farrell and Newman focus on the United States, their work raises a significant question: To what extent can revisionist states—states that seek, in whole or in part, to challenge the status quo—also weaponize interdependence? Can states such as Russia and China also exploit their position in global networks to challenge U.S. dominance and seek significant change?

Most liberal scholars argue that in an interdependent world, revisionism is unlikely. Unlike the revisionists of the nineteenth and twentieth centuries, emerging powers in global politics now face a system where their own wealth and power depends upon dense economic, security, and political networks. For this reason, some agree with John Ikenberry that "in the age of liberal order, revisionist struggles are a fool's errand."[2] But as other chapters in this volume argue, revisionists seem increasingly able and willing to use their structural position to contest U.S. dominance. Other great powers—especially China, but also Russia and the European Union (EU)—are finding weapons within their own networks. Thomas Cavanna, for example, suggests that China could weaponize Belt and Road Initiative (BRI) networks. Although he cautions that there are limits to China's power, the BRI's "energy and transit infrastructure could help China exert major 'panopticon effects,' that is, the ability to use 'physical access to or jurisdiction over hub nodes . . . to obtain information.' "[3] Adam Segal likewise notes that China has sought power positions in new 5G networks and, moreover, is seeking ways to dislodge the United States from a position where it can "choke" China's critical supply lines.[4] Amrita Narlikar contends that this increased power-political competition among the great powers will open up space for seemingly weaker powers to exploit their own network positions and exert influence. This is a very different picture than the conventional wisdom about interdependence and revisionist politics suggests.[5]

I would argue that much of the literature on revisionism and interdependence rests on two suspect assumptions: that revisionism was primarily about the use of military power to overturn the status quo; and that global networks were more likely to constrain rather than enable revisionist behavior. Below, I provide an overview of the literature on revisionist politics, with a brief discussion of China's behavior in an interdependent world. I discuss how it is that revisionism is equated with military force and misses the ways in which revisionists can exploit their network positions, giving them weapons of information, mobilization, and coercion that they can wield against rivals. Finally, I discuss how revisionist states come to occupy power positions where they can extract the resources necessary to play power politics.

Interdependence and the Persistence of Revisionist Ambition in an Interdependent World

As noted above, revisionists are states that seek to challenge, in whole or in part, the international institutional order, the "settled rules and arrangements between states that define and guide their interaction."[6] International order, as David Rapkin and William Thompson write, is established by "states at the top of the system's hierarchy" who "take advantage of their elite status and establish rules, institutions and privileges that primarily benefit themselves."[7] Over time, however, states that are dissatisfied with their subordinate positions—often as rising powers—will seek to "redraft the rules by which relations among nations work."[8] Of course, while many states harbor some ambitious aims, not all revisionist challengers are cut from the same cloth. Some revisionists are limited aims revisionists. These states may be dissatisfied with their position but hope to alter institutions in ways that preserve the foundations of the existing order. They may seek adjustments to territorial boundaries but still abide by the rules and norms that govern sovereignty and regulate conquest. They may demand more resources but ask for redistribution within the confines of economic institutions. They may seek recognition of their growing prestige but accept the legitimacy of an existing status hierarchy. Revolutionary revisionists, in contrast, challenge not the distribution of power or goods within the system, "but the system itself."[9] There is no within-system change acceptable to revolutionaries; for these revisionists to be satisfied, the institutional order itself must be transformed. At the extreme, revolutionary revisionists will destroy an existing system even at the cost of hegemonic war.

Scholars suggest that revisionist states are one of the engines of change, if not the most important, in international politics.[10] In the late nineteenth and early twentieth centuries, Wilhelmine Germany, believing itself denied imperial spoils, became more aggressive and revisionist in its aims, and willing to overturn the existing balance-of-power order. So, too, did Imperial Japan and Nazi Germany seek the destruction of the interwar system.[11] For this reason, understanding how and when revisionists emerge is crucial to understanding the future of the current liberal international order, the "far flung system of multilateral arrangements, multilateral institutions, alliances, trade agreements, and political partnerships,"[12] designed to strengthen liberal political and economic norms, undercut geopolitical competition, and, ensure stability in world politics.

Some argue that an interdependent world should limit revisionist ambitions, if not eliminate them altogether. Liberals suggest that when potential revisionists become dependent on dense economic, military, and diplomatic networks, this should limit or eliminate preferences to overturn the status quo for two reasons. First, once states become accustomed to the benefits of interdependence, they should have little rational interest in overthrowing the status quo. As Ikenberry argues, in the current international system, all of the potential revisionist states "gain from trade and integration within the world capitalist system. They all either are members of the WTO [World Trade Organization] or seek membership in it."[13] Second, once states are integrated into networks, interdependence can eliminate revisionism by socializing states. Constructivists, in particular, argue that when states are integrated into institutions, these rules and norms shape the boundaries of appropriate behavior.[14] The more embedded a state is into international networks, the more likely it is that the state will come to see the status quo as legitimate.

This logic shapes more than the world of theoretical debates. Arguably, it underpinned two decades of United States' strategy toward a rising China. This strategy of engagement wagered that a China integrated into and strengthened by global institutions would become a sated, status quo state and a "responsible stakeholder" in global politics. U.S. leaders hoped that integration would convince China to, as Robert Zoellick explained in 2005, "work with us to sustain the international system that has enabled its success." Over a period of decades, China became integrated into the interdependent order. It opened its markets and joined the WTO. It assumed a greater role in regional and global affairs. In 1966, China belonged to one intergovernmental organization (IGO); by 2003, it belonged to forty-six IGOs.

How have these arguments played out in practice? In particular, how has this increased interdependence shaped China's aims? The evidence remains unclear. On the one hand, much of China's behavior appears oriented around maintaining the status quo of liberal economic institutions. It frames its core economic projects, including the creation of the Asian Infrastructure Investment Bank (AIIB) and BRI, as largely "order consistent," designed to reinforce rather than undermine the economic order. In diplomatic relations, China has taken the lead on issues like climate change and recently has positioned itself as a core supporter of the World Health Organization (WHO). Even where China's actions have arguably been more assertive, as in the South and East China Seas, one could still say that without integration into global networks, China would have been far more aggressive, especially toward Taiwan.[15]

But on the other hand, China has also signaled it has a bolder and more revisionist agenda, especially under the leadership of President Xi Jinping. During the National Congress of the Chinese Communist Party in 2017, Xi proclaimed that China would pursue a strategy of "national rejuvenation." Concretely, he argued that China should double its per capita GDP from 2010 to 2020; have a military "capable of fighting and winning wars"; and meet the social welfare needs of the people.[16] Regardless of whether China has actually been more assertive in the South China Sea, it has been bolder in declaring the issue as one of China's "core interests." And while Xi promised that China would remain a "defender of international order," that it would continue to support "the multilateral trading system" and "promote economic globalization," the country has increasingly suggested that it will do so on its own terms and that it is ready to compete with the United States if necessary.

In other words, the effects of interdependence on China's revisionist ambitions seems mixed at best. China's strategy may be surprising to scholars who have stressed the restraining power of interdependence and integration into existing orders, yet it is consistent with the historical record of revisionist behavior. I have demonstrated in other work that, historically, even states dependent upon international networks still challenge the status quo, sometimes in revolutionary ways.[17] While this might suggest that interdependence has little to no effect on state behavior, it is not the case. While embedding states into an integrated world may not prevent them from challenging the status quo, it does affect two outcomes: how revisionist states build and disrupt the existing order, and which revisionists are more equipped to do so.

Interdependence and Strategies of Revisionism

One of the reasons why scholars and policymakers became so convinced that interdependence would squelch revisionism is the fact that, in an interdependent world, using military force to overturn an order has gone from being risky to being catastrophic, Most academics and policymakers equate revisionism with the use of military power. Certainly for foundational authors in the literature on revisionist powers, significant revisionist challenges come in the form of major power or even hegemonic war.[18] Only large-scale conflict, they argue, could destroy the status quo and create space for a new world order. It was for this reason that Napoleon attempted to overturn the eighteenth-century balance-of-power system through hegemonic war, and, in the twentieth century, Hitler and Japan ultimately pressed their revisionist claims through force. In each of these cases, revisionists who were dissatisfied with their position in the international system were willing to fight for dominance, even at great costs.

But that is not the world of today. Interdependence decreases the chance that states would go to war by increasing the value of trading over the alternative of aggression: simply put, states get more from trading than from fighting.[19] China's increased wealth is the result of its integration into the economy. Any attempt to overturn this order, especially through force, would be fundamentally irrational. As global supply chains become more complex, it is difficult to imagine an economy so autarkic that it could survive a conflict. Add to this the increasing cost of conventional force and the threat of nuclear war, and the intentional use of military force to overturn the status quo appears downright suicidal.[20] Interdependence, moreover, should decrease the possibility of inadvertent war between revisionist and status quo powers as well. The more interdependent states are, the more transparency there is about intentions and behavior—information that should mitigate security dilemmas in international politics.

Viewed through this lens, then, while there may be competition and efforts at reform, if military force is no longer useful, then any attempt "to build a new international order from the ground up is essentially impossible."[21] And indeed, this argument has been at the core of more optimistic predictions of revisionism in the current world order. It is true that China and Russia may be somewhat dissatisfied with institutional arrangements, and they may seek to reform them at the margins, but ultimately the cost of changing these forcefully is prohibitively high. Some argue that this assessment is far too optimistic, however. While they agree that major power war is unlikely, they contend that interdependence will not stop revisionists from using military force to alter the status quo. Over the next few decades, China, in particular, is unlikely to accept a continuing U.S. military presence in what it sees as its own backyard: interdependence will not alleviate China's fears of having its rival so close. While China will avoid direct conflict with the United States, realists predict that it will increasingly use its military power for coercion—for example, to expand its claims in the South China Sea, or to put pressure on key U.S. allies such as Japan and South Korea in the hopes of driving the United States out of the Asia-Pacific region.[22]

Despite their disagreements, all of these commentators share the assumption that revisionism rests on military power. But equating revisionism with military force fundamentally misconstrues the nature of revisionist politics and, indeed, of power politics more generally. Historically, many revisionist states—and most of the successful ones—have relied on nonmilitary instruments to overturn against the status quo.[23] When Bismarck sought to unite Germany and overturn the existing European order, it was his mobilization of nationalist networks—not the limited use of force—that proved essential. The Soviet Union intentionally avoided using force in its competition with the Western world. During the nineteenth and early twentieth centuries, the United States relied primarily on its economic networks to spread influence; when military force was used against European rivals, it was used sparingly and only against already weakened foes (such as Spain). Indeed, in some cases, using military force to overturn the status quo was not the preferred choice of revisionist states but, rather, a weapon of last resort.[24]

By focusing on the ways in which interdependence has made military force costly, scholars miss the ways in which interdependence creates new instruments of power politics, which revisionists may be able to use in their challenge to world order. Indeed, as Farrell and Newman's work suggests, power-political competition is likely to play out using instruments that stem from weaponized interdependence. These instruments can be grouped into three different categories. First, interdependence gives revisionists weapons of information. Farrell and Newman argue that the United States effectively weaponized its financial and internet networks to gain information about both friends and rivals. China's command of 5G technology could give that state similar capabilities.[25] Second, interdependence gives revisionists the capacity to mobilize against the hegemon. China has forged new economic and political ties through institutions like the Shanghai Cooperation Organization (SCO), the BRI, and the AIIB.[26] Scholars are right that these ties do not necessarily signal revisionist aims: they were largely formed in response to specific demands, not as a means to challenge the liberal order. But over time, these ties have given China increased social and material capital in global politics, and the ability to mobilize new coalitions to challenge the institutional order. Third, interdependence also creates new instruments of coercion. Much has been written about Russia's military power, or lack thereof, and its aggressive attacks on the institutional order in Crimea, Ukraine, and Syria. Yet, for all of the focus on its military power, Russia's use of economic and social-political instruments has been far more effective in its attempts to disrupt the institutional order. Even before the 2016 U.S. election, Putin was relying on ideological appeals and economic aid in an effort to split apart the European Union and NATO.[27]

Opportunities for Revisionism: The Rise of Power Positions

Even if revisionists have the instruments to challenge the status quo, this does not mean they will have the opportunity to do so. Interdependence, so the wisdom goes, restrains revisionists, placing constraints both on the rising powers who might otherwise seek to revise the status quo and on those potential allies who might aid the rising powers in their revisionist crusade.[28] As states become embedded in networks, so, too, does their wealth and security become linked to cooperation with others. Such "binding" effects are perhaps most clearly seen in international trade, where global supply chains quite literally link the production of goods across boundaries. In current chains, production processes are often spread across dozens of firms operating in multiple countries Clearly one cannot simply "delink" from these chains without dire consequences. And while binding may be most obvious in the economic realm, there are similar effects in security relations. European states, most notably, are currently "bound" to an interdependent NATO security order; their militaries can no longer operate autonomously from the alliance.[29]

In an interdependent world, a state's wealth and power depends upon maintaining these networks. In the conventional liberal argument, this binding process should dampen competition and increase collaboration in global politics.[30] Unable to increase their wealth or power unilaterally states—even those that harbor some revisionist aims—must instead act in concert. China's well-being is intricately tied to the functioning of global financial and trade networks to overturn them. And even if there was a will, there certainly is no way. If a revisionist state tried to overturn the system, it is unclear how it would build a coalition capable of doing so. Once a state is embedded in these networks, it is not simply costly to overturn the system; it makes significant revisionism impossible.

Certainly these constraining effects are real. But in focusing only on the constraints of interdependence, scholars have downplayed the ways in which interdependence can enable revisionist states and, indeed, increase the capacity of these states to play power politics. What liberals miss about interdependence is that an interdependent world is not flat, with power and vulnerability equally distributed among states. It is instead, as Farrell and Newman argue, composed of "asymmetric network structures [that] create the potential for 'weaponized interdependence,' in which some states are able to leverage interdependent relations to coerce others."[31] While Farrell and Newman focus on economic networks, there are myriad types of networks, defined as any "continuing series of transactions to which participants attach shared understandings, memories, forecasts, rights, and obligations"[32] in the international system that shape the distribution of structural power. Alliances, both permanent and temporary, are networks: they are a continuing series of transactions centered around the provision of security. Diplomatic exchanges, too, are a series of more or less institutionalized networks.

As Emilie Hafner-Burton, Alexander Montgomery, and Miles Kahler argue, these networks "form structures, which in turn may constrain and enable agents."[33] How networks constrain or enable depends on a state's position within these networks. For example, some states have more network access, defined as the number of strong ties a state has with other states in a network.[34] Actors within a network can be centrally positioned in a number of ways. States can possess high- or low-degree centrality, which is defined simply as the number of ties a state has with other states in a system. States can also possess high prestige centrality, defined as the number of ties a state has with states that also have a number of strong ties within the system (in other words, it is a state with ties to other well-positioned states). Other states might be positioned as brokers, or actors that bridge structural holes in fragmented networks; these states maintain ties with actors that would otherwise remain unconnected.[35] In economics, a broker might be an actor with ties to different firms. In politics, a broker might be an actor that maintains ties with rival coalitions, domestic or international. By bridging structural holes, brokers occupy central positions in a network structure, acting as nodes through which multiple transactions coalesce.

By focusing on these power positions, we can analyze the ways in which interdependence gives some states more capacity than others to practice power politics: It is these structural power positions that give states the ability to use the instruments of weaponized interdependence, gathering information, mobilizing coalitions, and coercing others to expand their influence. In Farrell and Newman's analysis, for example, the United States' power stems not only from its attributes—its military power and wealth—but also from its position. The United States is a hub in financial and internet communication networks, with far more access than other actors in the system. For this reason, the United States has been able to use its position for both information and coercive purposes—"using its network position to extract informational advantages vis-à-vis adversaries" in the former, and cutting "adversaries off from network flows" in the latter.[36]

While Farrell and Newman focus on hegemonic power, a network approach envisions how interdependence also augments potential revisionists' power. Indeed, a network approach suggests that interdependence, far from hindering revisionism, might actually facilitate revisionism in global politics. As noted above, China's economic welfare is tied to global financial networks and supply chains. But these ties have also allowed China to emerge as a competing hub in international politics. The AIIB places China at the core of new financial networks, which it has leveraged to mobilize new partners in Europe. China has used its position in the global supply chain to wield coercive power, as it demonstrated when it halted its rare earth exports to Japan to force that state's hand in the dispute over the Senkaku/Diaoyu islands.[37] And China's bid to dominate 5G networks would allow that state to occupy a hub position in communication, giving China increased information capacity.[38]

A network approach also suggests that Russia is in a position of relative weakness. However disruptive Putin's Russia is, it has less access to networks than either the United States or China. In the wake of the Cold War, Russia sought access to economic networks, becoming a member of the WTO and the Group of Eight (G-8), but it remains marginal to these organizations. Russia, moreover, has few alternative, exclusive economic and security ties to actors in the international system. Without a power position, Russia's revisionist projects have faltered. It has been outflanked by NATO and the EU in Eastern Europe, and China competes with Russia for influence in Central Asia. This does not mean Russia entirely lacks power, however. Lacking the resources to effectively challenge the existing order or build a new one, Russia relies on coercive action, using what ties it has to weaken the American alliance system and shore up its patron-client relations. But however grand Putin's claims about Russia's grand strategy and the liberal order, Russian instruments have proven to have limited success. The country's wedging efforts, for example, generally prove more successful in places where Moscow enjoys access to networks of collaborators—sometimes co-ethnics or co-ideologues with whom Putin's efforts resonate—and where they stand ready and able to mobilize on Russia's behalf. In areas where Russia lacks these resources (such as in Western Europe), its efforts have produced countermobilizing strategies that are likely to check its disruption in the future.

Conclusion

Liberal theorists are right that interdependence matters in revisionist power politics. But they have overstated the extent to which interdependence limits or constrains revisionist behavior. Rather, more analysis of how interdependence shapes the instruments and strategies of revisionist power politics is needed.

Indeed, arguably the ability of revisionists to weaponize interdependence is nothing new. As discussed above, some of the most successful examples of revisionist states—nineteenth-century Prussia or the twentieth-century United States—were actors that pursued their ambitions using only a limited use of force, utilizing social and economic networks to facilitate realpolitik in various forms. In the same vein, it is possible, if not likely, that China and Russia can continue to challenge the status quo without resorting to military force and instead use instruments drawn from their economic, security, and diplomatic networks. Revisionist states are likely to continue to weaponize interdependence to further their own ambitions.

Notes

1. See Robert O. Keohane and Joseph S. Nye Jr., *Power and Interdependence*, 4th ed. (New York: Longman, 2012); and Anne-Marie Slaughter, *The Chessboard and the Web: Strategies of Connection in a Networked World* (Yale University Press, 2017).

2. G. John Ikenberry, "The Illusion of Geopolitics: The Enduring Power of the Liberal Order." *Foreign Affairs* 93 (May/June 2014), p. 90.

3. Thomas P. Cavanna, "Coercion Unbound? China's Belt and Road Initiative," chapter 12 in this volume. Henry Farrell and Abraham L. Newman, "Weaponized Interdependence: How Global Economic Networks Shape State Coercion," *International Security* 44 (Summer 2019), pp. 42–79.

4. Adam Segal, "Huawei, 5G, and Weaponized Interdependence," chapter 8 in this volume.

5. Amrita Narlikar, "Must the Weak Suffer What They Must? The Global South in a World of Weaponized Interdependence," chapter 16 in this volume.

6. G. John Ikenberry, *Liberal Leviathan: The Origins, Crisis, and Transformation of the American World Order* (Princeton University Press, 2011), p. 12. See also Robert Gilpin, *War and Change in International Society* (Princeton University Press, 1981).

7. David P. Rapkin and William R. Thompson, "Power Transition, Challenge and the Reemergence of China," *International Interactions* 29 (2003), pp. 315–42.

8. A. F. K. Organski, and Jacek Kugler, *The War Ledger* (University of Chicago Press, 1980), p. 23.

9. Henry Kissinger, *A World Restored: Metternich, Castlereagh, and the Problems of Peace* (London: Weidenfield and Nicolson, 1957), p. 2.

10. E. H. Carr, *The Twenty Years Crisis* (New York: Harper Perennial, 1964).

11. See, for example, Michelle Murray, *The Struggle for Recognition in International Relations: Status, Revisionism, and Rising Powers* (Oxford University Press, 2018); Steven Ward, *Status and the Challenge of Rising Powers* (Cambridge University Press, 2017).

12. Ikenberry, *Liberal Leviathan.*

13. Ibid., p. 341.

14. See, for example, G. John Ikenberry and Charles A. Kupchan, "Socialization and Hegemonic Power," *International Organization* 44 (1990), pp. 283–315. Martha Finnemore and Kathryn Sikkink, "International Norm Dynamics and Political Change," *International Organization* 52 (1998), pp. 887–917.

15. See, for example, Alastair Iain Johnston, "How New and Assertive Is China's New Assertiveness?" *International Security* 37 (2013), pp. 7–48, https://doi.org/10.1162/ISEC_a_00115; Huiyun Feng, "Is China a Revisionist Power?" *Chinese Journal of International Politics* 2 (2009): 313–33.

16. Rush Doshi, "Xi Jinping Just Made It Clear Where China's Foreign Policy Is Headed," *Washington Post,* October 25, 2017, accessed April 22, 2020, at www.washingtonpost.com/news/monkey-cage/wp/2017/10/25/xi-jinping-just-made-it-clear-where-chinas-foreign-policy-is-headed/.

17. Stacie E. Goddard, "Embedded Revisionism: Networks, Institutions, and Challenges to World Order, *International Organization* 72 (2018), pp. 763–97.

18. See, for example, Gilpin, *War and Change in International Society.*

19. See, for example, Edward Deering Mansfield and Brian M. Pollins. *Economic Interdependence and International Conflict: New Perspectives on an Enduring Debate* (University of Michigan Press, 2009).

20. Robert Jervis. "Theories of War in an Era of Leading-Power Peace: Presidential Address, American Political Science Association, 2001," in *American Political Science Review* 96 (2002), pp. 1–14, https://doi.org/10 .1017/S0003055402004197.

21. Ikenberry, *Liberal Leviathan*, p. 346.

22. See, for example, John J. Mearsheimer, "Can China Rise Peacefully?" *National Interest*, October 25, 2014, https://nationalinterest.org/commentary/ can-china-rise-peacefully-10204.

23. Goddard, "Embedded Revisionism."

24. Ibid.

25. Segal, chapter 8 in this volume.

26. Cavanna, chapter 12 in this volume.

27. Stacie E. Goddard and Daniel H. Nexon, "The Dynamics of Power Politics: Realpolitik in Post-Paradigmatic Security Studies," *Journal of Global Security Studies* 1 (Winter 2016), pp. 4–18.

28. Farrell and Newman, "Weaponized Interdependence."

29. Patricia A. Weitsman, *Dangerous Alliances: Proponents of Peace, Weapons of War* (Stanford University Press, 2004), p. 22.

30. See, for example, Anne-Marie Slaughter, *A New World Order.* (Princeton University Press, 2005). On the argument that states purposefully create institutions to bind revisionists to rules see, for example, Joseph. M. Grieco, "The Maastricht Treaty, Economic and Monetary Union and the Neo-Realist Research Programme," *Review of International Studies* 21 (1995), pp. 21–40.

31. Farrell and Newman, "Weaponized Interdependence," p. 45

32. Charles Tilly, "Contentious Conversation," *Social Research* 65 (1998), pp. 456, 491–51.

33. Emilie Hafner-Burton, Alexander H. Montgomery, and Miles Kahler, "Network Analysis for International Relations," *International Organization* 63 (2009), p. 560.

34. Emilie Hafner-Burton and Alexander H. Montgomery, "Power Positions: International Organizations, Social Networks, and Conflict," *Journal of Conflict Resolution* 50 (2006), p. 2.

35. See, for example, Goddard, "Embedded Revisionism."

36. Farrell and Newman, "Weaponized Interdependence," p. 46.

37. Keith Bradsher, "China's Supply of Minerals for iPhones and Missiles Could Be a Risky Trade Weapon," *New York Times*, May 23, 2019.

38. Cavanna, chapter 12 in this volume; Segal, chapter 8 in this volume.

II

FINANCE

5

Weaponized Interdependence and International Monetary Systems

HAROLD JAMES

Weaponized interdependence, as defined by the editors of this volume, is a condition under which an actor can exploit its position in an embedded network to gain a bargaining advantage over others in the system. States with some sort of control over central economic nodes in a network "can weaponize networks to gather information or choke off economic and information flows, discover and exploit vulnerabilities, compel policy change, and deter unwanted actions."[1] There are two parts to the weaponization: the collection of information on network sensitivities, and the potential use of that information in a choking operation. But as Henry Farrell and Abraham Newman also note, there are limits on the exercise of power by such weaponization; there is a temptation to overuse it, and then the weapon starts to crumble as others realize the dangers and seek alternative mechanisms and alternative networks. Indeed, recent writing by Juan Zarate (see also Thomas Oatley in this volume) on the use of financial power suggests that hegemons can easily overuse their power. The nemesis of hegemony used to be overextension;[2] now it is overuse.

International monetary regimes have long been the subject of this kind of reflection. A striking example is Charles Kindleberger's famous categorization of the nineteenth-century gold standard as an era of British hegemony, Pax Britannica, and the late-twentieth-century analogue of a Pax Americana.[3] In this chapter, I look at the way in which a monetary regime requires a specific instrument or mechanism, and focus on two examples: the role of the bill of exchange in the international gold standard of the nineteenth century (the basis of the Pax Britannica; and for the twenty-first century, the intracentral bank payments system in the euro—a currency union that is commonly compared to the gold standard in the policy limitations it requires of national members, and that sometimes looked like a Pax Germanica. Network effects produced by the interactions of private economic agents generate coercive power that may be used by states. Both monetary orders had an inherent capacity to be weaponized, but once that capacity was unveiled—let alone really used—it produced a counterresponse that threatened and undermined the operation of the system. The networks are hub-dependent, but the hub needs to exist in a certain veiled discretion; when the curtain is lifted, the power effects can be challenged and ultimately eroded. A rules-based international order becomes vulnerable as the degree of complexity of the rules increases. Moments of transition in international order are accompanied by a heightened attention to the possibility of covert action to abuse the complexity of the rules-based system to the advantage of one particular power.[4]

This chapter examines two particular ways of gathering information arising out of multiple transactions: first, the payments mechanism of early modern commerce (which continued well into the modern era); second, the payments clearing mechanism used within a modern currency union. At first sight, each individual element is meaningless from the point of view of states thinking about coercive power; the power dynamic lies in the cumulation and in initially restricted knowledge about how the cumulation is managed.

The Bill of Exchange and the Gold Standard

The first case looks at the payments mechanism, the bill of exchange, that tied the international economy together in what is now generally seen as the first era of globalization, or fifty years before the First

World War. Cumulatively, the bills would produce critical strategic information about trade, including imports of basic foodstuffs and commodities needed for military production and mobilization. Control of that information would provide a basis for a new type of interdiction and economic warfare.

After the Franco-Prussian War of 1870–1871, more and more countries joined the gold standard. Joining involved a calculation of national advantage; no country thought that it was losing by participating in the new international monetary order. The gains came in the form of lower borrowing costs and access to an international capital market, which might allow financing of domestic development. The move involved a commitment to credible policies, including budgetary and financial sector restraint; a spending splurge or a credit boom would push the country off the gold standard. Maintenance of the tie to gold became what modern economists call the good housekeeping seal of approval, but the members did not, on the whole, think that they were laying themselves open to any particular pressure from the core country, the United Kingdom.[5]

The commitment to the gold standard, paradoxically, involved very little gold. The United Kingdom at the end of the nineteenth century had a gold reserve of only around £30–35 million, while GNP was £1,550 million and U.K. imports was £421 million (figures for 1890). In fact, U.K. policymakers worried constantly about whether that reserve was sufficient. However, the more credible the policy was, the less gold was needed. The actual practice of the gold standard consisted in a constant buying and selling of a financial instrument, the bill of exchange.

The four-party bill of exchange dated back to the later European Middle Ages as an instrument to make payments over long distances. Its ingenuity was such that weird conspiracy theories surfaced about its origins; for example, it was commonly but wrongly supposed that it had been devised by Portuguese Jews as a way of moving money out of Iberia.[6] The classic four-party bill was dependent on some degree of familiarity with the other parties and, in particular, on the existence of trust over long distances. A merchant in Venice would present an instrument of obligation bought in Venice from someone with whom the merchant regularly did business and payable in

London by a correspondent of the Venetian issuer of the instrument. That correspondent would look at the paper presented and also at the presenter, seeking assurance that both the document was genuine and the instrument had not been stolen in the course of the long journey by someone who was not permitted to use it.

Such bill exchanges would have been rather limited operations and actually not much of an improvement on a barter transaction, if not for the development of a market in which bills were traded. The bill needed a platform to become a truly powerful financial instrument; initially, that took place through trade fairs. Later, banks, specialized discount houses, or bill brokers dealt with bundled bills and made the physical assembly of merchants in the giant fairs unnecessary. The open platform of the bustling trade fair was replaced by a nonvisible, internalized platform. The bank cut down on travel costs, but it meant sacrificing an element of transparency about the process of bill broking. There were periodical outbreaks of panic and systemic worries about whether the banks could transform their bill holdings into "real" money; before the twentieth century, that almost always meant metallic money.

Central banking, as it is conceived in the modern world, developed out of the need to provide support at a time of panic. The idea was that a large institution with a special mandate from the government was in a position to take a longer-term view and discount or buy assets (bills) for which there existed no market liquidity but there was some confidence in the long-term asset value. This new function was taken on in the nineteenth century by two institutions in particular, the Banque de France and the Bank of England—banks originally established to manage government debt, which was in effect sold to the bank shareholders, who were compensated with a license to do other kinds of business. At the beginning, it is not clear that the Bank of England knew what it was doing. In the panic of 1825, the bank had been exceptionally enterprising, but its directors did not consider their action a long-term model. Yet, in 1866, after the collapse of a large and reputable London bank, Overend and Gurney, the Bank of England repeated the same sort of instinctive market support. The influential liberal periodical *The Economist* then set out a theory of how the bank was underpinning the whole London market. A bank director wrote in to *The Economist* to say that was not how the Bank of England considered its actions. *The Economist*'s editor, Walter Bagehot, who had written the original article (as he wrote much of the content of the paper), then fired back with an extensive treatment that quickly became a manual of central banking; it was adopted as a guide by Germans looking to manage money in the newly established German Empire and then by other monetary reformers, including the designers of the U.S. Federal Reserve System.

In the new world of banks, and of central banks that later acted as a kind of support, the operations of the bill market were no longer visible. The central bank was designed to be in a position to know the secrets of the banks without divulging them. In place of a platform there was now hidden operations in a black box that operated on confidence. The most famous contemporary description of the evolution of central banking, Bagehot's *Lombard Street* (1873), declared the City of London to constitute "the greatest combination of economic power and economic delicacy that the world has ever seen." He presented the development as a very recent phenomenon, deriving from the aftermath of the Franco-Prussian War, when the Paris market had been weakened. "Not only does this unconscious 'organisation of capital,' to use a continental phrase, make the English specially quick in comparison with their neighbours on the continent at seizing on novel mercantile opportunities, but it makes them likely also to retain any trade on which they have once regularly fastened."[7] The London market was both a choke point, in that all transactions went through it, and potentially a panopticon—but that vision was not realized until a substantial period of time had elapsed.

Eventually, an awareness grew that the information that was embedded in the bill of exchange constituted a valuable resource in itself (a panopticon). Individual bills were meaningless, but an overview of the aggregation of exchanges provided an accurate picture of what goods and quantities were imported and exported by a particular country. That information could be used in the case of military conflict (a choke point).

By the beginning of the twentieth century, the invisibility of bill operations produced a new calculation. Taken together, the bill market contained an enormous amount of information that had a strategic use at a time of escalating great power rivalry. The financial operations of the world in the early 1900s were concentrated in Britain, specifically in the City of London, and ultimately coordinated through the monetary policy of the Bank of England. Since exporters could not have financial agents in every city that imported from them, the trading finance of the world was run through London merchant banks. If merchants in Hamburg, Germany, or New York City wanted to buy coffee from Brazil, they would sign a commitment (a bill) to pay in three months' time upon the product's arrival in their port; the bill might be drawn on a local bank or be turned into cash by the exporter (discounted) at a London bank. A physical infrastructure, the transoceanic cable, provided the basis for the financial links. In addition, most of the world's marine insurance—even for commerce not undertaken in British ships or to British ports—was underwritten by Lloyds of London. Put together, as Nicholas Lambert brilliantly shows, this information was used by the British Admiralty to prepare for a blockade of strategic commodities going to European ports in the case of war.[8]

Instead of having one international platform provider, each strategically significant country wanted to have its own platform as a way of providing strategic information. That discussion occurred in the context of a heightened great power competition.

The panic of October 1907 showed the fast-growing industrial powers the desirability of mobilizing financial power. In particular, it convinced some American financiers that New York needed to develop its own commercial trading system that could handle bills in the same way as the London market.[9] The central figure on the technical side in pushing for the development of an American acceptance market was Paul Warburg, the immigrant younger brother of a great (fourth generation) Hamburg banker, Max Warburg, who was the personal adviser of the German autocrat Kaiser Wilhelm II.

Paul Warburg was a key player in the bankers' discussions held on Jekyll Island, Georgia, and then in drawing up the institutional design of the Federal Reserve System. The two banking brothers Warburg were, in fact, on both sides of the Atlantic energetically pushing for German-American institutions that would offer an alternative to the British industrial and financial monopoly. The brothers were convinced that Germany and the United States were growing stronger year by year while British power would erode.

The language of Paul Warburg's public appeals made analogies to armies and defense: "Under present conditions in the United States . . . instead of sending an army, we send each soldier to fight alone." His proposed reform would "create a new and most powerful medium of international exchange—a new defense against gold shipments."[10] The experience of U.S. financial crises in both 1893 and 1907, where there was a dependence on gold shipments from Europe, indicated a profound fragility. Building up a domestic pool of credit that could be used as the basis for issuing money was a way of obviating the dependence. The reform project involved the search for a safe asset, one not dependent on the vagaries and political interferences of the international gold market.

Meanwhile, brother Max galvanized the 1907 German Bankers' Association conference in Hamburg with a speech on "Financial Preparedness for War." The brothers Warburg attained their unique degree of political influence by having prepared a diagnosis, and also a remedy, before it was evident to outsiders that such extreme measures were needed. The German Warburg was concerned with a different sort of risk to financial stability than the concern of the American about overdependence on stock exchange loans. The risk to financial stability lay in the increasing diplomatic and military tensions in Europe after the First Moroccan Crisis of 1905, when Germany unsuccessfully challenged French influence in Morocco. Market participants were beginning to think about war and its potential consequences in an internationally interdependent system.

The underlying idea or vision of the two Warburgs was fundamentally pacific: that a better distribution of financial capacity would make the world a more balanced and, thus, more stable place. In their view, financial unipolarity or overdependence on Britain as the center of the financial order made the world inherently dangerous. The structures that they devised held out the possibility of a model of central banking that could be exported to a wide range of countries and would make for greater financial stability. In a similar spirit, in October 1913 the young Cambridge economist John Maynard Keynes drew up a memorandum on Indian currency reform in which he suggested that three banks in Calcutta, Bombay, and Madras form the head offices of a federal banking system analogous to the new U.S. Federal Reserve System or the German Reichsbank.[11]

The British strength, as well as the vulnerability elsewhere that the Warburgs had identified, increased because of the heightened concern of financial markets over security and the arms race. The logic of the Warburgs' argument required that other countries should develop their own financial infrastructure. A strong domestic financial system, underpinned by a safe asset, would produce a reserve, a defense against attack, or a deterrent. In the U.S. case, a mechanism would be built around the commercial bill or bill of exchange, and in the German case around government securities.

The Power and Fragility of TARGET2

TARGET2 is not a concept that many people, even in central banks, were familiar with before the global financial crisis. Like bill clearing in the operation of the pre-1914 gold standard, TARGET2 operated as a purely technical operation that was, for a long time completely, off the political radar screen. But it represents, in Bagehot's terms, both extraordinary power and terrifying fragility. It represents a powerful (but initially hidden) potential tool for political pressure. *TARGET* is an acronym for the "Trans-European Automated Real-time Gross Settlement Express Transfer System," which commenced with the institution of the euro as the single European currency in 1999; TARGET2 is simply the updated version, introduced in 2007. The European Central Bank (ECB) website rather blandly explains that "TARGET2 is the real-time gross settlement (RTGS) system owned and operated by the Eurosystem. Central banks and commercial banks can submit payment orders in euros to TARGET2, where they are processed and settled in central bank money, that is, money held in an account with a central bank. TARGET2 settles payments related to the Eurosystem's monetary policy operations, as well as bank-to-bank and commercial transactions."[12]

In normal, precrisis times, there were no large balances in TARGET2. If a Greek resident bought a German automobile, he or she made a payment, probably through a Greek bank, to a German bank. The payments were processed through a central clearing system in the Eurosystem of central banks, which operated just as the pre-1914 nexus of acceptance houses and central banks did. The claims had to regularly balance out if there was not to be pressure on the exchange between the Greek and German sides, so a German bank would give a credit to a Greek bank. There was thus a perfect balance. But after 2008, and especially in the euro debt crisis after 2010, the interbanking system seized up and there were no offsetting flows. So a transaction like the one described above would lead to a German claim on the central clearing system (TARGET) and a Greek liability. The makers of the euro had not envisaged a situation in which such a breakdown could occur. They simply assumed that the banking system would always finance imbalances.

In the new environment, very substantial imbalances built up. The largest imbalances occurred for Italy and Spain (see figure 5-1). Most of the amounts corresponded to movements in capital markets, with the sale of securities reflecting a growing renationalization of finance. Thus, for instance, the Banca d'Italia would have incurred a liability to the Bundesbank via the Eurosystem when a foreign holder of an Italian government bond sold it to the Italian central bank and maintained the proceeds in Frankfurt. There was also an element of capital flight. Especially since 2015, Italians built up portfolios of foreign securities and other assets (including real estate) while foreign individuals and institutions stopped buying Italian government bonds.

The chronology of TARGET2 is the fever curve of the European debt problem. The imbalances built up from the outbreak of the crisis in 2010 to reach a high point in August 2012. They then fell as a new policy stance, articulated by ECB president Mario Draghi in the summer of 2012, reassured markets; by 2015, the reversal was interpreted as a major sign of success by the ECB and the policy community more generally. However, with the introduction of the ECB's quantitative easing (QE) program in [2015], the balances started to expand again.

The topic of TARGET2 discussion was likely raised by the one participant who was there in the early days of Eurozone planning and, at age ninety (in 2014), was still part of discussions about the travails of the Euro. Former Bundesbank president Helmut Schlesinger,

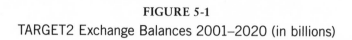

FIGURE 5-1

TARGET2 Exchange Balances 2001–2020 (in billions)

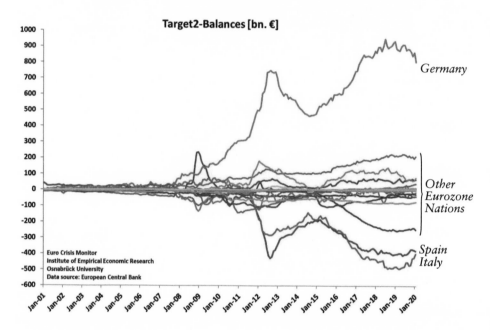

an austerely intellectual but paternal figure, inspired in particular his successor as Bundesbank president, Jens Weidmann (only half his age), and the Munich economics professor who was widely seen as the most influential German economist, Hans-Werner Sinn. In 2011, Sinn and an associate, Timo Wollmershäuser, started to document the development of the buildup of TARGET2 claims and liabilities.[13] At this point, the discussion flared into a polemic as journalists and politicians, especially in Germany, took up the case. The TARGET2 balances could be presented as a potential instrument—a weaponized monetary mechanism—in that the implicit liability of the German state and the German taxpayer, as the ultimate owner of the German Bundesbank, would become an open loss if any of the deficit countries left the euro, and thus also their liabilities in the Eurosystem. The balances could be used to pressure the ECB to extend other sorts of credit or to make asset purchases.

At this stage, there was no widespread knowledge of the TARGET2 imbalances and no way of calculating them. Sinn and Wollmer-shäuser began by using some data reported by individual European national central banks and linking that data with data separated out of reports to the International Monetary Fund (IMF).[14] The ECB did not provide such information, since it regarded it as irrelevant (that was the public stance) and the discussion as dangerous and possibly fatal to the euro project (the internal stance). Only much later did the ECB move to a greater openness, when it became more plausible to argue that the origins of the problem were purely "technical."

TARGET2 imbalances become important in the event of an exit from the currency union. As such, they measure the exposure of the rest of the system to a particular national central bank should its country exit the euro. For example, Greek citizens who transfer bank deposits from a Greek bank to a German bank account run up TARGET2 claims. By transferring funds to a German account, the Greek citizens avoid devaluation losses, as they hold "German euros." However, if Greece left the Eurosystem, these devaluation losses would show up as losses for the other national central banks in the form of lost TARGET2 claims if there was no hope that the Greek central bank would repay its TARGET2 liabilities after the exit.

The risk of an exit revealed another vulnerability. Importantly, even the chance of an exit opens up the possibility of a speculative attack. Investors and speculators alike might run and push the country toward exit from the currency union. In other words, the threat of an exit can be self-fulfilling. There is one equilibrium in which investors believe no exit will occur and, for example, a Greek euro has the same value as a German euro. But there is also another equilibrium in which doubts about the homogeneity of the eurozone induces speculators to bet on an exit. When the exit risk starts to materialize, prudent investors hedge this redenomination/exit risk, leading them to short sell Greek euros and buy German ones, thereby contributing to the likelihood of the exit. As long as both euros trade one-for-one, the cost of such a trade is only the interest rate differential—earning the low German interest rate and foregoing the higher Greek interest rate. Ultimately, however, the exit equilibrium might prevail.

Unlike in the intense period of the euro crisis, 2010–2012, the new soaring of TARGET2 imbalances after 2015 was not linked to a rise in risk perception as reflected in sovereign credit default swaps (CDS) or in divergent government bond yields. Most commentators—notably in the official central banking world—interpreted the increase as a purely technical business. Thus, for instance, one frequent explanation tells how the Banca d'Italia, as part of its implementation of the ECB asset purchasing program, would buy securities from a London bank that connects to TARGET2 system via a correspondent bank located in Germany. The purchase amount would be credited to the account of the German correspondent bank at the German central bank, producing an increase in Germany's TARGET2 claims and in the Banca d'Italia's liabilities.[15]

Awareness of the technical details transformed the debate about the euro and its implication for members states and their national interest. For both sides, it looked as if TARGET2 held out the possibility of blackmail. The information—as it became available—provided a panopticon that everyone could see. It created an awareness of the choke points. For Germans and other creditors (such as the Netherlands and Luxembourg), the choke point was the ability to compel policy change by threatening large losses. In 2015, it looked at times as if this was the game plan of the Syriza government in Greece and, particularly, of Finance Minister Yanis Varoufakis.[16] For the Southern Europeans, the choke point lay in the possibility of the ECB limiting access to the facilities of the Eurosystem or limiting supplies of physical cash, which became a bottleneck for Greece in the crisis moments of 2012 and 2015, or of other goods. In 2020, the debate refocused on whether Germany would allow the shipment of medical goods to Italy in response to the COVID-19 emergency.

Conclusion

The awareness of a highly technical mechanism that is at the heart of interdependence changes the debate when many participants realize what is actually seen in the panopticon. First, countries subject to the exercise of power learn that they need to evolve analogous mechanisms, to copy particular instruments, and to reduce the extent of their vulnerability; that is the Warburg lesson. Second, countries that feel constrained by a linkage system that is exposed an in the open want to cut those ties. Thus, the Sinn lesson from the euro crisis was the same as the eventual Varoufakis calculation: the need to uncouple and reduce interdependence. The Warburg vision of how to respond to the security consequences of financial interdependence was about altering the form of the coupling to make it more balanced. By contrast, the Sinn-Varoufakis approach is about building resilience by destroying a dangerous interdependence. The risk, however, is that in destroying interdependence, a great deal of baby (gains from cooperation) is thrown out with the interdependent bathwater.

It is possible to make the argument that modern information technology (IT) allows a quicker and more complete bundling of information that in previous ages. But Thomas Piketty has recently claimed that, despite big data, more information is actually concealed or unavailable now than before the IT revolution.[17] The evidence suggests, however, that it is always a crisis—the 1907 financial panic, the euro debt crisis, or the current COVID-19 medical emergency—that prompts a rethinking of what data matter for the security of states. A new dynamic emerges as previously obscure or neglected data become the subject of widespread discussion and of political controversy.

Notes

1. Henry Farrell and Abraham L. Newman, "Weaponized Interdependence: How Global Economic Networks Shape State Coercion," *International Security* 44 (Summer 2019), p. 45.

2. Famously in Paul Kennedy, *The Rise and Fall of the Great Powers: Economic Change and Military Conflict from 1500 to 2000* (New York: Vintage Books, 1989).

3. Charles P. Kindleberger, *The World in Depression, 1929-1939* (University of California Press, 1973).

4. See the argument of Harold James, "Cosmos, Chaos: Finance, Power and Conflict," *International Affairs* 90 (January 2014), pp. 37–57.

5. Michael D. Bordo and Hugh Rockoff, "The Gold Standard as a 'Good Housekeeping Seal of Approval,'" *Journal of Economic History* 56 (June 1996), pp. 389–428.

6. See Francesca Trivellato, *The Promise and Peril of Credit: What a Forgotten Legend about Jews and Finance Tells Us about the Making of European Commercial Society* (Princeton University Press, 2019).

7. Walter Bagehot, *Lombard Street: A Description of the Money Market* (London: H. S. King & Co., 1873).

8. Nicholas Lambert, *Planning Armageddon: British Economic Warfare and the First World War* (Harvard University Press, 2012).

9. The general theme (but without a consideration of the security aspects) is handled in J. Lawrence Broz, *The international Origins of the Federal Reserve System* (Cornell University Press, 1997).

10. Paul M. Warburg, "Defects and Needs of Our Banking System," *Proceedings of the Academy of Political Science in the City of New York* 4 (July 1914).

11. Robert Skidelsky, *John Maynard Keynes: Hopes Betrayed, 1883–1920*, vol. 1 (London: Macmillan, 1983), p. 280.

12. European Central Bank, "What is TARGET2?" www.ecb.europa.eu/paym/target/target2/html/index.en.html.

13. Hans-Werner Sinn and Timo Wollmershäuser, "Target Loans, Current Account Balances and Capital Flows: The ECB's Rescue Facility," *CESifo Working Paper Series 3500*, 2011; Hans-Werner Sinn and Timo Wollmershäuser, "TARGET Loans, Current Account Balances and Capital Flows: The ECB's Rescue Facility," *NBER Working Paper* no. 17626, November 2012.

14. Hans-Werner Sinn, *Die Target-Falle: Gefahren für unser Geld und unsere Kinder* (Munich: Hanser, 2012), pp. 171–72.

15. See Raphael Auer, "What Drives TARGET2 Balances? Evidence from a Panel Analysis," *Economic Policy* 29 (2014), pp. 139–97; ECB, "TARGET Balances and Monetary Policy Operations," *Monthly Bulletin*, May 2013; and Stephen Cecchetti, Robert McCauley and Patrick McGuire, "Interpreting TARGET2 Balances," *BIS Working Papers* no. 393 (December 2012).

16. Yanis Varoufakis, *Adults in the Room: My Battle with the European and American Deep Establishment* (New York: Farrar, Straus and Giroux, 2017).

17. Thomas Piketty, *Capital and Ideology* (Harvard University Press, 2019), pp. 677–79.

6

Weaponizing International Financial Interdependence

THOMAS OATLEY

The international financial system offers one of the clearest illustrations of weaponized interdependence. Over the last twenty years, U.S. policymakers have exploited the leverage generated by America's central position in global financial networks to advance their foreign policy objectives.[1] Officials began to weaponize financial interdependence during the late 1990s as they sought to extraterritorialize U.S. anti-money laundering law to safeguard the integrity of the American financial system. The U.S. Treasury Department expanded the scope of this effort after the attacks of September 11, 2001, to interrupt financial support for terrorist networks. In 2007, the United States expanded this scope still further, drawing on the need for global banks to retain relationships with U.S.-based banks to bring North Korea and then Iran back to multilateral negotiations on their respective nuclear programs. In 2014, the United States responded to Russia's role in the Ukraine by leveraging U.S. financial power to sanction Russian banks and threaten to exclude Russia from the Society for Worldwide Interbank Financial Telecommunications (SWIFT) network, a threat Russian Prime Minister Dmitry Medvedev called equivalent to a declaration of war.[2]

The American decision to weaponize its global financial centrality has produced mixed results. On the plus side of the balance sheet, the United States denied terrorist groups access to traditional channels of financial transfers. In addition, most commentators have concluded that financial sanctions played a central role in bringing North Korea and Iran back to multilateral negotiations on their respective nuclear programs. On the minus side, however, sanctions imposed on Russia have yet to produce the desired results and have served only to further antagonize the regime. Moreover, and more broadly, the willingness to weaponize U.S. financial status has led to significant uneasiness throughout the system, even among America's traditional allies. This unease has produced sustained discussion about creating alternative networks that would reduce America's centrality and thereby render states less vulnerable to American financial power.

In their efforts to weaponize America's central position in the global financial system, policymakers have employed a variety of tools to pursue a range of objectives. Henry Farrell and Abraham Newman focus on one such tool, the leveraging of SWIFT, the Belgium-based network that was established in the 1970s to transmit payment instructions between banks located in different jurisdictions.[3] Farrell and Newman point out that SWIFT has served as a panopticon to the United States by providing information with which to track terrorist financing and thereby uncover terrorist planning; and it has also functioned as a choke point by providing a single point of access to the international financial system that can be closed to banks that engage in illicit activity.

This chapter explores these American efforts to weaponize its central position in the global financial system. I focus most of my attention on the choke-point effect, the ability to exploit a position within a network to deny others access to the resources it offers. The chapter is organized into three sections. I first describe the network structure of the global financial system, with an emphasis on the role of the dollar as the primary reserve currency and the network of interbank relationships that have developed around the dollar's role. I then trace the emergence and development of American efforts to weaponize its central position with the global financial network to support the War on Terror and ongoing negotiations with regimes in North Korea,

Iran, and Russia, and highlight how targeted states have responded to American financial power. The final section draws a few general conclusions.

The Network Structure of the Global Financial System

The global financial system is a hierarchical network.[4] Hierarchical networks exhibit a clear hub-and-spoke structure; all the nodes in the network—in this case, national economies—are connected to a single central country (or hub), with only a few national economies also connected directly to each other. In the postwar era, the United States has occupied the hub while most of the rest of the world is in the periphery, connected directly to the United States but not to each other. Financial flows across the system between any two national economies, such as a flow from France to Iran, thus must pass through the United States. This gives to the United States the ability to exclude any country from the global financial system simply by denying it the ability to transact with banks based in the United States. The American financial system thus constitutes a choke point of global finance.

The network structure that places the United States at the center of the global financial system derives ultimately from the dollar's role as the system's primary reserve asset, a role it assumed in the immediate postwar period. The basic details are familiar but bear repeating.[5] The dollar is the most heavily traded currency in foreign exchange markets, involved in 85 to 89 percent of all transactions between 1999 and 2016.[6] Nearly 64 percent of all global foreign exchange reserves are held in dollars. This is three times more than the second most widely held currency, the euro. In addition, international trade is invoiced in dollars at a far higher rate than is justified by the U.S. share of global imports and exports. Roughly 40 percent of all global debt securities are denominated in dollars. The dollar also accounts for almost 60 percent of all cross-border bank liabilities, making it "the currency that underpins the global banking system."[7] As Benjamin Cohen and Tabitha Benney summarize, "Today there is only one currency—the dollar—that plays all [important] roles in virtually every part of the world. Even now, decades after World War II, the greenback remains unique, a truly global money."[8]

The dollar's central role has meant that large globally oriented banks located outside the United States have steadily increased their dollar-based activities. Indeed, the rate of growth in foreign dollar-based positions is rather astonishing. Between 1980 and 2010, banking systems in industrial democracies increased their foreign currency assets and liabilities from less than $1 trillion to more than $18 trillion, with the dollar accounting for more than two-thirds of this increase.[9] Economist Hyun Song Shin argues that in 2008, foreign banks held more dollar-denominated assets than the entire U.S.-based commercial banking sector; "it is as if an offshore banking sector of comparable size to the U.S. commercial banking sector" emerged at the center of the U.S. financial system to intermediate dollar claims and obligations.[10] Consequently, half of the assets of the prime U.S. money market funds were short-term obligations of foreign banks, European banks the dominant debtors in this market.[11] Access to dollars is thus fundamentally important everywhere, and the survival of practically every bank in the world rests on the continued ability to access the U.S. financial system to acquire, transmit, and settle dollar-denominated payments.

This global financial structure is characterized by significant network externalities that stabilize it even in the face of potential threats. The dollar's global role ensures that almost every institution or individual involved in cross-border trade and finance uses dollars, and holds significant dollar balances. Rather than keeping these balances in cash, foreign entities acquire a variety of low-risk and highly liquid dollar-denominated assets, among which U.S. government debt is the preferred instrument. The dollar's role as a reserve and transactional currency thus encourages private and public entities from across the world to pool liquidity in the U.S. money market.[12] And because the American money market is so liquid, it is often a cheaper and more attractive place to raise funds than other financial markets, and it attracts more business. As a result, the dollar-centered global financial system has been remarkably resilient even as potential rivals have emerged.

Academics and policymakers alike have long recognized what the French famously called the exorbitant privilege America derives from the dollar's global centrality.[13] For the most part, however, previous scholarly work has conceptualized these benefits in terms of diffuse macroeconomic and financial processes that relax constraints on American policy trade-offs. Benjamin Cohen, for instance, argues that the dollar's global role allows the United States to delay and deflect current account adjustment.[14] It can delay adjustment because the world's appetite for low-risk dollar denominated assets enables the United States to borrow in large amounts for an extended period and at very low interest rates. It can deflect adjustment by forcing currency realignments that devalue the dollar and thereby induce surplus countries to import more U.S. goods. Combined, this monetary power provides America with the capacity to pursue ambitious foreign and domestic policy goals simultaneously, while pushing some of the costs of these policies on to the rest of the world in the form of monetary and financial instability. President Lyndon Johnson's simultaneous pursuit of the Great Society at home and escalation of the Vietnam War abroad provides the classic example, but the George W. Bush administration's decision to cut taxes massively while simultaneously embarking on the Global War on Terrorism.[15]

Weaponizing American Financial Centrality in the War on Terror

In spite of the widespread recognition that the global financial system was centered upon the United States and therefore operated as an instrument of American power, it was only following the terrorist attacks of 9/11 that American policymakers began to explore whether and how they might manipulate access to the American financial system in support of their political objectives.[16] Officials working in the U.S. Treasury recognized that deepening financial interdependence was creating "a new ecosystem" in which banks were becoming "acutely sensitive to their reputations and the risks of doing business with suspect individuals and entities. . . . Banks were willing to cut . . . relations with rogue regimes, criminals, and terrorists given the right conditions."[17] This ecosystem "could be leveraged uniquely to American advantage."[18] And indeed, from 2003 forward, Treasury began to leverage this system in pursuit of two broad objectives: ending the flow of finance to terrorist groups, and trying to isolate North Korea and Iran by denying them access to the global financial system.

The initial objective, characterized by the Treasury team that led it as the "Bad Banks Initiative," identified specific banks that occupied central nodes in the global financing of illicit activity, with a particular focus on banks that financed terrorist groups. Once Treasury identified such banks, officials used the authority provided by Section 311 of the Patriot Act to label them "primary money laundering concerns" and block them from transacting with banks based in the United States.[19] Once labeled as a primary money laundering concern, a bank became a high-risk partner for other foreign banks, because these banks might themselves become unwitting participants in the labeled bank's illicit activity and wind up being excluded from U.S. markets themselves. The belief was that banks would decide the income generated through business with bad banks was not sufficient to run the risk of being excluded from the United States. Hence, the targeted bank would lose direct and indirect access to dollar-based transactions until such time as it ceased to engage in the illicit activity. Under this initiative, the United States focused first on five targets: two Burmese banks, the Commercial Bank of Syria, the First Merchant Bank of the Turkish Republic of Northern Cyprus, and InfoBank of Belarus.

This early initiative was essentially an exercise in law enforcement and in extraterritorializing the U.S. legal structure regarding anti-money laundering and terrorist financing. In particular, the United States sought to induce the home country government of the targeted banks to introduce more effective anti-money laundering frameworks. And while the initiatives were broadly considered to have been successful, American officials made little effort to tie the exercise to specific U.S. foreign policy objectives.

Targeting Rogue Regimes

As Treasury officials discovered how easily they could shut banks out of the global financial system, they sought ways to widen the application of this financial weapon. The course they elected to follow focused on providing support to the U.S. government's efforts to end nuclear programs in North Korea and Iran. In contrast to prior actions, this leveraging of American financial centrality was an exercise in cost imposition intended to change state policy. North Korea was the first target. The Treasury Department identified Macau-based Banco Delta Asia (BDA) as the critical node that tied the North Korean regime and North Korean banks to the global banking system. Treasury then sought to sever BDA's ties to the global system by labeling BDA a primary money laundering concern. This action triggered a dramatic panic and a global bank run. Almost immediately following the U.S. designation, depositors fled BDA, foreign banks closed their accounts, and BDA was rendered insolvent. Regulators in Macau assumed control of the bank and froze $25 million in assets held there on behalf of various North Korean entities, including the ruling regime. Thus the regime was effectively cut off from the global financial system; it had no access to dollars to pay for desired imports and no way to purchase dollar-denominated assets. Juan Zarate argues that the resulting financial isolation was one of the major factors that drove the North Korean regime back to the bargaining table.[20]

Iran became America's second target, with financial leverage exerted to induce Iran to accept international constraints on its nuclear program.[21] The first wave of America's Iran policy was a "whisper campaign" in which Stuart Levey (who at the time was under secretary for terrorism and financial intelligence at the U.S. Department of Treasury) met with foreign bank executives and outlined the risks they faced in continuing to do business directly with Iran, as well as in doing business indirectly by transacting with entities that were doing business with Iran. According to a GAO report, "the Department of the Treasury made overtures to 145 banks in 60 countries, including several visits to banks and officials in the UAE, and convinced at least 80 foreign banks to cease handling financial transactions with Iranian banks."[22] Levey and his team used these meetings with banks to present information that outlined how the Iranian regime tried to hide the source and destination of its financial activities, and to document specific accounts and transactions handled by the particular bank that supported Iran's illicit activity. The whisper campaign was not well received by many European governments or by many bank executives, who viewed the meetings as briefings in which Levey threatened, in subtle and not-so-subtle ways, to impose sanctions and fines on (largely European) banks that continued to do business with certain entities. Treasury officials denied making such threats, claiming instead that they merely provided information about illicit activity; and because "Treasury was feared and respected for what it could do," bank executives listened and acted.[23]

The second wave of the Iranian policy started in 2006 in the Bush administration and carried into the Barack Obama administration. In this phase, Treasury began to designate specific Iranian banks as primary money laundering concerns. In September 2006, Treasury cut off Bank Saderat Iran (BSI) from the U.S. market by pulling the exemption under which the bank was allowed to engage in U-turn transactions. Treasury then designated the Iranian institution Bank Sepah as a problem bank in January 2007, under the antiproliferation finance executive order. Similar designations occurred for other banks, including Bank Mellat, Mellat Bank SB CJSC, and Persian International Bank PLC. In July 2010, the U.S. Congress passed the Comprehensive Iran Sanctions, Accountability, and Divestment Act (CISADA), which made it illegal for banks that provide services to Iran to operate in the United States. The United States enforced these restrictions by striving to identify and fine foreign banks that were moving Iranian-controlled dollars through the American financial system. One authoritative account indicates that between 2004 and late 2019, the Treasury Department and other U.S. agencies imposed fines totaling about $12.8 billion on ten large European banks.[24] The list of banks that were fined reads like a who's who of the industry: ING, ABN Amro, UBS, Credit Suisse, and BNP Paribas, to name just a few.

America's Iran policy culminated in a declaration by the Obama administration in late 2011 that Iran itself constituted a primary money laundering concern.[25] By taking this rather remarkable step, the U.S. Treasury "identified the entire Iranian financial sector, including Iran's Central Bank, private Iranian banks, and branches, and subsidiaries of Iranian banks operating outside of Iran, as posing illicit finance risks for the global financial system." It was in the context of this campaign that the United States and the European Union (EU) blocked participation of Iranian banks in SWIFT. Zarate and others suggest that this tightening of financial sanctions induced the Iranian regime to return to the bargaining table and was thus critical to the ability to arrive at the Joint Comprehensive Plan of Action (JCPOA) in 2015. Once this agreement was reached, Iranian banks were allowed back into SWIFT and the United States relaxed other elements of its financial sanctions regime.[26]

The Donald Trump administration reimposed many of the sanctions after it withdrew from the JCPOA.[27] In May 2018, the U.S. Treasury named Valiollah Seif, who at the time was Iran's central bank, and Ali Tarzali, the assistant director of the bank's international department, for facilitating financial transfers in support of terrorist activities (specifically, Hezbollah). In November 2018, Treasury named Rasul Sajjad and Hossein Yaghoobi, other officials in the Iranian central bank's international department, for conducting financial transactions for the Islamic Revolutionary Guards Council and Quds Force. Alongside these actions, the administration pressured SWIFT to exclude most Iranian banks from the messaging network.[28] In September 2019, in response to the attack on a Saudi oil refinery, the administration listed Bank Markazi and Iran's National Development Fund as entities engaged in illicit activity that financed terrorism.[29] As of this writing, the Trump administration's sanctions regime remains in place.

The important role that financial sanctions played in bringing Iran back to negotiations led the Obama administration to rely heavily upon similar measures as a central component of its response to Russia's 2014 annexation of Crimea. Targeting Russia was a departure from prior actions in two ways. First, Russia is the first great power that the United States has targeted. Second, American goals were broader, aiming to force Russia to "abide by its international obligations and return its military forces to their original bases and respect Ukraine's sovereignty and territorial integrity." By 2018, the U.S. Treasury's Office of Foreign Assets Control (OFAC) had placed "680 individuals, entities, vessels, and aircraft" on its Specially Designated Nationals (SDN) and Sectoral Sanctions Identification (SSI) Lists.[30] In addition, during the summer of 2014, the Obama administration and David Cameron's U.K. government, with support from a European Parliament resolution developed in the summer and enacted in September 2014, pressured SWIFT to deny Russian banks access to its service. All parties recognized that pushing Russia out of SWIFT would constitute a major escalation of the conflict. As Kurt Volker, the American special envoy to the Ukraine, explained in 2018: "People refer to it as a nuclear option. It would have costs for everybody involved. Big costs for Russia, but big costs for allies as well. Ultimately, we have to keep it on the table as a possibility because we just can't continue to see Russia launch further steps of aggression in its neighborhood like this."[31] However, SWIFT management resisted the pressure from governments, in 2014 and again in 2018, and the United States and EU quietly dropped the campaign. For now, Russian banks continue to enjoy access to the system.

The United States' determination to weaponize its financial centrality has created discomfort among governments about the current structure of the global financial system. This apprehension has produced efforts to create alternative structures that would reduce American financial centrality. Observers regularly predict the emergence of a global currency that could diminish the dollar's importance, yet none of the most likely contenders—a list that includes the euro, the yen, and now China's renminbi (RMB)—has made significant inroads. Nor have efforts to create alternatives to the SWIFT system been especially successful. Russia created a new payment system as an alternative in 2014. This network, known as SPFS (service for transfer of financial messages), functions predominantly inside Russia, but the Putin government has sought to extend participation to China, India, Iran, and Turkey. China launched the Cross-Border Interbank Payment System (CIPS) in 2015 to facilitate the settlement of cross-border trade denominated in RMB in response to sanctions on Iran. Even America's traditional European allies have felt vulnerable to American financial power. They created the Instrument in Support of Trade Exchanges (INSTEX) in response to the Trump administration's decision to reimpose sanctions on Iran, in an attempt to enable EU-based companies to transact with Iran without violating U.S. sanctions. At the moment, however, these alternatives pose little challenge to SWIFT. Russia's SPFS functions primarily as an internal clearing system with limited international functionality. Although CIPS has attracted significant international participation, especially among actual and potential targets of American sanctions, total processed RMB transactions remain a small fraction of the dollar transactions processed by SWIFT.[32] The EU's INSTEX only just processed its first transaction in March 2020 and remains dedicated to transactions with Iran. Moreover, its reliance on barter makes it a very unappealing settlement system for global trade. None of these alternative systems currently constitutes a substantial challenge to SWIFT's centrality. Network externalities are likely at work here; thus, the U.S.-centered system will remain the dominant structure in the future because it is the dominant structure at the moment.

Conditions for Successful Weaponization

During the past twenty years, the United States has become increasingly willing to leverage its central position in the global financial network to advance its foreign policy objectives. This initiative began as law enforcement aimed at maintaining the integrity of financial institutions and the financial system, and then became a critical element in the War on Terror. Success on these fronts led the United States to use financial power for more ambitious foreign policy objectives. This brief review of these American efforts suggests three primary conclusions. First, the U.S. control of a critical choke point in the global financial network confers considerable power upon American policymakers. As we have seen, they can influence the decisions and activities of global banks by doing little more than threatening to name them as a bank engaged in illegal and illicit activity. We see this clearly in the system-wide reaction to the BDA listing as well as to the response of banks to the U.S. Treasury's whispering campaign. Moreover, during the past twenty years, the United States has used its network position to bring about changes in the policies and behaviors of foreign governments. Sanctions that targeted North Korea's financial interests and a set of financial measures that cut Iran off from the global financial system proved critical in bringing both regimes back to international negotiations on their nuclear programs.

Second, the cases examined here also suggest that weaponized financial interdependence has been most effective under three conditions. (1) Financial sanctions are most likely to succeed against small actors such as individual banks (BDA) and small states (North Korea), and less likely to succeed when applied to great powers (Russia). The

United States shut down BDA with little collateral damage; but in April 2018, U.S. sanctions on Rusal, a large Russian aluminum firm, rattled global markets so dramatically that the United States removed the sanctions less than a year later. Thus, some private entities may be too big to sanction. (2) Finance can be more effectively weaponized when the target does not itself occupy an alternative choke point that it can use for retaliation. In the Russian case, for instance, Putin's control of the flow of natural gas to Western Europe offered an effective retaliation in the event that Russia was expelled from SWIFT, and this threat may have been an important deterrent to European governments. Russia's control of direct energy flows provided it with leverage that Iran lacked and may thus have been an important reason for the different treatment. (3) Weaponizing finance against a large power requires broad agreement among Western governments about ends and means. Iran could be excluded from SWIFT, for example, because Western governments agreed on the importance of constraining the Iranian nuclear program through the P5+1 talks. In contrast, Russia could not be excluded from SWIFT, because Western governments disagreed about the severity of the Russian threat as well as about how best to manage this threat; this division—one that Putin may have exploited and widened—prevented the tightening of financial constraints.

Third, the last two decades indicate that there are a limited number of arrows in the financial sanctions quiver. As former U.S. secretary of the treasury Jacob Lew has said, if sanctions "make the business environment too complicated—or unpredictable, or if they excessively interfere with the flow of funds worldwide, financial transactions may begin to move outside of the United States entirely—which could threaten the central role of the U.S. financial system globally, not to mention the effectiveness of our sanctions in the future."[33] And this is more than a hypothetical. Banks, for instance, are de-risking their activities, preferring to shut down "entire lines of business rather than incur the increased compliance costs" or run the risk of a large fine.[34] States react to the weaponization of finance by creating alternative payments systems and turning to other currencies.

Notes

1. Daniel W. Drezner, "Targeted Sanctions in a World of Global Finance," *International Interactions* 41 (2015), pp. 755–64.

2. Quoted in "Cutting Russia Off from SWIFT Would Mean Declaration of War—Russian PM," *RT,* December 5, 2019, www.rt.com/business/475089 -russia-swift-ban-war/.

3. Henry Farrell and Abraham L. Newman, "Weaponized Interdependence: How Global Economic Networks Shape State Coercion," chapter 2 in this volume.

4. Thomas Oatley and others, "The Political Economy of Global Finance: A Network Model," *Perspectives on Politics* 11 (2013), pp 133–53.

5. This discussion draws heavily on Thomas Oatley and Bilyana Petrova, "The Global Deregulation Hypothesis," Tulane University, February 2020.

6. Bank for International Settlements, "Triennial Central Bank Survey of Foreign Exchange and Derivatives Market Activity in 2013" (Basel, Switzerland: Bank for International Settlements, 2015), www.bis.org/publ/ rpfx13.htm.

7. Hyun Song Shin, "Global Banking Glut and Loan Risk Premium," *IMF Economic Review* 60 (2012), p. 166.

8. Benjamin J. Cohen and Tabitha M. Benney, "What Does the International Currency System Really Look Like?" *Review of International Political Economy* 21 (2014), p. 1021.

9. Valentina Bruno and Hyun Song Shin, "Cross-Border Banking and Global Liquidity," *Review of Economic Studies* 82 (2013), pp. 535–64.

10. Shin, "Global Banking Glut and Loan Risk Premium," p. 163–64.

11. Iñaki Aldasoro and Torsten Ehlers, "The Geography of Dollar Funding of Non-U.S. Banks," *BIS Quarterly Review* (December 2018), pp. 15–26; Patrick McGuire and Peter von Goetz, "The U.S. Dollar Shortage in Global Banking," *BIS Quarterly Review* (March 2009), pp. 47–61.

12. Pierre-Olivier Gourinchas and Helene Rey, "From World Banker to World Venture Capitalist: U.S. External Adjustment and the Exorbitant Privilege," in *G7 Current Account Imbalances: Sustainability and Adjustment,* edited by Richard Clarida (University of Chicago Press, 2007), pp. 11–66; Matteo Maggiori, "Financial Intermediation, International Risk Sharing, and Reserve Currencies," *American Economic Review* 107 (2017), pp. 3038–71.

13. Benjamin J. Cohen, *Currency Power: Understanding Monetary Rivalry* (Princeton University Press, 2015); Barry J. Eichengreen, *Exorbitant Privilege: The Rise and Fall of the Dollar and the Future of the International Monetary System* (Oxford University Press, 2011); Carla Norrlof, "Dollar Hegemony: A Power Analysis," *Review of International Political Economy* 21 (2014), pp. 1042–70; Thomas Oatley, *A Political Economy of American Hegemony* (Cambridge University Press, 2015).

14. Benjamin J. Cohen, "The Macrofoundations of Monetary Power," in *International Monetary Power*, edited by David Andrews (Cornell University Press, 2006), pp. 31–50.

15. Oatley, *A Political Economy of American Hegemony*.

16. Thus, as Michael Mastanduno argues, fear was an important trigger for the effort to weaponize financial interdependence. Michael Mastanduno, "Hegemony and Fear: The National Security Determinants of Weaponized Interdependence," chapter 3 in this volume.

17. Juan Zarate, *Treasury's War: The Unleashing of a New Era of Financial Warfare* (New York: PublicAffairs, 2013), p. 150.

18. Ibid., p. 151.

19. Section 311 of the Patriot Act gave the "Treasury Secretary discretionary authority to impose one or more of five new 'special measures against foreign jurisdictions', foreign financial institutions, transactions involving such jurisdictions or institutions, or one or more types of accounts (including foreign accounts), that the Secretary determines to pose a 'primary money laundering concern to the USA." Alexander Kern, "Extraterritorial U.S. Banking Regulation and International Terrorism: The Patriot Act and the International Response," *Journal of International Banking Regulation* 3 (2002), pp. 307–326.

20. Zarate, *Treasury's War*.

21. Much of the authority for the Iranian campaign came from legislation that specifically targeted Iran. For instance, the Comprehensive Iran Sanctions, Accountability, and Divestment Act (CISADA) of 2010 "prohibits U.S. banks from maintaining correspondent accounts for foreign financial institutions if those institutions knowingly process transactions related to Iranian weapons or nuclear programmes, or transactions with already designated Iranian banks and entities." Aaron Arnold, "The True Costs of Financial Sanctions," *Survival* 58 (2016), p. 84. The National Defense Authorization Act of 2012 prohibited "U.S. banks from establishing new correspondent and payable-through accounts and [required] them to severely restrict existing accounts with any foreign bank that knowingly engages in transactions with the Central Bank of Iran (CBI) or any designated Iranian bank." See Suzanne Katzenstein, "Dollar Unilateralism: The New Frontline of National Security," *Indiana Law Journal* 90 (2015), p. 319.

22. Kenneth Katzman, *Iran Sanctions*, CRS Report no. 20871 (Washington: Congressional Research Service, 2020).

23. Zarate, *Treasury's War*, p. 302.

24. Katzman, *Iran Sanctions*, p. 30.

25. U.S. Department of the Treasury, "Fact Sheet: New Sanctions on Iran," November 11, 2011, www.treasury.gov/press-center/press-releases/Pages/tg1367.aspx.

26. "Iranian Banks Reconnected to SWIFT Network After Four-Year

Hiatus," Reuters, February 17, 2016, www.reuters.com/article/us-iran-banks
-swift/iranian-banks-reconnected-to-swift-network-after-four-year-hiatus
-idUSKCN0VQ1FD; U.S. Department of the Treasury, "Frequently Asked
Questions Relating to the Lifting of Certain U.S. Sanctions Under the Joint
Comprehensive Plan of Action (JCPOA) on Implementation Day," January
16, 2016, www.treasury.gov/resource-center/sanctions/Programs/Documents/
jcpoa_faqs.pdf.

27. U.S. Department of the Treasury, "U.S. Sanctions Iran's Central Bank
and National Development Fund," September 20, 2019, https://home.treasury
.gov/news/press-releases/sm780.

28. Eli Lake, "Trump Bank Sanctions Will Hit Iran Where It Hurts,"
Bloomberg, November 2, 2018, www.bloomberg.com/opinion/articles/2018
-11-02/trump-s-iran-bank-cutoff-from-swift-will-make-u-s-sanctions-hurt.

29. U.S. Department of the Treasury, "U.S. Sanctions Iran's Central Bank
and National Development Fund."

30. Katzman, *Iran Sanctions*, p. 9.

31. Marissa Melton, "U.S. Diplomat: Russia Should Release Ukrainian
Sailors by Christmas," VOA, December 5, 2018, www.voanews.com/europe/
us-diplomat-russia-should-release-ukrainian-sailors-christmas.

32. Kazuhiro Kida, Masayuki Kubota, and Yusho Cho, "Rise of the
Yuan: China-based Payment Settlements Jump 80%," *Nikkei Asian Business
Review*, May 20, 2019, https://asia.nikkei.com/Business/Markets/Rise-of-the
-yuan-China-based-payment-settlements-jump-80.

33. "U.S. Treasury Secretary Jacob J. Lew on the Evolution of Sanctions
and Lessons for the Future," speech to the Carnegie Endowment for International Peace, March 30, 2016, https://carnegieendowment.org/2016/03/
30/u.s.-treasury-secretary-jacob-j.-lew-on-evolution-of-sanctions-and-lessons
-for-future-event-5191. See also Jacob Lew and Richard Nephew, "The Use
and Misuse of Economic Statecraft," *Foreign Affairs* 97 (November/December
2018), pp. 139–49.

34. Arnold, *The True Costs of Financial Sanctions*, p. 88.

III

TECH

7

Internet Platforms Weaponizing Choke Points

NATASHA TUSIKOV

Fans of the Houston Rockets basketball team had front-row seats to the coercive power of the Chinese government in October 2019, when the team's general manager, Daryl Morey, tweeted his support for pro-democracy protestors in Hong Kong. Morey quickly deleted the tweet and apologized, as did the National Basketball Association (NBA), but the damage was done. Basketball is big business in China, with a rapidly growing fan base and lucrative sponsorship deals. In response to Morey's tweet, the Chinese Basketball Association and Chinese sponsors rapidly suspended their partnerships with the NBA. Underscoring the Chinese government's direct involvement in the case, Chinese state television canceled broadcasts of games, and government officials demanded that the NBA commissioner fire Morey.[1]

Chinese internet companies also lashed out. Tencent, the massive e-commerce conglomerate and operator of the WeChat social media platform, temporarily suspended all NBA preseason broadcasts. The marketplace giant Alibaba removed Houston Rockets merchandise from its popular Taobao and Tmall marketplaces, as did the online marketplace JD.com. U.S. politicians, both Democrats and Republicans, condemned the Chinese government for using its economic clout over the NBA to silence critics in the United States.

While the full economic repercussions are not yet fully known, the losses to the NBA and the Rockets measure in the millions. Chinese companies also suffered a serious financial blow. Tencent, for example, lost revenue from streaming and advertising NBA games. Just months earlier, in July 2019, Tencent had secured a five-year partnership with the NBA for US$1.5 billion for the exclusive rights to stream NBA games in China.[2]

In the terminology of this volume, the Houston Rockets' case can be understood as a particular type of coercive interdependence that, in the book's conclusion, Henry Farrell and Abraham Newman term "points of control," in which states leverage networks against private actors. China used its media and technology industries, both state-run and private, as a tool of economic retaliation against a major U.S. sporting franchise to condemn a U.S. business leader's political speech on Hong Kong's anti-government protests, a topic of high political sensitivity in China. This case is a continuation of China's global efforts to control political speech in regard to Hong Kong and Taiwan, among other issues. The Rockets' example illustrates how states can extend their power by enrolling private industry, particularly in this case of enacting choke points to control or block information flows.

While weaponized interdependence is a new concept within the mainstream international relations literature, the concept describes long-recognized tendencies within the internet governance and regulatory literatures. Drawing from these literatures to enrich the discussion of weaponized interdependence, this chapter argues that states with the capacity to co-opt and coerce key internet platforms can extend state control beyond traditional jurisdictional boundaries. Leveraging large platforms, however, is primarily the domain of powerful states like the United States and China, which can pressure their domestic industries and use the draw of their large markets to compel industry cooperation. *Platforms* here refers to entities, often from the private sector, that provide important commercial and technical services to enable the effective functioning of the internet, like payments or the domain name system. Platforms' withdrawal of critical services can enable states to control global flows of information or render websites commercially nonviable, essentially cutting them off from the global economy.

Contextualizing Weaponized Interdependence

Weaponized interdependence, as set out by Farrell and Newman, describes a situation in which a state leverages network structures to induce or compel specific actors to control flows of information or alter behavior to gain an advantage over other actors.[3]

Scholars from internet governance, communications, and socio-legal studies have long analyzed the state's strategic exploitation of information and communications infrastructure.[4] However, for too long there have been fruitful discussions within these disciplines but not enough cross-disciplinary engagement among internet governance, communications, and socio-legal studies with international relations. While there have been efforts from international relations scholars to bridge disciplinary divides,[5] deeper engagement is needed to see how weaponized interdependence may engender scholarship in other fields and what ideas international relations can adapt to further develop weaponized interdependence.

In the internet governance literature, the manner in which states might extend control over the budding internet infrastructure—including control over internet firms that provide increasingly critical services of search, payment, and domain name functions—has been a topic of considerable discussion since the late 1990s. Scholars in this field stress the inherent regulability of the internet and warn of the state's interest in, and capacity for, exploiting communications technologies and internet infrastructure, particularly by co-opting or coercively pressuring private-sector service providers.[6]

Three key ideas from the internet governance literature explain how conceptions of the internet rapidly shifted from one of an ungovernable space to a highly regulable space where states and, importantly, private-sector actors could exert authority. First, rules can be set within technology to govern behavior, a concept captured by the well-known phrase "code is law."[7] This refers to the capacity of actors, principally private-sector technology companies, to set rules within technical architecture (or code) in software that controls the various systems, applications, and protocols that compose the internet. Depending on the nature of the rules and systems governed, the rule makers may be able to deter or even prevent certain activities, or monitor or block information flows.

Second, the growth of key, often private-sector-operated nodes within networks that supply the internet's technical and commercial services offer an attractive leverage point for states, but only certain states have the capacity to exert control. While states initially took a laissez-faire approach to internet governance, in the early 2000s they began recruiting and co-opting these nodes.[8] States' ability to secure the cooperation of these nodes varies widely, as does the nodes' capacity and desire to resist attempts to compel cooperation.

Third, jurisdiction still matters online. States can achieve extraterritorial reach by tapping into private transnational networks. Control key actors, the argument goes, and one can control the provision and operation of important online services and infrastructure.[9] Jurisdiction remains important for states in relation to internet platforms, as governments may have greater influence over companies that operate within or are headquartered in their territory.

Platforms' Choke-Point Effects

Depending upon the type of services provided, platforms that command dominant market share can institute what I elsewhere have defined as access or revenue choke points.[10] By withdrawing payment services, platforms can disable websites' capacity to process payments or receive advertising funds, thereby "choking" the websites' revenue streams. Platforms can also disrupt users' ability to locate and access targeted websites by interfering with search and domain services, and they can remove sales listings from marketplaces, making it difficult to sell goods and services. The intention is to render the targeted entities commercially nonviable by impeding the sites' proper functioning. Given their operational scope and provision of important services, these dominant platforms can have a regulatory capacity similar to or even exceeding that of typical state regulators.

In recognition of the role that large, mostly U.S. companies play in providing vital commercial and technical services on the internet, scholars have referred to platforms' provision of key services as choke points,[11] natural points of control,[12] or bottlenecks.[13] A handful of U.S. companies dominate the provision of important technical and commercial services including payment (PayPal, Visa, MasterCard), advertising (Google and Facebook), domain name (GoDaddy), and marketplace (eBay and Amazon). These actors are dominant because of their transnational and, in some cases, near-global platforms; their significant market share; and their regulatory capacity that stems, in part, from "their positions at the nexus points between communications networks."[14] U.S. platforms are only rivaled by their Chinese counterparts, which generate most of their revenue in China; Tencent, Alibaba, and Baidu collectively dominate the provision of payment, marketplace, search, and social media services.

Internet platforms' capacity to enact choke points on behalf of states stems from the platforms' legal authority and business models. In terms of the former, platforms grant themselves considerable latitude through their contractual terms-of-use agreements with their users to draft, interpret, and enforce rules in ways that suit the platforms' business models and commercial interests. Platforms' implementation and enforcement of these rules, typically undertaken with little independent oversight or public disclosure, constitute a form of private ordering. Through these agreements, platforms can act of their own initiative in the absence of formal legal orders or involvement by law enforcement. A standard element of these agreements is a discretionary provision granting platforms the ability to remove content or terminate services even when the act in question is lawful. Platforms can also rapidly institute new rules, or change existing ones, governing their services, and studies show that few users read—or they struggle to understand—the updated legal agreements.[15]

In terms of business models, the regulatory capacity of a platform relies on its routine surveillance of its users' activities and transactions as part of its data-intensive business practices that are characteristic of surveillance capitalism.[16] Platforms employ surveillance not only to police users for violations of platform policies, but also, more importantly, to collect and interpret data on users to serve the platforms' commercial interests. This mass accumulation of data presents a tempting target for governments intent on surveilling or controlling their citizens online.

Weaponizing Choke Points

The concept of online choke points gained public prominence in 2010, when the U.S. government sought to destroy WikiLeaks after its publication of thousands of classified U.S. diplomatic cables leaked by whistleblower Chelsea Manning. Claiming the publication would harm U.S. national security interests, the U.S. government pressured key internet companies to sanction WikiLeaks. In response, companies withdrew their services, citing WikiLeaks for violating their terms-of-service agreements. Amazon stopped providing WikiLeaks with cloud-storage facilities, and EveryDNS withdrew its domain name services, meaning that users would not be able to find WikiLeaks online. PayPal, MasterCard, and Visa discontinued payment processing—a critical blow, as the WikiLeaks site relied on donations and struggled to replace its payment services.[17]

The U.S. government's campaign against WikiLeaks was the first high-profile case of what legal scholar Yochai Benkler described as a "denial-of-service attack" aimed at halting the "technical, payment, and business process systems to targeted sites."[18] Prior to its use on WikiLeaks, denial of service (DoS) was also used to block revenue from and freeze funds related to terrorist organizations.[19]

Lessons from Setting Choke Points

The attack on WikiLeaks was not a singular case: it was the forerunner in the normalization of state pressure on platforms to withdraw their technical and commercial services to targeted entities. States use platforms to enact choke points against private actors to serve their strategic interests, as highlighted in the cases of WikiLeaks and the Houston Rockets. Drawing from socio-legal studies and the regulatory studies literatures, there are six important lessons to learn regarding weaponized interdependence.

First, states' capacity to recruit or coerce platforms to enact choke points varies widely. State capacity disproportionately favors powerful states that can compel involvement by exerting political or legal pressure, particularly over their domestic industry. As Michael Mastanduno finds in his chapter in this volume, weaponized interdependence is a tool of strong states that have control over critical networks. States with dominant platforms headquartered in their jurisdictions have the home-court advantage.

In the wake of WikiLeaks, the United States, United Kingdom, and European Commission pressured large, mostly U.S. internet platforms to withdraw their services from targeted websites and businesses. The targets were websites involved in illegal gambling, the unlawful distribution of tobacco, child pornography, counterfeit goods, and the distribution of copyright-infringing movies, software, and music.[20] These state actors were successful because they credibly threatened to lay criminal charges or enact legislation if platforms did not agree to institute choke points "voluntarily" in the absence of legislation or formal legal orders.[21] China has also applied considerable political and legal pressure on its platforms, given the tight control the Chinese government exerts over its internet and domestic technology companies.[22]

However, even powerful states face limits in their capacity to compel action from platforms. For example, the European Commission and the United Kingdom were only successful in directing U.S.-based platforms to set choke points within their respective jurisdictions regarding the distribution of counterfeit goods and copyright-infringing content.[23] In these cases, pushback from platforms contributed, in part, to the jurisdictional limits on the regulatory efforts. As Adam Segal finds in his chapter on the U.S. government's campaign against Huawei, successfully leveraging the global supply chain is a difficult task complicated by Huawei's diversification of its suppliers and by U.S. companies' exploitation of boycott loopholes to maintain business with Huawei.

Second, states can use access to their domestic markets as leverage to compel platforms to enact choke points. The United States has a significant advantage, given the size of its domestic market, but the European Union (EU) and China can also use access to their markets as a way to secure industry cooperation. China is interested in leveraging its domestic internet platforms to serve its economic and political interests, as the Houston Rockets case shows. But given that its platforms largely operate within China, its choke-point capabilities are currently limited to inside China. With the continued expansion of Chinese platforms, China may have a future capacity to use platforms to set choke points that affect the provision of commercial and technical services beyond its borders.

In contrast to powerful states, smaller countries have few options to coerce action from global platforms. In Canada, for example, Google banned election-related advertising rather than comply with a new law regulating elections, concluding that the Canadian market was too small to merit the trouble of making the required changes.[24]

Third, states' interest in seeking to leverage specific private actors may stem from private actors' actual or perceived specialized technical or industry knowledge, and greater access to markets.[25] Working with platforms, particularly in the absence of legislation, can also offer states the benefits of flexibility and extraterritorial reach. As platforms operate through their contractual terms-of-service agreements, their rule setting and enforcement is generally more rapid, secretive, and adaptable than legislation or legal orders. Therefore, states may perceive corporate actors to be more responsive, cost-effective, and efficient actors than government agencies in certain areas.[26] By working through third parties, governments can also have deniability of certain industry-facilitated choke points or may be able to operate at a scale unfeasible for government agencies.

Fourth, private actors have varying interests in working with states to enact choke points, such as preventing an association of their platforms with criminality or entities perceived to be a threat to the state. Platforms, particularly those operating globally, are vulnerable to state pressure in the form of threats of legislation or legal action where they operate in an uncertain regulatory environment. Finally, private actors may view collaboration with the state as a way to curry favor with state officials, secure an advantage over commercial rivals, or expand their operations.

Fifth, conflicts between states and private actors—and among private actors—are inevitable. States and platforms have shared interests, although sometimes differing goals, in expanding their control over the internet. Concepts such as "surveillance capitalism" and "platform capitalism" underscore the importance of controlling information flows.[27] States may prioritize economic, military, or security interests, while platforms follow their commercial imperatives.[28] When state and corporate interests conflict, such as in the case of Apple refusing to circumvent its encryption at the request of the U.S. Federal Bureau of Investigation (FBI), states may shift to more coercive tactics like legal action, legislation, or threats of withdrawing market access but face the possibility of industry opposition, as was the case with Apple.[29]

In addition to state-corporate conflict, there may also be conflict within states as to the necessity, viability, or effectiveness of weaponized interdependence, or when, if at all, states should resort to this tactic. As Mastanduno argues in his chapter, the weaponization of structural power should be reserved for clear, justifiable emergencies such as national security crises. He notes that, in an environment of competition and conflict among the great powers, shifts in regional power, and the continued instability of foreign policy under the Donald Trump administration, the challenge is that weaponized interdependence may become a frequent rather than exceptional tool, at least for the United States.

Sixth, and finally, the effectiveness of choke points depends upon the degree of concentration in the industry sector in question and the availability of replacement service providers. Some services are relatively easy to replace, while in some industry sectors there are few viable commercial alternatives. The online payment provider industry, for example, is highly concentrated with a small number of dominant players—PayPal, Visa, MasterCard, and, in China, Tencent's WeChat Pay and Alibaba's AliPay. There are also a host of smaller players, like Apple Pay, but these often rely on the large players' payment systems. Payment providers are the most successful regulators because they can effectively defund targeted entities. Further, given the due-diligence requirements for payment providers to vet their users before granting accounts, it can be difficult to replace payment services, as WikiLeaks found.

There are dominant actors in other online sectors: Google and Facebook for digital advertising; Google for search; Amazon and eBay, along with Alibaba's Taobao and Tmall in China, for marketplaces; and GoDaddy for domain registrars. However, in contrast to the online payment industry, these sectors are more diversified and their services are easier to replace. Unlike replacing online payment services, it is a relatively simple process to secure alternative providers for advertising, marketplaces, social media, web hosting, or cloud services. Many websites, for example, can function without advertising revenue; if a dominant search engine like Google removes search results from its index, people can use other search engines. Similarly, if a marketplace removes sales listings for certain products, as Taobao did with listings for Houston Rockets' paraphernalia, sellers can move to another trading platform.

Future Research

Developing the concept of weaponized interdependence will no doubt be of value to international relations, bringing greater theoretical and empirical understanding to the state's leveraging of network capabilities. The concept may be able to provide insight on how and under what conditions states can leverage private actors to achieve their strategic objectives against other states, as well as when private actors are most likely to comply or resist. These contributions from international relations would likely provoke fertile cross-disciplinary engagement and contribute to scholarship within internet governance, communications, and socio-legal studies, as well as other disciplines.

More broadly, the case needs to be made for the utility of the concept of weaponized interdependence outside the United States. The United States has used its structural power for decades to achieve its political, security, and economic interests. Only recently has the United States realized that it can also be affected by weaponized interdependence, as Daniel Drezner notes in this book's introduction. The rest of the world, however, has a deep familiarity with what it means to be in an interdependent relationship with a more powerful country and, in particular, has long experienced the ability of the United States to exert this type of power on allies and enemies alike. To what extent does this concept serve to explain to U.S. policymakers the newly discovered vulnerability of the United States to weaponized interdependence employed by other states, and how can it be best developed for usefulness to non-American and non-international relations scholars and policymakers?

In terms of a more specific research agenda related to internet and digital technologies, there are several fruitful lines of inquiry for future choke-point research. Scholarship should consider what other areas of commercial or technical services on the internet might be vulnerable to choke-point effects. Cloud infrastructure, for example, is a highly concentrated industry with major U.S. companies holding key market share, especially Amazon Web Services, Microsoft Azure, IBM, and Google Cloud Platform, along with China's Alibaba Cloud (Aliyun) and Tencent Cloud. What might be the effects of choke points within cloud infrastructure, and which companies might be most amenable or resistant? With an increasing number of commercial and government services dependent upon the cloud, including education, health care, and military services, disruptions to this sector could be consequential.

Scholarship also needs to examine the potential for choke points in the physical infrastructure making up the internet, the protection of which has been a long-standing national security concern in the United States, as well as in many other countries. Control of the internet's physical infrastructure takes on a new urgency with research demonstrating that the ownership and operation of core elements of the global internet infrastructure is shifting away from the United States toward Europe and Brazil, Russia, India, China, and South Africa.[30] These elements include the fiber-optic submarine cables, autonomous system numbers, and internet exchange points that constitute the "pipes" of the internet. A consortium of public and private actors is building and controlling internet infrastructure in the Asia-Pacific and African regions, but the short- and long-term implications of these developments, particularly in terms of continued U.S. hegemony over the internet, are not clear.[31]

Analyzing choke points in the online environment requires a careful examination of the Chinese government's interest in and capability to enact choke points. The rapid growth of Chinese internet platforms over the past decade has generated friction between the United States and China, as only China has internet platforms that rival those in the United States. In addition to having national security implications, the U.S.-China trade dispute is also a technological dispute, with both parties wanting to dominate global markets in advanced technologies like robotics, autonomous vehicles, and artificial intelligence.[32] The Chinese government has strategically cultivated its national technology champions, in part by banning foreign competitors and using policy incentives to favor domestic firms, which has resulted in a symbiotic partnership between the Chinese government and its commercial internet firms.[33] China's tech giants operate largely within China but control industry sectors: Baidu dominates search; Tencent operates the popular WeChat social media platform and WeChat Pay application; and the Alibaba Group's Taobao and Tmall platforms are the dominant retail marketplaces in China, while Alibaba's AliPay system competes with WeChat Pay for dominance of China's online payment sector. Tencent and Alibaba are also expanding within Europe and Asia, with investments in cloud infrastructure, artificial intelligence, and payment services, raising concerns in the United States.[34]

How and in what industry sectors might the Chinese government impose choke points to serve its political and economic interests, and with what effects? Since Chinese platforms remain reliant on foreign capital, particularly from the United States, for continued growth,[35] how might this constrain the effectiveness of the Chinese government's use of choke points? How might China employ choke points to gain technological dominance in areas of strategic interest to itself and the United States, especially in robotics, autonomous vehicles, and artificial intelligence?[36]

Finally, this focus on the United States and China prompts a final critical question: How are other countries affected by weaponized interdependence? Research is needed not just on states that have the capacity and intent to wield choke points, but also in assessing how affected countries might best respond to, resist, or deter state-sanctioned choke points. How might smaller countries without dominance over economic networks, like Canada, Brazil, or Australia, resist or respond to choke points? This research agenda should consider the role of the EU in facilitating or responding to weaponized interdependence. The European Union does not have a domestic internet industry that rivals that of the United States or China, but the

EU is attempting to position itself as a regulatory superpower, in part through its May 2018 implementation of the General Data Protection Regulation (GDPR), its groundbreaking privacy law.

Next Steps

The use of choke points will continue because globally operating internet platforms are an attractive and valuable tool for states to extend their control. The United States has a particular advantage, given the commercial dominance of its platforms across various industry sectors and its capacity to compel cooperation from its platforms. China, however, has its own internet giants over which the government exerts considerable control. The Houston Rockets' case is a likely prelude to future scenarios in which China capitalizes upon its growing internet sector to extend its political and economic control.

This chapter is structured around the Houston Rockets case because it highlights an important factor in why U.S. academics and policymakers are concerned about weaponized interdependence: a country other than the United States can now leverage networks to exert choke-point power to serve its interests. As Drezner notes in the introduction, U.S. policymakers have been slow to recognize that the United States can be affected by weaponized interdependence, and now they need to consider how they might respond to choke points targeting U.S. political, security, or economic interests. Outside the United States, the practice of weaponized interdependence is quite familiar. Countries like Canada can provide advice and counterstrategies because they have experienced the United States wielding its structural power for decades. With the United States finally experiencing the negative effects of weaponized interdependence, might U.S. policymakers consider prioritizing alternative forms of statecraft?

Notes

1. Patrick Blennerhassett, "NBA Boss Adam Silver Says Chinese Government Asked Him to Fire Houston Rockets General Manager Daryl Morey," *South China Morning Post*, October 18, 2019, www.scmp.com/sport/basketball/article/3033476/adam-silver-said-chinese-government-asked-him-fire-houston-rockets.

2. Tony Xu, "China's Tech Giants Hit Pause on NBA Ties after Executive's Hong Kong Tweet," *TechNode*, October 9, 2019, https://technode.com/2019/10/09/chinas-tech-giants-hit-pause-on-nba-ties-after-executives-hong-kong-tweet/.

3. Henry Farrell and Abraham L. Newman, "Weaponized Interdependence: How Global Economic Networks Shape State Coercion," *International Security* 44 (Summer 2019), pp. 42–79.

4. See, for example, David Harvey, *The New Imperialism* (Oxford University Press, 2003).

5. See Henry Farrell, "Regulating Information Flows: States, Private Actors, and E-Commerce," *Annual Review of Political Science* 9 (2006), pp. 353–74.

6. See Michael D. Birnhack and Niva Elkin-Koren, "The Invisible Handshake: The Reemergence of the State in the Digital Environment," *Virginia Journal of Law and Technology* 8, no. 6 (2003), pp. 1–57; Lawrence Lessig, *Code and Other Laws of Cyberspace* (New York: Basic Books, 1999); Joel R. Reidenberg, "Lex Informatica: The Formulation of Information Policy Rules through Technology," *Texas Law Review* 76 (1998), pp. 553–93.

7. Lessig, *Code and Other Laws of Cyberspace*.

8. Birnhack and Elkin-Koren, "The Invisible Handshake."

9. Annemarie Bridy, "Internet Payment Blockades," *Florida Law Review* 67, no. 5 (2015), pp. 1523–68; Uta Kohl, "Google: The Rise and Rise of Online Intermediaries in the Governance of the Internet and Beyond (Part 2)," *International Journal of Law and Information Technology* 21, no. 2 (2013), pp. 187–234; Natasha Tusikov, *Chokepoints: Global Private Regulation on the Internet* (University of California Press, 2017).

10. Tusikov, *Chokepoints*.

11. Laura DeNardis, *The Global War for Internet Governance* (Yale University Press, 2014); Tusikov, *Chokepoints*.

12. Jonathan A. Zittrain, "A History of Online Gatekeeping," *Harvard Journal of Law and Technology* 20, no. 1 (2006), pp. 253–98, at p. 254.

13. Oren Bracha and Frank Pasquale, "Federal Search Commission? Access, Fairness, and Accountability in the Law of Search," *Cornell Law Review* 93 (2008), pp. 1149–1210, at p. 1161.

14. Andrew Murray, "Nodes and Gravity in Virtual Space," *Legisprudence* 5 (2011), pp. 195–221, at p. 220.

15. Jonathan A. Obar and Anne Oeldorf-Hirsch, "The Biggest Lie on the Internet: Ignoring the Privacy Policies and Terms of Service Policies of Social Networking Services," *Information, Communication & Society* 23, no. 1 (2018), pp. 128–47.

16. Shonsana Zuboff, *The Age of Surveillance Capitalism: The Fight for a Human Future at the New Frontier of Power* (New York: PublicAffairs, 2019).

17. Yochai Benkler, "WikiLeaks and the Protect-IP Act: A New Public-Private Threat to the Internet Commons," *Daedalus* 140, no. 4 (2011), pp. 154–64.

18. Ibid, p. 155.

19. Ibid.

20. See Tusikov, *Chokepoints.*

21. Ibid.

22. See Aofei Lv and Ting Luo, "Authoritarian Practices in the Digital Age: Asymmetrical Power Between Internet Giants and Users in China," *International Journal of Communication* 12 (2018), pp. 3877–95.

23. See Tusikov, *Chokepoints.*

24. Tom Cardoso, "Google to Ban Political Ads Ahead of Federal Election, Citing New Transparency Rules," *The Globe and Mail*, March 4, 2019, www .theglobeandmail.com/politics/article-google-to-ban-political-ads-ahead-of -federal-election-citing-new/.

25. Claire A. Cutler, Virginia Haufler and Tony Porter, *Private Authority and International Affairs* (SUNY Press, 1999).

26. Fabrizio Cafaggi, editor, *Enforcement of Transnational Regulation: Ensuring Compliance in a Global World* (Cheltenham, United Kingdom: Edward Elgar Publishing, 2012).

27. See Zuboff, *The Age of Surveillance Capitalism;* Nick Srnicek, *Platform Capitalism* (Cambridge, United Kingdom: Polity, 2017).

28. Shawn M. Powers and Michael Jablonski, *The Real Cyber War: The Political Economy of Internet Freedom* (University of Illinois Press, 2015).

29. Lily Hay Newman, "This Apple-FBI Fight is Different from the Last One," *Wired*, January 16, 2020, www.wired.com/story/apple-fbi-iphone -encryption-pensacola/#:~:text=For%20all%20the%20FBI's%20 posturing,to%20crack%20it%20for%20them.

30. Dwayne Winseck, "Internet Infrastructure and the Persistent Myth of U.S. Hegemony," in *Information, Technology and Control in a Changing World: Understanding Power Structures in the 21st Century*, edited by Blayne Haggart, Kathryn Henne, and Natasha Tusikov (New York: Palgrave Macmillan, 2019), pp. 93–120.

31. Ibid.

32. See Natasha Tusikov, "How U.S.-Made Rules Shape Internet Governance in China," *Internet Policy Review* 8, no. 2 (2019), pp. 1–22.

33. Min Jiang and King-Wa Fu, "Chinese Social Media and Big Data: Big Data, Big Brother, Big Profit?" *Policy & Internet* 10, no. 4 (2018), pp. 372–92.

34. Philippe Le Corre, "On China's Expanding Influence in Europe and Eurasia," testimony to the U.S. House of Representatives Foreign Affairs Committee, Subcommittee on Europe, Eurasia, Energy, and the Environment, Washington, May 9, 2019.

35. Lianrui Jia and Dwayne Winseck, "The Political Economy of Chinese Internet Companies: Financialization, Concentration, and Capitalization," *International Communication Gazette* 80, no. 1 (2018), pp. 30–59.

36. See Kim Min-hyung, "A Real Driver of U.S.–China Trade Conflict: The Sino–U.S. Competition for Global Hegemony and Its Implications for the Future," *International Trade, Politics and Development* 3, no. 1 (2019) pp. 30–40.

8

Huawei, 5G, and Weaponized Interdependence

ADAM SEGAL

The competition between China and the United States over 5G and the next generation of communication technology is perhaps the clearest illustration of the structure and processes of weaponized interdependence. The Chinese and U.S. economies had been connected by global information and communication technologies supply chains that policymakers in both countries believed fostered innovation and economic growth. Moreover, the resulting interdependence had been seen as a stabilizing influence in the bilateral relationship.

Over the last decade, however, leaders in both countries began to question whether the vulnerabilities created by interdependence outweighed the vulnerabilities to panopticon and choke-point threats. Decisionmakers in Beijing and Washington have wielded the tools of weaponized interdependence and traditional economic statecraft, exerting greater control over supply chains while also exploring options to constrain the free flow of talent, goods, and capital, to block market access, and to punish individual firms. In an effort to reduce the ability of U.S. intelligence agencies to gather information and the potential of the U.S. military to launch more disruptive cyber operations, Beijing has moved to make information and communication technologies (ICT) more "secure and controllable," to support indigenous innovation, and to replace foreign technology with domestic suppliers.

In the terms of Michael Mastanduno's chapter in this volume, the Donald Trump administration was willing to bear the costs of weaponized interdependence because it was uncommitted to the liberal international order and viewed the international environment as threatening.[1] For the last decade, Washington has grown increasingly concerned that China was not only exploiting the openness of the U.S. innovation system to accelerate its own science and technology development, but that it could soon replace the United States at the center of global communication platforms. U.S. officials worried that the panopticon effects that had flowed to the United States in the internet's first four decades would be captured by China as it built out 5G networks around the world. Moreover, once economies became dependent on these networks for the internet of Things (IoT), self-driving cars, and other data-dependent next-generation internet services, Beijing would wield leverage by threatening to disrupt them.

These policy concerns and their manifestation in weaponized interdependence crystallized in the Trump administration's campaign against Huawei, the Chinese telecom giant. Huawei owns more standard essential patents in 5G than any other company, has submitted more than twice the number of standard protocols than Qualcomm, and spends more on research and development (R&D) than its chief rivals, Ericsson and Nokia, combined.[2] Huawei and another Chinese company, ZTE, account for about 40 percent of global 5G infrastructure, and Huawei has over ninety commercial contracts to build 5G equipment.[3]

Alarmed by the company's reach, the White House relied on many tools of economic statecraft to wound Huawei, including blocking its access to the U.S. market; filing a criminal case against Chief Financial Officer Meng Wanzhou for sanctions violations, and against the company for intellectual property theft; and pressuring friends and allies to use alternative suppliers of 5G networks.

The White House also weaponized interdependence, cutting the company off from critical supply chains and components by placing it on the U.S. Commerce Department's entity list, which restricts the export, reexport, and transfer of specific items to foreign entities.[4]

The first stage of the process, which ran from the announcement of sanctions in May 2019 until May 2020, when a second set of provisions were rolled out, demonstrated many of the domestic and international dynamics that determine the success or failure of weaponized interdependence. While the United States leveraged choke points in the global supply chain—especially in semiconductors and, to a lesser extent, in mobile operating systems—Huawei survived the U.S. onslaught by producing its own components, stockpiling parts, and diversifying suppliers. Important suppliers, and Taiwan Semiconductor Manufacturing Company (TSMC) in particular, remained outside the first wave of U.S. efforts. Beijing also responded to the threat and mobilized a national effort to lessen the dependence on foreign chips.

In addition, domestic actors complicated (if not weakened) the administration's initial efforts. For instance, U.S. technology companies exploited loopholes in export control laws to continue selling products to Huawei. There was bureaucratic resistance to tightening controls, most notably from the Pentagon, which worried about the impact of lost revenues on the innovation capabilities of American technology companies. President Trump's messaging about the threat of the company often contradicted official policy. Huawei's 2019 revenues were up 17 percent from 2018 and net profits increased by $9 billion, though growth slowed sharply and the company was more reliant on domestic markets.[5] In May 2020, however, the White House announced changes in export control laws that more effectively cut Huawei off from chips produced by TSMC.

Despite its erratic start, the Huawei case is likely to be a successful example of the United States weaponizing interdependence to slow the emergence of a new set of networks that could be more easily weaponized by Beijing. Without access to advanced chips, Huawei's central role in 5G networks outside of China becomes more tenuous. Moreover, despite Beijing's efforts to produce chips domestically, it is likely to remain behind the cutting edge for another decade at least.

Global Innovation

China and the United States have built and joined globalized networks of innovation because they were mutually advantageous. By opening up their science and technology systems to the world, both countries have addressed weaknesses in their respective domestic innovation ecosystems. The United States responded to the challenge from Japan in the 1980s by breaking electronics and computer sectors value chains into multiple components and locating them throughout Asia. U.S. technology firms transferred ever more sophisticated production tasks to specialized suppliers located in complex ecosystems.[6] The iPhone became the archetypical example of the use of multinational supply chains, with parts sourced in forty-three countries, including China, Japan, and South Korea.[7] As competition became more intense over time, technology firms shifted more complicated tasks such as product R&D to the supply chain. Since the 1990s, for example, the distribution of R&D investment from U.S. companies across countries has shifted dramatically away from Europe toward China, India, and Israel.[8]

The semiconductor supply chain has become especially global and complex. The Semiconductor Industry Association notes that an American firm can have up to 16,000 suppliers, with over half located outside the United States.[9] In the integrated design manufacturer model, companies like Intel and Samsung distribute design, manufacturing, assembly, testing, and packaging around the world. In the fabless-foundry model, the production process is split between design companies known as "fabless" because they focus on design for specialized uses and then contract out fabrication to foundries. The world's biggest foundry company is TSMC, which supplies the world's leading tech companies, including Apple, Qualcomm, and Nvidia as well as Huawei and Alibaba.

As it opened to the world, China became deeply enmeshed in these global value chains. Beijing reinforced and accelerated the reform of its domestic science and technology system through access to foreign technology. Initially, China traded market access for technology; later, it welcomed foreign investment in numerous sectors, especially electronics assembly, with the expectation that they would help to develop the capabilities of domestic firms. Chinese firms developed extensive connections to foreign customers, investors, and suppliers. But although several prominent Chinese companies have moved up the value chain, the majority of Chinese firms continue to be low-value suppliers with high dependence on foreign technology and intellectual property.

Policymakers and analysts on both sides of the Pacific also saw technological interdependence as a stabilizing feature of the bilateral relationship, acting as a restraint against wide swings when tensions flared over issues such as Taiwan. The U.S. business community, in particular, has been an important supporter of stable bilateral relations. For both sides, a dynamic of "mutually assured economic destruction" created a level of restraint against potential escalation.[10]

The Threat of Collection and Disruption

Over the last five years, leaders in both countries have questioned whether the asymmetries and vulnerabilities created through global supply chains and interdependence outweigh the benefits. While a wide range of strategic and economic motivations have spurred the disentangling of the two sides, Chinese and U.S. policymakers and analysts have referred to concepts akin to panopticon and chokepoint threats to justify their efforts.

Chinese leaders have long assumed that a reliance on U.S. technology has left the country vulnerable to cyber operations. The revelations of U.S. National Security Agency (NSA) contractor Edward Snowden in 2013 reinforced these beliefs and energized efforts to replace foreign technology, develop domestic cybersecurity institutions and regulations, and foster innovation in quantum information and other emerging technologies. Chinese officials and press reports have often used Snowden to highlight U.S. intelligence collection capabilities and what they see as U.S. hypocrisy for its criticism of Beijing's own cyber-enabled theft of intellectual property. In a February 2019 *Financial Times* op-ed, for example, Guo Ping, one of Huawei's rotating chairpersons, wrote that Washington saw the company as a threat because documents leaked by Snowden showed "how the NSA's leaders were seeking to 'collect it all' — every electronic communication sent, or phone call made, by everyone in the world, every day. Those documents also showed that the NSA maintains 'corporate partnerships' with particular U.S. technology and telecom companies that allow the agency to 'gain access to high-capacity international fibre-optic cables, switches and/or routers throughout the world.'" The reason the United States was so worried about Huawei, Guo continued, was "the more Huawei gear is installed in the world's telecommunications networks, the harder it becomes for the NSA to 'collect it all.' Huawei, in other words, hampers U.S. efforts to spy on whomever it wants."[11]

U.S. officials, of course, have not emphasized that reliance on Huawei could result in significant losses for American intelligence collection. Rather they highlight the espionage threats from China. These officials have mirrored the argument that Stacie Goddard makes in this volume—that a revisionist China could use networks to augments its power, striving "to occupy a hub position in communication that would give it increased information capacity."[12] Though officials have occasionally referred to reports from third-party cybersecurity companies that argue the company has poor security practices or intentionally left vulnerabilities unpatched, their primary argument is not technical. Rather, U.S. officials have argued that Huawei exists within a political system in which the Chinese Communist Party (CCP) has broad discretionary tools that may be used to compel assistance with national security matters and that it could force Huawei to deliberately place security backdoors, vulnerabilities unknown to the user that would allow access by intelligence agencies. Secretary of State Mike Pompeo, for example, told Maria Bartiromo, "If it's the case that the Chinese Communist Party wanted to get information from technology that was in the possession of Huawei, it is almost certainly the case that Huawei would provide that to them."[13] Similarly, in response to a question from a journalist about European use of Huawei technology, Deputy Assistant Secretary of State Rob Strayer said, "We think that as technology used in [smart] cities is integrated into broader wireless networks, that would be a cause for concern because that data could end up back in places such as Beijing where it would not be used for the purposes that we want to see all of our data subject to which is protected uses, limited uses, and not to be exploited for authoritarian purposes."[14]

The widespread use of encryption and authentication in 5G networks would address many of the risks of collection, so U.S. officials and analysts have also invoked the threat of choke points. Rob Joyce, a senior NSA official, warned that the threat was not just espionage but the ability of the Chinese to create a cyber "effect"; at the February 2019 Mobile World Congress in Barcelona, Spain, Deputy Assistant Strayer warned, "With the transformational critical services that 5G will empower, we cannot risk having those services being disrupted or manipulated by authoritarian regimes."[15] Erica Borghard and Shawn Lonegran argue there is a threat to U.S. military operations in areas of interest to China, since Beijing could leverage Huawei to deny military communications or "limit the U.S. military's ability to conduct precision targeting that leverages signals intelligence collection on 5G telecommunications network."[16] Thomas Donohue echoes this threat, noting that while the risk of disruption may not be high during normal times, it has to be considered "on the worst possible day in a conflict with a peer adversary."[17] John Hemmings argues that the bundling of 5G and smart port technologies could allow China to "create a deniable, surgical sanctions system by interdicting or slowing the container traffic of states or their leaders."[18]

The Application of Weaponized Interdependence

It is through the use of the Commerce Department's entity list that Washington most clearly has exploited its position in an embedded network to gain a bargaining advantage over Huawei and Beijing, especially in regard to semiconductors. In 2014, China's State Council set a plan to raise the country's semiconductor capabilities, and the "National Guidelines for the Development and Promotion of the IC Industry" provided new backing for advances in semiconductors, with reported investments totaling between $100 billion and $150 billion in public and private funds. Semiconductors were also a central focus of the "Made in China 2025" plan, which set the goal of growing the country's integrated circuit (IC) industry to a self-sufficiency rate of 40 percent by 2020, increasing to 70 percent by 2025. Yet, in 2020, China was importing more chips, not fewer. In 2018, China depended on imported semiconductors, worth $311 billion, for 84 percent of its demand; of the 16 percent produced in China, only half were produced by Chinese firms.

Chinese capabilities are mainly in low-end chips.[19] The dominant semiconductor companies, with the exception of NXP in the Netherlands and Toshiba in Japan, are headquartered in the United States and South Korea, with U.S. companies dominating semiconductor design and South Korea dominating memory chip production. The United States retains significant influence over the markets for graphics processing units (GPUs) and field-programmable gate arrays (FPGAs) needed for artificial intelligence (AI) platforms, as well as relatively tight control on semiconductor manufacturing equipment and semiconductor electronic automation design tools. But China has made progress in some areas, especially memory chips. In April 2020, for example, Yangtze Memory Technologies Company announced that it had developed a type of advanced memory chip for data storage, called 128-layer 3D-NAND—reducing the technological gap with incumbents to about a year.[20] Still, Chinese firms continue to be weak in leading-edge multicore processors, memory devices, semiconductor equipment, and design tool services.[21] For example, China is about five years behind the technological edge in dynamic random-access memory (DRAM) chips used for processing code.

The United States has wielded this dependence on U.S. chips against several Chinese technology firms. The process has been very similar to the weaponization of interdependence on the internet as described in the Natasha Tusikov chapter in this volume, with Washington pressuring domestic companies and using the lure of the domestic market to compel industry compliance. In April 2018, the Commerce Department banned U.S. companies from selling components and software to ZTE for seven years, after the company was found violating an agreement on punishing employees, which was reached after ZTE was caught illegally shipping U.S. goods to Iran. The company, which purchased about $1.5 billion in chips from U.S. manufacturers in 2017 and relied on Qualcomm for chips inside its smartphones, Android for its operating system, and a range of other U.S. suppliers, announced in May 2018 that it was "ceasing major operations."

The company was saved by a June deal with President Trump, but Fujian Jinhua Integrated Circuit, a state-owned Chinese memory chip maker, was not as fortunate. In September 2018, the U.S. Department of Justice unsealed charges against Jinhua and United Microelectronics Corporation, its Taiwanese partner, for stealing trade secrets from Micron Technology. Then the Commerce Department, claiming that "Jinhua poses a significant risk of becoming involved in activities that are contrary to the national security interests of the United States," announced restrictions on American firms selling to the company in October.[22] Cut off from essential equipment and materials from suppliers such as Applied Materials, Lam Research, and KLA-Tencor, Jinhua stopped production in March 2019.[23]

The Commerce Department placed Huawei on the entity list in May 2019, describing it as "engaged in activities that are contrary to U.S. national security or foreign policy interest," and blocking the company from buying parts from U.S. companies without government approval. At that time, Commerce issued temporary licenses that allowed some sales to continue, and the licenses were extended multiple times. In 2018, Huawei procured $11 billion worth of goods from American suppliers, including semiconductors from Qualcomm, Intel, and Texas Instruments; radio frequency chips from Skyworks Solutions and Qorvo; memory chips from Micron; integrated circuit design tools from Synopsys and Cadence Design Systems; and the Android mobile phone operating system from Google.[24] A number of high-profile suppliers, such as Google and the U.K.-based chip design firm ARM Holdings, stopped supplying the company, but others like Qualcomm, Micron, and Intel decided that the ban did not affect the products they were selling to Huawei because the technology transferred to the Chinese telecom owed less than 25 percent of its origin to U.S.-based activities.[25] As a result, critical components continued to flow to Huawei.

China Fights Back

Huawei was defiant in the face of U.S. pressure. The company stockpiled goods, diversified supply chains, and increased its efforts to develop its own technologies. In the wake of the sanctions on ZTE, for example, Huawei stockpiled several months' worth of Xilinx's FPGAs, which are essential to its 5G base stations. Huawei also began telling suppliers that it wanted to build up a year's worth of other components and increased purchases of capacitors, integrated circuits, flash memory, and camera-related parts from Japanese suppliers.[26]

Company officials also told suppliers to increase production in China. HP reportedly agreed to build a new production complex in the Chinese city of Yueyang, and Huawei asked Taiwanese firms Unimicron and Nan Ya Printed Circuit Board to help it build new production capacity in China. The company requested that Taiwan's ASE Technology Holding and King Yuan Electronics, its top chip-packaging and -testing providers, relocate most production to sites in mainland China. The company also increased its participation in open-source software projects, which are less subject to U.S. export controls.

Huawei accelerated efforts to develop its own substitutes for U.S. products. The company increased the amount it spends on R&D, hitting $15 billion in 2018, which placed it among the top five spenders on research in the world. In April 2019, Huawei announced that it would establish an Institute of Strategic Research and invest US$300 million each year for the next five to ten years to fund research in basic science and technology; the company also introduced new lines of AI chips.[27] In addition, Huawei started developing its own operating system, Harmony (HongMeng), which might eventually be adapted to smartphones, and released Huawei Mobile Services (HMS) as a substitute for the Google Play Store, Google Maps, Google Chrome, YouTube, and other apps.

In the first year of the sanctions, this strategy kept the firm afloat. According to outside analysts, Huawei managed to replace critical U.S. parts with other suppliers for the Mate 30 smartphone, which the company unveiled in September 2019. In an interview with the *Wall Street Journal*, John Suffolk, the company's top cybersecurity official, said that Huawei was capable of producing—without U.S. components—the 5G base stations that are a key part of the infrastructure needed for high-speed networks: "All of our 5G is now America-free."[28]

Huawei's efforts to reduce dependence on foreign suppliers was echoed and amplified by the mobilization of national resources.[29] In a series of speeches after the ZTE ban, Xi Jinping highlighted China's need for innovation and technological self-determination. In May 2018, at a joint annual conference of the Chinese Academy of Sciences and the Chinese Academy of Engineering, for example, Xi exhorted the gathered scientists and engineers to redouble their efforts, stating, "Self-determination and innovation is the unavoidable path ... to climb to the world's top as a leading player in technology." The country accelerated 5G rollout, signaling that it would not let either U.S. sanctions nor the COVID-19 crisis slow development. Chinese state-owned telecoms directed business to Huawei, and the company secured $4 billion in orders from China Mobile in 2020, beating out Ericsson and ZTE to win more than half of the 5G contracts.[30]

In October 2019, Beijing established a new semiconductor fund of $29 billion, $9 billion more than a similar fund it launched in 2014. Chinese semiconductor firms lured talent away from Taiwan, reportedly recruiting 300 senior engineers in 2018 with higher pay, free travel between the island and mainland, and subsidized apartments.[31] Chinese big tech also signaled that they would follow the government's lead. As Alibaba's chief executive officer, Jack Ma, said, "Big enterprises have an important responsibility. If we do not master the core technologies, we will be building roofs on other people's walls and planting vegetables in other people's yards."[32] Alibaba launched its semiconductor division, Pingtouge, in September 2018 and Baidu released its smart chip, Kunlun, in July 2019.

Beijing also signaled that it could retaliate against individual U.S. firms. The Ministry of Commerce reportedly prepared an "unreliable-entity list" of foreign businesses and individuals that would face restrictions in their dealings with Chinese counterparts. In response to the White House's pressure on Huawei, Eric Xu, the company's chairperson, warned, "The Chinese government will not just stand by and watch Huawei be slaughtered. I believe it would take countermeasures. Why would the Chinese government not use similar cyber security concerns to ban the use of U.S. 5G chips ... in the Chinese market?"[33]

The United States Tightens the Noose

Despite U.S. influence over global supply chains, China hawks in the U.S. administration were frustrated with their inability to deliver a more damaging blow to Huawei in the first year. Messaging was inconsistent, with the president tweeting in February 2020 that the United States should not use national security as an excuse for export controls and that the country "wants to sell products and goods to China and other countries."[34] U.S. firms continued supplying Huawei, which spent $18.7 billion with U.S. companies in 2019, up from $11 billion in 2018.[35] In addition, TSMC continued working with Huawei's chip design arm, HiSilicon.

These loopholes were closed in May 2020 as U.S. officials announced two rule changes to expand U.S. authority to block the sales of technology to China. The first closed the door to most U.S. suppliers. The previous rules allowed for sales of products that contained less than 25 percent of U.S.-made content; officials dropped this down to 10 percent, which prevented U.S. companies from shipping to Huawei from outside of the United States. The Pentagon reportedly opposed tighter restrictions, fearing they would hurt defense suppliers and U.S. innovation, but eventually dropped its opposition.[36]

The second provision had an even more dramatic impact. The Commerce Department extended licensing requirements to foreign companies producing semiconductor products for HiSilicon that use U.S. technology as part of the manufacturing process. Almost all HiSilicon-designed chips were made by TSMC using technology from U.S. companies, in particular electronic design automation software and semiconductor manufacturing equipment. As noted earlier, the markets for these two technologies are extremely concentrated, so the measure effectively crippled the ability of Huawei to supply advanced equipment across its products lines, including smartphones and 5G base stations. The new restrictions also eliminated the company's capabilities to design and produce advanced semiconductors into the foreseeable future.

This tightening of a critical choke point is likely to accomplish a central U.S. policy goal and slow the adoption of Huawei in markets outside of China. Cut off from a reliable supply of advanced chips, foreign network operators will be concerned about the company's ability to build out and update networks and are likely to shift some of their Huawei business to Nokia, Ericsson, or Samsung. Moreover, the May 2020 announcement strengthened Washington's efforts to pressure friends and allies to not use Huawei equipment. In particular, the United Kingdom—which had originally said it would limit Huawei to 35 percent of the 5G market in Britain and exclude the company from providing equipment for the sensitive core of the networks—announced that it would revisit the decision and that it wanted to organize an alliance of ten democracies to create an alternative pool of suppliers of 5G equipment.[37] In this instance, weaponized interdependence has bolstered a more traditional tool of economic statecraft.

The Future of Weaponized Interdependence

While the campaign against Huawei has certainly accelerated Chinese efforts to reduce dependence on the United State, weaponized interdependence in the area of advanced chips is likely to be fairly durable and sustainable. The 2020 sessions of the National People's Congress and the Chinese People's Political Consultative Conference were filled with exhortations to increase China's scientific and technological capabilities. The government also announced that it will invest close to $2 trillion over five years in high-tech infrastructure.

In addition, U.S. pressure may spur institutional reform. One of the weaknesses of the Chinese system, especially compared with the United States in the AI chip sector, is that there is very little contact between academic research and Chinese industry. However, U.S. technology controls are forcing China to strengthen basic and applied research, and Chinese agencies are trying to overcome the fragmentation of the innovation system. As Dieter Ernst argues, "Ironically, U.S. technology export restrictions are thus forcing a reform of China's technological investment and innovation policy, which may help China to correct one of the fundamental weaknesses of its innovation system in AI."[38]

Still, U.S. control over the most advanced chip technologies, especially electronic design automation software and semiconductor manufacturing equipment, is well entrenched. Moreover, policymakers and industry are using competition with China to further reinforce the United States' advantages by supporting greater federal funding for semiconductor manufacturing and R&D in the United States.[39] Thus, China will remain vulnerable to weaponized interdependence and externally imposed supply disruptions for the foreseeable future.

Notes

1. Michael Mastanduno, "Hegemony and Fear: The National Security Determinants of Weaponized Interdependence," chapter 3 in this volume.

2. Dan Strumpf, "Where China Dominates in 5G Technology," *Wall Street Journal*, February 26, 2019, www.wsj.com/articles/where-china-dominates-in-5g-technology-11551236701.

3. Katie Benner, "China's Dominance of 5G Networks Puts U.S. Economic Future at Stake, Barr Warns," *New York Times*, February 6, 2020, www.nytimes.com/2020/02/06/us/politics/barr-5g.html; Dan Strumpf, "Huawei's Revenue Growth Slowed Sharply by Coronavirus, U.S. Blacklisting," *Wall Street Journal*, April 21, 2020, www.wsj.com/articles/huaweis-revenue-growth-slowed-sharply-by-coronavirus-u-s-blacklisting-11587456003.

4. Henry Farrell and Abraham Newman, "Weaponized Globalization: Huawei and the Emerging Battle over 5G Networks," *Global Asia*, September 26, 2019, www.globalasia.org/v14no3/cover/weaponized-globalization-huawei-and-the-emerging-battle-over-5g-networks_henry-farrellabraham-newman.

5. Huawei Investment & Holding Co., Ltd, *2019 Annual Report*, www-file.huawei.com/-/media/corporate/pdf/annual-report/annual_report_2019_en.pdf?la=en).

6. Richard Baldwin, *The Great Convergence: Information Technology and the New Globalization* (Cambridge: Belknap Press, 2017).

7. Magdalena Petrova, "We Traced What It Takes to Make an iPhone, from Its Initial Design to the Components and Raw Materials Needed to Make It a Reality," CNBC, December 14, 2018, www.cnbc.com/2018/12/13/inside-apple-iphone-where-parts-and-materials-come-from.html.

8. Science & Engineering Indicators, "Cross National Comparisons of R&D Performance," National Science Foundation, https://ncses.nsf.gov/pubs/nsb20203/data.

9. Quoted in "The Chips are Down: The Semiconductor Industry and the Power of Globalisation," *Economist*, December 1, 2018, www.economist.com/briefing/2018/12/01/the-semiconductor-industry-and-the-power-of-globalisation.

10. For an early usage of the concept of "mutually assured economic destruction," see James Dobbins, "Conflict with China: Prospects, Conse-

quences, and Strategies for Deterrence," RAND Occasional Paper, 2011, www.rand.org/content/dam/rand/pubs/occasional_papers/2011/RAND_OP344.pdf.

11. Guo Ping, "The U.S. Attacks on Huawei Betray Its Fear of Being Left Behind," *Financial Times*, February 27, 2019, www.ft.com/content/b8307ce8 -36b3-11e9-bb0c-42459962a812.

12. Stacie E. Goddard, "The Road to Revisionism: How Interdependence Gives Revisionists Weapons for Change," chapter 4 in this volume.

13. Secretary of State Mike Pompeo, interview with Maria Bartiromo on *Mornings with Maria*, Fox Business Network, May 28, 2019, www.state.gov/ interview-with-maria-bartiromo-of-mornings-with-maria-on-fox-business -network-5/.

14. Press briefing with Deputy Assistant Secretary Robert Strayer, Cyber and International Affairs and Information Policy, Bureau of Economic and Business Affairs, May 2019, www.state.gov/press-briefing-with-deputy-assis tant-secretary-robert-strayer-cyber-and-international-affairs-and-infor mation-policy-bureau-of-economic-and-business-affairs-2/.

15. Sean Lyngaas, "No 'Smoking Gun' Evidence Coming on Huawei, NSA Official Says," *Cyberscoop*, March 7, 2019, www.cyberscoop.com/ huawei-no-smoking-gun-nsa-rsa/; Ellen Nakashima and Brian Fung, "U.S. Allies Differ on Difficulty of Containing Huawei Security Threat," *Washington Post*, March 3, 2019, www.washingtonpost.com/technology/2019/03/06/us -allies-are-skeptical-trump-administrations-huawei-argument/.

16. Erica Borghard and Shawn Lonegran, "The Overlooked Military Implications of the 5G Debate," *Net Politics*, April 25, 2019, www.cfr.org/ blog/overlooked-military-implications-5g-debate.

17. Thomas Donohue, "The Worst Possible Day: U.S. Telecommunications and Huawei," *Prism* 8, no. 3 (January 9, 2020), https://ndupress.ndu.edu/ Media/News/News-Article-View/Article/2053215/the-worst-possible-day-us -telecommunications-and-huawei/.

18. John Hemmings, "Reconstructing Order: The Geopolitical Risks in China's Digital Silk Road," *Asia Policy*, vol. 15, no. 1 (January 2020).

19. Edward White, "China's ability to make computer chips still 'years behind' industry leaders," *Financial Times*, January 21, 2019, www.ft.com/ content/a002a9e4-1a42-11e9-b93e-f4351a53f1c3.

20. Jacky Wong, "Beijing Still Wants Microchips Made in China," *Wall Street Journal*, April 17, 2020, www.wsj.com/articles/beijing-still-wants -microchips-made-in-china-11587125377.

21. Junko Yoshida, "U.S.-China Crisis: Fallout for Chip Industry," interview with Dieter Ernst, *EETimes*, February 24, 2019, www.eetimes .com/u-s-china-crisis-fallout-for-chip-industry/#.

22. Kate O'Keefe, "U.S. to Restrict Chinese Chip Maker from Doing Business with American Firms," *Wall Street Journal*, October 29, 2018, www

.wsj.com/articles/u-s-restricts-state-owned-chinese-chip-maker-from-doing-business-with-american-firms-1540837561?mod=article_inline.

23. Kathrin Hille, "Trade war Forces Chinese Chipmaker Fujian Jinhua to Halt Output," *Financial Times*, January 28, 2019, www.ft.com/content/87b5580c-22bf-11e9-8ce6-5db4543da632.

24. Mathieu Duchatel, "Huawei's 5G Supply Chain: Taiwan Winning Twice?" *Institut Montaigne*, October 29, 2019, www.institutmontaigne.org/en/blog/huaweis-5g-supply-chain-taiwan-winning-twice.

25. Dan Strumpf and others, "American Tech Companies Find Ways around Huawei Ban," *Wall Street Journal*, June 25, 2019, www.wsj.com/articles/american-tech-companies-find-ways-around-huawei-ban-11561517591.

26. Chen Ting Fang, Lauly Li, and Coco Liu, "Exclusive: Huawei Stockpiles 12 Months of Parts Ahead of U.S. Ban," *Nikkei Asian Review*, May 17, 2019, https://asia.nikkei.com/Economy/Trade-war/Exclusive-Huawei-stockpiles-12-months-of-parts-ahead-of-US-ban.

27. Dan Strumpf, "China's Huawei Seeks to Chip Away at Silicon Valley's AI Supremacy," *Wall Street Journal*, October 10, 2018, www.wsj.com/articles/chinas-huawei-seeks-to-chip-away-at-silicon-valleys-ai-supremacy-1539160300.

28. Asa Fitch and Dan Strumpf, "Huawei Manages to Make Smartphones without American Chips," *Wall Street Journal*, December 1, 2019, www.wsj.com/articles/huawei-manages-to-make-smartphones-without-american-chips-11575196201?mod=searchresults&page=1&pos=2.

29. Adam Segal, "Seizing Core Technologies: China Responds to U.S. Technology Competition," *China Leadership Monitor*, June 1, 2019, www.prcleader.org/segal-clm-60.

30. "Shunned by U.S., Huawei Winning China's $170 Billion 5G Race," *Bloomberg*, April 21, 2020, www.bloomberg.com/news/articles/2020-04-21/shunned-by-u-s-huawei-winning-in-china-s-170-billion-5g-race.

31. Yimou Lee, "China Lures Chip Talent from Taiwan with Fat Salaries, Perks," Reuters, September 4, 2018, www.reuters.com/article/us-china-semiconductors-taiwan-insight/china-lures-chip-talent-from-taiwan-with-fat-salaries-perks-idUSKCN1LK0H1.

32. "Alibaba's Jack Ma on Developing Core Technologies Post-ZTE," *Shanxi Evening News*, April 24, 2018, http://baijiahao.baidu.com/s?id=1598613211326939453&wfr=spider&for=pc.

33. Joe McDonald, "China's Huawei Warns More U.S. Pressure May Spur Retaliation," AP, March 31, 2020, https://apnews.com/2127b0cc3f91afa6176a2381d77bdbed.

34. Joseph Marks, "The Administration's Huawei Policy Has a Trump Problem," *Washington Post*, February 19, 2020, www.washingtonpost.com/news/powerpost/paloma/the-cybersecurity-202/2020/02/19/the-cyber

security-202-the-administration-s-huawei-policy-has-a-trump-problem
/5e4c21db88e0fa5fb3f8b086/.

35. Nic Fildes, James Kynge, and Yuan Yang, "Huawei Spending with U.S. Companies Surges Despite Sanctions," *Financial Times*, March 31, 2020, www.ft.com/content/42a0ed8d-c77a-4acd-93d5-676a656a2a0a.

36. Ana Swanson, "Tougher Huawei Restrictions Stall After Defense Department Objects," *New York Times*, January 24, 2020, www.nytimes.com/2020/01/24/business/economy/huawei-restrictions.html.

37. Lucy Fisher, "Downing Street Plans New 5G Club of Democracies," *The Times*, May 29, 2020, www.thetimes.co.uk/article/downing-street-plans-new-5g-club-of-democracies-bfnd5wj57.

38. Dieter Ernst, "Competing in Artificial Intelligence Chips: China's Challenge amid Technology War," Centre for International Governance Innovation, March 2020, www.cigionline.org/publications/competing-artificial-intelligence-chips-chinas-challenge-amid-technology-war.

39. Bob Davis, Asa Fitch, and Kate O'Keeffe, "Semiconductor Industry to Lobby for Billions to Boost U.S. Manufacturing," *Wall Street Journal*, May 31, 2020, www.wsj.com/articles/semiconductor-industry-to-lobby-for-billions-to-boost-u-s-manufacturing-11590919201.

IV

ENERGY

9

Weaponizing Energy Interdependence

EMILY MEIERDING

As oil prices collapsed in spring 2020, causing bankruptcies and mass unemployment in the American oil patch, energy analysts bemoaned the loss of American "energy dominance."[1] This concept, introduced by the 2017 U.S. National Security Strategy (NSS), refers to the geopolitical windfall that was purportedly conveyed by the dramatic increase in U.S. oil and natural gas production over the preceding decade.[2] In the heady, pre–price crash days, commentators asserted that the United States' surging output would bolster its energy security at home and its ability to defeat adversaries abroad.[3]

These commentaries conceptualized energy dominance in extremely narrow terms. By asserting that the United States' dominance rests on its energy production, the 2017 NSS implies that power in global energy networks is derived solely from market share: that the states that sell or buy the most energy resources—and, particularly, the most oil and gas resources—are the most powerful. In this conceptualization, as Henry Farrell and Abraham Newman note, "Power and vulnerability are characterized as the consequences of aggregate market size or bilateral interdependencies."[4]

This chapter, in contrast, observes that the global oil and gas sector consists of multiple, interrelated networks. It evaluates the

United States' dominance in three energy networks—trade, transportation, and financial transactions—using the concept of weaponized interdependence. It finds that the United States' energy dominance varies across the three energy networks. Ironically, even before the oil price crash, the United States was least dominant in the network that has been most emphasized by popular commentators and the NSS: energy trade.

In contrast, the United States is partially dominant in the energy transportation network. Although it cannot interrupt pipeline transportation, the United States' exceptional naval power, coupled with its ability to impose crippling secondary sanctions on private shipping and insurance companies, enables it to interrupt maritime energy shipments to and from most states. The United States is only truly energy dominant, however, in the energy financial transaction network. The historical pricing of oil in dollars, coupled with the dollar clearing system and countries' reliance on the Society for Worldwide Interbank Financial Telecommunications (SWIFT) messaging service, allows the United States to weaponize interdependence in this arena. The United States' energy dominance in this network is also likely to persist.

Energy Security, Independence, or Dominance?

Energy security, defined by the International Energy Agency as "the uninterrupted availability of energy sources at an affordable price," has been a core U.S. national security concern since at least 1945, when President Franklin D. Roosevelt purportedly established an "oil for security" pact with Saudi Arabia.[5] The United States' energy security concerns intensified in 1973, when Arab members of the Organization of the Petroleum Exporting Countries (OPEC) imposed a partial embargo on oil sales to the United States. The Iranian Revolution and Soviet invasion of Afghanistan heightened anxieties, especially because the United States was becoming increasingly dependent on Middle Eastern energy supplies.

To assuage these concerns, all American presidents since Richard Nixon have promoted the concept of "energy independence." At its extreme, energy independence implies that a state is entirely self-sufficient in energy sources and engages in no international energy trade. In a milder version of energy independence, a state is a net exporter of energy resources but continues to trade with other countries.[6] Between the 1970s and the first decade of the 2000s, the United States achieved neither type of energy independence. The country's oil and gas consumption continued to rise, while domestic production continued to fall in what was perceived as an irreversible decline.

In the past decade, however, American energy independence became more viable. Advances in extractive technologies—specifically, improvements in hydraulic fracturing—precipitated the U.S. "shale revolution." American oil production doubled from five million barrels per day (MMb/d) in 2008 to over ten MMb/d a decade later, making the United States the world's leading crude oil producer. In 2017, the United States became a net exporter of natural gas resources and, in late 2019, a net exporter of crude oil and petroleum products.[7] While the United States will never achieve the maximalist version of energy independence because it must import certain crudes to maintain the efficiency of its refineries, it had achieved the minimalist version.

The concept of energy dominance goes further than energy independence or energy security. According to the 2017 NSS, energy dominance is "America's central position in the global energy system as the leading producer, consumer, and innovator." Although the NSS refers to a wide range of energy resources, its language of "leading producer, consumer, and innovator" suggests an oil and gas emphasis. The NSS claims that energy dominance will enhance U.S. energy security, economic growth, and power. Energy dominance will also "ensure that markets are free and U.S. infrastructure is resilient and secure." Finally, energy dominance will "help our allies and partners become more resilient against those that use energy to coerce," by diversifying global energy "supplies and routes."[8]

The NSS's version of energy dominance focuses on trade; it presents the United States as a buyer and seller of energy resources. In this conventional conceptualization, states exert power (or are coerced) purely through purchases and sales of energy resources. The United States was a victim of such coercion in 1973. However, it has also wielded the oil weapon against its adversaries—most prominently, against Japan before World War II.[9] The United States has also exerted its market power as a consumer by refusing to purchase oil from certain producers, like Iran and Venezuela.

Trade is nonetheless only one vector through which a state can potentially exercise energy dominance. The energy sector consists of multiple interrelated networks that a state could attempt to weaponize. The next three sections present the topography of the three energy networks (trade, transportation, and financial transaction), identify how they could be weaponized, and evaluate the United States' ability to weaponize each. Like the NSS, this assessment focuses on oil and natural gas.

The Energy Trade Network

Over 70 percent of oil and almost 25 percent of natural gas resources are traded internationally rather than consumed by the countries that produce them.[10] The nodes in the global energy trade network are the actors that buy and sell oil and gas resources. On the supplier side, the nodes are private or state-owned energy companies. On the customer side, the main nodes are refineries (for crude oil) and electrical utilities (for gas). National governments are also customers when they import crude oil for their strategic petroleum reserves or to fuel their armed forces and federal installations. The network's ties are the contracts that suppliers and customers establish for oil and gas deliveries.

To weaponize this network, states exploit choke-point mechanisms to prevent suppliers and customers from establishing or fulfilling contracts. A state can interrupt resource purchases by embargoing energy sales, as the Roosevelt administration did when it blocked U.S. oil sales to Japan in 1941. Alternatively, a state can interrupt resource sales by sanctioning energy suppliers, as the Bill Clinton administration did by halting U.S. oil purchases from Iran in 1995. It is easier for governments to restrict energy trade when resource suppliers or customers are state-owned enterprises. However, as the U.S. examples demonstrate, governments are also capable of directing privately owned firms' trade decisions.

States' capacities to weaponize the energy trade network are uneven. In order for trade restrictions to harm a targeted country enough to compel it to change its behavior, states must block a large portion of the target's resource sales or purchases. Accordingly, the only states that can effectively, unilaterally weaponize the energy trade network are major hubs in the system: globally dominant importers or exporters, or states that, for some other reason, monopolize energy trade with a targeted country.

The United States was historically capable of weaponizing the energy trade network. In 1940, it was responsible for over two-thirds of global oil production and was the dominant oil supplier for some countries. For example, before World War II, 80 percent of Japan's oil imports came from the United States. These positions gave the United States enormous coercive power. The 2017 NSS alludes to this era when it claims that the United States has become an energy-dominant state, "[f]or the first time in generations."[11]

The NSS gets history right, but the present wrong. Although the United States is currently the world's leading oil and gas producer, it is responsible for only 10 percent of global oil exports and 8 percent of global gas exports. Additionally, over three-quarters of U.S. gas exports flow to its North American neighbors, Canada and Mexico.[12] Thus, the United States is not a significant node in the global gas trading network outside of its immediate region. In the global oil trading network, the United States' reach is broader because it is an important supplier of crude oil and petroleum products to many countries in the Western Hemisphere, as well as a few countries outside of it. However, U.S. oil is not irreplaceable, especially during a glut. If the United States unilaterally places an embargo on a country, its customers can easily find alternative suppliers who will be eager to increase their resource sales. Accordingly, as an oil and gas exporter, the United States does not have a dominant position in most of its bilateral trade relationships, let alone the energy trade network as a whole.

The United States is also unable to dominate the energy trade network through its oil and gas imports. American customers obtain over 95 percent of their gas imports from Canada, so the United States cannot successfully, unilaterally sanction any other gas-exporting countries. American customers import oil from a larger number of states and consume a substantial share of the crude oil exports of some of them, including Canada, Mexico, Guatemala, Trinidad and Tobago, Colombia, and Ecuador. These countries would lose a substantial amount of revenue if the United States blocked imports of their oil, especially because they would struggle to find alternative customers during an oil glut. That being said, exerting coercive power over a handful of states using conventional bilateral sanctions is different from weaponizing interdependence and does not qualify as energy dominance.

The United States could attempt to weaponize the energy trade network multilaterally, by persuading other countries to join it in sanctioning or embargoing a targeted state. However, as Daniel Drezner's introduction to this volume observes, it is very difficult to implement effective multilateral trade restrictions. The limited panopticon opportunities in the energy trade network, in which contracts are notoriously secret, further inhibit international monitoring and punishment. Even with allied support, trade is no longer a realm of U.S. energy dominance.

The Energy Transportation Network

The global energy transportation network physically moves oil and gas resources from supplier states to customer states. It has two modalities: pipelines and seaborne transit. Most oil resources travel by sea; approximately 40 MMb/d of crude oil, as well as substantial amounts of refined petroleum products, are shipped daily.[13] Most gas travels by pipeline. However, the share of gas that travels by sea, in the form of liquified natural gas (LNG), is increasing annually.

Both transportation modes share a similar topography. Their nodes are the facilities through which energy resources exit supplier states and enter consumer states. In seaborne transportation, export and import terminals dispatch and receive energy resources. Pipelines' international exit and entry points may include pumping or monitoring stations. Both sets of nodes are owned and operated by private or state-owned companies.

The network's ties are the routes that energy resources travel between international exit and entry points. Some international pipeline routes, like the notorious Keystone XL oil pipeline between Canada and the United States, navigate only two states (cross-border pipelines). Others navigate three or more, fully traversing at least one (transit pipelines). Prominent transit pipelines include the Baku–Tbilisi–Ceyhan (BTC) oil pipeline, traveling from Azerbaijan to Turkey via Georgia, and the Yamal gas pipeline, traveling from Russia to Western Europe via Belarus. Authority over oil and gas pipelines is shared by multiple actors: the companies that own and operate them, and the national governments that host them. International pipelines are geographically fixed and, due to the cost of constructing them, few in number. If one is shut down, regional oil or gas transportation is significantly disrupted.

Seaborne oil and gas resources travel by tanker along standard global sea routes. Portions of these routes traverse the high seas, which are outside any state's jurisdiction. Some pass through international straits, where all ships enjoy the right of innocent passage. The most significant international straits for oil and LNG transportation are the Strait of Hormuz and Strait of Malacca. Over 17 MMb/d of crude oil transit the Strait of Hormuz, while over 15 MMb/d of crude transit the Strait of Malacca.[14] Most maritime energy transportation routes are more flexible than pipeline transportation routes, because ships can change course. Nonetheless, there are exceptions—most prominently, the Strait of Hormuz. Deviating from other standard sea routes extends voyage lengths and marginally raises shipping costs.

Choke points are the key mechanism for weaponizing the energy transportation network. To choke off pipeline energy transportation, a state can physically suspend pipeline operations by activating shut-off valves and deactivating pumping stations. Only transit state governments are likely to attempt this maneuver, because energy suppliers' and customers' governments want to keep resources flowing. Transit state governments, in contrast, may want to increase transit fees or compel a supplier's or customer's government to change its behavior. To shut down pipeline transportation, a transit state government must wrest control from the pipeline's operator, unless the operator is a transit state-owned enterprise.

To choke off seaborne energy transportation, a state has two options. First, it can physically interdict oil and gas shipments, preventing tankers from completing their journey from exporting to importing states. International straits are the most likely locale for implementing this strategy, but a state could alternatively implement a near blockade of the targeted state's export or import terminals. Second, a state can interrupt the energy transportation network through commercial choke-point mechanisms. Specifically, it can induce the private companies involved in oil and gas transportation to isolate a targeted state. For example, the coercer may persuade tanker companies to refuse shipments to or from the targeted state. Or, it may convince insurance companies to refuse to cover these shipments. For either of these commercial strategies to succeed, the coercer must possess very compelling arguments or the ability to punish any companies that fail to comply.

The United States can partially weaponize the energy transportation network. Its ability to weaponize the pipeline transportation network is limited by geography; it is not a transit state. The U.S. government's interests in this network are therefore aligned with those of its customers and suppliers. Also, if the U.S. government wanted to restrict energy trade with Mexico or Canada, it would be far more likely to impose trade restrictions than to seize control over privately operated pipelines.

The United States can, however, weaponize much of the seaborne energy transportation network. Physically, the United States possesses the world's dominant navy. Its tonnage is at least twice that of China's, despite the latter's recent building spree, and far exceeds any other country's forces.[15] Since World War II, the United States has also developed a global naval presence as the self-designated protector of international sea lanes.[16] Although the United States has generally used these capabilities to facilitate the free flow of maritime transportation, it can also employ them to physically interdict oil and gas shipments traveling to or from targeted states. The U.S. Navy can also exploit panopticon opportunities in the maritime transportation network, since the International Maritime Organization requires all tankers to be equipped with transponder systems and thus, their locations can be tracked. Even if tankers go dark, most of them can be traced using satellite imagery.

Commercially, the United States can block maritime energy shipments by dissuading tanker companies from accepting cargo destined to or originating from targeted states, or by discouraging insurance companies from covering these shipments. These strategies are likely to succeed if the United States threatens secondary sanctions against tanker or insurance companies that do not comply. The prospect of losing access to the U.S. financial system is sufficient to induce private companies to refuse even the most lucrative oil and LNG shipments, as the United States demonstrated when it targeted Iran's maritime oil transportation system over the last decade.[17]

When it comes to China, however, the United States' ability to weaponize the maritime energy transportation network is circumscribed. Over the last fifteen years, China has built a sizeable domestic tanker fleet. If it imports oil and LNG using these ships, and insures them through state-owned insurance companies, China can neutralize the United States' commercial network weaponization capabilities.[18]

The obstacles to physically interdicting China-bound energy shipments are also considerable, even for the U.S. Navy. The United States' ability to implement a distant blockade, intercepting ships as they travel through choke points like the Strait of Malacca, is impeded by limitations to the network's panopticon opportunities. Although it is usually possible to determine tankers' origins using tracking systems, these methods cannot ascertain their destinations—nor can direct visual contact. Consequently, American sailors would need to board every tanker traveling through the choke point and consult its documentation to determine which ones to seize. All oil and LNG tankers are required to carry bills of lading, stating their origin and destination. However, documents can be forged or resource cargoes can be resold during transit, legitimately changing their destination after they pass through a U.S. blockade.[19]

Tankers can also attempt to evade a distant blockade by rerouting or by resisting U.S. interdiction. If Beijing ordered its domestic tanker fleet to run a blockade, American sailors would need to forcefully board or sink Chinese ships, significantly raising the blockade's enforcement and environmental costs.[20] Moreover, while the Chinese military currently lacks the capacity to respond directly to a distant blockade, it can retaliate in other ways, including attacking targets closer to home.[21] Finally, a U.S. attempt to block China's energy supplies would prompt widespread international opprobrium and resistance.

A near blockade implemented close to China's oil import terminals would eliminate the panopticon problems mentioned above. From that location, it would be easy to determine where tankers are headed. Some analysts also claim that the United States' attack submarine advantage would enable it to intercept energy shipments while evading China's anti-access/area-denial (A2AD) systems, if the U.S. Navy were willing to sink tankers rather than seize them.[22] However, the escalation risks associated with that strategy are evident. For this reason, while analysts disagree about the physical viability of blockading Chinese energy shipments, most of them assume that the United States would only attempt a near or distant blockade in the context of a larger Sino-American conflict. The United States cannot physically weaponize the maritime energy transportation network against China without precipitating a broader war.

In sum, while the United States is energy dominant against most countries in the maritime energy transportation network, its coercive power against China is limited.

The Energy Financial Transaction Network

To buy foreign oil and gas resources, energy customers must be able to pay energy suppliers. Historically, an enormous amount of money has changed hands in these transactions, due to the volume and value of international energy sales. In 2018, OPEC's net oil export revenues alone were valued at $711 billion.[23] The total value of global oil exports was likely over $3 trillion.[24] International gas sales raise the figure even higher.

Banks are the nodes in the energy financial transaction network. They include suppliers' banks, where oil companies collect payments for oil and gas sales, and customers' banks, where these payments originate. The financial transaction network also includes intermediary banks, which are essential to the network's functions. The vast majority of international oil sales are denominated in dollars, regardless of where the resources originate. Consequently, for resource payments to clear, they must pass through the U.S. financial system—either through branches of the suppliers' and customers' banks in the United States, or through these institutions' U.S. correspondent banks. It is extremely difficult for dollar-denominated energy sales to bypass the U.S. system, because offshore dollar clearing facilities usually lack the liquidity to reliably handle transactions of this scale. Accordingly, almost all oil and gas transactions eventually pass through the United States, at which point they fall under U.S. jurisdiction.[25]

The ties in the energy financial transaction network are the messages sent between the suppliers', customers', and intermediary banks. Although no dollars physically move in these transactions, each bank must be able to instruct others to debit or credit their customers' and suppliers' accounts. As Newman and Farrell observe, the Belgium-based SWIFT system handles the lion's share of this interbank messaging.[26]

A state that aims to weaponize the energy financial transaction network can therefore exploit two choke points: the SWIFT messaging system and the U.S. dollar clearing system.[27] In both, the actor prevents oil and gas customers from paying suppliers. A state can weaponize the financial messaging system by inducing SWIFT's managers to block targeted banks' access to its services. Alternatively, a government can weaponize the dollar clearing system by compelling U.S. financial institutions that handle energy transactions to refuse to do business with targeted banks. Either choke point is likely to be highly effective at blocking energy sales and purchases.

The United States is the only country in the world that can weaponize the energy financial transaction network, giving it unquestioned energy dominance in this arena. It can prohibit U.S. banks from conducting business with an adversary's banks, as it did against Iran in the last decade.[28] Blocking targeted banks' access to the U.S. financial system severely restricts their ability to buy or sell oil, because they lose the ability to clear dollar-denominated transactions. States without access to the dollar clearing system can only buy or sell energy resources by finding suppliers or customers that are willing to denominate transactions in other currencies, or to trade oil and gas on a barter basis. However, the United States can also discourage these trades by threatening secondary sanctions against the actors that conduct them. Finally, the United States has demonstrated that it can persuade SWIFT's managers to block targeted banks' access to its messaging system.

Conclusion: Sustaining Energy Dominance

The global oil and gas sector is not a single network. Instead, it is comprised of at least three interrelated networks, and the United States' ability to weaponize interdependence varies across them. Contrary to the NSS's intimations, the United States cannot unilaterally weaponize the energy trade network. It does not supply sufficient shares of most countries' energy imports, or purchase sufficient shares of most countries' energy exports, for unilateral trade restrictions to affect the global network or harm most targeted countries. The United States could attempt to weaponize the energy trade network multilaterally. However, multilateral trade restrictions often fail.

In contrast, the United States can partially weaponize the global energy transportation network. Although its geographic location prevents it from effectively interfering with international pipeline transportation, it can impede most countries' maritime energy transportation by deploying the U.S. Navy or by compelling tanker and insurance companies to shun shipments to or from targeted states. However, the United States' ability to choke off energy transportation to China, its major adversary, is uncertain. The one arena in which the United States can reliably weaponize interdependence is the energy financial transaction network. By blocking targets' access to the U.S. dollar clearing system or to the SWIFT financial messaging service, the United States can prevent them from buying or selling energy resources.

Claims of U.S. energy dominance were therefore exaggerated, even before the 2020 oil price crash. Despite the massive increase in U.S. oil and gas production over the past decade, the United States cannot fulfill many of the energy-related promises articulated by the 2017 NSS. The United States does not export enough oil or gas to protect its allies and partners against coercion by energy producers. Nor, as recent events have shown, does U.S. energy output ensure national economic growth. That being said, the United States can interrupt most countries' maritime energy shipments and restrict all countries' access to the energy financial transaction network.

If the United States continues to aggressively exploit these capabilities, however, its energy dominance may degrade even further. Prospective targets are already taking steps to protect themselves against energy networks' weaponization. Beijing is checking the United States' ability to physically and commercially interrupt China-bound energy shipments by constructing a domestic tanker fleet, expanding its blue-water navy, and enhancing its A2AD capabilities. The United States is likely to lose this point of leverage in the near future, if it has not already.

Foreign governments are also attempting to undercut the United States' dominance in the energy financial transaction network. Some are trying to bypass SWIFT by establishing their own financial messaging systems. In September 2019, Russia and Iran announced that they were linking their domestic messaging systems, SPFS and SEPAM, to facilitate bilateral financial communications.[29] Russian state media has also claimed that Moscow is establishing alternative messaging systems with Turkey and China.[30]

Other states are attempting to bypass the dollar clearing system in their energy transactions. Rosneft, Russia's leading national oil company, announced in August 2019 that it would denominate all oil export contracts in euro rather than in dollars.[31] Chinese customers have paid for some Russian, Venezuelan, and Iranian resource shipments in yuan.[32] Other states, including Iran, have developed barter-based systems for trading energy resources.[33] Venezuela has been supplying oil to China in exchange for food staples.[34]

Displacing the dollar in international energy transactions will nonetheless be an uphill battle. In January 2019, over 99 percent of crude oil payments were still conducted in dollars, and most suppliers and customers have no incentive to move away from this system.[35] Oil has historically been traded in dollars because they are abundant and reliable. No other currency—including the yuan or ruble—can compete in terms of liquidity and stability. Accordingly, only countries that expect to be targeted by the United States are likely to seek alternatives. While these countries may be able to de-dollarize some of their resource sales and purchases, it is unlikely that they can dedollarize all of them.

The United States will therefore sustain some degree of energy dominance over the coming decades. However, it will look very different from what current national security documents and commentators have imagined. Moreover, as Bruce Jentleson's contribution to this volume perceptively notes, weaponizing a network does not guarantee successful coercion. If states like Iran continue to resist U.S. demands despite energy network weaponization, claims of energy dominance will ring even hollower.

Notes

1. Gregory Brew, "Energy Dominated: Why the Price Shock Shatters the Myth of American Oil Independence," *Responsible Statecraft*, March 13, 2020, https://responsiblestatecraft.org/2020/03/13/why-the-price-shock-shatters-the-myth-of-american-oil-independence/.

2. White House, *National Security Strategy of the United States*, December 2017, pp. 22–23.

3. Meaghan L. O'Sullivan, *Windfall: How the New Energy Abundance Upends Global Politics and Strengthens America's Power* (New York: Simon and Schuster, 2017).

4. Henry Farrell and Abraham L. Newman, "Weaponized Interdependence," *International Security* 44, no. 1 (2019), p. 43.

5. International Energy Security (IEA), "Energy Security," www.iea.org/topics/energy-security.

6. O'Sullivan, *Windfall*, pp. 90–95.

7. Unless otherwise stated, all oil and gas data are from the U.S. Energy Information Agency (EIA).

8. White House, *National Security Strategy of the United States*, p. 22.

9. Emily Meierding, *The Oil Wars Myth: Petroleum and the Causes of International Conflict* (Cornell University Press, 2020), chapter 7.

10. Data from BP, *Statistical Review of World Energy*, 68th edition, 2019, www.bp.com/en/global/corporate/energy-economics/statistical-review-of-world-energy.html.

11. White House, *National Security Strategy of the United States*, p. 22.

12. BP, *Statistical Review of World Energy*.

13. UN Conference on Trade and Development (UNCTAD), "World Seaborne Trade by Types of Cargo and by Group of Economies, Annual," https://unctadstat.unctad.org/wds/ReportFolders/reportFolders.aspx.

14. EIA, "More than 30% of Global Maritime Crude Oil Trade Moves through the South China Sea," August 27, 2018, www.eia.gov/todayinenergy/

detail.php?id=36952; EIA, "The Strait of Hormuz Is the World's Most Important Oil Transit Chokepoint," June 20, 2019, www.eia.gov/today inenergy/detail.php?id=39932.

15. Ian Livingston and Michael O'Hanlon, "Why China Isn't Ahead of the U.S. Navy, Even with More Ships," *Brookings*, September 10, 2018, www .brookings.edu/blog/order-from-chaos/2018/09/10/why-china-isnt-ahead-of -the-us-navy-even-with-more-ships/.

16. Joshua Rovner and Caitlin Talmadge, "Hegemony, Force Posture, and the Provision of Public Goods: The Once and Future Role of Outside Powers in Securing Persian Gulf Oil," *Security Studies* 23, no. 3 (2014), pp. 548–81.

17. Juan Zarate, *Treasury's War: The Unleashing of a New Era of Financial Warfare* (New York: PublicAffairs, 2015), pp. 304–5, 329–30, 334, 339.

18. Jennifer Lind and Daryl G. Press, "Markets or Mercantilism? How China Secures its Energy Supplies," *International Security* 42, no. 4 (2018), pp. 170–204.

19. Gabriel B. Collins and William S. Murray, "No Oil for the Lamps of China," *Naval War College Review* 61, no. 2 (2008), pp. 21–22.

20. Lind and Press, "Markets or Mercantilism?" p. 198.

21. Collins and Murray, "No Oil for the Lamps of China," p. 89.

22. Llewelyn Hughes and Austin Long, "Is There an Oil Weapon? Security Implications of Changes in the Structure of the International Oil Market," *International Security* 39, no. 3 (2015), p. 180.

23. EIA, "OPEC Revenues Fact Sheet," updated August 20, 2019, www. eia.gov/international/analysis/special-topics/OPEC_Revenues_Fact_Sheet.

24. Calculation based on the information that OPEC supplied approximately 32 percent of global oil exports in 2018. Alex Lawler, "OPEC's Market Share Sinks—and No Sign of Wavering on Supply Cuts," Reuters, August 22, 2019, www.reuters.com/article/us-oil-opec-graphic/opecs-market -share-sinks-and-no-sign-of-wavering-on-supply-cuts-idUSKCN1VC0U4.

25. Zarate, *Treasury's War*, p. 25.

26. Farrell and Newman, "Weaponized Interdependence."

27. For details, see Thomas Oatley, "Weaponizing International Financial Interdependence," chapter 6 in this volume.

28. Suzanne Katzenstein, "Dollar Unilateralism: The New Frontline of National Security," *Indiana Law Journal* 90 (2015), pp. 293–351.

29. "Russia & Iran to Switch to SWIFT-Free Banking System," RT, September 17, 2019, www.rt.com/business/469007-russia-iran-swift-alterna tive/.

30. Alan Rappeport and Katie Rogers, "Trump's Embrace of Sanctions Irks Allies and Prompts Efforts to Evade Measures," *New York Times*, November 15, 2019, www.nytimes.com/2019/11/15/us/politics/trump-iran -sanctions.html.

31. Elliot Smith, "Russia's Bid to Ditch the U.S. Dollar Is Slowly Working,

But Obstacles Remain," CNBC, September 27, 2019, www.cnbc.com/2019/09/27/russias-bid-to-ditch-the-us-dollar-is-slowly-working-but-obstacles-remain.html.

32. Maha Kamel and Hongying Wang, "Petro-RMB? The Oil Trade and the Internationalization of the Renminbi," *International Affairs* 95, no. 5 (2019), pp. 1131–48.

33. Zarate, *Treasury's War*, pp. 341, 371.

34. Corina Pons and Mayela Armas, "Exclusive: Venezuela in Talks with China over Support amid Pandemic, Oil Price Drop—Sources," Reuters, March 25, 2020, www.reuters.com/article/us-health-coronavirus-venezuela-china-ex/exclusive-venezuela-in-talks-with-china-over-support-amid-pandemic-oil-price-drop-sources-idUSKBN21C2LB.

35. David Dollar and Samantha Gross, "China's Currency Displacing the Dollar in Global Oil Trade? Don't Count on It," *Brookings*, April 19, 2018, www.brookings.edu/blog/order-from-chaos/2018/04/19/chinas-currency-displacing-the-dollar-in-global-oil-trade-dont-count-on-it/.

10

Russia's Gazprom

A Case Study in Misused Interdependence

MIKHAIL KRUTIKHIN

Relations between Russia as a supplier of natural gas and Europe as a gas consumer have been a perfect example of mutually beneficial interdependence for decades. Until recently, all involved parties respected the interests of each other and protected this interdependence from internal misunderstandings and external problems.

In the Soviet era, gas supplies to Europe played an invaluable role for Moscow—not merely as a source of income in hard currency, but also as a factor that enhanced the image of the Soviet Union as an indispensable and reliable economic partner, and helped to create a background for détente. Even the Soviet invasion in Afghanistan in 1979 was unable to hinder the gas trade between the Soviet Union and Europe as both sides became increasingly dependent on each other in this respect. Neither geopolitical considerations nor U.S. economic sanctions could make a dent in the solid framework of the Soviet-European natural gas trade.[1]

Russia changed its "all-quiet-on-the-Western-front" attitude when Vladimir Putin, the leader of a coterie of KGB colleagues and former Communist Party officials with connections in organized crime, came to power in Moscow. Putin's views on Russia as the successor to the Soviet Union's global greatness and a "separate civilization"[2] became a monkey wrench thrown into the works of this functional, interdependent trade system.

Understanding the huge role of controlling oil and gas flows as potential leverage over their recipients, Putin has done all he could to weaponize Gazprom, the state-controlled monopoly of natural gas transportation and exports, often to the detriment of its value to Russia's economy. Under Putin's guidance, the gas industry of Russia has resisted attempts at liberalization and privatization, and Gazprom has remained a monopoly in natural gas transportation and exports.[3]

The president's personal control over the company, however, keeps exposing Gazprom to two types of pressure, which make it a special business entity not resembling a regular commercial company. One type of pressure on Gazprom comes from Putin's interest in exploiting the company's gas transportation infrastructure for power mongering in former Soviet republics and beyond the ex-Soviet borders. On presidential orders, Gazprom has had to plan and undertake exorbitant, politicized, and economically nonfeasible megaprojects. These include the Streams pipeline bypassing Ukraine in the Baltic Sea and Black Sea, the Power of Siberia pipeline to China, and a pipeline from Sakhalin Island to the Chinese border near Vladivostok. Such projects are an extremely large and commercially unjustified burden on Gazprom's finances.

Another type of pressure on Gazprom is its function as a source of profit for the oligarchs around Putin. It is open to speculations whether Putin chooses the most expensive and noneconomical options for projects of Gazprom because of his incompetence in the gas business or under the influence of his oligarch friends who get lucrative contracts for building redundant gas pipelines (and reportedly charge exaggerated fees for the job). In fact, Gazprom is both a political weapon for Putin and a means of transporting state-controlled funds into the private pockets of Putin's friends.[4] Paradoxically, the Russian institutions that permit Putin to use Gazprom as a tool of weaponized interdependence also undercut it as an instrument of statecraft. These structures are corrupt and highly personalized by Putin, which helps to explain why they have not been effective. This confirms Henry Farrell and Abraham Newman's thesis that domestic capabilities affect this instrument of statecraft.

Weaponizing the gas trade interdependence with Europe has failed to help Putin reach his geopolitical goals (unlike the "crony oligarchs" and the pecuniary goals that have made them quite a lot of money on pipeline construction contracts). Dismayed with Gazprom's politically motivated "monopolistic practices," the European Union (EU) has adopted a series of resolutions and regulations to make the Russian gas supplier behave like a civilized business entity. Significant efforts have been made by the EU and Turkey to diversify gas supply sources and decrease their dependence on Russian gas. The Nord Stream and Turkstream (formerly South Stream) projects have not been able to undermine Ukraine's economy and subjugate this former Soviet republic to the wills and whims of Moscow. And Putin's idea of obtaining an extra leverage over Europe by building a pipeline link to China and switching the gas flows from one destination to the other also failed when it became clear that China does not need gas from Russia.

The experience has shown that attempts at weaponizing interdependence can be resisted, weakened, or neutralized by concerted efforts aimed at decreasing dependence on the challenger and by disciplining the challenger with introduction of stricter norms and regulations. The EU has relied on its market and jurisdictional power to resist Russian pressure. Assistance by an outsider, such as the United States, can also help, as the Europeans understood when Gazprom had to suspend the construction of the Nord Stream 2 bypass around Ukraine and sign a commercial agreement with Ukraine to continue natural gas transit across that country.

A Brief History of Energy Interdependence in Europe

Russian deliveries of gas to Eastern European countries began after the Second World War and to the western part of Europe, in the latter part of the 1960s.[5] A trailblazing Soviet-Austrian gas contract was signed in June 1968, followed by contracts with Italy, Germany, and others. Neither the Soviet invasion in Czechoslovakia in 1968 nor disapproval by the United States could stop the projects of Soviet gas pipelines in Europe. In the early 1980s, the Ronald Reagan administration fiercely opposed a new gas pipeline deal between Western Europe and the Soviet Union. Western European consumers' interest in gas supplies from the east was so great that the Yamal pipeline through Poland to Germany was built and commissioned in 1999 in addition to the first Brotherhood pipeline, which transits Ukraine.[6]

Today, the prevailing opinion in Germany, for example, is still in favor of cooperation with Russia in natural gas trade, as some energy researchers point out: "For more than 40 years, German-Russian natural gas relations have been embedded into a broader relationship, in which détente, confidence, and trust-building were perceived as a function of economic interdependence, and the gas-for-pipes deal became part of the *Ostpolitik*."[7] Dependence on Russia as a major gas supplier is seen there, somewhat paradoxically, as a way toward economic independence.

For Russia's economy, the European gas market is indispensable. The Russian budget is increasingly dependent on commodities exports, and energy plays the main role. Oil and gas sales in 2019 accounted to 40.8 percent of Russia's federal revenues.[8] Foreign sales of gas that year fetched a total of $41.6 billion; that was 15.3 percent less than a year earlier, but natural gas and liquefied natural gas (LNG) still contributed 13.5 percent to Russian export revenues.[9]

Russia, and the Soviet Union before it, has spent tremendous sums on building and maintaining gas transportation infrastructure that targets consumers in Europe. As of the beginning of 2020, the overall throughput capacity of Russia's western cross-border pipelines has exceeded 260 billion cubic meters (bcm) a year, excluding Nord Stream 2 (another 55 bcm a year), which has not been completed. In addition to the Soviet-era northern and southern gas transmission corridors on Russian territory, Gazprom has built new high-capacity corridors from the Yamal Peninsula toward the Baltic Sea and Black Sea where the Nord Stream and Turkstream projects begin.[10] Compared with China's Belt and Road Initiative or the U.S. effort to develop its LNG sector, Russia has a more fully developed network of transit pipelines.[11] The scope of its infrastructure projects demonstrates the importance of gas trade with Europe for Russia—and that importance is impossible to underestimate.[12]

Just as Russia relies on an influx of revenues from those gas sales, Europe heavily relies on Russian gas supply. In the first semester of 2019, for example, Russia supplied 39.4 percent of gas imported by the EU members.[13] The dependence on Russian gas is a cause of concern in some European countries,[14] even though Russia is also critically dependent on gas trade with Europe as a good source of replenishing its budget revenues.

Russian Institutions for Weaponized Interdependence

The monopoly status of Gazprom—a government-controlled corporation that remains the largest producer of natural gas in the country, the sole owner of the nationwide gas transmission system, and the exclusive exporter of piped gas—is also a sign of the importance that the Russian leadership assigns to the gas sector of the economy and especially to its export potential. Gazprom is a pampered and cherished source of revenues, and an instrument of strengthening and expanding Russia's footprint in the economies of European nations. The latter quality has prompted Putin to sacrifice Gazprom's economic functions for the sake of weaponizing the company.[15]

As Fiona Hill and Clifford Gaddy note in their excellent analysis of Putin's approach to governance:

> The people who brought Vladimir Putin from St. Petersburg to Moscow never cared about his credentials as a specialist in *developing* business. For them he was an expert in *controlling* business. . . . His goal was to make sure that Russia's own new class of capitalists did not predate on each other and on the Russian state. He was to try to harness them to be "bigger and better" and make more money in the service of Russia—not just for themselves.[16]

Having bestowed a geopolitical role on Gazprom, Putin assumed full control over the company, which operates without any consideration to governmental bodies such as the ministry of economic development or ministry of energy.[17] The company is an instrument of an autocratic ruler who issues orders—often on the basis of incomplete, simplified, and incompetent reports delivered by his old friend and companion, Alexey Miller, the chief executive officer of

Gazprom.[18] The company's board of directors functions as little more than a rubber stamp for Putin's instructions, readily approving costly projects that have no commercial value but are desired by the Russian president.

It would seem a simple arrangement: Putin issues political orders to Gazprom through Miller, and Gazprom does what the president wants. The scheme, however, includes another element, a small group of Putin's old-time friends—notably, Arkady Rotenberg and Gennady Timchenko as far as Gazprom is concerned. These friends have made a fortune on contracts to supply large-diameter steel pipes and build pipelines plus ancillary infrastructure for Gazprom's megaprojects. It is hard to see how much Putin's management of Gazprom is influenced, if not dictated, by those entrepreneurs, but the results usually benefit the duo more than anyone else.[19]

Two possible explanations of the actions of the president and his cronies can be offered. Putin might be sincerely pursuing the elusive idea of Russia's imperial greatness, and the group around him parasitizes on his ideology to make money. Or, Putin is knowingly involved in the money-making schemes of the group and simply uses imperial rhetoric to disguise the real pecuniary interests of the ruling elite. His actual motivation is of little importance for the purpose of this chapter, but some of Putin's decisions have proved to be so reckless and arrogant that the second explanation appears to be realistic. For instance, he ordered Gazprom to launch the Nord Stream and South Stream projects, and invest billions of dollars in them, before obtaining absolutely necessary, and highly improbable, permissions from the European market regulators; and he had the company build a pipeline from Sakhalin to the Chinese border, even though there was no gas supply capacity at one end of the pipeline and no sufficient demand at the other end. The only logical rationale of such decisions was, evidently, the opportunity to generate profits to contractors of Gazprom—that is, Rotenberg and Timchenko. The geopolitical component of these projects was an impossible dream from the very beginning.

The European Response

Recipients of Russian gas do not seem to be willing to weaponize[20] this interdependence and use their importance for the Russian economy as a tool for promoting any political or other interests. It is the Russian political leadership that has demonstrated such intentions for quite a long while.[21] On multiple occasions, the Russian government has used gas supply as a weapon in Europe.[22] Russia has repeated the tactic in the Kremlin's political conflicts with Ukraine, Belarus, and Turkmenistan, and Gazprom has served as a tool of tougher or milder political pressure on the Baltic States, Armenia, Bulgaria, Serbia, and other countries.

Two examples of countries where Gazprom has helped Putin achieve political results are Armenia and Serbia. Armenia was unable to pay Gazprom for gas deliveries in cash and, instead, gradually transferred equity stakes in its gas transmission and distribution facilities to the Russian monopoly. Now, Gazprom sells gas to its own subsidiary in that country, and the subsidiary sells gas to Armenian consumers. It was one of the reasons that Armenia accepted Moscow's offer to become a member of the Eurasian Economic Union (EAEU), an alliance of a few former Soviet republics under the aegis of the Kremlin.[23]

In Serbia, Gazprom has invested heavily in upgrading local gas infrastructure and in construction and sports projects. Despite minimal investment in the rest of Serbia's economy, Gazprom has become a significant source of foreign direct investment in that country's energy sector. The current political course of Serbia, as a result, tends to be pro-Russian.[24]

However, the strategy failed to fetch significant results in Bulgaria, which until recently depended almost fully on Russian gas supply. Regardless of pressure from the powerful local pro-Russian lobby, the Bulgarian government has opted to receive natural gas from Azerbaijan (through Turkey) and from Greece (from Greek LNG terminals). A pipeline link between Greece and Bulgaria is being built.[25]

Another example of resistance is Turkmenistan. Russia promised to build a new pipeline from that country across Kazakhstan and pay European prices for Turkmenian gas. Instead, Turkmenistan opted for cooperation with China, which has provided loans, helped develop new gas reserves, and built three pipelines going from Turkmenistan as far as China's eastern regions.

Belarus is also resisting Russian pressure. Policymakers in Moscow openly say they will only supply natural gas to Belarus at huge discounts if that country accepts Russian terms of integration into the EAEU. Thus far, Belarus has rejected these proposals.[26]

In Western Europe, Gazprom often becomes an instrument of enhancing Russia's political influence through bribery of policymakers ("Schroederization," named after former Federal Chancellor of Germany Gerhard Schroeder, who was hired by Gazprom immediately after he left the state position in Berlin and was believed to be a lobbyist of the Russian gas company during his job in the government)[27] and other unconventional methods.[28] This approach has failed in such countries as Poland and Lithuania but appears to be making an impact on political leanings in Germany and Austria. Since the "shale revolution" in the United States, when an influx of LNG flooded the global energy market, depressed energy prices, and offered cheaper and easier alternatives to Russian gas supply, the influence of Gazprom-subsidized lobbies in the EU has diminished dramatically. The Russian gas monopoly seems to have lost the political battle in Europe.

In fact, the Kremlin's overt attempts at weaponizing interdependence made the Europeans react well before the arrival of cheap LNG. The European Commission (EC) has adopted a series of regulatory documents to liberalize the gas market in the EU and constrain Gazprom's predatory behavior on the gas market. The First Gas Directive was enacted in 1998.[29] The second one followed in 2003,[30] and the Third Gas Directive and Regulation 715 on access to gas networks were adopted in 2009 as parts of the so-called Third Energy Package.[31] Gazprom vehemently protested the anti-monopoly regulations but has had to comply, especially after the European Commission threatened in 2012 to penalize "monopoly practices" of the Russian company.[32] A separate EC resolution obliged Gazprom to enable free flow of gas at competitive prices,[33] And other, similar protective directives are expected to follow.

The European governments' desire to switch to a greener and

cleaner energy through decarbonization does not bode well for Russia's Gazprom either. The attitude of the Russian government vis-à-vis this tendency became clear when, in May 2019, Putin signed into effect the Doctrine of Energy Security of the Russian Federation.[34] The document states that the substitution of petroleum products with other types of energy, higher energy efficiency, and energy saving—as well as an increase of global production of LNG and development of global gas trade, along with international efforts of switching to green energy and climate-saving measures—are only challenges rather than examples of worldwide tendencies that Russia could follow. The document also says that international legislative changes that restrict activities of Russian energy entities under pretexts of supply diversification and climate control are threats to Russia's energy security. The doctrine shows that Russian policymakers do not intend to accept the idea of decarbonization and are determined to keep using exports of oil and natural gas to ensure Russia's role in the international energy balance.

Explaining Russian Failure

Moscow's tactic of using its gas trade with Europe as a weapon may be regarded from different angles. The weaponization attempts might be an ancillary part of a larger picture where the main goal is to expand gas trade so that Gazprom can maintain and enhance its influence as a major commercial player on the European gas market, and can disarm possible competitors.

For observers who focus on commercial interests of Gazprom, it is a challenge to offer a plausible rationale for activities of the Russian gas monopoly. Jonathan Stern, for example, comments on Gazprom's efforts aimed at increasing its export capacity in Europe:

> There are various explanations for such behavior in the face of falling European gas demand. The main one is Gazprom's—and perhaps more importantly President Putin's—determination to bypass Ukraine and create sufficient "transit arbitrage," in other words, the need to create sufficient transit alternatives that no single country will be able to obtain leverage over Russian gas exports to Europe.

Another explanation relates to Gazprom's—and general Russian—view that European efforts to decarbonize energy balances are an expensive fashion requiring huge subsidies which cannot be afforded, and which will be abandoned in favor of much greater gas use. A third explanation is that the Russian leadership elites need Gazprom to build these new pipelines because this is how they are able to obtain corrupt payments by means of equipment and construction contracts.[35]

Stern's third explanation, considering Russian practices, appears to be a priority motivation for Gazprom's megaprojects that, in the final run, have no commercial value. The previous two explanations lay out the pretext for promoting the pecuniary interests of Putin's cronies.[36]

On the other hand, the Kremlin may consider the gas trade itself as merely one of many possible tools for promoting ambitious political aims—and, thus, resorts to weaponizing the gas trade's interdependence status with this goal in mind.

It is not hard to see that all major moves of Gazprom always begin with some strategic geopolitical goal set by Vladimir Putin. The Russian president is the initiator of a strategy—and then the management of the company and close friends of Putin (who monetize this relationship by obtaining Gazprom's lucrative contracts without any competition) draft specific projects to help implement the president's geopolitical ideas. It is not important whether such geopolitical ideas are conceived in Putin's mind or are planted there by someone in the president's closest circle. Once an idea is embedded, it becomes a justification for further actions, a foundation for making practical decisions aimed at its implementation. Often enough, even in critical situations, the decisionmaking is based on a combination of "distorted data and fanciful beliefs," as Pavel Baev notes in his analysis of the way the Kremlin was reacting to the COVID-19 pandemic.[37]

Putin's efforts aimed at disciplining Ukraine for its independent attitude and unwillingness to accept Moscow's leadership in the ex-Soviet territories have not been limited to subversive activities or military intervention in Crimea and Donbass. The Nord Stream and South Stream gas pipeline projects became instruments of punishment that were supposed to deprive Ukraine of its revenues from transportation of Russian gas to the Western Europe.[38]

The Streams program has cost Gazprom a lot of cash that could have been used for a more profitable purpose. According to calculations of Gazprom's main research and development (R&D) body, Gazprom VNIIGAZ, the new gas transmission corridor from Arctic fields on the Yamal Peninsula required between $79 billion and $93 billion to build (based on a segment of 2,100 kilometers, about three-quarters of the complete route, not reaching the Black Sea and Baltic Sea coasts).[39] The same document stated that Yamal gas sales would not be commercially feasible until 2035.[40] It was a purely geopolitical project from the very beginning and had no economic value for either Gazprom or Russia's budget at all.

Another case of Vladimir Putin's policy of weaponized interdependency is the Russian president's idea of connecting Russian gas fields in Arctic with China and switching the export flows of gas from the west to the east and back, depending on the Kremlin's priorities at any given moment. This desire to make Russia an important node for manipulation of energy flows throughout Eurasia was also devoid of economic value but based on a false geopolitical vision.[41]

In September 2016, Putin admitted that Gazprom was planning to link Russia's western grid of gas pipelines with the eastern grid. "If any difficulties arise in Europe, we will easily switch the flows to the East," he explained.[42] And Gazprom CEO Miller said earlier that the volume of Russian gas deliveries to China would "in a mid-term perspective" be equal with the volume of gas exported to Europe.[43] The idea of the link, which would enable Moscow to switch the gas flows and thus obtain a geopolitical opportunity to blackmail both the Europeans and Chinese with a threat of depriving either of Russian gas supply, was hardly practical, given the huge capacity of Russian gas pipelines that go to Europe and the very small capacity of the single pipeline (Power of Siberia) that reaches China. Besides, Putin and Miller overestimated China's appetite for Russian gas.

The geopolitical goals that Putin was pursuing in Ukraine and China by weaponizing the interdependence of Russia and its trade partners on the common gas transportation infrastructure have failed. Ukraine has retained its role as the principal transit territory for Russian gas deliveries to the west,[44] and China has diversified its gas requirements, making Russia's Power of Siberia pipeline an ancillary, and relatively unimportant, source of supply.[45] In the end, only the Putin cronies who encouraged the president's oversized geopolitical ambitions and parasitized on those ambitions have reaped billions of dollars from Gazprom contracts.[46]

Conclusion

Vladimir Putin and Russia's current political establishment have attempted to use Gazprom as an instrument of weaponized interdependence despite incurring economic and diplomatic costs. These factors are not a priority when one of the players is driven by reckless personal ambitions, as many authoritarian politicians are. Those ambitions are encouraged, and capitalized on, by a close and corrupt circle around the chief decisionmaker. And a system where government-controlled companies do not mind losing money to satisfy the personal whims of the national leader is a perfect environment for weaponizing any interdependence.[47]

This is a challenge for the other parties involved in the interdependence arrangement, and they have proven they can resist and diminish the negative effects of Putin's weaponization. The obvious means have been the European Union's anti-monopoly legislative measures; an investigation of Gazprom's monopoly practices (with possible penalties of billions of euros); diversification of gas supply sources; expansion of the European capacity for imports of liquefied natural gas; construction of cross-border interconnectors; and a joint plan of emergency response to possible disruptions of Russian gas supply. Political support by the United States has also helped Europe resist the pressure of Gazprom (against the will of some Europeans).[48] In the final run, Europe is witnessing a disarmed Gazprom that is unable to play the role of Putin's political weapon, and a more civilized environment in the natural gas trade with Russia.

The sort of interdependence that has been developing for decades in Russia's natural gas trade with Europe has demonstrated a great endurance potential. It has foiled Vladimir Putin's attempts at domineering and imposing his political will on consumers of Russian natural gas. In fact, the weaponizing of this interdependence by Russia has accelerated the evolution of a more resilient and sustainable energy sector in Europe, which is gradually becoming less dependent on the whims and wills of its unreliable and unpredictable Russian partner.

Notes

1. Bruce W. Jentleson, *Pipeline Politics: The Complex Political Economy of East-West Energy Trade* (Cornell University Press, 1986).

2. "Putin nazval Rossiyu otdel'noi tsivilizatsiyei," *RIA Novosti*, May 17, 2020, https://ria.ru/20200517/1571580444.html.

3. Chris Miller, *Putinomics: Power and Money in Resurgent Russia* (University of North Carolina Press, 2018), pp. 48–56.

4. Leonid Bershidsky, "A Fired Analyst Got Too Close to Gazprom's Truth," *Bloomberg*, May 23, 2018, www.bloomberg.com/opinion/articles/2018-05-23/sberbank-analyst-got-too-close-to-gazprom-s-truth.

5. A good study of the evolution of Soviet gas exports to Western Europe can be found in Per Högselius, *Red Gas: Russia and the Origins of European Energy Dependence* (Basingstoke, United Kingdom: Palgrave Macmillan, 2013).

6. Madalina Sisu Vicari, "How Russian Pipelines Heat Up Tensions: From Reagan's Battle over Yamal to the European Row on Nord Stream 2," *Vocal Europe*, April 21, 2016, www.vocaleurope.eu/how-russian-pipelines-heat-up -tensions-from-reagans-battle-over-yamal-to-the-european-row-on-nord -stream-2/.

7. Aurélie Bros, Tatiana Mitrova, and Kirsten Westphal, "German-Russian Gas Relations: A Special Relationship in Troubled Waters," research paper (Berlin: Stiftung Wissenschaft und Politik German Institute for International and Security Affairs, December 2017), p. 7.

8. "Minfin podschital dolu dokhodov budzheta . . . ," *Prime*, September 19, 2019, https://1prime.ru/state_regulation/20190919/830338839.html.

9. "Russian Foreign Trade in 2019," Russian Foreign Trade, February 14, 2020, https://en.russian-trade.com/reports-and-reviews/2020-02/russian -foreign-trade-in-2019/.

10. See an overview of Russia's gas export pipelines at Gazprom's website, at www.gazprom.com/projects/#pipeline.

11. See Thomas P. Cavanna, "Coercion Unbound? China's Belt and Road Initiative," chapter 12 in this volume; Emily Meierding, "Weaponizing Energy Interdependence," chapter 9 in this volume.

12. Tatiana Mitrova, "The Political and Economic Importance of Gas in Russia," in *The Russian Gas Matrix: How Markets Are Driving Change* (Oxford University Press, 2014), pp. 6–38.

13. "EU Imports of Energy Products—Recent Developments: Statistics Explained," Eurostat, June 2020, https://ec.europa.eu/eurostat/statistics-ex plained/pdfscache/46126.pdf.

14. Andres Mäe, "European (Energy) Security and Russian Natural Gas," International Centrefor Defence and Security, Estonia, https://icds.ee/euro pean-energy-security-and-russian-natural-gas/.

15. Valeriy Panyushkin and Mikhail Zygar, with Irina Reznik, *Gazprom: Novoye Russkoye Oruzhiye* (Moscow: Zakharov Books, 2008).

16. Fiona Hill and Clifford G. Gaddy, *Mr. Putin, Operative in the Kremlin* (Brookings Institution Press, 2013), p. 166.

17. See, for example, Macey A. Bos, "Gazprom: Russia's Nationalized Political Weapon and the Implications for the European Union," thesis (George-town University, 2012), https://repository.library.georgetown.edu/handle/10 822/557642.

18. See also "Putin. Corruption. An Independent White Paper," translated from Russian by Dave Essel, 2011, www.putin-itogi.ru/putin-corruption-an -independent-white-paper/.

19. Anders Aslund, "The Illusions of Putin's Russia," Atlantic Council, May 6, 2019, www.atlanticcouncil.org/blogs/ukrainealert/the-illusions-of -putin-s-russia/.

20. Henry Farrell and Abraham L. Newman, "Weaponized Interdependence: How Global Economic Networks Shape State Coercion," *International Security* 44 (Summer 2019), pp. 42–79.

21. Daniel W. Drezner, *The Sanctions Paradox: Economic Statecraft and International Relations* (Cambridge University Press, 2010).

22. Gabriel Collins, "Russia's Use of the 'Energy Weapon' in Europe," Rice University's Baker Institute for Public Policy, issue brief, July 18, 2017, www.bakerinstitute.org/media/files/files/ac785a2b/BI-Brief-071817-CES_ Russia1.pdf.

23. Vahram Ter-Matevosyan and others, "Armenia in the Eurasian Economic Union: Reasons for Joining and Its Consequences," *Eurasian Geography and Economics* 58, no. 3 (2017), www.tandfonline.com/doi/abs/10 .1080/15387216.2017.1360193?src=recsys&journalCode=rege20.

24. Christopher Hartwell, "Serbia's cooperation with China, the European Union, Russia and the United States of America" (Brussels: European Parliament, 2017), www.europarl.europa.eu/cmsdata/133504/Serbia%20cooper-ation%20with%20China,%20the%20EU,%20Russia%20and%20the%20 USA.pdf.

25. Aleksia Petrova, "Bulgaria to Diversify Half of Its Gas Consumption by End-2020," *SeeNews*, January 28, 2020, https://seenews.com/news/bul garia-to-diversify-half-of-its-gas-consumption-by-end-2020-energy-min -685128.

26. Vusala Abbasova, "Belarus Seeks Lower Gas Price from Russia Amid

Negotiations," *Caspian News,* May 16, 2020, https://caspiannews.com/news -detail/belarus-seeks-lower-gas-price-from-russia-amid-negotiations-2020-5 -15-44/.

27. Max de Hadelvang, "Putin's Relationship with Germany's Ex-Leader Has Created a New Word for Corruption," *Quartz,* March 20, 2018, https:// qz.com/1232384/putins-relationship-with-germanys-ex-leader-has-created-a -new-word-for-corruption/.

28. Heather A. Conley and others, "The Kremlin Playbook: Understanding Russian Influence in Central and Eastern Europe" (Washington: Center for Strategic & International Studies, 2016); and Heather A. Conley and others, "The Kremlin Playbook 2: The Enablers" (Washington: Center for Strategic & International Studies, 2019).

29. Directive 98/30/EC, of the European Parliament and of the Council, June 22, 1998.

30. Directive 2003/55/EC of the European Parliament and of the Council, June 26, 2003.

31. Directive 2009/73/EC of the European Parliament and of the Council, July 14, 2009. See also Katja Yafimava, "The Third EU Package for Gas and Gas Target Model," working paper NG75 (Oxford Institute for Energy Studies, April 2013).

32. Marco Siddi, "The Antitrust Dispute between the European Commission and Gazprom: Towards an Amicable Deal," Finnish Institute of International Affairs, April 2017 www.fiia.fi/wp-content/uploads/2017/11/ comment9_the_antitrust_dispute_between_the_european_commission_and _gazprom.pdf.

33. European Commission, "Antitrust: Commission Imposes Binding Obligations on Gazprom to Enable Free Flow of Gas at Competitive Prices in Central and Eastern European Gas Markets," May 24, 2018. https://ec.europa .eu/commission/presscorner/detail/en/IP_18_3921.

34. Ministry of Energy, "Doktrina Energeticheskoy Bezopasnosti," Russian Federation, 2019, https://minenergo.gov.ru/node/14766.

35. Jonathan Stern, "The Impact of European Regulation and Policy on Russian Gas Exports and Pipelines," in *The Russian Gas Matrix: How Markets Are Driving Change* (Oxford University Press, 2014), p. 103.

36. Leonid Bershidsky, "A Fired Analyst Got Too Close to Gazprom's Truth," *Bloomberg Opinion,* May 23, 2018, www.bloomberg.com/opinion/ articles/2018-05-23/sberbank-analyst-got-too-close-to-gazprom-s-truth.

37. Pavel K. Baev, "Distorted Data and Fanciful Beliefs Inform Russia's Crisis Mismanagement," *Eurasia Daily Monitor* 17, no. 69 (May 18, 2020), https://jamestown.org/program/distorted-data-and-fanciful-beliefs-inform -russias-crisis-mismanagement/.

38. Glenn Diesen, *Russia's Geoeconomic Strategy for a Greater Eurasia* (London: Routledge, Taylor & Francis Group, 2018), p. 150.

39. Gazprom VNIIGAZ, "Program for Comprehensive Development of Yamal Peninsula Reserves," 2007, p. 179.

40. Ibid., p. 185.

41. Mikhail Krutikhin, "Russia and the West: Energy Warfare," in *The Russia File: Russia and the West in an Unordered World,* edited by Daniel S. Hamilton and Stefan Meister (Johns Hopkins University Press, 2017), p. 70; and James Henderson, "Asia: A Potential New Outlet for Russia Pipeline Gas and LNG," in *The Russian Gas Matrix: How Markets Are Driving Change* (Oxford University Press, 2014), pp. 216–45.

42. "Gaz dlya Yevropy v Aziyu," *EurAsia Daily,* September 2, 2016, https://eadaily.com/ru/news/2016/09/02/gaz-dlya-evropy-v-aziyu-gazprom -planiruet-globalno-upravlyat-potokami-golubogo-topliva.

43. "Miller: Postavki gaza iz RF v KNR . . . ," NTV, November 9, 2014, www.ntv.ru/novosti/1260944/comments/.

44. Mikhail Krutikhin, "A Truce in a Gas War," *Forbes Russia,* December 23, 2019, www.forbes.ru/biznes/390009-peremirie-v-gazovoy-voyne-kto-vyi gral-i-kto-proigral-ot-soglasheniya-s-ukrainoy-po.

45. Mikhail Krutikhin, "The Chinese Are Happy," *Current Time,* December 2, 2019, www.currenttime.tv/a/russia-china-gas/30304037.html.

46. Anders Åslund, *Russia's Crony Capitalism: The Path from Market Economy to Kleptocracy* (Yale University Press, 2019).

47. Mikhail Krutikhin, "The Core Principle of a Russian State-Controlled Comopay Is Maximization of Costs," *NEWSru.com,* April 15, 2020, https:// blog.newsru.com/article/14apr2020/sechin.

48. See, for example, "Nord Stream 2: Trump Approves Sanctions on Russia Gas Pipeline," BBC News, December 21, 2019, www.bbc.com/news/ world-europe-50875935.

V

STATE-OWNED NETWORKS

11

Weaponized Weapons

The U.S. F-35 and European Eurofighter Networks

FLORIAN DAVID BODAMER

KAIJA E. SCHILDE

As modern armaments become more technologically complex, states find it increasingly difficult to sustain the costs and technology necessary for developing advanced weapons platforms. While some states import advanced weapons, others form or join transnational projects to codevelop and coproduce them, creating public-private networks of complex interdependence and allowing member states to achieve market scale through supply chains and investments.[1] Transnational arms development projects are state-centric networks with high political, economic, and security externalities, comparable to China's Belt and Road Initiative (BRI) discussed by Thomas Cavanna in this volume.[2] Arms networks can be asymmetrical, led by core states; others are more symmetrical, where states have more equal power. State-centric arms networks probe the boundaries of the weaponized interdependence (WI) framework, specifically the relationship between the state power, network structure and centrality, and weaponization. States willingly join state-centric networks—both symmetrical and asymmetrical—but with complex legal safeguards of network and supply chain design. Even state-centric networks built under this threat of WI, however, can be weaponized for domestic political purposes.[3]

Adding nuance to WI scope conditions, this chapter evaluates two weaponization attempts: the 2019 expulsion of Turkey from the U.S.-dominated F-35 project, and the 2018 export stop of the Eurofighter Typhoon from the United Kingdom to Saudi Arabia via Germany. Arms projects are the largest interdependent networks in contemporary international politics. For example, the United States' costs for the F-35 project are $1.6 trillion, not counting international partner investments, compared to China's $1.3 trillion spread across all BRI projects and regions.[4] Conceptually, state-centric networks exist under the threat of WI and trigger more wariness than non-state networks, resulting in network designs to insure against weaponization.[5] Arms networks are technologically sophisticated, fixed-cost networks with high network externalities, where states join to drive down the cost of the network good. However, while the threat of WI makes weaponization less likely, states still attempt to weaponize arms networks. The costs of weaponization—which Michael Mastanduno also discusses in this volume[6]—appear to be high in both cases, due to political and supply chain interdependence. We also find evidence that arms network weaponization attempts look less like intentional acts of statecraft and more like unstrategic outcomes of domestic political processes.

F-35 Network

The F-35 is a U.S.-developed and Lockheed Martin-manufactured fighter jet. The F-35 network is highly asymmetric: the United States is the main investor and buyer, and sets the technical requirements and standards. This hierarchical network structure creates a strong future threat of WI. Lockheed built 134 of the jets in 2019 and plans to produce 160 per year by 2023.[7] The F-35 program was designed as an international partnership both to control costs by achieving larger market scale and to address alliance interoperability concerns. Nine countries (United States, United Kingdom, Italy, Netherlands, Turkey, Canada, Australia, Denmark, and Norway) developed and coproduce the F-35. The program gives states access to high technology, interoperability with U.S. systems, and supply-chain opportunities for domestic defense firms. Partner states have had concerns about the F-35 program, including high costs, delays, data surveillance, and issues around the quality of the final product. Indeed, multiple states have threatened to pull out of the F-35 program over panopticon issues, due to the F-35 logistics database that surveils sovereign military data in all training and operations. Partner states have addressed this concern by developing separate databases, using software that filters out sensitive data, and even setting up independent national data monitoring labs at Eglin Air Force Base in Florida.[8]

Turkey joined the consortium as a Tier III partner in 2001, and received (for pilot training use within the United States only) its first two F-35s in June 2018.[9] As a NATO member, Turkey's strategic assets to the alliance include Incirlik Air Base, hosting missile defense radar systems, and storing U.S. nuclear weapons. Turkey invested $1.2 billion in the F-35s, for a total market value of $9 billion (in 2019 dollars).[10] As an international partner in the F-35 program, Turkey was both a buyer and a supply chain contributor. By 2019, ten Turkish firms had produced over 900 components for the F-35, including parts of the airframe structure, landing gear, engine, and wiring systems.[11] Some Turkish firms were critical, including single-source industry producers of key engine components and a secondary producer of fuselage.[12] The value of the program to Turkish industry was around $12 billion.[13] Turkish firms also supported F-35 operations and maintenance, with Turkey hosting the main European hub for engine repair and overhaul.[14]

2018–2019: Weaponization of F-35 Network

By 2019, Turkey was on target to buy a hundred F-35s. However, shifts in Turkey's domestic stability and regional security altered its alliance relations. U.S.-Turkish ties were increasingly strained by Turkish President Recep Tayyip Erdoğan's consolidation of regime power and deterioration of the rule of law after the 2016 coup attempt, as well as conflicting strategy over Syria, the U.S.-Kurdish relationship, Iran sanctions, and Turkey's detention of U.S. evangelical pastor Andrew Brunson and U.S. consular staff.[15] In 2018, Turkey signaled that it intended to purchase the Russian S-400 surface-to-air missile defense system.[16] The United States considers the S-400 and F-35 systems incompatible, because the S-400 can "learn" the stealth features of the F-35 if both systems are operating and training in the same location, generating military intelligence data about the NATO missile defense network. [17] According to the Pentagon, the "S-400 is a Russian system designed to shoot down an aircraft like the F-35, and it is inconceivable to imagine Russia not taking advantage of that (intelligence) collection opportunity."[18]

Initially, the U.S. government was split between Congress seeking to punish Turkey and the Donald Trump administration trying to maintain the status quo. The State Department attempted to prevent the S-400 deal in 2018 by approving a $3.5 billion Raytheon Patriot missile defense platform export to Turkey, touting U.S. technology and NATO interoperability.[19] Erdoğan rejected the deal, saying Raytheon had not "given us an offer as good as the S-400s," a $2.5 billion deal.[20] The United States warned Turkey that "an S-400 acquisition could potentially trigger actions under the Countering America's Adversaries Through Sanctions Act (CAATSA), created in 2017 to address Russian interference in U.S. elections."[21] Congress grappled with how to sanction Turkey over the issue; because F-35 sales are not conducted government-to-government, but rather through a complex public-private international consortium, Congress did not have direct legal authority to block the sale. Ultimately, a bipartisan bill prohibited the military logistics for transferring F-35s to Turkey and blocked intellectual property for maintenance support, rendering any existing Turkish F-35s unusable.[22] Under congressional pressure, the Pentagon slowly began ratcheting up consequences to Turkey. It blocked Turkish pilot training, uninvited Turkey from the annual F-35 roundtable, and threatened to evict Turkish pilots from the United States; however, the Trump administration strongly signaled that it did not want to fully evict Turkey.[23] While the Pentagon's opposition to Turkish expulsion was to protect the F-35 network, the White House's opposition to expulsion was based on personal ties to Erdoğan. Indeed, Defense Secretary James Mattis resigned in late 2018 over disapproval of the intimate

Erdoğan-Trump coordination in reversing U.S. policy and withdrawing troops from Syria.[24]

In response to U.S. pressure, Turkey accelerated the delivery of
the S-400 from 2020 to July 2019 but proposed a compromise: It
"would operate the system independent of its integrated air defense,"
and personnel would train in Russia instead of Turkey.[25] Turkish officials downplayed the S-400 intelligence risks, because they planned
a separate data system with no Russian or NATO interoperability.
They also pointed to the precedence of Israeli F-35s already operating
in close proximity to the S-400 in Syria.[26] But by mid-2019, the Pentagon officials who had actively prevented the Turkish expulsion had
resigned, which allowed the domestic politics initiated by congressional actions to prevail.[27] In response to the July 2019 delivery of the
S-400, the Pentagon announced that Turkey would be expelled from
the F-35 program by March 2020.

The unwinding of Turkey from the program involved multifaceted
logistics and supply chain issues. A critical concern was the already-
built Turkish F-35s, stored for pilot training at Luke Air Force Base,
in addition to twenty-four other jets in various stages of production.[28]
The United States declared that it had the power to keep the planes,
even though they were owned and paid for by Turkey.[29] No provision
in the U.S.-Turkey memorandums of understanding (MOUs) "prevent[ed] the U.S. from suspending F-35 transfers to Turkey, despite
Turkey's role in production."[30]

Costs of Weaponization

In the lead-up to the U.S. decision, officials warned of unaccept-
able blowback costs to the United States, particularly to F-35 supply
chains, timelines, and affordability. Indeed, House legislation stopped
far short of prohibiting F-35 sales to Turkey, because—according to
a Republican aide—"such a restriction would hurt the U.S. and its
allies more than it would affect Turkey."[31] NATO officials were concerned that the move would be "a strategic risk and setback to NATO
in the global race to deploy the fifth-generation stealth fighters, particularly as other world powers are rushing to deploy theirs."[32] In
2018, U.S. Defense Secretary Mattis cautioned that "removing

Turkey could trigger a major supply chain disruption for the U.S. military" resulting in increased costs and delays of "18–24 months to re-source parts and recover."[33] The F-35 program manager claimed that "approximately 3,000 suppliers working on the F-35" would also be impacted, and that they were already "struggling with the demand signal on them" as more planes entered service and older ones were increasingly in need of repair.[34] Lockheed also admitted that while "we do have alternate sources for some of the material already . . . if we lost [Turkey] . . . the other two remaining sources are [in]sufficient for capacity."[35]

While warnings of blowback were widespread, some officials downplayed risks and even highlighted potential future opportunities. The post-Mattis Pentagon claimed that Turkey's expulsion would minimally impact the F-35 program, because most parts were from "predominantly U.S. sources"[36] and "secondary sources of supply for Turkish-produced parts are now in development."[37] Some U.S. officials claimed that ejecting Turkey provided new enticements to help sell the stealth fighter jet to other allies, because subcontracts could be "re-marketed"[38] and Turkey's jets resold to prospective customers such as Japan and Poland.[39] It remained unclear which F-35 partners, "if any, would be willing to buy the F-35s already in production for Turkey."[40]

The Pentagon acknowledged some up-front costs. Initial costs were estimated at "$500–600 million in nonrecurring engineering in order to shift the supply chain" to U.S. sources.[41] It also reappropriated over $200 million from the Navy's F-35 spare parts budget, even though parts shortages have exacerbated existing F-35 readiness problems.[42] Ultimately, U.S. officials had to acknowledge short-term dependence on Turkish parts and delayed the transition to U.S. suppliers. Six key Turkish-made F-35 components, including the jet's fuselage and landing gear, were already paid for and could not be substituted.[43] The Pentagon announced in February 2020 that the consortium would continue to procure Turkish parts through 2020.[44] A March 2020 audit by the Government Accountability Office (GAO) estimated that the short-term supply chain costs to the United States would exceed $1.5 billion and that fifteen key parts were not substitutable, a conclusion not yet accounting for additional COVID-19-related supply chain disruptions.[45]

The medium- and long-term costs of the Turkish expulsion are not yet known. Even when domestic suppliers are identified, they will be costlier than Turkish subcontractors. However, it is likely that the costs will extend to the sustainability of the F-35 program. The plane has been especially vulnerable to quality and cost issues, with its unit cost a particular vulnerability in acquisition decisions.[46] The program was predicated on Lockheed's 2001 promise of a market demand for 5,179 domestic and international planes, which determined cost programming and planning.[47] Even before the Turkish expulsion, the total market size of the F-35 program was downgraded to "up to" 3,500 planes.[48] The F-35 also faces a domestic down cycle of budgetary demand; in 2019, despite Defense Department budget increases, the U.S. military ordered fewer F-35s than expected. In particular, the U.S. Air Force, the F-35's largest customer, requested only 48 F-35s per year for fiscal years 2020 to 2025, after originally promising to buy 60 per year. Finally, Lockheed had to announce in May 2020 that it would fall 18 to 24 jets short of the 141 scheduled for delivery,[49] further complicating Lockheed's goals to keep the cost per jet under $80 million and to lower sustainment costs on par with fourth-generation fighters.[50]

In addition, Turkey is expected to take retaliatory legal action to recoup its investments. It has signaled that it will look to China or Russia for fighter jet alternatives or develop its own fighter jet project.[51] However, it is the loss of Turkey as a buyer that may have the greatest long-term impacts on the F-35 program. Its success has always been linked to scaling its market to bring down per-unit costs. A double hit of a contracting market and increasing unit costs—in addition to quality issues still haunting the program—might leave a lasting mark on the United States' premier defense project.

Eurofighter Network

The Eurofighter is a fourth-generation, multirole fighter jet. The network structure of the Eurofighter is best described as symmetric, because no state holds a majority or a major plurality of network ownership, and the "single-source principle" holds for the supply chain. Eurofighter Jagdflugzeug GmbH, the entity that "coordinates the design, production and upgrade of the [Eurofighter]," is owned by four partner states: Germany and the United Kingdom (33 percent each), Italy (21 percent), and Spain (13 percent).[52] A single-source production structure requires that parts be "produced at only one location and exchanged for other parts or components made elsewhere."[53] For example, once central fuselages are completed in Germany, they are sent for final assembly to the other states' assembly lines. Due to the partners' equal network centrality, each state has significant choke-point and panopticon leverage over the entire network, even beyond traditional state control over defense industrial collaboration, because the states only share assembly of the plane itself rather than combining elements of the supply chain.

However, during the initial stages of the Eurofighter project, the network structure looked different. In the late 1970s to early 1980s, France joined Germany, the United Kingdom, and Italy in negotiating codevelopment and production of a fighter jet, then called the European Fighter Aircraft (EFA). By 1983, negotiations had progressed toward a general partner-nation agreement, including a proportional share of cost and work agreement based on the number of planes ordered by each state.[54] During negotiations, however, France pushed for a greater participation share based on domestic pressure for "the chief engineer, lead firm, and overall design and management responsibility [to] all be French, that the headquarters be located in France, and that all planned exports be added to the French work share."[55] This would have made the EFA network more asymmetric, with one actor in control of a significant portion of the program, enabling France to more easily weaponize the network in the future. Other states, particularly Germany, opposed this. As a result, France decided to pursue its own project. With France's departure, the German, British, and Italian program structure became more equally aligned. Even when Spain later joined, the four states pursued a symmetrical network, without a clear lead state.[56] The network was designed with the intent that "no country can intervene unitarily in the four-sided program,"[57] partially mitigating the threat of future WI. Each network participant was equally interdependent, illustrated by the United Kingdom's concerns over a potential 1990s German exit from the program, fearing that the project "would be disrupted if 33 per cent of the project is removed."[58] Additionally, the partner states worked proactively to maintain the network balance when Spain had issues maintaining its financial commitment, by offering promises of additional domestic work for the Eurofighter and other projects.[59]

2018–2020: Weaponization of the Eurofighter Network

The German government strictly regulates the export of weapons. Article 26(2) of German Basic Law says that "weapons designed for warfare may be manufactured, transported or marketed only with the permission of the Federal Government,"[60] and Article 2(2) of Germany's War Weapons Control Act states that the transfer of armaments, which encompasses exports, requires a license.[61] The Federal Ministry of Economic Affairs and Energy is responsible for authorizing arms exports except in sensitive cases that are handled by the Bundessicherheitsrat (Federal Security Council), consisting of the German chancellor and eight cabinet officials.[62] In 2000, the left-wing government, consisting of the socialist Sozialdemokratische Partei Deutschlands (SPD) and the Greens, stated that it wanted to "shape a restrictive arms exports policy," especially toward non-NATO and non-European Union (EU) states.[63] This position was reiterated in 2019 by the centrist government, consisting of the Christian Democratic Union/Christian Social Union (CDU/CSU) and the SPD,[64] but only after the arms exports to those states had increased significantly in the preceding decade under the "Merkel Doctrine,"[65] which stood in contrast to German citizens' overwhelmingly critical views of arms exports.

The political debate over arms exports escalated with the onset of civil war in Yemen in 2015, especially with evidence of Saudi Arabia's involvement and the conflict's increasing civilian toll. Yemen was frequently discussed in the Bundestag, where parliamentarians became increasingly vocal in their concerns "that further German weapons are [being] delivered to commit mass murder in Yemen."[66] After the September 2017 general election, SPD pressure on the center-right CDU/CSU ensured that Germany was on the "path to prevent deliveries [of weapons] to states participating in the Yemen War" in the new coalition agreement.[67] On March 12, 2018, the parties reached an agreement that included the "Yemen clause," stating that the government would "immediately no longer authorize [arms] exports to states as long as they are directly involved in the Yemen War."[68] Despite this, deliveries of German armaments continued in the first half of 2018, with the German government in only "an assessment and advisory process" regarding armaments exports to war participants by late July.[69] The political agreement was simply not implemented.[70]

However, a turning point occurred with the October 2018 disappearance of the journalist Jamal Khashoggi. After Saudi Arabia admitted responsibility in November 2018, the German government announced an immediate stop of weapons exports to Saudi Arabia, formalizing the earlier political agreement.[71] The decision resulted in the stop of not only German weapons exports to Saudi Arabia, but also German parts in European weapons designated for export to Saudi Arabia. Germany's decision thus weaponized the Eurofighter network to prevent the export of weapons to Saudi Arabia, just as British defense company BAE Systems was negotiating a sale of forty-eight Eurofighters to Saudi Arabia.[72]

This weaponization of the Eurofighter network was unexpected; MOU #1, signed in 1986, says that "none of the partner-nations [can prevent] the sale of products or systems of the program to third parties."[73] Although the German-Saudi ban was originally slated to last for a short period, it was renewed in March and September 2019 for six months, and again in March 2020 for nine months.[74] After the first extension, the German government allowed for domestic parts to be exported to allies but not incorporated into new armaments designated for Saudi Arabia.[75]

The rationale for and outcome of the German weaponization of the Eurofighter network remain elusive. It is unclear to what degree the German state intentionally blocked domestic parts for export platforms and anticipated the network consequences, or whether the consequences were unintentional outcomes of domestic political processes. However, the network implications were clear almost immediately. As the export stop went into its second month, Chancellor Angela Merkel noted "that of our European partners only very few are adopting a similar policy"[76] and later said that Germany was torn "between [its] commitment and dependability as a part of European armaments policy and at the same time [its] political goals."[77] The German government clearly saw itself as part of a larger European defense industry network.

Outcomes of Weaponization

If measured only in terms of blocking Eurofighters to Saudi Arabia, German network weaponization has been incredibly successful. Since November 2018, Saudi Arabia has not been able to continue its negotiations with BAE for the purchase of an additional forty-eight fighter jets.[78] However, there is also negative blowback. Most importantly, Germany's reputation as a reliable partner for international armaments projects is in jeopardy, at both state and firm levels. After the export stop, a German parliamentarian noted that "all of [our partners] are questioning [cooperation on armament projects with Germany] because you are saying if there is a German share, then it cannot be exported anymore."[79] Although currently only Saudi Arabia is blocked from German armaments, Great Britain and France are concerned about Germany's future behavior and willingness to act alone, especially with France closely working with Germany on a sixth-generation fighter jet as well as a next-generation main battle tank. Indeed, the French ambassador to Germany warned that companies may "prefer 'German-free' armaments projects without German components," something companies like Airbus have already pursued by redesigning parts of the C295 military transport aircraft.[80]

Conclusion

Our findings add additional nuance and complexity to the WI framework. By illustrating weaponization attempts in arms networks, we demonstrate the conditions under which technologically sophisticated, fixed-cost, high externality, state-centric networks become weaponized. State-centric networks should be less vulnerable to weaponization attempts, due to the heavy hand of the state in the network and the wariness of other actors in joining the network.[81] While state-centric weaponization should then be less probabilistically likely, weaponization attempts that do occur may rapidly escalate because states hold the levers in their existing statecraft toolkit, and need no new policies or powers to weaponize them. State policymakers with access to weaponization options may even be unaware of the powers and consequences of those tools. Because state-centric networks are already "in house," weaponization can be implemented quickly, but perhaps without being well designed or thought through, leading to unintentional outcomes. Indeed, we observe variation in our cases along these lines. The Eurofighter network was particularly easy to weaponize, possibly because the consortium of firms that manufacture the platform are partially state-owned. The decision, once it filtered out, was implemented faster than policy could catch up with it. In contrast, the F35 is manufactured by a privately owned firm, Lockheed Martin. Thus, U.S. officials had initial difficulty weaponizing the F-35 because they were not in direct control of aircraft production, and they instead had to find alternative choke-point and panopticon mechanisms such as intellectual property controls or access to U.S. bases for training.

Our cases also suggest that there is more to weaponization attempts than just network power and hierarchy: Even states without major network power, like Germany, can weaponize a symmetrical network. This aligns with Stacie Goddard's point in this volume about the importance of network centrality, which might have allowed Germany to weaponize a symmetrical network without being a central node.[82] Our cases also suggest that weaponization may reflect domestic political interests rather than rational "unitary" statecraft. Weaponization outcomes also appear costly, with effects uncertain to even the actors initiating them, and cannot be described as successful in the short or medium term. These findings enhance the WI framework, particularly by illustrating the conditions that lead to network weaponization and outcomes, justifying further research and analysis to decouple the idea of interdependence and structure from weaponization.

Notes

1. Srdjan Vucetic and Kim Nossal, "The International Politics of the F-35 Joint Strike Fighter," *International Journal* 68 (2012), pp. 3–12.

2. Thomas P. Cavanna, "Coercion Unbound? China's Belt and Road Initiative," chapter 12 in this volume.

3. Stéfanie von Hlatky and Jeffrey Rice, "Striking a Deal on the F-35: Multinational Politics and U.S. Defence Acquisition," *Defence Studies* 18 (March 2018), pp. 19–38.

4. Jonathan Caverley, Ethan Kapstein, and Srdjan Vucetic, "F-35 Sales Are America's Belt and Road," *Foreign Policy,* July 12, 2019, https://foreignpolicy.com/2019/07/12/F-35-sales-are-americas-belt-and-road/.

5. Daniel W. Drezner, "Introduction: The Uses and Abuses of Weaponized Interdependence," chapter 1 in this volume.

6. Michael Mastanduno, "Hegemony and Fear: The National Security Determinants of Weaponized Interdependence," chapter 3 in this volume.

7. Marcus Weisgerber, "Ejecting Turkey from the F-35 Effort Will Cost At Least Half a Billion Dollars," *Defense One,* July 17, 2019, www.defenseone.com/business/2019/07/ejecting-turkey-f-35-effort-will-cost-least-half-billion-dollars/158500/.

8. Valerie Insinna, "Two F-35 Partners Threatened to Quit the Program. Here's Why They Didn't," *Defense News,* June 13, 2019, www.defensenews.com/smr/hidden-troubles-f35/2019/06/12/two-f-35-partners-threatened-to-quit-the-program-heres-why-they-didnt/.

9. Aaron Mehta, "Turkey Officially Kicked Out of F-35 Program, Costing U.S. Half a Billion Dollars," *Defense News,* July 17, 2019, www.defensenews.com/air/2019/07/17/turkey-officially-kicked-out-of-f-35-program/.

10. Jarod Taylor, "The F-35 Dispute and Tensions in the U.S.-Turkey Relationship," *Lawfare* (blog), May 2, 2019, www.lawfareblog.com/f-35-dispute-and-tensions-us-turkey-relationship.

11. Weisgerber, "Turkey Will Make F-35 Parts Throughout 2020."

12. Aaron Stein, "The Clock Is Ticking: S-400 and the Future of F-35 in Turkey," Atlantic Council, July 24, 2018, www.atlanticcouncil.org/blogs/menasource/the-clock-is-ticking-s-400-and-the-future-of-f-35-in-turkey/.

13. Lara Seligman and Jen DiMascio, "Should U.S. Block F-35 Deliveries to Turkey?" *Aviation Week & Space Technology*, May 15, 2018, https://aviationweek.com/defense-space/should-us-block-f-35-deliveries-turkey.

14. Ibid.

15. Stein, "The Clock Is Ticking."

16. Phil Stewart, "Exclusive: U.S. Will Not Accept More Turkish F-35 Pilots over Russia Defenses—Sources," Reuters, June 6, 2019, www.businessinsider.com/exclusive-us-will-not-accept-more-turkish-f-35-pilots-over-russia-defenses-sources-2019-6.

17. Seligman and DiMascio, "Should U.S. Block F-35 Deliveries to Turkey?"

18. Phil Stewart and Humeyra Pamuk, "The U.S. Laid Out Its Plan to Kick Turkey Out of the F-35 Program If It Buys Russia's S-400," Reuters, June 7, 2019, www.businessinsider.com/us-starts-unwinding-turkey-from-f-35 -fighter-jet-program-2019-6.

19. Defense Security Cooperation Agency, "Turkey—Patriot Missile System and Related Support and Equipment," press release, December 18, 2018, https://dsca.mil/major-arms-sales/turkey-patriot-missile-system-and-re lated-support-and-equipment.

20. Stewart and Pamuk, "The U.S. Laid Out Its Plan to Kick Turkey Out."

21. Seligman and DiMascio, "Should U.S. Block F-35 Deliveries to Turkey?"

22. Ibid.

23. Valerie Insinna, "Turkish Suppliers to Be Eliminated from F-35 Program in 2020," Defense News, June 7, 2019, www.defensenews.com/air /2019/06/07/turkish-suppliers-to-be-eliminated-from-f-35-program-in-2020/.

24. Julian Borger, "Mattis Resignation Triggered by Phone Call between Trump and Erdoğan," Guardian, December 21, 2018, www.theguardian. com/us-news/2018/dec/21/james-mattis-resignation-trump-erdogan-phone -call.

25. Stein, "The Clock Is Ticking."

26. Ragip Soylu, "Turkey Extends S-400 Offer to Washington," Daily Sabah, June 28, 2018, www.dailysabah.com/columns/ragip-soylu/2018/06/28/ turkey-extends-s-400-offer-to-washington.

27. Idrees Ali and Phil Stewart, "U.S. Removing Turkey from F-35 Program after Its Russian Missile Defense Purchase," Reuters, July 17, 2019, www.reuters.com/article/us-turkey-security-usa-idUSKCN1UC2DD.

28. Weisgerber, "Turkey Will Make F-35 Parts Throughout 2020."

29. Mehta, "Turkey Officially Kicked Out of F-35 Program."

30. Taylor, "The F-35 Dispute."

31. Seligman and DiMascio, "Should U.S. Block F-35 Deliveries to Turkey?"

32. Adam Bensaid, "NATO and F-35 Program Put at Risk by U.S. F-35 Suspension to Turkey," TRT World, July 18, 2018, www.trtworld.com/maga zine/nato-and-f-35-program-put-at-risk-by-us-f-35-suspension-to-turkey -19930.

33. Anthony Capaccio and Roxana Tiron, "Mattis Urges Congress Not to Hit Turkey with Lockheed F-35 Ban," Bloomberg, July 19, 2018, www. bloomberg.com/news/articles/2018-07-19/mattis-urges-congress-not-to-hit -turkey-with-lockheed-f-35-ban.

34. Paul McLeary, "F-35 Production Hurt If Turkey Kicked Out of Program: Vice Adm. Winter," Breaking Defense, April 4, 2019, https://break

ingdefense.com/2019/04/f-35-production-hurt-if-turkey-kicked-out-of
-program-vice-adm-winter/.

35. Weisgerber, "Turkey Will Make F-35 Parts Throughout 2020."

36. Weisgerber, "Lockheed: We Could Easily Sell Turkey's F-35s to Other
Customers," *Defense One*, May 29, 2019, www.defenseone.com/politics
/2019/05/lockheed-preps-give-turkish-f-35s-other-customers/157326/.

37. Mike Stone and Mumeyra Pamuk, "Despite Ankara's Claims, U.S.
Can Make F-35 without Turkish Parts," Reuters, March 28, 2019, www.
reuters.com/article/us-usa-turkey-f35-idUSKCN1R90CY.

38. Ali and Stewart, "U.S. Removing Turkey from F-35 Program."

39. Weisgerber, "Lockheed: We Could Easily Sell Turkey's F-35."

40. Jacqueline Feldscher, "White House Kicks Turkey Out of Fighter Jet
Project," *Politico*, July 17, 2019, www.politico.com/story/2019/07/17/white
-house-turkey-f35-program-1597407.

41. Ibid.

42. Joseph Trevithick, "Pentagon Will Raid F-35 Spare Parts Budget to
Help Pay for Kicking Turkey Out of the Program," *The Drive*, July 11, 2019,
www.thedrive.com/the-war-zone/28940/pentagon-will-raid-f-35-spare-parts
-budget-to-help-pay-for-kicking-turkey-out-of-the-program.

43. Weisgerber, "Turkey Will Make F-35 Parts Throughout 2020."

44. Feldscher, "White House Kicks Turkey Out."

45. U.S. Government Accountability Office, "Weapon System Sustainment:
DOD Needs a Strategy for Redesigning the F-35's Central Logistics System,"
GAO-20-316, March 2020, www.gao.gov/assets/710/705154.pdf.

46. Valerie Insinna, "Inside America's Dysfunctional Trillion-Dollar
Fighter-Jet Program," *New York Times*, August 21, 2019, www.nytimes.com
/2019/08/21/magazine/f35-joint-strike-fighter-program.html.

47. Flight International, "F-35's Supply-and-Demand Paradox," *Flight
Global*, April 13, 2015, www.flightglobal.com/opinion/opinion-f-35s-supply
-and-demand-paradox/116475.article.

48. Kenneth Eps, "The Size of the F-35 Market Is Overstated," Project
Ploughshares, briefing 10-4, November 2010, http://ploughshares.ca/pl_
publications/the-size-of-the-f-35-market-is-overstated/.

49. Valerie Insinna, "Lockheed Slated to Miss F-35 Delivery Target in
2020 as Supply Chain Struggles to Keep Up," *Defense News*, May 19, 2020,
www.defensenews.com/breaking-news/2020/05/19/lockheed-to-slow-f-35
-production-as-supply-chain-struggles-to-keep-up/.

50. Valerie Insinna, "The U.S. Air Force, Not Turkey, Is Frustrating
Lockheed Execs on the F-35 Program," *Defense News*, April 23, 2019, www
.defensenews.com/industry/2019/04/23/the-us-air-force-not-turkey-is
-frustrating-lockheed-execs-on-the-f-35-program/.

51. "Turkey, Kicked Out of F-35 Program, Calls on U.S. to Reverse
Decision," *Sydney Morning Herald*, July 19, 2019, www.smh.com.au/world/

middle-east/turkey-kicked-out-of-f-35-program-calls-on-us-to-reverse
-decision-20190719-p528r1.html.

52. Eurofighter GmbH, "About Us" (2020), www.eurofighter.com/about
-us.

53. Ulrich Pabst, "Eurofighter Has Commenced Production," *Air & Space Europe* 1 (September–December 1999), p. 15.

54. House of Commons, Committee of Public Accounts, "Management of the Typhoon Project," April 15, 2011, https://publications.parliament.uk/pa/cm201011/cmselect/cmpubacc/860/860.pdf); Andrew Moravcsik, "Armaments among Allies; European Weapons Collaboration, 1975-1985," in *Double-edged Diplomacy: International Bargaining and Domestic Politics*, edited by Peter Evans, Harold Haran Jacobson, and Robert Putnam (University of California Press, 1993), p. 138.

55. Ibid., p. 142.

56. Ibid.

57. Deutscher Bundestag, "Stenographischer Bericht 204. Sitzung," Plenarprotokoll 13/204, November 14, 1997, p. 18497, http://dipbt.bundestag.de/dip21/btp/13/13204.pdf.

58. House of Commons, Debates and Oral Answers, column 612, July 9, 1992, https://publications.parliament.uk/pa/cm199293/cmhansrd/1992-07-09/Debate-12.html.

59. Deutscher Bundestag, "Stenographischer Bericht 113. Sitzung," Plenarprotokoll 11/113, December 11, 1988, p. 8184, http://dipbt.bundestag.de/dip21/btp/11/11113.pdf.

60. Bundesamt für Justiz, "Basic Law for the Federal Republic of Germany," May 23, 1949, www.gesetze-im-internet.de/englisch_gg/englisch_gg.html#p0143.

61. Bundesamt für Justiz, "Ausführungsgesetz zu Artikel 26 Abs. 2 des Grundgesetzes (Gesetz über die Kontrolle von Kriegswaffen)," April 20, 1961, www.gesetze-im-internet.de/krwaffkontrg/BJNR004440961.html.

62. Deutscher Bundestag, "Antrag, Mehr Transparenz bei Rüstungsexportentscheidungen sicherstellen," Drucksache 18/1334, May 7, 2014, http://dipbt.bundestag.de/dip21/btd/18/013/1801334.pdf.

63. Bundesregierung, "Politische Grundätze der Bundesregierung für den Export von Kriegswaffen und sonstigen Rüstungsgütern," January 8, 2000, www.bundesregierung.de/resource/blob/975280/432334/19eafb41a78dc5a3afb61e92511c9f2f/2015-09-22-ruestungsrichtlinien-data.pdf?download=1.

64. Bundesministerium für Wirtschaft und Energie, "Politische Grundsätze der Bundesregierung für den Export von Kriegswaffen und sonstigen Rüstungsgütern," June 6, 2019, https://www.bmwi.de/Redaktion/DE/Downloads/P-R/politische-grundsaetze-fuer-den-export-von-kriegswaffen-und-sonstigen-ruestungsguetern.pdf?__blob=publicationFile&v=4.

65. "German Weapons for the World: How the Merkel Doctrine is Changing Berlin Policy," *Der Spiegel*, December 12, 2012, www.spiegel.de/international/germany/german-weapons-exports-on-the-rise-as-merkel-doctrine-takes-hold-a-870596.html.

66. Deutscher Bundestag, "Stenographischer Bericht 3. Sitzung," Plenarprotokoll 19/3, November 22, 2017, p. 163, http://dipbt.bundestag.de/dip21/btp/19/19003.pdf.

67. Deutscher Bundestag, "Stenographischer Bericht 16. Sitzung," Plenarprotokoll 19/16, February 28, 2018, p. 1360, http://dipbt.bundestag.de/dip21/btp/19/19016.pdf.

68. Bundesregierung, "Koalitionsvertrag zwischen CDU, CSU und SPD," March 12, 2018, www.bundesregierung.de/resource/blob/975226/847984/5b8bc23590d4cb2892b31c987ad672b7/2018-03-14-koalitionsvertrag-data.pdf?download=1.

69. Deutscher Bundestag, "Stenographischer Bericht 41. Sitzung," Plenarprotokoll 19/41, June 27, 2018, p. 4048, http://dipbt.bundestag.de/dip21/btp/19/19041.pdf.

70. Ibid.

71. Bundeskanzlerin, "Pressekonferenz von Bundeskanzlerin Merkel und dem tschechischen Ministerpräsidenten Andrej Babiš," October 26, 2018, www.bundeskanzlerin.de/bkin-de/aktuelles/pressekonferenz-von-bundeskanzlerin-merkel-und-dem-tschechischen-ministerpraesidenten-andrej-babi%C5%A1-1542722.

72. BAE Systems, "Memorandum of Intent between the Kingdom of Saudi Arabia and the U.K. Government," March 9, 2018, www.baesystems.com/en/article/memorandum-of-intent-between-the-kingdom-of-saudi-arabia-and-the-uk-government.

73. Deutscher Bundestag, "Antwort: Deutsche Anteile am Eurofighter und dessen Einsatz im Jemenkrieg," Drucksache 19/4028, August 27, 2018, p. 4, http://dipbt.bundestag.de/dip21/btd/19/040/1904028.pdf.

74. Bundesministerium für Wirtschaft und Energie, "Schriftliche Frage an die Bundesregierung im Monat September 2019 Fragen Nr. 194," September 23, 2019, www.bmwi.de/Redaktion/DE/Parlamentarische-Anfragen/2019/9-194.pdf?__blob=publicationFile&v=2; "Der Rüstungsexportstopp nach Saudi-Arabien gilt weiter," *DeutscheWelle*, March 23, 2019, www.dw.com/de/der-r%C3%BCstungsexportstopp-nach-saudi-arabien-gilt-weiter/a-52893125.

75. Deutscher Bundestag, "Stenographischer Bericht 93. Sitzung," Plenarprotokoll 19/93, April 5, 2019, p. 11208, http://dipbt.bundestag.de/dip21/btp/19/19093.pdf.

76. Bundeskanzlerin, "Befragung der Bundesregierung mit Bundeskanzlerin Merkel," December 12, 2018, www.bundeskanzlerin.de/bkin-de/aktuelles/befragung-der-bundesregierung-mit-bundeskanzlerin-merkel-1560426.

77. Bundeskanzlerin, "Befragung der Bundesregierung mit Bundeskanzlerin Merkel," April 10, 2019, www.bundeskanzlerin.de/bkin-de/aktuelles/befragung-der-bundesregierung-mit-bundeskanzlerin-merkel-1599752.

78. Sarah Young, "BAE Systems Predicts 2020 Growth Despite Saudi Ban," Reuters, January 20, 2020, www.reuters.com/article/us-bae-systems-results/bae-systems-predicts-2020-growth-despite-saudi-ban-idUSKBN 20E0S0.

79. Deutscher Bundestag, "Stenographischer Bericht 62. Sitzung," Plenarprotokoll 19/62, November 9, 2018, p. 7129, http://dipbt.bundestag.de/dip 21/btp/19/19062.pdf.

80. Anne-Marie Descôtes, "Vom 'German-free' zum gegenseitigen Vertrauen," *Arbeitspapier Sicherheitspolitik* Nr. 7/2019, p. 1, www.baks.bund.de/de/arbeitspapiere/2019/vom-german-free-zum-gegenseitigen-vertrauen; Andrea Shalal, "Unpredictable German Export Policies Threaten Arms Projects with France: French Envoy," Reuters, March 25, 2019, www.reuters.com/article/us-germany-france-arms/unpredictable-german-export-policies-threaten-arms-projects-with-france-french-envoy-idUSKCN1R 62MA.

81. Drezner, "Introduction," chapter 1 in this volume.

82. Stacie E. Goddard, "The Road to Revisionism: How Interdependence Gives Revisionists Weapons for Change," chapter 4 in this volume.

12

Coercion Unbound?

China's Belt and Road Initiative

THOMAS P. CAVANNA

This chapter investigates how the concept of weaponized interdependence applies to China's Belt and Road Initiative (BRI) in the domains of energy and transit. Since BRI's launch in 2013, many scholars, experts, and officials have denounced it as a geoeconomic instrument that aims to upend the U.S.-led liberal order, thanks to massive investments, skyrocketing trade flows, and soaring debts.[1] Yet, most of those studies only approach Belt and Road as a vehicle for bilateral coercion that produces immediate and tangible effects. Despite valuable insights, this narrative misses the real story. By contrast, this chapter argues that the main impact of the BRI's expansion in the domains of energy and transit is to gradually empower China's nascent asymmetric global networks (finance, data, and so on) and to slowly degrade the sources of America's weaponization of interdependence. While less commonly understood, those (mostly) immaterial dynamics could generate potent strategic gains in the long term.

The chapter proceeds in four sections. First, it discusses the natural affinities between the Belt and Road Initiative and the concept of weaponized interdependence. Second, it explores the structural limitations of the Chinese endeavor's coercion potential. Third, it investigates the panopticon and choke-point effects that BRI could yield over time. Fourth, it examines how Belt and Road erodes the foundations of America's weaponization of interdependence. The chapter's conclusion discusses scholarly and policy implications.

BRI and Weaponized Interdependence: Natural Affinities

At first sight, the BRI seems propitious to the use of weaponized interdependence, which Henry Farrell and Abraham Newman define as a state's ability to "leverage [asymmetric] network structures as a coercive tool."[2] As a global network linking hundreds of nodes (ports, airports, reactors, and so on) with countless ties (roads, railways, pipelines, and more) that all lead to Beijing, the Chinese endeavor possesses a genuine potential for interdependence. Exploiting unique assets such as massive foreign reserves and an enormous and fast-growing market, China has already convinced about 150 countries to endorse BRI, although some of those endorsements have not yet translated into concrete projects.[3] As of mid-2019, Belt and Road's investments totaled $575 billion, 46 percent of which were allocated to energy and electric power, and 25 percent to transportation and shipping.[4]

The appeal of BRI derives from powerful dynamics. On the one hand, the world suffers from an infrastructure investment gap estimated at $15 trillion for 2019 to 2040, a deficit particularly pronounced among developing countries.[5] On the other hand, China is ramping up its international economic profile to satisfy growing needs and ambitions. In the energy domain, Beijing should become the world's top oil consumer by 2030;[6] its public and private actors are expected to spend $6 trillion on green technologies by 2040;[7] and its investments accelerate Eurasia's "ever-tightening mutual energy embrace."[8] Transit sectors have recorded similar dynamics. For instance, Chinese companies handle 39 percent of the traffic of the top ten global port operators;[9] new Eurasian railways enabled more than 11,000 freight trains to connect China and Europe in 2011–2018;[10] and Beijing signed a memorandum of understanding (MOU) with the African Union in 2015 for the construction of highways, airports, and other transportation infrastructure to link the continent's fifty-four countries to one another.[11] Besides enormous economic capabilities, China has "legal and regulatory institutions" that enable and optimize the weaponization of interdependence.[12] Indeed, thanks to its inherent centralization of power, which President Xi Jinping has enhanced in recent years, Beijing's authoritarian regime can easily mobilize national resources, bend existing regulations, pass new legislation, and shape domestic perceptions to push strategic objectives without excessive domestic resistance.[13]

Limitations of BRI's Short-Term Coercion Potential

There are structural limits to the application of the concept of weaponized interdependence to Belt and Road in energy and transit sectors. First, the BRI as a whole has drawn severe skepticism. Many experts have dismissed the Chinese endeavor as a mere slogan driven by domestic politics, have stressed its continuities with past investment patterns, and have emphasized Beijing's misleading statistics.[14] Moreover, ambiguities, flaws, and uncertainties abound even if one assumes that Xi Jinping advances a genuine strategic vision. Belt and Road's implementation is influenced by competing domestic bureaucratic actors and business leaders, as well as myriad foreign recipients, who all seek the funds and stamp of legitimacy provided by the BRI to pursue their own interests.[15] Highlighting China's recent economic difficulties and long string of failed projects abroad, some critics have also questioned the BRI's financial sustainability.[16] Meanwhile, others point at the multiple controversies observed on the ground, contending that a growing number of partner states and local communities are rising up against Beijing's economic, social, political, and environmental abuses.[17] Finally, many states across the world (especially in the West) have declined to join the BRI, although some may change course later on.

Another limitation derives from the fact that the energy and transit domains themselves are not entirely conducive to the emergence of highly "asymmetric network structures."[18] Indeed, these domains differ in three ways from the sectors of financial messaging and internet communications that Farrell and Newman explored in their article. To begin, transit and energy are deeply rooted in the real world, and rely on physical assets that are scattered across the globe and, hence, difficult to place under any single centralized state control. Likewise, although geography constrains a state's strategic calculations, it usually allows national leaders to diversify the lines of communication supposed to secure their country's access to natural resources and economic centers across the globe.[19] Finally, attempts to project influence abroad must cope with geographic distance and with the "loss of strength gradient force" that it implies.[20] Altogether, those factors inhibit any state's ability to achieve the global asymmetric position necessary for a full-fledged weaponization of interdependence. Consider, for example, that there is no such thing as a worldwide pipeline, a global gas market (although that might partly change with the rise of liquified natural gas, LNG), or (with a few exceptions) a unique route from country A to country B.[21] Along similar lines, Farrell and Newman point out that "oil markets are sufficiently diversified [to ensure that there is] no single point of control."[22] More broadly, they even emphasize that "market transfers of commodities with a significant number of suppliers and no need for network infrastructure are unlikely to be subject to [weaponized interdependence]."[23]

The last factor concerns the United States (and the West writ large). Although in relative decline, America's hegemony is likely to reduce the impact of any Chinese weaponization of interdependence, if not deter any such attempt or blunt Beijing's efforts to attain sufficient asymmetric network power in the first place. To begin, Washington has long entrenched its influence in or near most of the planet's energy-rich countries. Admittedly, many of those countries have developed strong economic relations with Beijing in recent years. Yet, for all the uncertainties (fiscal constraints, war fatigue, the shale gas revolution, and so on) surrounding its grand strategy, the United States is still able to blunt China's pull, thanks to its significant financial appeal and to its central security role in the "maintenance" of the global energy system.[24] Second, America's military can capitalize on its "command of the commons," the closest equivalent to an asymmetric network structure in the domain of worldwide shipping.[25] Were a high-intensity conflict to erupt because of a Chinese attempt to weaponize interdependence, the United States could potentially disrupt the vital lines of communication that link China's territory to Middle Eastern oil and gas resources via the Straits of Hormuz and Malacca.[26] Third, despite the Donald Trump administration's inward turn, Western actors still have the upper hand over Beijing in global governance institutions and worldwide foreign direct investment (FDI) levels.[27] Finally, the great powers that worry about China's rise have all recently launched their own connectivity initiatives, including the U.S.-led Blue Dot Network, the Indo-Japanese Asia-Africa Growth Corridor, and the European Union's (EU's) Eurasia connectivity plan.[28] Although unlikely to reach the Belt and Road Initiative's mammoth scale, those endeavors are bound to curb Beijing's geoeconomic appeal and to reduce "exit costs" for BRI members willing to escape China's orbit.

Second Order Consequences: Panopticon and Choke-Point Effects

The above-mentioned reservations notwithstanding, there are undeniable affinities between Belt and Road and the concept of weaponized interdependence. First, the Chinese initiative's resilience should not be underestimated. Although Beijing's FDI levels have been less exuberant since 2016, recent trends suggest a deepening of China-centric global networks along key BRI routes and sectors of activity. Beijing signed Belt and Road contracts worth $128 billion in the first eleven months of 2019 (+41 percent)[29] and its commerce with other members reached $1.34 trillion during that year, an increase of 10.8 percent (compared to 3.4 percent for the country's aggregate foreign trade growth).[30] Second, although state and substate actors can still hijack BRI money and abuses still occur on the ground, Xi Jinping's government has tightened its oversight and tried to address some critics.[31] Third, in contrast with the private entities that drive Western global FDI, China's outward investments, which mostly emanate from state-owned enterprises or from companies close to the government, can more easily be calibrated for strategic purposes.[32] Fourth, energy and transit infrastructures work in tandem with other facets of the BRI, including telecommunications, finance, and military expansion.[33] Last, as it expands, Belt and Road augments China's influence over global standards (high-speed trains, ultra-high voltage, and more), which might help it develop asymmetric network structures in the long term.[34]

In light of those elements, and provided that one relaxes the initial boundaries of the concept of weaponized interdependence, it is possible to argue that the BRI generates a certain degree of structural coercion. Although the latter may not reach the threshold set by Farrell and Newman, it could both affect BRI members' strategic calculations and erode Washington's ability to weaponize interdependence against China (or third parties). In investigating those dynamics below, one should note that many of the described scenarios constitute potentialities that remain hotly debated and might not ever materialize, given the shrouds of secrecy, controversy, and uncertainty that surround the BRI.

Belt and Road's energy and transit infrastructures could help China exert major panopticon effects—that is, the ability to use "physical access to or jurisdiction over hub nodes . . . to obtain information."[35] Contrary to America and the EU, whose democratic systems create significant (albeit far from insurmountable) domestic constraints, Beijing's authoritarian regime can easily leverage its huge national security apparatus, disregard for intellectual property, and disrespect of privacy norms to conduct pervasive surveillance activities against foreign actors.[36]

Several examples come to mind in the energy domain. Although the creation of a Eurasian network appears unrealistic, investments in southern European electricity grids (for example, in Italy, Greece, and Portugal) could allow China to extract private data from millions of local citizens.[37] In a different vein, investments in nuclear reactors (such as in Britain or Romania) and nuclear joint ventures (with French companies) could enable industrial espionage.[38] Transit sectors have witnessed similar patterns. The Chinese government could leverage its projects on Israeli ports, railways, and tunnels to spy on local economic actors and collect intelligence in the eastern Mediterranean region.[39] Likewise, as is currently being discussed, if Chinese companies were to contribute to Britain's future HS2 high-speed railway network, Beijing might be able to deploy espionage devices along the railway's branches.[40] More broadly, the economic bonds cemented by Chinese energy and transit infrastructures help to promote the "Digital Silk Road," which could yield massive panopticon effects thanks to China-built optic cables and 5G internet systems.[41]

Beijing may also use Belt and Road to wield choke-point effects—that is, "limit or penalize use of hubs by third parties (e.g., other states or private actors)."[42] This assessment applies to the global shipping industry.[43] As it acquires more terminals worldwide, China may redirect a growing share of international traffic toward BRI facilities, which could then give preferential access to Chinese transport companies.[44] Combined with the unmatched "rate of completed construction . . . volume of new orders, and . . . volume of holding orders" of Beijing's shipbuilding industry,[45] and with its ability to reorient shipbuilding supply chains thanks to an unparalleled purchasing power, those dynamics could weaken Western competitors.[46] Under that scenario, China would bolster its leverage over many littoral states. This phenomenon could also occur continentally as Chinese-funded roads and railways provide landlocked countries such as Central Asian Republics with key pathways to the rest of the world.[47] Similar trends may unfold in the domain of energy. As Beijing uses BRI to increase its share of the planet's "strategic metals and minerals," it could impact the world's most developed economies, as shown by the pull that its grip over cobalt resources exerts on the German automobile industry.[48] Likewise, if successful, the construction of a network of dams in China, Laos, Myanmar, and other states could boost Beijing's strategic leverage over all of the South and Southeast Asian countries located downstream.[49] China will not necessarily use those energy and transit assets for coercive purposes. But other states will be more inclined to take its strategic interests into account in the first place.

In addition, BRI might translate into the seizure of strategic infrastructure. China's massive money infusions could potentially compromise the financial solvency of numerous partner states. In recent years, more and more experts have denounced Beijing's so-called debt-trap diplomacy, or FDIs designed to aggravate recipients' bilateral debt so as to force them to make substantial concessions, such as Sri Lanka's leasing of the port of Hambantota to China for ninety-nine years in December 2017.[50] Additionally, some believe that, in time of major crisis, Beijing might curtail the activities of (or even assume control over) other states' critical infrastructure (ports, railways, and so on) to influence their policy or curtail enemy maneuvers.[51] Finally, BRI disputes are settled in Chinese courts, which may give China another channel of action to confiscate foreign assets.[52]

However, those nightmare scenarios deserve some perspective. Although worthy of attention, most are based on worst assumptions mitigated by BRI's weaknesses, the West's alternative connectivity plans, and Beijing's likely unwillingness to engage in reckless behaviors that could prove disastrous from both strategic and reputational standpoints. For instance, despite its popularity with many scholars and decisionmakers, the debt-trap diplomacy thesis has its limits.[53] First, triggering waves of bankruptcies abroad would deal a lethal blow to China's precarious financial system. Second, Beijing's investments in Africa and Latin America have had largely positive effects in the last few decades.[54] Third, for all its denunciations of China's practices, the West has long neglected poor countries while imposing development standards designed to increase recipients' dependency and advance its own interests.[55] To be sure, Beijing has indulged in abuses, and BRI accentuates its coercion potential. Yet the problem should not be exaggerated, and China's intentions may not warrant a systematic demonization.

Second Order Consequences: Erosion of America's Weaponization of Interdependence

Beyond panopticon and choke-point effects, a more indirect link exists between the BRI and the concept of weaponized interdependence. Indeed, regardless of whether Beijing attains the latter's required degree of asymmetric network power, BRI could gradually curtail the United States' ability and willingness to weaponize interdependence against China (and third parties).

For instance, Beijing's energy and transit investments could erode Washington's ability to weaponize its military command over the pathways used by China's key global shipping networks. Belt and Road helps diversify Beijing's maritime itineraries, and its new terrestrial routes and pipelines reduce the country's vulnerability to the U.S. Navy. The initiative's transit and energy infrastructures participate in the emergence of a global Chinese intelligence network that has already incited Washington to approach some of its operations and strategic partnerships more cautiously.[56] Additionally, as Beijing increases its economic presence near the world's choke points, local leaders may become more resistant to any efforts to cut Chinese lines of communication.[57] More broadly, the growing military contributions that China makes to protect its sea lines of communication (SLOC) along BRI itineraries are likely to cast a shadow over America's monopoly on the provision of global public goods such as the free flow of oil.[58]

This pushback is visible in the financial sector as well. Belt and Road's development strengthens Beijing's long-standing ambition to erode the United States' monetary dominance.[59] China's investments and trade flows in the realms of energy and transit help internationalize the renminbi (RMB); the petro-yuan, created in 2018, bolsters the credibility of the Chinese currency.[60] The massive Sino-European trade and investment relationship offers both parties incentives to work against Washington's monetary hegemony and extra-regional sanctions.[61] Along similar lines, joint projects such as oil pipelines and the "Polar Silk Road" facilitate China and Russia's collaboration on new payment systems that circumvent U.S. networks.[62] Admittedly, Beijing is unlikely to rival America's global financial position in the near future, if at all. Nonetheless, the alternative channels that it promotes may suffice to gradually reduce Washington's ability to weaponize interdependence in the financial domain.

Conclusion

Despite notable caveats, applying the concept of weaponized interdependence to the BRI's expansion in the domains of energy and transit offers a unique window into the Sino-American strategic competition. For all of its problems and ambiguities, BRI could give China a certain degree of asymmetric network power over time. Beijing's endeavor is unlikely to yield the full-blown weaponized interdependence potential that the United States has attained in sectors like financial messaging and internet communications. But the Belt and Road Initiative's energy and transit dimensions may gradually generate potent panopticon and choke-point effects while eroding America's ability to weaponize interdependence against China (and third parties).

This analysis has important policy implications. Given Beijing's economic might and authoritarian institutions, U.S. leaders must brace for a relative decline of America's weaponized interdependence potential. In the meantime, to protect third parties, they should mount a geoeconomic response that protects nonphysical asymmetric global networks (5G internet, finance, and others), secures the transmission belts connecting physical infrastructure to those networks, and focuses on the states that are most "integrated into the international economy."[63] However, given the depth of Washington's first-mover advantage and the difficulty of creating alternative asymmetric global networks, an overly belligerent approach is unwarranted. In fact, an effective response to China's rise will require addressing the significant frustrations that America's heavy-handed use of weaponized interdependence has caused among allies and partners to avoid tempting them to drift toward Beijing to resist the United States.

Finally, this analysis opens promising avenues for future research. The concept of weaponized interdependence both contradicts the realist paradigm on the limited fungibility of economic power, and highlights the gaps of the economic trade and conflict literature on coercion and global asymmetric networks.[64] Those literatures now need to be connected and cross-fertilized to achieve a better understanding of the BRI, China's geoeconomics, and twenty-first-century great power competition. This will necessitate more studies that systematically investigate how asymmetric global economic networks emerge and operate, their interactions with real-world power dynamics at multiple levels (local, national, regional), and the potent synergies that those interactions can yield in the long term.

Notes

1. *Bruno Maçães, Belt and Road: A Chinese World Order* (London: Hurst & Company, 2018), pp. 5–8; Farah N. Jan and Justin Melnick, "China's Challenge to America's Economic and Political Liberal Order," *National Interest*, January 6, 2020; Brahma Chellaney, "China's Debt-Trap Diplomacy," *Project Syndicate*, January 23, 2017.

2. Henry Farrell and Abraham L. Newman, "Weaponized Interdependence: How Global Economic Networks Shape State Coercion," *International Security* 44, no. 1 (Summer 2019), p. 43.

3. On China's geoeconomic assets, see Robert D. Blackwill and Jennifer M. Harris, *War by Other Means: Geoeconomics and Statecraft* (Harvard University Press, 2016), pp. 129–51; William J. Norris, *Chinese Economic Statecraft: Commercial Actors, Grand Strategy, and State Control* (Cornell University Press, 2016), pp. 58–65.

4. Michele Ruta and others, "Belt and Road Economics: Opportunities and Risks of Transport Corridors," *The World Bank*, 2019, p. 38.

5. Anita George, Rashad-Rudolf Kaldany, and Joseph Losavio, "The World Is Facing a $15 Trillion Infrastructure Gap. Here's How to Bridge It," *World Economic Forum*, April 11, 2019; Branko Milanovic, "The West Is Mired in 'Soft' Development. China is Trying the Hard Stuff," *Guardian*, May 17, 2017.

6. Kent E. Calder, *Super Continent: The Logic of Eurasian Integration* (Stanford University Press, 2019), p. 81.

7. Amy Myers Jaffe, "Green Giant: Renewable Energy and Chinese Power," *Foreign Affairs* 97, no. 2 (March/April 2018), p. 87.

8. Kent E. Calder, *The New Continentalism: Energy and Twenty-First Century Eurasian Geopolitics* (Yale University Press, 2012), p. 2.

9. James Kynge and others, "How China Rules the Waves," *Financial Times*, January 12, 2017.

10. "China Sends a Record 6,300 Cargo Trains to Europe in 2018," *Global Times*, January 4, 2019.

11. Alice Ekman and others, "Three Years of China's New Silk Roads: From Words to (Re)action?" *Institut Français des Relations Internationales*, February 2017, p. 63.

12. Farrell and Newman, "Weaponized Interdependence," p. 57.

13. Matt Schrader, "Domestic Criticism May Signal Shrunken Belt and Road Ambitions," *Jamestown Foundation*, August 10, 2018; on BRI and Xi Jinping's centralization of power, see Elizabeth C. Economy, *The Third Revolution: Xi Jinping and the New Chinese State* (Oxford University Press, 2018).

14. Min Ye, "Fragmentation and Mobilization: Domestic Politics of the Belt and Road in China," *Journal of Contemporary China* 28, no. 119 (2019), pp. 696–711; Eyck Freymann, " 'One Belt, One Road' Is Just a Marketing

Campaign," *The Atlantic*, August 17, 2019; Jonathan E. Hillman, "China's Belt and Road Is Full of Holes," Center for Strategic and International Studies, September 4, 2018.

15. Lee Jones and Yizheng Zou, "Rethinking the Role of State-Owned Enterprises in China's Rise," *New Political Economy* 22 (2017), p. 744.

16. Lily Kuo, "Belt and Road Forum: China's 'Project of the Century' Hits Tough Times," *The Guardian*, April 24, 2019; Chris Horton, "The Costs of China's Belt and Road Expansion," *The Atlantic*, January 9, 2020.

17. Jonathan E. Hillman, "Corruption Flows along China's Belt and Road," Center for Strategic and International Studies, January 18, 2019; James Kynge, "Chinese Contractors Grab Lion's Share of Silk Road Projects," *Financial Times*, January 24, 2018.

18. Farrell and Newman, "Weaponized Interdependence," p. 45.

19. See Jakub J. Grygiel, *Great Powers and Geopolitical Change* (Johns Hopkins University Press, 2006).

20. Kenneth E. Boulding, *Conflict and Defense: A General Theory* (New York: Harper, 1962); Patrick Porter, *The Global Village Myth: Distance, War, and the Limits of Power* (Georgetown University Press, 2015).

21. Mikkal Herberg, "Pipeline Politics in Asia: Implications for the United States," in *Pipeline Politics in Asia: The Intersection of Demand, Energy Markets, and Supply Routes, National Bureau of Asian Research*, edited by Mikkal Herberg, special report no. 23 (September 2010), p. 69.

22. Farrell and Newman, "Weaponized Interdependence," p. 76.

23. Ibid., p. 50, note 26.

24. Doug Stokes and Sam Raphael, *Global Energy Security and American Hegemony* (Johns Hopkins University Press, 2010), pp. 1–2, 15; Daniel W. Drezner, "Military Primacy Doesn't Pay (Nearly as Much as You Think)," *International Security* 38 (Summer 2013), pp. 67–77.

25. Barry R. Posen, "Command of the Commons: The Military Foundations of U.S. Hegemony," *International Security* 28 (Summer 2003), pp. 5–46.

26. John Garver, "China–Iran Relations: Cautious Friendship with America's Nemesis," *China Report* 49 (2013), p. 73; Marc Lanteigne, "China's Maritime Security and the 'Malacca Dilemma,'" *Asian Security* 4 (2008), pp. 143–61.

27. James X. Zhan and others, "World Investment Report 2019: Key Messages and Overview," *United Nations Conference on Trade and Development*, 2019, p. 4.

28. Matthew P. Goodman, Daniel F. Runde, Johnathan E. Hillman, "Connecting the Blue Dots," Center for Strategic and International Studies, February 20, 2020; Anit Prakash, "The Asia-Africa Growth Corridor: Bringing Together Old partnerships and New Initiatives," Observer Research Foundation, April 25, 2018; Robin Emmott, "In Counterweight to China, EU-Japan Sign Deal to Link Asia," Reuters, September 27, 2019.

29. Keith Bradsher, "China Renews Its Belt and Road Push for Global Sway," *New York Times*, January 15, 2020

30. "China's Trade with BRI Countries Booms in 2019," *XinhuaNet*, January 14, 2020.

31. Nadège Rolland, "Beijing's Response to the Belt and Road Initiative's Pushback: A Story of Assessment and Adaptation," *Asian Affairs* 50 (2019), pp. 216–35.

32. Lee Jones and Yizheng Zhou, "Rethinking the Role of State-Owned Companies in China's Rise," *New Political Economy* 22 (November 2017), pp. 743–60.

33. Thomas P. Cavanna, "Unlocking the Gates of Eurasia: China's Belt and Road Initiative and its Implications for U.S. Grand Strategy," *Texas National Security Review* 2 (May 2019), pp. 11–37.

34. "Power Play: China's Ultra-High Voltage Technology," *Paulson Institute*, April 2015, pp. 14–26; Peter Cai, "Understanding China's Belt and Road Initiative," *Lowy Institute*, March 2017, p. 10; Jaffe, "Green Giant," p. 90; Andrew Polk, "China Is Quietly Setting Global Standards," *Bloomberg*, May 6, 2018.

35. Farrell and Newman, "Weaponized Interdependence," p. 55.

36. Murray Scott Tanner, "Beijing's New National Intelligence Law: From Defense to Offense," *Lawfare*, July 20, 2017; Charlie Campbell, " 'The Entire System Is Designed to Suppress Us.' What the Chinese Surveillance State Means for the Rest of the World," *Time*, November 21, 2019.

37. James Kynge and Lucy Horny, "China Eyes Role as World's Power Supplier," *Financial Times*, June 6, 2018; Miguel Otero-Iglesias and Manuel Weissenegger, "Motivations, Security Threats and Geopolitical Implications of Chinese Investment in the EU Energy Sector: The Case of CDP Reti," *European Journal of International Relations*, first published September 12, 2019, p 16.

38. Steve Thomas, "China's Nuclear Export Drive: Trojan Horse or Marshall Plan?" *Energy Policy* 101 (February 2017), p. 690.

39. Yossi Melman, "China Is Spying on Israel to Steal U.S. Secrets," *Foreign Policy*, March 24, 2019; Admiral Shaul Chorev and others, "The Eastern Mediterranean in the New Era of Major Power Competition: Prospects for U.S.-Israeli Cooperation," *Hudson Institute*, September 2019, pp. 20–22.

40. Thomas, "China's Nuclear Export Drive," p. 690.

41. Jeremy Page, Kate O'Keeffe, and Rob Taylor, "America's Undersea Battle with China for Control of the Global Internet Grid," *Wall Street Journal*, March 12, 2019; Eli Huang, "China's Cable Strategy: Exploring Global Undersea Dominance," *Real Clear World Politics*, December 4, 2017; James Vincent, "Don't Use Huawei Phones, Say Heads of FBI, CIA and NSA," *The Verge*, February 14, 2018.

42. Farrell and Newman, "Weaponized Interdependence," pp. 55–56.

43. Matthieu Duchâtel, "China's Port Investments: The Flag behind the Trade," *Institut Montaigne*, June 2019.

44. Frans-Paul van der Putten, "European Seaports and Chinese Strategic Influence: The Relevance of the Maritime Silk Road for the Netherlands," *Clingendael*, December 2019, pp. 15–18; Cullen Hendrix, "Rough Patches on the Silk Road? Security Implications of China's Belt and Road Initiative," in *China's Belt and Road Initiative: Motives, Scope, and Challenges*, edited by Simeon Djankov and Sean Miner, Peterson Institute for International Economics, March 2016, p. 26.

45. Devin Thorne and Ben Spevack, "Harboured Ambitions: How China's Port Investments Are Strategically Reshaping the Indo-Pacific," *Center for Advanced Defense Studies*, 2017, p. 18.

46. Jonathan Holslag, *The Silk Road Trap, How China's Trade Ambitions Challenge Europe* (Cambridge, United Kingdom: Polity Press, 2019), pp. 102–5, 112.

47. "Central Asia's Economic Evolution from Russia to China," *Stratfor*, April 5, 2018.

48. Susan Crawford, "China Will Likely Corner the 5G Market—and the U.S. Has No Plan," *Wired*, February 20, 2019; Henry Sanderson, "China Tightens Grip on Global Cobalt Supplies," *Financial Times*, March 14, 2018; *Wolfgang Münchau*, "China Gains the Upper Hand over Germany," *Financial Times*, March 3, 2019.

49. Yaw Bawm Mangshang and Ashley South, "China, India, and Myitsone: The Power Game to Come," *Frontier Myanmar*, March 1, 2019.

50. Kari Lindberg and Tripti Lahiri, "From Asia to Africa, China's Debt Trap Diplomacy Was Under Siege in 2018," *Quartz*, December 28, 2018.

51. Andrea Kendall-Taylor, Hearing on "China's Expanding Influence in Europe and Eurasia," prepared statement, U.S. House Subcommittee on Europe, Eurasia, Energy, and the Environment, May 2019, p. 6.

52. "A Belt-and-Road Court Dreams of Rivalling the West's Tribunals," *The Economist*, June 6, 2019; Jonathan Hillman and Matthew Woodman, "China's Belt-and-Road Court to Challenge Current U.S.-led Order," *Financial Times*, June 24, 2018.

53. Deborah Brautigam, "A Critical Look at Chinese 'Debt-Trap Diplomacy': The Rise of a Meme," *Area Development and Policy 5* (2020), pp. 1–14; Jacob Mardell, "China's Belt and Road Partners Aren't Fools," *Foreign Policy*, May 1, 2019.

54. Axel Dreher and others, "Aid, China, and Growth: Evidence from a New Global Development Finance Dataset," AidData, working paper 46 (October 2017).

55. W. Gyude Moore, "2018 FOCAC: Africa in the New Reality of Reduced Chinese Lending," Center for Global Development, August 31, 2018; Daron Acemoğlu and James Robinson, "The Economic Impact of Colonial-

ism," Center for Economic and Policy Research, policy portal, January 20, 2017; Joseph E. Stiglitz, *Globalization and Its Discontents* (New York: W.W. Norton, 2002).

56. Leah Dreyfuss and Mara Karli, "All That Xi Wants: China Attempts to Ace Bases Overseas," Brookings, September 2019, pp. 5–6; Michael Wilner, "U.S. Navy May Stop Docking in Haifa After Chinese Take Over Port," *Jerusalem Post*, December 15, 2018; Shira Efron and others, "The Evolving Israel-China Relationship," Rand Corporation, 2019, pp. 107–9.

57. Jennifer Lind and Daryl G. Press, "Markets or Mercantilism? How China Secures Its Energy Supplies," *International Security* 42 (Spring 2018), pp. 191–99.

58. Michael Clarke, "The Belt and Road Initiative: Exploring Beijing's Motivations and Challenges for its New Silk Road," *Strategic Analysis* 42 (2018), p. 86.

59. Gregory T. Chin, "True Revisionist: China and the Global Monetary System," in *China's Global Engagement: Cooperation, Competition and Influence in the 21st Century*, edited by Jacques deLisle and Avery Goldstein, (Brookings Institution Press, 2017), pp. 35–66.

60. John A. Mathews and Mark Selden, "China's Petro-Yuan Is Going Global, and Gunning for the U.S. Dollar," *South China Morning Post*, December 4, 2018.

61. Frances Coppola, "Europe Circumvents U.S. Sanctions on Iran," *Forbes*, June 30, 2019; Nicola Casarini, "The Internationalization of the Renminbi and the Role of the Euro," *China-U.S. Focus*, January 8, 2014; Chin, "True Revisionist," pp. 46–47, 51–52.

62. Karen Yeung, "Could China, Russia Ditch the U.S. Dollar with New Payment System to Avoid Sanction," *South China Morning Post*, November 22, 2018.

63. Farrell and Newman, "Weaponized Interdependence," p. 76.

64. Robert S. Ross, "On the Fungibility of Economic Power: China's Economic Rise and the East Asian Security Order," *European Journal of International Relations*, first published March 16, 2018, pp. 302–27.

VI

RESPONSES TO WEAPONIZED INTERDEPENDENCE

13

Weaponized Interdependence, the Dynamics of Twenty-first Century Power, and U.S. Grand Strategy

BRUCE W. JENTLESON

What are the implications of weaponized interdependence for overall thinking about American grand strategy, both within international relations theory and for policy applicability? And what are the counterpart implications of grand strategy for the utility of weaponized interdependence?

A main value of weaponized interdependence (WI), Henry Farrell and Abraham Newman contend, is as a structural theory of power based on economic interactions operating through networks in which private actors play crucial roles, such that states "with political authority over the central nodes in the international networked structures . . . are able to leverage interdependent relations to coerce others."[1] While I agree that WI has significant power compared to more traditional theories of international power, it too has the limits inherent in structural theories: that is, it insufficiently distinguishes between power as the possession of resources and influence as the capacity to wield those resources to achieve state policy objectives.[2]

Farrell and Newman do acknowledge an aspect of this—the importance of "appropriate institutions" to harness private-sector actors and their asymmetrically interdependent networks for state objectives. But they leave its general theoretical bases and empirical validation underdeveloped. In the spirit of friendly amendment, I flesh out the theoretical bases and delve into the United States as a validating case study.

More critically, in not considering the array of counterstrategies by which targeted states can reduce economic impact or absorb it but resist being coerced into policy changes, the theory of WI is too static and insufficiently interactive. To the extent that Farrell and Newman acknowledge target state strategies, it is more about economic autonomy measures than political and strategic ones, which are no less and arguably even more crucial. Notwithstanding that networks are broader than state-state dyads common in economic sanctions cases, propositions in the sanctions literature about "target state defenses" bear on this point.[3] The global finance–Iran case, which Farrell and Newman use as a central WI example, shows the importance of a more interactive approach.

For WI's structural theory of power to bridge that power-influence gap, greater attention must be paid to "harnessing" and "countering" to the domestic constraints a coercer state must overcome to wield WI power, and to the interactive action-reaction with target state counterstrategies that determine the extent of influence achieved. I develop these analyses in the next two sections. The final section puts WI in the broader context of grand strategy and overall twenty-first-century systemic dynamics, including interconnecting with other chapters in this volume and, while continuing the focus on the United States, with broader significance for major power grand strategy in general.

Harnessing Weaponized Interdependence: U.S. Domestic Constraints

Farrell and Newman assert that "Variation in domestic institutions in terms of capacity and key norms may limit their states' ability to use these coercive tools."[4] They rightly position domestic institutions as an independent variable affecting coercer state WI capacity. But domestic institutions also need to be cast as a dependent variable so as to assess the key factors shaping that harnessing capacity. This is important both for understanding the WI power that a particular state can exert and for cross-state comparisons of how respective domestic structures enhance or constrain state capacity to use WI as part of their grand strategies.

I am drawn back to the domestic structures framework developed by Peter Katzenstein, Stephen Krasner, and others. Their focus was on 1970s advanced industrial democracies—otherwise rather similar political systems but for which they found significant differences along a strong/weak state continuum in how respective domestic structures shape foreign economic policy. Krasner's case study of the United States put it very much in the weaker state category, with its central feature being "the fragmentation and dispersion of power and authority," making it "very difficult for American central decision makers to change the behavior of non-state domestic actors."[5] This tracks with work by Theodore Lowi and other American politics scholars, and traces back to foundational pillars of the American constitutional order, such as separation of powers, federalism, and the core Lockean precept that "government that governs least governs best."[6] For all the virtues that Daron Acemoglu and James Robinson see in how societal norms and political-legal mechanisms promote liberty by "shackling" the American version of Leviathan, they also show concern for the ways in which public authority is constrained from developing effective public policy.[7]

Issues and situations in which the national security rationale can be invoked have provided state-empowering exceptions. During World War I, for example, President Woodrow Wilson requested, and Congress approved, powers over the economy that were "more extensive than those possessed by any other ruler in the Western world," in the view of noted historians Samuel Eliot Morison and Henry Steele Commager.[8] Franklin Roosevelt's wartime powers were even more sweeping, such as the War Production Board, with its broad power over industry, and the Office of Price Administration, which set prices and rationed the most basic consumer goods. During the Cold War, with its overarching specter of nuclear war, what Daniel Yergin called "the gospel of national security" provided the basis for enormous expansion of governmental and, especially, presidential authority. Michael Mastanduno points out in his chapter in this volume, the broad scope of authority that the 1949 Export Control Act granted based on the Cold War rationale.[9] The 1950 Defense Production Act provided President Harry Truman with quite extensive powers during the Korean War—and, as has been more than noted, could have provided comparable authority and capacity during the 2020 COVID-19 crisis had President Donald Trump invoked it sooner and more systematically.[10]

Yet, while highly elastic, the national security rationale has not been infinitely so. When, in response to the 1979 Soviet invasion of Afghanistan, the Jimmy Carter administration sought to weaponize America's nearly 75 percent share of Soviet grain imports, opposition from American farmers was a factor in Carter's 1980 reelection defeat. The politics can be even more blatant, as with President Trump's personal intervention to block possible criminal penalties for Iran sanctions violations against Halkbank, one of Turkey's largest state-owned banks and thus a source of potential leverage, but with which Trump political cronies had lucrative lobbying contracts.[11]

Indeed, the private profit interests of American companies have diverged from U.S. foreign policy, national security, and geostrategic interests with some frequency. To go back to another 1970s seminal work, *U.S. Power and the Multinational Corporation*, Robert Gilpin questions the widespread assumption that American hegemony and MNC expansion were "overlapping and complementary interests":

> We live in a world in which technological knowledge diffuses to America's foreign competitors at a faster and faster rate. . . . The paradox of an interdependent world economy is that it creates sources of insecurity and competition . . . [which] cause anxieties and suspicions which exacerbate international relations.[12]

Fast forwarding about fifty years, American companies are stashing some 20 percent of corporate profits earned from global investments in foreign tax havens (ten times more than in the 1980s) to keep them beyond the reach of the same U.S. government that negotiated the investment treaties and other agreements that make such earnings possible.[13] Tech firms and investors are involved with China's face recognition and other "Orwellian state" technology developments and deployments. Netflix censored a show critical of Saudi crown prince Mohammed Bin Salman to keep its market access. McKinsey has worked with some of the very Russian companies against which sanctions have been imposed.[14] While, in some of these cases, the Trump administration has not been all that unhappy with such relationships, the public-private interest divergence pattern preceded Trump and will continue after him, significantly constraining WI harnessing capacity.

In sum, notwithstanding its formidable power endowments and favorable transnational hub positionings, American WI harnessing capacity faces significant internal constraints. What, though, of the financial sector, which Farrell and Newman argue is a domain in which the United States holds a particularly potent position, both choke point and panopticon?

Countering Target State Strategies: Limits of U.S. Financial Coercion against Iran

The Barack Obama administration considered the 2015 Iran nuclear nonproliferation agreement, formally known as the Joint Comprehensive Plan of Action (JCPOA), one of its major foreign policy successes. The Farrell and Newman account of how U.S. choke-point capacity through the Society for Worldwide Interbank Financial Telecommunications (SWIFT)—combined with the dollar's centrality to international finance—was a key factor in achieving the JCPOA both tracks with other accounts and is consistent with the broader literature on the particular utility of financial sanctions.[15] The United States had worked the diplomacy with the P5+1 coalition (consisting of China, Russia, France, the United Kingdom, and the United States as the five permanent members of the UN Security Council, plus Germany for its role in earlier negotiations with Iran). The council's Resolution 1929 was passed in June 2010, tightening financial and other sanctions on Iran on a multilateral basis. Within those sanctions, the United States had directly targeted SWIFT as a lever. Iranian oil exports were brought down from 2.5 million barrels per day (MMb/d) in 2011 to 1.1 MMb/d in 2015, and then allowed to increase to 2.1 MMb/d post-JCPOA. Iran's GDP growth rates, once as low as -9 percent, boomed to 13 percent post-JCPOA. Inflation, as high as 60 percent, fell to single digits in 2016. The rial foreign exchange rate, down by over 200 percent, started to level off.

Why, then, has Trump's "maximum pressure" strategy not achieved its policy objectives despite inflicting even harsher economic costs? Iranian oil exports were squeezed to less than 300,000 barrels per day (b/d). GDP was down -10 percent, and inflation back up to 40 percent. Youth unemployment was 29 percent. The rial had to be so devalued that the regime renamed it the toman, with a unit revaluation of 10,000 to 1.[16]

Consistent with choke-point theory, European efforts to route around American secondary sanctions have had limited impact. Even with the European Union's (EU's) August 2018 "blocking statute" seeking to protect European firms from the Trump sanctions, firms still saw greater risks in not complying with the U.S. measures. A month later, Germany, France, and Britain joined with Russia and China in creating a "special purpose vehicle" (SPV) to facilitate trade with Iran by avoiding dollar-denominated transactions or other exposure to the U.S. market. In January 2019, this vehicle was officially registered as the Instrument for Supporting Trade Exchanges (INSTEX). Yet, it was not until March 31, 2020, that INSTEX actually completed its first transaction.[17]

The 200 percent increase in domestic gasoline prices and supply rationing that the Iranian government was forced to impose in November 2019 as part of sanctions-induced austerity set off the most intense and widespread political unrest since the 1979 Iranian Revolution. As many as 450 protesters were killed by Iranian security forces, over six times as many as in the 2009 "green revolution" and election fraud protests.[18] "The United States of America supports the brave people of Iran who are protesting for their FREEDOM," Trump tweeted. "The United States is with you," Secretary of State Mike Pompeo added. Regime change advocates inside and outside the administration felt like they could taste victory.[19]

But it did not come. Not then, and not in late December 2019 or early January 2020, when another round of protests were set off by the Iranian government's attempt to cover up responsibility for shooting down a Ukrainian passenger plane amid the back and forth following the American assassination of Islamic Revolutionary Guard

Corps (IRGC) chief Qassem Soleimani. In April 2020, U.S. naval exercises in the Persian Gulf were met by IRGC speedboat challenges at an "unprecedented" scale.[20] And once COVID-19 hit, while the Iranian regime bore plenty of responsibility for the disease's severity in its country, American sanctions so further hindered access to drugs and medical equipment that humanitarian ethical critiques were intensified.[21]

So, yes, interdependence was intensively weaponized. Substantial costs were imposed. But no significant policy change resulted. Not renegotiating of the JCPOA on the highly concessionary terms the Trump administration demanded. Not significant reduction of Iranian involvement in Iraq, or Syria, or Yemen. And not regime change. Why?

This is where we need a more interactive formulation that starts with the coercer state's stronger structural position in the networks but takes into account three sets of factors: target state counterstrategies, bargaining dynamics, and negative carryforward effects on the coercer state's power.

One target state counterstrategy is mobilizing the political will to resist. This can be generalized, per the sixteenth-century political theorist Jean Bodin's formulation, as "the best means for preserving a State, to prevent rebellion . . . and to maintain the good will of subjects is to have an enemy."[22] With reference to the 1960s UN sanctions against Rhodesia, Johan Galtung criticized "naïve theories of economic warfare" that ignored the politically integrative effect feeding the will to resist despite the economic costs being borne.[23] While the mass protests in Iran manifested the limits of any politically integrative effect in Iran, polls also showed resistance to conceding to American demands.[24]

The Iran case very much fits the crucial role that key domestic elites play as either "circuit breakers" or "transmission belts."[25] To the extent that their interests are served by resisting coercer state pressures for policy change, elites act as circuit breakers that block the external pressures. If on the other hand those elites' interests are significantly damaged by the economic coercion or otherwise served by making the policy concessions demanded, they serve as transmission belts that pass on and even intensify the pressure on the regime to comply.

While some transmission effect was evident in the major political protests, Iranian elites had some offsetting through black markets and other sanctions busting, as well as government subsidies. Moreover, the elites whose interests were most at risk had little compunction against resorting to violent repression to break those circuits.[26]

The Iran case also shows how target states can counter with cross-domain retaliations and provocations—as in, "if you are going to cut off our capacity to export oil, we are going to make it harder and more expensive for others to sell you or anyone else oil." In May 2019, within days of Trump having further ratcheted-up sanctions, Iranian-planted mines blew holes in four oil tankers in the Gulf of Oman. In June, an American espionage drone was shot down. In September, two Saudi oil processing facilities were attacked. An American base in Iraq was attacked in retaliation for the Soleimani assassination. And initial steps were taken to restart the Iranian nuclear weapons program.

Bargaining theory also helps to explain why the more limited Obama economic pressure led to substantial policy gains but Trump maximalism has not. While Thomas Schelling and others do stress clarity of demands as a key factor in bargaining, when maximalist demands are made, it does not matter whether they are explicit or kept implicit. For bargaining success, there has to be a means-ends proportionality between the severity of the coercive means used and the scope of objectives pursued, as well as a degree of reciprocity such that both sides gain from resolving the conflict short of further escalation. Obama's strategy had proportionality between sanctions as a limited coercive instrument and nonproliferation as a significant but still limited policy concession. The reciprocity was in the United States and the P5+1 gaining from reducing, if not eliminating, the prospect of Iranian nuclear proliferation, and Iran gaining sanctions relief. The Trump strategy's disproportionality, with such an expansive objective as regime change and the lack of a serious diplomatic process for moving from opening positions to bases for reciprocity, squandered any prospect for WI success.

Negative carryforward effects also need to be considered. European discontent with Trump's Iran policy reached the point that Britain, France, and Germany refused to support UN Security Council extension of the arms embargo or re-imposition ("snap-back" in the parlance) of sanctions lifted with the JCPOA. This "says a lot," tweeted Gerard Arnaud, the highly regarded former French ambassador to the United States and the United Nations, "about the world status of the U.S. today."[27] China gained openings to grow closer to Iran, including colluding on sanctions-busting oil trade plans for $400 billion in Belt and Road Initiative (BRI) deals in the energy and other sectors, as well as progress toward a long-term comprehensive strategic partnership.[28] In return for sanctions cooperation, countries like India and Turkey have leveraged various Trump concessions contrary to other U.S. interests. Gulf allies like the United Arab Emirates shifted from wondering whether Obama was insufficiently anti-Iran to worrying that Trump is so recklessly anti-Iran that the Emirates even tried to open its own diplomatic channel with Iran, only to face U.S. pressure to quash it.[29]

Of broader relevance to financial sanctions is whether yet another instance of America wielding dollar centrality to coerce other states to comply with a policy that is counter to their own interests will provide further incentive for efforts to reduce U.S. financial power. As Thomas Oatley notes in his chapter in this volume, U.S. efforts to weaponize its financial power go back to late 1990s anti-money laundering and especially the post-9/11 Global War on Terrorism. True, repeated predictions of fallout from overuse of financial sanctions leading to larger roles for other currencies can seem akin to Paul Samuelson's quip about economists predicting nine of the last five recessions.[30] The dollar still represents 63 percent of global foreign currency reserves and 40 percent of international payments transactions.[31] Still, one wonders whether there is a "sandpile effect," in which this or the next grain of sand is the one to topple the pile.[32] Oatley, while cautious, cites former Treasury Secretary Jacob Lew's concern along these lines, and Mark Carney, governor of the Bank of England, adds "the growing asymmetry between the importance of the U.S. dollar in the global financial system and the increasingly multi-polar nature of global economic activity."[33] For China, the Iran financial leveraging comes on top of the United States' financial crisis in 2008, which prompted a shift in Chinese strategy from just "decrying U.S. dollar hegemony to more confidently seeking ways to blunt it." The strategy includes more bilateral currency swap agreements using the renminbi in trade deals, as well as initial steps for the Cross-Border Interbank Payment System (CIPS).[34] It is not that the dollar would be replaced, but that it may finally lose its quasi-monopoly position in international finance.

Along with the state-driven efforts to reduce dollar dominance, a May 2020 U.S. Justice Department indictment of shell companies and banks for laundering $2.5 billion to North Korea shows financial sanctions busting is rather robust.[35] Shell companies in China and Russia plus Austria, Libya, Kuwait and Thailand, and banks in the United States and Europe as well as in China, were all involved in breaking that WI choke point and blocking the WI panopticon reach. Bitcoin and other cryptocurrencies have been involved in this as well as other efforts, as documented in a UN report showing North Korea "using 'widespread and increasingly sophisticated' cyberattacks to steal from banks and cryptocurrency exchanges."[36] A U.S.-based cybersecurity firm draws the impact out more widely, stating that "North Korea has developed a model that leverages the internet as a mechanism for sanctions circumvention that is distinctive, but not exceptional. This model is unique but repeatable, and most concerningly can serve as an example for other financially isolated nations, such as Venezuela, Iran, or Syria, for how to use the internet to circumvent sanctions."[37]

In sum: While WI structural power endowed the United States with the capacity to impose substantial costs on Iran, coercing policy compliance was limited by interactive dynamics with Iranian counterstrategies. As to the implications for U.S. WI financial power more generally, fallout from this case may well feed into other factors such that the dollar finally does begin to lose its quasi-monopoly position.

WI, Twenty-first Century Power, and U.S. Grand Strategy

Grand strategy sure has become a growth industry. Some of this is due to a touch of self-aggrandizement—the idea that we scholars (*mea culpa* included) do something "grand" while others do mere "policy." Still, while any such strategizing is well short of some master plan—for all the heralding of containment, George Kennan himself became one of its biggest critics as containment became over-militarized and over-globalized[38]—going beyond the ad hoc and transactional and getting at foundational questions such as the nature of power does have utility.[39]

The concept of WI makes three important contributions to thinking about grand strategy. First is its core critique that liberal theory leans too much toward a positive view of interdependence as a basis for order. Second is its emphasis on private-sector networks, not just states. Third is the need to bridge international security and international political economy in ways that still leave some topics as distinct to the respective subfields, while stressing the value of greater conceptual and theory integration—something the COVID-19 crisis, which puts "pandemic mass destruction" (PMD) right up there with WMDs (weapons of mass destruction), is making even more evident.[40]

The traction that WI has gotten—this book being one but far from the only manifestation—speaks to its impressive impact, in the policy world as well as the academic community. My analysis is less about its "abuse" than about limits of its effective "use." My main questions have been about how much of a source of power WI provides to even those states that are structurally well positioned at key nodes. While WI eases some of "the necessary conditions for coercion," as Daniel Drezner argues in the introduction to this book, other conditions remain no less constraining than for economic sanctions and other forms of economic statecraft. Whether a state has the domestic governance capacity to harness its national private-sector actors that provide the networks, and whether it can overcome target state counterstrategies that offset or deflect, requires a more interactive relational approach to if and how the possession of structural power does or does not get converted to the influence necessary to achieve policy goals.

This analysis syncs with those of other colleagues in this volume and their questions about WI effectiveness. Mastanduno pushes for a net assessment that weighs gains made against costs incurred to American external power and position. Stacie Goddard shows how the very asymmetries that get weaponized can further spur revisionist state challenges to the order on which the structural power is based. Amrita Narlikar argues that counterstrategies similar to those in the

Iran case are available broadly to the global south. Charli Carpenter brings in nongovernmental organization-based (NGO-based) networks with their own power, including technology-enabled reverse-panopticon effects turned back on powerful states.

While I have focused mostly on the United States, Thomas Cavanna's chapter shows how China is able to do some weaponization through its BRI but on a more limited basis than often ascribed, given target-recipient state pushbacks. Compliance on issues important to China but peripheral to recipient countries (for example, relations with Taiwan) has been one thing, but being leveraged on issues important to the countries' own interests and to overall global geopolitics is quite another. Leaving aside politicized China-bashing, in both the ways it handled the original coronavirus outbreak and its promises of help belied by defective equipment, the COVID-19 crisis has prompted serious questioning of the risks of being too dependent on China.[41] Moreover, China has its own internal weaknesses coming out of COVID-19, slowed economic growth, and issues like Hong Kong and the Uighurs.

To also bring Russia in, as Mikhail Krutikhin shows, there have been repeated WI attempts with its natural gas supplies. Yet, as Drezner observes, past efforts "yielded uneven efforts at best," particularly with regard to Western Europe.[42] Russian economic decline and stagnation, evident in an anemic 1.3 percent GDP growth rate (2018), has been further exacerbated by the 2020 cratering of world oil prices. Even Russian officials are beginning to acknowledge the burdens from ostensible gains like Syria, with which, as experienced Russian diplomat Alexander Aksenyonok acknowledges, "it is becoming increasingly obvious that the [Bashar al-Assad] regime is reluctant or unable to develop a system of government that can mitigate corruption and crime and go from a military economy to normal trade and economic relations."[43]

Indeed, if we extend beyond the economic to other domains also bearing on grand strategy, we see power being, as Moises Naim puts it, "easier to obtain and harder to use."[44] In the absence of an overarching shared security threat like the Cold War nuclear deterrence era, military power is being diluted in two respects. Without that shared security threat, extended deterrence, forward basing, military aid, and other forms of military protection bring strong states less leverage over weaker states. In addition, the gap has widened between military superiority as measured by traditional indicators and the limited operational utility of that superiority for achieving strategic objectives given the prevalence of asymmetric and other irregular warfare, as evidenced by the Afghanistan and Iraq wars.

As to traditional diplomatic power, even under Obama—a president and an administration inclined to emphasize diplomacy—it was not just a matter of the United States leads and others follow. For all the enthusiasm Obama drew, NATO was divided over the 2011 Libya intervention; Pakistan still sheltered the Taliban; both the Israelis and the Palestinians resisted efforts to restart the peace process.[45] And this was all before Trump.

In some respects, these other trends may make states even more inclined to try to wield WI. Costs can still be imposed. Claims of action can still be made, and not just through talks-based diplomacy. Risks tend to be less than those of using military force. But for success beyond that, the points herein about overcoming domestic constraints and taking target state counterstrategies into account need to be part of WI strategizing.

Finally, it's worth thinking about how WI's coercive potential could be used in pursuit of more collective global goals—say, if the United States or China, or the United States and China together, were to use its global networks to mobilize global pandemic preparation, opening choke points to cooperating countries and tightening against those that do not, while enhancing panopticon observational reach with a World Health Organization (WHO) empowered in ways that can be a win-win-win. Or imagine these and other countries wielding WI for climate-change mitigation or other global goals. WI, like most other forms of power, is not inherently good or bad. It depends on how it is used.

Notes

Thanks to Elise Bousquette and Andrew Trexler for their research assistance.

1. Henry Farrell and Abraham L. Newman, "Weaponized Interdependence: How Global Economic Networks Shape State Coercion," *International Security* 44 (Summer 2019), p. 45.

2. See, for example, Robert A. Dahl, "The Concept of Power," *Behavioral Science* 2, no. 3 (1957), pp. 201–15.

3. Bruce W. Jentleson, *Pipeline Politics: The Complex Political Economy of East-West Energy Trade* (Cornell University Press, 1986) and "Economic Sanctions and Post-Cold War Conflicts: Challenges for Theory and Policy," in Paul C. Stern and Daniel Druckman (eds.), *International Conflict Resolution After the Cold War* (Washington: National Academy Press, 2000).

4. Farrell and Newman, "Weaponized Interdependence," p. 58; see also pp. 45, 56, 57, 75–76.

5. Stephen D. Krasner, "United States Commercial and Monetary Policy: Unravelling the Paradox of External Strength and Internal Weakness," in Peter J. Katzenstein (ed.), *Between Power and Plenty: Foreign Economic Policies of Advanced Industrial States* (University of Wisconsin Press, 1978), p. 61.

6. Theodore J. Lowi, *The End of Liberalism: Ideology, Policy and the Crisis of Public Authority* (New York: W.W. Norton, 1969).

7. Daron Acemoglu and James A. Robinson, *The Narrow Corridor: States, Societies and the Fate of Liberty* (New York: Penguin Press, 2019), pp. 26–27, 304–37.

8. Samuel Eliot Morison and Henry Steele Commager, *The Growth of the American Republic,* vol. 2 (Oxford University Press, 1940), p. 471.

9. See also Michael Mastanduno, *Economic Containment: CoCom and the Politics of East-West Trade* (Cornell University Press, 1992).

10. Dan Else, "The History of the Defense Production Act and What It Means for COVID-19," War on the Rocks, 2020, https://warontherocks. com/2020/04/the-history-of-the-defense-production-act-and-what-it-means -for-covid-19/.

11. Eric Lipton and Alan Rappeport, "Bolton Book Puts New Focus on Trump's Actions in Turkey and China Cases," *New York Times,* January 28, 2020, www.nytimes.com/2020/01/28/us/politics/bolton-book-trump-china -turkey.html.

12. Robert Gilpin, *U.S. Power and the Multinational Corporation: The Political Economy of Foreign Direct Investment* (New York: Basic Books, 1975), pp. 141, 167, 256.

13. Jennifer Harris, "Making Trade Address Inequality," *Democracy: A Journal of Ideas,* Spring 2018, https://democracyjournal.org/magazine/48/ making-trade-address-inequality/.

14. Lindsay Gorman and Matt Schrader, "U.S. Firms Are Helping Build China's Orwellian State," *Foreign Policy,* March 19, 2019, https://foreignpolicy .com/2019/03/19/962492-orwell-china-socialcredit-surveillance/?utm_ source=PostUp&utm_medium=email&utm_campaign=11875&utm_ term=Editor#39;s%20Picks%20OC; Ben Sisario, "Netflix Blocks Show in Saudi Arabia Critical of Saudi Prince," *New York Times,* January 1, 2019,

www.nytimes.com/2019/01/01/business/media/netflix-hasan-minhaj-saudi
-arabia.html; Walt Bogdanovich and Michael Forsythe, "How McKinsey Has
Helped Raise the Stature of Authoritarian Governments," *New York Times,*
December 15, 2018, www.nytimes.com/2018/12/15/world/asia/mckinsey-china
-russia.html.

15. William J. Burns, *The Back Channel: A Memoir of American Diplomacy and The Case for Renewal* (New York: Random House, 2019); Richard
Nephew, *The Art of Sanctions: A View from the Field* (Columbia University
Press, 2017).

16. Congressional Research Service, *Iran Sanctions* (updated January 20,
2020), pp. 52–53, 66.

17. One Iranian diplomat responded to the first INSTEX transaction
by saying that it was "too little, too late, but still good." Giorgio Cafiero and
Maysam Behravesh, "U.S.-EU Tensions Set to Escalate over Iran's Coronavirus
Crisis," Atlantic Council, April 29, 2020, www.atlanticcouncil.org/blogs/
iransource/us-eu-tensions-set-to-escalate-over-irans-coronavirus-crisis/.

18. Farnaz Fassihi and Rick Gladstone, "With Brutal Crackdown, Iran Is
Convulsed by Worst Unrest in 40 Years," *New York Times*, December 3, 2019,
www.nytimes.com/2019/12/01/world/middleeast/iran-protests-deaths.html.

19. Nahal Toosi, "Trump Team Scours Intel Sent by Iranians as It Weighs
New Sanctions," *Politico*, December 3, 2019, www.politico.com/news/2019
/12/03/donald-trump-sanctions-iran-074961; Richard Goldberg, "Trump
Has an Iran Strategy. This Is It," *New York Times*, January 24, 2020, www.
nytimes.com/2020/01/24/opinion/trump-iran.html.

20. Farzin Nadimi, "Iran Gets Aggressive in the Northern Gulf Following
U.S. Military Exercises," Washington Institute for Near East Policy, April 21,
2020, www.washingtoninstitute.org/policy-analysis/view/iran-gets-aggres
sive-in-the-northern-gulf-following-u.s.-military-exercises.

21. "Maximum Pressure: U.S. Economic Sanctions Harm Iranians' Right
to Health," Human Rights Watch, October 29, 2019, www.hrw.org/report
/2019/10/29/maximum-pressure/us-economic-sanctions-harm-iranians-right
-health; Congressional Research Service, *Iran Sanctions* (updated January 20,
2020), p. 68; Erin Cunningham, "As Coronavirus Cases Explode in Iran, U.S
. Sanctions Hinder Its Access to Drugs and Medical Equipment," *Washington
Post*, March 29, 2020, www.washingtonpost.com/world/middle_east/as-coro
navirus-cases-explode-in-iran-us-sanctions-hinder-its-access-to-drugs-and
-medical-equipment/2020/03/28/0656a196-6aba-11ea-b199-3a9799c54512_
story.html.

22. Cited in Edward L. Morse, *Modernization and the Transformation of
International Relations* (New York: Free Press, 1976), p. 32.

23. Johan Galtung, "On the Effects of International Economic Sanctions,
with Examples from the Case of Rhodesia," *World Politics* XIX (April 1967),
p. 389.

24. In polls jointly conducted by the Chicago Council on Global Affairs and the Toronto-based Iran poll, 75 percent of Iranians sampled agreed with exceeding the JCPOA limits on nuclear weapons development in response to the Trump abrogation, and 59 percent with retaliating militarily if the United States were to attack. Dina Smeltz and Amir Farmanesh, "Majority of Iranians Oppose Development of Nuclear Weapons But Support Iran's Decision to Exceed Enriched Uranium Limits, " The Chicago Council On Global Affairs, March 2020, www.thechicagocouncil.org/sites/default/files/report_majority -iranians-oppose-nuclear-weapons-development_20200331.pdf.

25. Bruce W. Jentleson and Christopher A. Whytock. "Who 'Won' Libya? The Force-Diplomacy Debate and Its Implications for Theory and Policy," *International Security* 30, no. 3 (Winter 2005–2006).

26. Beyond the usual talk of moderates and reformers, Kim Ghattas so much more incisively captures the essence of Iranian politics and culture, as she does for so much of the Middle East in her exceptional book, *Black Waves: Saudi Arabia, Iran and the Forty-Year Rivalry That Unraveled Culture, Religion, and Collective Memory in the Middle East* (New York: Henry Holt, 2020).

27. Gerard Araud on Twitter, August 20, 2020, https://twitter.com/ gerardaraud/status/1296539217334603780.

28. Anjali Singhvi, Edward Wong, and Denise Lu, "Defying U.S. Sanctions, China and Others Take Oil from 12 Iranian Tankers," *New York Times*, August 3, 2019, www.nytimes.com/interactive/2019/08/03/world/middleeast/ us-iran-sanctions-ships.html?action=click&module=Intentional&pg type=Article; Kevjn Lim, "With COVID-19, Iran's Dependence on China Grows," Washington Institute, March 27, 2020, www.washingtoninstitute. org/policy-analysis/view/with-covid-19-irans-dependence-on-china-grows; Alam Sayeh and Zakiyah Yaszdanshenas, "Iran's Pact with China Is Bad News for the West," *Foreign Policy,* August 9, 2020, https://foreignpolicy .com/2020/08/09/irans-pact-with-china-is-bad-news-for-the-west/.

29. Mark Mazzetti, Ronen Bergman, and Farnaz Fassihi, "How Months of Miscalculation Led the U.S. and Iran to the Brink of War," *New York Times*, February 13, 2020, www.nytimes.com/2020/02/13/us/politics/iran -trump-administration.html.

30. Steve Liesman, "Can the Markets Predict Recessions? What We Found Out," CNBC, February 4, 2016, www.cnbc.com/2016/02/04/can-the-markets -predict-recessions-what-we-found-out.html.

31. "Germany Urges SWIFT End to U.S. Payments Dominance," *DW .com,* www.dw.com/en/germany-urges-swift-end-to-us-payments-dominance /a-45242528; Jo Harper, "Germany Urges SWIFT End to U.S. Payments Dominance," *Deutsche Welle*, August 27, 2018, www.dw.com/en/germany -urges-swift-end-to-us-payments-dominance/a-45242528.

32. In his book *Deep Survival* (New York: W.W. Norton, 2003), Laurence

Gonzales recounts the research of Danish physicist Per Bak, who simulated a pile of sand to which new grains are continuously added, as in an hourglass. As new grains are added, the pile steadily grows until that additional grain causes it to collapse. My thanks to my research assistant Andrew Trexler for making this insight.

33. Mark Carney, "The Growing Challenges for Monetary Policy in the Current International Monetary and Financial Systems," Bank of England, August 23, 2019, www.bankofengland.co.uk/-/media/boe/files/speech/2019/the-growing-challenges-for-monetary-policy-speech-by-mark-carney.pdf.

34. Rush Doshi, "China's Ten-Year Struggle against U.S. Financial Power," *National Bureau of Asian Research*, January 6, 2020, www.nbr.org/publi cation/chinas-ten-year-struggle-against-u-s-financial-power/; Christopher Smart, "Could the Renminbi Challenge the Dollar?" *Project Syndicate*, February 2, 2018, www.project-syndicate.org/onpoint/could-the-renminbi-challenge-the -dollar-by-christopher-smart-2018-02?barrier=accesspaylog.

35. Katie Benner, "North Koreans Accused of Laundering $2.5 Billion for Nuclear Program," *New York Times*, May 28, 2020, www.nytimes.com /2020/05/28/us/politics/north-korea-money-laundering-nuclear-weapons. html?action=click&module=Latest&pgtype=Homepage.

36. Michelle Nichols, "Exclusive: U.N. Sanctions Experts Warn—Stay Away from North Korea Cryptocurrency Conference," Reuters, January 15, 2020, www.reuters.com/article/us-northkorea-sanctions-un-exclusive/exclu sive-u-n-sanctions-experts-warn-stay-away-from-north-korea-crypto currency-conference-idUSKBN1ZE0I5; Morgen Peck, "What North Korea Really Wants from Its Blockchain Conference," *IEEE Spectrum*, February 13, 2020, https://spectrum.ieee.org/tech-talk/computing/software/north -korea-blockchain-conference; Jason Brett, "Trend Continues for Countries Looking to Evade U.S. Sanctions Using Crypto," *Forbes*, January 29, 2020, www.forbes.com/sites/jasonbrett/2020/01/29/trend-continues-for-countries -looking-to-evade-us-sanctions-using-crypto/#49c3fe0f59ff.

37. Insikt Group, "How North Korea Revolutionized the Internet as a Tool for Rogue Regimes," Recorded Future, February 2020, https://go. recordedfuture.com/hubfs/reports/cta-2020-feb.pdf.

38. See, for example, Wilson D. Miscamble, *George F. Kennan and the Making of American Foreign Policy, 1947-1950* (Princeton University Press, 1992), pp. 133–34.

39. Hal Brands, *What Good Is Grand Strategy?* (Cornell University Press, 2014); Rebecca Friedman Lissner, "What Is Grand Strategy? Sweeping a Conceptual Minefield," *Texas National Security Review* (November 2018); Richard K. Betts, "The Grandiosity of Grand Strategy," *Washington Quarterly* 42, no. 4 (Winter 2020); Daniel Drezner, Ronald R. Krebs, and Randall Schweller, "The End of Grand Strategy," *Foreign Affairs* 99, no. 3 (May/June 2020).

40. Bruce W. Jentleson, "Refocusing U.S. Grand Strategy on Pandemic and Environmental Mass Destruction," *Washington Quarterly* 43, no. 3 (Fall 2020), pp. 1–23.

41. See, for example, Steven Erlanger, "Global Backlash Builds Against China Over Coronavirus," *New York Times,* June 17, 2020, www.nytimes.com/2020/05/03/world/europe/backlash-china-coronavirus.html; Minxin Pei, "China's Deepening Geopolitical Hole," *Project Syndicate,* July 16, 2020, www.project-syndicate.org/commentary/china-uk-huawei-ban-another-diplomatic-setback-by-minxin-pei-2020-07?utm_source=Project+Syndicate+Newsletter&utm_campaign=6a78f0e5f0-sunday_newsletter_19_07_2020&utm_medium=email&utm_term=0_73bad5b7d8-6a78f0e5f0-93696481&mc_cid=6a78f0e5f0&mc_eid=2fe32546ed.

42. Jentleson, *Pipeline Politics.*

43. Alexander Aksenyonok, "War, the Economy and Politics in Syria: Broken Links," Valdai Discussion Club, April 17, 2020, https://valdaiclub.com/a/highlights/war-the-economy-and-politics-in-syria-broken-links/.

44. Moises Naim, *The End of Power: From Boardrooms to Battlefields and Churches to States, Why Being in Charge Isn't What It Used to Be* (New York: Basic Books, 2013), p. 158.

45. The paradox of negative reputation leading to noncooperation more than positive reputation makes for cooperation is discussed in a 2009 task force report, "U.S. Standing in the World: Causes, Consequences and the Future," American Political Science Association, October 2009, www.apsanet.org/PUBLICATIONS/Reports/Task-Force-on-US-Standing-in-World-Affairs-2.

14

Investment Screening in the Shadow of Weaponized Interdependence

SARAH BAUERLE DANZMAN

On October 4, 2019, U.S. Senator Marco Rubio sent a letter to U.S. Treasury Secretary Steven Mnuchin requesting that the Committee on Foreign Investment in the United States (CFIUS) investigate the Chinese-owned short-video social media application TikTok and its 2017 acquisition of the U.S. businesses of a video-sharing platform called Musical.ly for national security risks.[1] Senator Rubio argued that TikTok's growing presence in Western markets provided the Chinese government with a platform through which to censor information unflattering to the Chinese Communist Party (CCP) and to shape media narratives to its benefit. The letter came just five days after Daryl Morey, the general manager of the Houston Rockets, tweeted his support of pro-democracy protestors in Hong Kong. After the National Basketball Association's (NBA's) uncoordinated response of first chastising Morey before supporting his right to free expression, Chinese state media retaliated by cutting off broadcasts of NBA games. Cutting the NBA's access to the China market put at risk substantial revenue streams—an estimated $500 million annually; in September 2019, the NBA's China business was valued at $5 billion.[2]

This example is perhaps the perfect microcosm of growing concerns among U.S. foreign policymakers that thickening networks of multinational production, ownership, and consumption have generated novel national security risks, by endowing adversaries—such as the People's Republic of China (PRC)—with the ability to control production and distribution networks to deter governments, corporations, and individuals from taking policy positions against their interests. The COVID-19 pandemic has heightened these fears by exposing previously ignored fragilities in global health supply chains and increasing concerns that PRC-connected businesses may take advantage of the economic fallout to buy distressed firms in sensitive sectors. In March 2020, NATO's deputy secretary-general Mircea Geoană warned NATO governments to prevent distressed critical assets from falling under the control of non-allies, saying "Free markets need to continue to operate, but you have to make sure [of] the crown jewels, the . . . industries and infrastructures that are indispensable for making sure we stay safe irrespective of the circumstances."[3] Many advanced economies have responded by introducing new or strengthening existing investment screening mechanisms to guard against foreign takeovers with adverse national security implications.[4]

The question for this chapter is whether investment screening broadly, and the United States' recently strengthened CFIUS in particular, can be usefully explained through the lens of weaponized interdependence (WI). Investment screening could be an offensive tool of WI if governments use their screening authorities to proactively shape global material and informational networks. Screening could also be a defensive tool to prevent rivals from obtaining the structural power necessary to weaponize networks. While a substantial number of countries now have investment screening mechanisms, I center the analysis in this chapter on CFIUS. Due to the size of the U.S. economy and the resources available to the U.S. government to conduct investment review, CFIUS represents a "most likely" case of weaponization of investment regulation. If any country has the capacity to use investment screening as a tool of or against WI, it would be the United States.

Below, I develop three points. First, investment screening for national security is most usefully conceptualized as an exercise of market power rather than of WI. Second, investment screening could more closely approximate an exercise of WI if governments chose to embrace more expansive interpretations of national security, impose more aggressive and extraterritorial mitigation conditions, and coordinate investment screening more closely with allies. Third, governments are unlikely to take the policy steps necessary to make screening a tool of WI, because doing so would create substantial financing constraints for domestic firms, reducing domestic capacity for technological innovation. It would also require a dismantling of open markets and cross-border economic networks simultaneously with a significant increase in international cooperation among partners and allies to effectively control technological and infrastructural choke points.

While my primary argument is that CFIUS, and investment screening broadly, as currently practiced is more usefully conceptualized through market power than WI terms, it is important to recognize some ambiguities here. By definition, national security-centered investment screening assesses the security implications of foreign investment, and functions to mitigate risks as they arise and block transactions that present unresolvable risks. Accordingly, the threat of WI operates as a background condition. CFIUS may deem a transaction risky because it provides a "threat actor"—meaning an entity tied to an adversarial government—with control over a critical technology or infrastructure network, conferring the adversary with choking power. CFIUS could also identify a national security risk if a transaction provided a rival with panopticon power through entry into a virtual network that it could use for surveillance. The underlying point is not that CFIUS is disinterested in or entirely incapable of responding to such national security threats. Instead, CFIUS provides the U.S. government with circumscribed abilities to respond to such risks; these authorities are directed specifically at individual firms and transactions rather than at broader networks or governments; and these limits on CFIUS are purposeful. Imbuing CFIUS with the authorities necessary to render it a tool of and against WI would undermine key U.S. foreign and economic policy interests in maintaining a mostly open global economy. As yet, the U.S. government is not willing to make such a costly trade. If it were, it is an open question whether the tools it would gain would be worth the price paid.

CFIUS: An Overview

Created by an executive order in 1975, CFIUS is an interagency body tasked with reviewing the national security implications of foreign acquisitions of U.S.-based companies, negotiating agreements with transaction parties to mitigate any risks arising from the transaction, and advising the U.S. president when it believes a transaction presents a nonmitigatable national security risk to the country and should be prohibited. CFIUS is not a sector or country screen; it can review any controlling investment into any U.S. business in any sector, by a foreign investor from any country. The Department of Treasury chairs the committee, and eight other agencies participate as voting members: Energy, Justice, Homeland Security, State, Defense, Commerce, the U.S. Trade Representative, and the Office of Science and Technology Policy. The breadth of CFIUS's membership is important to the functioning of the committee because this "whole-of-government" approach ensures that transactions before the committee are seen and discussed from a variety of different policy perspectives.

Until changes brought by the 2018 Foreign Investment Risk Review Modernization Act (FIRRMA), CFIUS review only covered controlling acquisitions, and filings were voluntary rather than compulsory.[5] FIRRMA broadens CFIUS coverage to also include noncontrolling, nonpassive investments in so-called TID businesses — those involved in critical technology, critical infrastructure, and sensitive personal data—while providing dispensation for investors from "excepted states," a list that currently includes the United Kingdom, Australia, and Canada. FIRRMA also mandates filings for investments in certain technologies and when a foreign government exerts substantial control over an acquiring party. Still, the choice to appear before the committee remains largely voluntary, and many covered transactions are never reviewed by CFIUS. For example, in 2018, commercial parties filed 229 notices while the total number of cross-border acquisitions of U.S.-based businesses that year was 1,233.[6]

Still, companies choose to file—particularly transactions that are very large or especially sensitive—because clearing CFIUS review confers safe harbor to transacting parties, meaning the U.S. government cannot review transactions it previously cleared. Without obtaining CFIUS clearance, firms leave themselves legally vulnerable to requests by the committee to submit post-closing transactions for review, which could result in the president demanding that the transaction be unwound. Four of the seven CFIUS presidential prohibitions since 1975 have been divestiture requirements.[7] Unwinding transactions post-closing can be especially costly to parties that may face challenges finding a CFIUS-approved buyer on a short timeline and therefore need to sell at a steep discount.

Although CFIUS review is mostly a voluntary process, the committee is widely considered to be quite powerful, and its strength emanates from its ability to block covered transactions. Only the president has the authority to legally prohibit a transaction on national security grounds, an authority used a mere seven times over CFIUS's forty-five-year history. In practice, CFIUS blocks transactions more frequently than the presidential prohibition record suggests. Most parties abandon a transaction when CFIUS informs them it has identified an unmitigable risk.[8] Parties do this to avoid negative publicity; while the CFIUS process is subject to strict rules prohibiting government officials from discussing transactions before the committee, presidential prohibitions are made public. Despite the fact that CFIUS reviews sometimes result in parties abandoning their transaction, CFIUS has demonstrated a strong preference toward clearing cases when possible. From 2005 to 2018, CFIUS reviewed 1,876 transactions, of which it cleared 1,452 cases or 77 percent of transactions before the committee.

CFIUS as Market Power

Many commentators point to CFIUS as an example of a policy tool to defend against attempts by adversaries—particularly the PRC—to obtain control of structurally important nodes in infrastructure, information networks, and supply chains.[9] With such control, competitors could have the capability to leverage their network position and exercise power by cajoling private firms beholden to their supply chain to act in certain ways or by threatening the U.S. government into a policy concession. The rhetoric surrounding FIRRMA has fueled such interpretations.[10] Even prior to FIRRMA, CFIUS case load grew by 358 percent from 2005 to 2018, as table 14-1 illustrates. Presidential prohibitions have also become more frequent. Before 2012, the president blocked one transaction; since then, the president has used his legal authority under CFIUS to prohibit six transactions—all involving acquirers with some connection to China.

Yet, a more careful consideration of typologies of power suggest that CFIUS is better conceptualized as a tool of market power than of WI.[11] The nature of CFIUS review is case specific and tied to the acquiring commercial party rather than to a government. Moreover, the actual exercise of power in a CFIUS review manifests in its ability to deny a highly circumscribed form of market access to foreign firms. This authority is tied exclusively to foreign acquisitions or investments in preexisting commercial enterprises. CFIUS can only exercise this power when it can link a clearly articulated and supportable national security concern to a specific transaction. Importantly, national security is a distinct concept from foreign policy, and CFIUS is not empowered to block a transaction in support of broader foreign policy goals.[12] This scoping of regulatory authority provides the U.S. government with a domestic institutional structure that limits coercive power over market actors to their actions within U.S. borders and only authorizes the exercise of that power through a narrow interpretation of national security.[13]

The United States is able to effectively wield investment regulatory authority because its internal market is large enough to confer a great deal of market power.[14] Countries lacking large internal markets cannot easily use screening authorities to compel foreign acquirers to change their operations or corporate governance structures to satisfy regulators' national security concerns, because firms are less likely to agree to pay the costs associated with such measures if the benefits of domestic operations are low.[15] The United States' power projection in this issue domain is quite different from financial payments networks or internet governance, in which its power emanates quite clearly from its central position in a hierarchical network. One might argue that the ability to prevent foreign entities from acquiring U.S.-

TABLE 14-1

CFIUS Case Statistics, 2005–2018

Year	Total M&A Deals	Notices	Notices as % Total Deals	Withdrawn During Review	Investigations	Withdrawn During Investigation	Transactions Abandoned	Transactions Mitigated	Presidential Decisions	Total Transactions Affected by CFIUS Review	As % of Total M&A Deals
2005	944	64	7%	1	1	1			0	0	0%
2006	1,099	111	10%	14	7	5		15	2	17	2%
2007	1,355	138	10%	10	6	5	2	14	0	16	1%
2008	1,149	155	13%	18	23	5	3	2	0	5	0%
2009	737	65	9%	5	25	2	3	5	0	8	1%
2010	887	93	10%	6	35	6	5	9	0	14	2%
2011	976	111	11%	1	40	5	0	8	0	8	1%
2012	833	114	14%	2	45	20	9	8	1	18	2%
2013	765	97	13%	3	48	5	7	11	0	18	2%
2014	1,054	147	14%	3	51	9	12	9	0	21	2%
2015	1,136	143	13%	3	66	10	5	11	0	16	1%
2016	1,225	172	14%	6	79	21	12	18	1	31	3%
2017	1,383	237	17%	7	172	67	30	29	1	60	4%
2018	1,233	229	19%	2	158	64	26	29	1	56	5%

Notes: Total (number of) M&A Deals from annex tables to UNCTAD's 2019 *World Investment Report.* All other data from Treasury's public CFIUS reports to Congress, 2008–2020. CFIUS rejected one filing each in 2014 and 2015. These rejections are added to the total abandoned transactions for their respective years. Total Transactions Affected by CFIUS Review is the sum of transactions abandoned, mitigated, and prohibited through presidential decisions.

based businesses provides the U.S. government with structural power through choke-point effects, but this interpretation is only correct in that CFIUS has the power to choke foreign firms out of acquisitions markets for U.S. businesses. It does not have the authority to prevent acquisitions of businesses operating in other jurisdictions, and it has no power to review greenfield investments in the United States. If a Chinese company with PRC ties wanted to construct a new semiconductor manufacturing plant in the United States, CFIUS would not have the authority to prevent the investment.[16]

CFIUS has evolved as a narrowly scoped domestic authority because its primary policy objective is to preserve as open an investment climate as possible while maintaining minimally necessary guardrails against investments that generate national security vulnerabilities. This mandate follows from the ideological and material commitments of most U.S. policymakers and the domestic interest groups that push for limited investment regulation.[17] The preamble to FIRRMA begins by outlining the substantial economic benefits that inward foreign direct investment (FDI) affords U.S. businesses and workers; states that the vast majority of FDI to the United States comes from its allies; and invokes a 1954 speech by President Dwight Eisenhower that explicitly ties American military power to an open investment environment.[18] Throughout CFIUS's legislative history, security hawks have clamored for more expansive authority over acquisitions with negative economic implications, greenfield investment, outbound investment, and even total bans on investments from certain countries. Yet, advocates for fundamentally open investment environments have consistently won the argument that these more expansive authorities—which could transform the committee into a tool of WI—would undermine open markets. This is a trade-off that the U.S. government has yet to be willing to make, despite a current rhetorical environment that would suggest otherwise.

CFIUS case statistics provide a concrete illustration of why WI is a problematic lens through which to interpret U.S. investment screening. If the United States used investment screening as a tool of or against WI, then CFIUS might be used frequently and assertively to shape production and ownership networks to the government's preferences. Yet, table 14-1 illustrates that CFIUS affects only a small percentage—3 percent, on average—of cross-border mergers and acquisitions (M&As) of U.S.-based companies. And, although reviews as a percentage of M&A activity has increased since 2012, they have hardly skyrocketed.[19] When considering the number of transactions materially affected by CFIUS reviews—abandonments, mitigations, and presidential decisions—they have never amounted to more than 5 percent of M&A.

CFIUS case statistics also reveal a preference for allowing transactions to proceed while entering into risk-mitigation agreements with parties when possible, rather than prohibiting any transaction that presents a security risk. Statute does not require the committee to mitigate transactions when feasible; it only provisions that the committee may do so.[20] From 2006 to 2018, parties abandoned 114 transactions while CFIUS cleared 168 transactions with mitigation. This represents about 9 percent of filings, a rate that has remained relatively steady over time. CFIUS's use of mitigation, despite the lack of a statutory requirement to do so, suggests that the committee prefers to clear transactions when it can, rather than acting as a more aggressive obstacle to foreign acquisitions of U.S.-based businesses.[21] This preference is the opposite of what we would expect if CFIUS functioned as a tool of WI. If this were the case, the goal would be more to shape the network than to find ways to eliminate national security risks to approve a foreign acquisition.

CFIUS and Defensive WI

While CFIUS is better characterized as an expression of market power than a tool of WI, it operates within a context of increasingly complex global supply chains and networked infrastructure. This means investment screening operates in the shadow of WI because some of the risks to national security that regulators must confront develop from WI dynamics. The national security risks CFIUS seeks to minimize may arise when foreign entities gain control over U.S. businesses that could confer choking or surveillance power to a rival. Accordingly, CFIUS as well as the investment screening mechanisms of other countries could operate as defensive tools to prevent adversaries from gaining the structural position needed to effectively weaponize ownership networks. CFIUS can prevent foreign threat actors from accessing or controlling critical infrastructure within the United States when a national security risk is identified. In these circumstances, investment screening can serve as a defensive tool against WI. Yet, this power is attenuated because CFIUS can only act if it identifies a specific national security risk from the transaction; a policy objective of preventing foreign ownership of critical infrastructure to guard against national security concerns that may arise in the future would not be grounds for prohibiting a transaction.

One could imagine an investment review tool grounded more clearly in the logic of WI. First, such a mechanism would leverage the size and centrality of the U.S. economy—and particularly, the U.S. technology sector—to reshape the ownership and licensed use of sensitive technology to the U.S. government's own liking. Because so many critical technologies are inherently dual-use in ways that cannot easily be disentangled or even immediately recognized, a more aggressive review mechanism would need to block or mitigate transactions involving technologies that may not have clear or current military uses.[22] This would require expanding the scope of review beyond national security to include a net economic and technological benefit assessment. Doing so would empower CFIUS to preemptively counter adversaries' advancements in both commercial and military spaces.

Second, the mechanism would expand mitigation and prohibition measures extraterritorially. CFIUS scoping currently limits the reach of the committee to business activities that occur within the U.S. and its territories. For example, suppose a foreign acquirer of a U.S. business that collects its customers' biometric data used untrusted wireless vendors such as Huawei or ZTE in its overseas operations. CFIUS might identify a risk of biometric data transfer to a malicious third actor if any data traversed wireless connections that use those vendors. But the committee would not be able to require the acquirer to remove all untrusted wireless vendors from its global operations.[23] Because CFIUS review and mitigation is scoped to the national security risk arising from the transaction, the committee would only be able to require, as a condition of the transaction, that the acquirer refrain from using untrusted vendors in wireless communication or virtual storage of biometric data collected from the U.S.-based operations. Thus, CFIUS can demand acquirers to structure U.S.-internal informational and material networks to the U.S. government's liking, but the committee currently cannot require acquirers to restructure their global business operations in a similar fashion.

A weaponized CFIUS would allow the committee to impose mitigation terms extraterritorially into the offshore business practices and vendor relationships of corporate entities that have any business in the U.S. market. This would leverage the centrality of the U.S. market to the strategic plans of most transnational businesses by prohibiting untrusted vendors in any part of their global operations, effectively starving entities deemed untrustworthy of a large customer base. Relatedly, a weaponized CFIUS would empower the committee to prohibit transactions when acquirers have investments from businesses in adversarial states in any of their global subsidiaries or affiliates— even associated business units with separate governance structures that have no U.S. business presence. Such a rule could force business groups to choose between operating in the U.S. market or accepting investment from firms connected to adversarial states, in any part of their activities.

Finally, a weaponized CFIUS would require substantial coordination among like-minded partners and allies. This would be necessary if the U.S. economy were to remain open to benign foreign investors while also using CFIUS as a more purposeful tool of defensive WI. In the absence of such coordination, a firm headquartered in an allied country could acquire a U.S.-based firm, import its emerging technology or know-how to the parent's headquarters, and then sell the parent to a firm with problematic ties to a rival such as the PRC. The recent FIRRMA legislation perhaps opened a door to such coordination through its "excepted state" list, which incentivizes states to develop robust national security-oriented investment screening mechanisms to gain easier access to U.S. investment markets. However, the possibility of a critical mass of countries developing investment review authorities and then agreeing with the United States' risk assessments over filings is hard to find realistic.

Limitations of Weaponized Investment Screening

Just because we can imagine the contours of a CFIUS tooled to defend against WI does not mean that the U.S. government could or should empower its investment screening committee in such a way. Domestic politics make it highly unlikely that CFIUS would ever be so empowered. U.S. corporations would certainly lobby vigorously against legislation that would expand the committee's power so significantly, as it would make it increasingly challenging for their businesses to engage in global trade and financial networks.[24] A committee with such power would likely ultimately reduce U.S national security by hamstringing the very industries that propel U.S. dominance in technological development, and by shutting U.S. firms out of global supply chains.[25]

Moreover, CFIUS's central policy objective—openness with limited controls justified on national security grounds—depends on continued trust that the United States will not use the leverage it accrues through cooperative efforts to secure sensitive economic activities against its allies. Without completely shutting off from international trade and production networks, the United States cannot safeguard its sensitive technology alone. One growing concern is that perceptions that the United States has abused its centrality in global economic networks to weaponize interdependence in other domains could cause partners and allies to rethink the benefits and costs of an open system. To effectively advocate for strengthened CFIUS-like review mechanisms across partner economies—mechanisms that take technology transfer risks seriously while still scoping review to relatively narrow conceptions of national security—the U.S. government will need to consider how its aggressive use of WI tactics in other areas could undermine CFIUS's efforts.

By statute and practice, CFIUS reflects a purposeful balancing of the risks and benefits of an open investment climate to national security and economic prosperity. FIRRMA's increasing focus on protecting TID businesses reflects an uncomfortable reality that national security and economic competitiveness are becoming increasingly challenging to delineate. The legislative history of CFIUS-related measures illustrates this balancing act; globally oriented lawmakers and bureaucrats have consistently won the argument that CFIUS authorities must be narrowly constrained to national security issues and not venture into the realm of economic benefit tests. Moving forward, the consequential policy developments in CFIUS will be how the committee negotiates its role as novel national security threats obfuscate the line between national security and economic policy.[26]

Conclusion

In this chapter, I have forwarded three arguments. First, investment screening mechanisms like CFIUS are better explained as expressions of market power than of WI because power is expressed bilaterally at private actors rather than at states through networks. Second, investment screening tools could be modified to become more explicit tools of, or safeguards against, WI. Third, the changes necessary to transform investment screening into manifestations of WI are unlikely to survive domestic political processes and also would likely undermine state power in other ways. In particular, it would be extremely challenging to weaponize CFIUS while simultaneously deepening international cooperation to secure sensitive economic activities.

The specific case of CFIUS highlights how careful consideration of the sources of power and influence in a complex global economic network leads to greater precision in discussions of what does and does not constitute WI. In a world defined by complex networks, it is tempting to view all risks and all exercise of power through the prism of WI. Yet, doing so can stretch the concept beyond usefulness. Overuse of WI concepts may also lead scholars to discount the many ways in which governments are constrained by domestic and transnational forces. Particularly when it comes to global financial markets, any analysis of state power must consider how business interests complicate governments' ability to leverage economic power for influence. Markets are not just complex but also complicated, meaning that states' have limited ability to orchestrate private behavior toward public policy goals, at least in market-oriented democracies.[27] Moreover, attempts to weaponize networks have real and enduring trade-offs that further confound and confuse foreign policy practices around enabling open economic exchange or insulating economic activity from adversaries. This policy dilemma presents a rich and exciting research agenda on how governments and society can, and do, navigate the boundaries of national security and economic engagement in the shadow of WI.

Notes

1. Marco Rubio, "Rubio Requests U.S. Review of TikTok After Reports of Chinese Censorship," press release, October 9, 2019, www.rubio.senate.gov/public/index.cfm/2019/10/rubio-requests-cfius-review-of-tiktok-following -reports-of-chinese-censorship.

2. Jeff Zillgitt and Mark Medina, "As Impasse over Pro-Hong Kong Tweet Simmers, What's at Stake for the NBA in China?" *USA Today*, October 9, 2019, www.usatoday.com/story/sports/nba/2019/10/09/nba-china-hong-kong -whats-at-stake/3912447002/.

3. Teri Schultz, "NATO Warns Allies to Block China Buying Spree," *Deutsche Welle*, April 17, 2020, www.dw.com/en/nato-warns-allies-to-block -china-buying-spree/a-53167064.

4. United Nations Conference on Trade and Development, "Investment Policy Responses to the COVID-19 Pandemic," *Investment Policy Monitor*, May 4, 2020, www.unctad.org/en/PublicationsLibrary/diaepcbinf2020d3_en .pdf.

5. James Jackson, "The Committee on Foreign Investment in the United States," *Congressional Research Service Reports*, February 26, 2020, https://crsreports.congress.gov/product/pdf/RL/RL33388/93.

6. See table 14-1 this chapter for data sources.

7. Jackson, "The Committee on Foreign Investment in the United States," p. 21. See also White House website for most recent prohibition at www.whitehouse.gov/presidential-actions/order-regarding-acquisition-stayntouch -inc-beijing-shiji-information-technology-co-ltd/.

8. For instance, U.S.-based Esko Bionics Holdings, Inc., released a press statement on May 20, 2020, indicating its intention to terminate a joint venture (JV) with Zhejiang Youchuang Venture Capital Investment Co., Ltd., after CFIUS reportedly informed them that it had determined the national security concerns endangered by the JV could not be mitigated; see "Ekso Bionics Announces CFIUS Determination Regarding China Joint Venture," press release, May 20, 2020, www.ir.eksobionics.com/press-releases/detail/685/ekso-bionics-announces-cfius-determination-regarding-china.

9. See, for example, Henry Farrell and Abraham L. Newman, "Chained to Globalization: Why It's Too Late to Decouple," *Foreign Affairs* 99 (January/February 2020), pp. 77–78.

10. Anthea Roberts, Henrique Choer Moraes, and Victor Ferguson, "Toward a Geoeconomic Order in International Trade and Investment," *Journal of International Economic Law* 22 (December 2019), pp. 655–76.

11. See Henry Farrell and Abraham L. Newman, "Weaponized Interdependence and Networked Coercion: A Research Agenda," the final chapter of this volume.

12. National security is not defined in statute, but Section 721(f) of the Defense Production Act provides a list of factors for the committee to consider when evaluating transactions for national security risks. Implications for broader foreign policy objectives are not included on this list.

13. Henry Farrell and Abraham L. Newman, "Weaponized Interdependence: How Global Economic Networks Shape State Coercion," *International Security* 44 (Summer 2019), pp. 42–79.

14. Beth Simmons, "The International Politics of Harmonization: The Case of Capital Market Regulation," *International Organization* 55 (Autumn 2001), pp. 589–620; Daniel W. Drezner, *All Politics Is Global: Explaining International Regulatory Regimes* (Princeton University Press, 2007).

15. For more on the determinants of FDI screening cross-sectionally, see Anastasia Ufimtseva, "The Rise of Foreign Direct Investment Regulation in Investment-Recipient Countries," *Global Policy* 11 (April 2020), pp. 222–32.

16. Depending on the exact foreign entity and the specific technology involved, the United States could have other authorities, such as export controls, to prevent technology transfer.

17. Matthew J. Baltz, "Institutionalizing Neoliberalism: CFIUS and the Governance of Inward Foreign Direct Investment in the United States Since 1975," *Review of International Political Economy* 24 (2917), pp. 859–80.

18. Dwight D. Eisenhower, "Recommendations Concerning U.S. Foreign Economic Policy," *Department of State Bulletin* 30 (1954), p. 602.

19. CFIUS activity did increase rather substantially in 2017 and 2018. For a number of reasons, filings and investigations are likely inflated. This is because investigations and withdrawals tend to compound each other. If the committee needs more time to investigate a transaction—perhaps to negotiate mitigation terms or because staffing issues make it challenging for the committee to complete action on cases in a timely manner—parties will often voluntarily agree to withdraw and refile the transaction to provide the committee more time.

20. Section 721 of the Defense Production Act of 1950, as amended, 50 U.S.C. § 4565, Sec. 7(a).

21. It likely also reflects a sensitivity to due process, especially after Chinese-owned wind energy developer Ralls Corporation sued the U.S. government over its decision to prohibit Ralls's investment in an Oregon wind farm. While CFIUS review decisions are immune to legal rulings, the case did proceed on the basis of a due process claim, and the committee has em-

phasized its commitment to conducting reviews and investigations carefully to avoid the appearance of lack of due process or arbitrariness of decisions.

22. Christian Brose, "The New Revolution in Military Affairs: War's Sci-Fi Future," *Foreign Affairs* 98 (May/June 2019), pp. 122–34.

23. Indeed, if CFIUS authority did extend extraterritorially in this way, a bipartisan group of U.S. lawmakers would likely view the proposed NET-WORKS Act, which would block U.S. firms from engaging in significant financial transactions with Huawei, to be redundant. See the draft legislation at the website of Representative Mike Gallagher, https://gallagher.house.gov/sites/gallagher.house.gov/files/Networks%20Act%203.10.20.pdf.

24. Sarah Bauerle Danzman, *Merging Interest: When Domestic Firms Shape FDI Policy* (Cambridge University Press, 2019).

25. Robert D. Williams, "In the Balance: The Future of America's National Security and Innovation Ecosystem," *Lawfare* (blog), November 30, 2018, www.lawfareblog.com/balance-future-americas-national-security-and-innovation-ecosystem.

26. J. Benton Heath, "National Security and Economic Globalization: Toward Collision or Reconciliation?" *Fordham International Law Journal* 42 (2019), pp. 1431–49.

27. Thomas Oatley, "Toward a Political Economy of Complex Interdependence," *European Journal of International Relations* 25 (2019), pp. 957–78.

15

Weaponized Interdependence and Human Rights

CHARLI CARPENTER

In the midst of an unfolding geopolitical crisis in January 2020, U.S. President Donald Trump tweeted a threat to bomb Iran's cultural sites.[1] International organizations and commentators immediately pushed back, pointing out this would be a war crime.[2] And many of them criticized Trump not only for indicating he would violate international law, but also for allegedly undermining the law itself. Eric Post, writing for *Katoikos*, argued "*such threats reject international legal norms*, weakening global efforts to limit civilian suffering and societal destruction during warfare" (emphasis added).[3] This type of criticism was not leveled at Iran during the crisis, though it had arguably committed atrocities in the run-up, accidentally shot down a civilian airliner during the height of tensions, and repressed student protests in the aftermath.[4] A few days later, amid the outcry, Trump backed away from his threat.[5]

What is happening here? Does the concept of weaponized interdependence, popularized to describe power dynamics in economic and technological networks, travel to issue areas like human rights and the laws of war? This question is important because if a concept is of broad theoretical utility, it ought to be applicable when exported to myriad issue areas in world politics.

In this chapter, I advance three arguments. First, the way to think about weaponized interdependence in the area of human rights is not simply as an exercise of structural power due to material centrality, but of productive power due to ideational centrality.[6] Second, the concept of weaponized interdependence not only can be applied to the human rights regime, but also can help to illuminate some important and paradoxical recent regime dynamics—including the tendency of powerful liberal democracies to contest or sabotage regime norms.[7] Third, while powerful liberal democracies may attempt to weaponize their perceived disproportionate centrality to the human rights regime to rewrite regime norms, their efforts often fail for two reasons: (1) such states overestimate the constitutive and causal effects of ideational weaponization; and (2) they face reverse-panopticon effects wielded by weaker networked actors, including human rights activists.

The chapter proceeds in two parts. In the first, I outline how the concept of weaponized interdependence can be applied to the human rights regime, highlighting the disproportionate ideological location of powerful Western liberal democracies—and particularly, the United States—in that regime and the way in which this confers disproportionate structural power onto these states. I discuss ways in which such states may attempt to use their ideational centrality to exercise productive power over regime norms to suit their material interests. Next, I discuss why this strategy often fails, given the way in which weaker actors can use ideational, institutional, and technological leverage to disrupt ideational choke points with reverse-panopticon effects of their own. Throughout, I illustrate the plausibility of this model with references to two decades of recent U.S. foreign policy under three different U.S. presidents.[8] I conclude the concept of weaponized interdependence is of utility in the human rights domain, but with caveats, and I suggest avenues for further research.

Weaponized Ideational Interdependence and Its Limits

Although weaponized interdependence is a concept that was originally applied to economic and technological networks, it is possible to observe this kind of power exerted in the human rights area. Henry Farrell and Abraham Neumann begin their discussion in this volume with an example of U.S. president Donald Trump pulling out of the Joint Comprehensive Plan of Action (JCPOA) and the knock-on effects on firms and states. A similar example is Trump's pulling back as a leader in the area of refugee protection. As Amrita Narlikar notes in this volume, a closed border creates a kind of choke-point effect on refugee flows, choking not only the refugees but also the contiguous states that must now deal with them.[9] And the very ability to wield such institutional or compulsory power arises in part from the United States' structural position as a destination of choice for refugees—a hub for refugee protection whose withdrawal from that role complicates matters, not just for refugees but also for transit countries.

But choking power is being exercised in this example at another, deeper level—in the form of efforts to exercise productive power over shared meanings about what refugee protection entails, who is a refugee and who is a migrant, what is "legal" and "illegal," what constitutes a "safe third country," and what the rules of the refugee regime in fact require both of asylum seekers, host countries, and transit countries.[10] In this sense, Trump might be said to use his structural position to exercise not only compulsory and institutional power over refugees, but also productive power over the meanings associated with the refugee regime.

The United States as an Ideational Hub

The advantage enjoyed by the United States in the human rights regime is not like its role as home to the internet, its influence over the financial trading architecture of SWIFT (Society for Worldwide Interbank Financial Telecommunications), or even solely its position as a concrete destination of choice for refugees—matters that depend as much on brute facts of technology and territory as on social facts.[11] As constructivist scholars have long indicated, international ethical norms such as human rights standards are intersubjective and therefore rely on productive relations of what we might call ideational interdependence.[12] Notions of due process, relief to war victims, rules regarding detainees, or free speech rights exist to the extent that many nations acknowledge they exist and citizens invoke their existence.[13] The meanings of these rights and how they will be implemented are consistently renegotiated through a dialectic between speech acts, judicial or quasi-judicial review, and state practice.[14]

Just as there exist structural asymmetries in trade or technological networks, actors occupy asymmetrical positions in the human rights regime. Some organizations operate as ideational hubs in the human rights network.[15] And some states—particularly powerful liberal democracies whose putative ideology has always been at the core of the international human rights regime—also occupy disproportionate influence in this ideational web. To some extent, this is with good reason: democracies are more likely to comply with human rights;[16] to name and shame human rights violators;[17] to use preferential trade agreements and foreign aid to promote human rights;[18] and to serve as headquarters for major human rights organizations.[19] These brute facts feed into a widespread, socially constructed, not wholly accurate yet politically consequential perception that powerful democracies are, and are expected to be, norm leaders in the human rights regime.

The United States, in particular, is viewed as having bankrolled and propped up the liberal international order, including the human rights regime first articulated by U.S. first lady Eleanor Roosevelt. But other Western liberal democracies are also perceived to be standard-bearers of fundamental freedoms.[20] Consequently, the behavior of powerful liberal democracies is seen by norm advocates to matter more to the promulgation of regime norms than does the behavior of more authoritarian states. When dictatorships violate human rights, it is seen as a threat to the human security of those tortured, disappeared, or executed, and the dictatorships are shamed as norm violators—yet, this behavior is, in some ways, expected (and even the accession of dictatorships to human rights treaties is often treated as a puzzle).[21] When democracies violate human rights (and especially when they justify doing so), it is viewed as a threat to the human rights regime norms themselves: such countries are viewed as norm contesters whose words and deeds are perceived to weaken not their own legitimacy through disgraceful noncompliance, but instead the very concept of human rights.

Empirically, it seems that when Western liberal democracies violate human rights standards, they are far likelier to be on the receiving end of condemnation by human rights NGOs than non-democracies. For example, James Meernik and others show that the United States, by far, is the nation most targeted with Amnesty International "Urgent Action" campaigns in the Western Hemisphere.[22] In the Middle East, as Jim Ron and Howard Ramos show, it is Israel who is most often condemned by human rights watchdogs.[23] This is true even though research by Cullen Hendrix and Wendy Wong has shown that NGOs are driven by a logic of effectiveness, and also that naming and shaming is actually less effective on democracies than on authoritarian regimes.[24]

Scholars sometimes explain this disproportionate attention by human rights watchdogs to liberal democracies and their allies as a function of media coverage,[25] NGO presence,[26] or leverage politics.[27] But these all logically covary with another meaningful reason for the disproportionate attention to liberal democracies: the belief that violations of human rights by democracies (or tolerance of such violations) are more threatening to the regime because the regime relies on these states to set an example for others.

This structural importance of liberal democracies to the human rights regime norms gives—or appears to give—countries like the United States, Canada, the United Kingdom, and Israel a particular kind of implicit productive power: a disproportionate power to define, through their own good or bad actions, the meaning of human rights. This power can be, and often is, thrown around in an effort to reconstitute and align international norms more closely with powerful states' brute political interests. Powerful liberal democracies realize that human rights norms are dependent on intersubjective understandings.

In the case of the United States, this ideational interdependence has often been weaponized, exploiting its relative power to attempt to shift human rights norms over time as suits the country's strategic needs. It is also possible to understand Trump's establishment of the Commission on Unalienable Rights in this way: by assuming the right to define human rights, he is also able to define away any rights his administration considers "alienable." This constitutes a weaponization of the structural centrality of the United States to the meanings associated with the concept of human rights.

Caveats

I suggest three qualifications to this observation. First, in weaponizing human rights, powerful states are not simply doing what they can while others either suffer what they must or react or resist as they may. Powerful states are also reacting to interdependence by seeking ways to weaponize it rather than undo it. What we see are efforts to duck constraints—which is one of the best indicators that the constraints are seen as real, even by the powerful. Although the United States has not signed onto many human rights conventions, it has (until rather recently) generally complied or acted as if it felt obligated to comply.[28] For example, the civilian immunity norm and requirement to conduct Article 36 reviews of new weapons are now enshrined in U.S. military culture, despite the fact that the United States resisted both these rules during their drafting and never signed the 1977 Additional Protocol to the Geneva Conventions.[29]

This is why even powerful liberal democracies generally do not, as the Athenians did at Mílos, violate ethical standards openly. They are much more likely to do so through a series of diplomatic maneuvers that aim to place their violations somehow outside the scope of regime norms[30]—what Nicole Dietelhoff and Lisbeth Zimmerman call "applicatory justification."[31] Instead of accounting for rule violations with denials, excuses, or apologies, these powerful democracies reinterpret the meaning of the law.[32] Thus, in the Qasem Soleimani case, the United States drastically expanded the definition of "self-defense" to justify violations of the norm against extrajudicial execution. In some cases, states follow the letter of the law while violating its spirit.[33] According to various scholars, this behavior can lead to the death or decay of norms[34]—thus, provoking particular concern by norm defenders.

In reinterpreting these norms, liberal democracies' stated rationale is often, in part, to protect themselves against the vagaries of ideational interdependence—the ability of less high-minded actors to use rules against them.[35] After 9/11, George W. Bush attempted to loosen the restrictions on and later rewired the meaning of "torture," claiming that it was impossible to combat terrorism without extracting actionable intelligence through so-called enhanced interrogation methods, often carried out at black sites.[36] The justification was that the Geneva Conventions and human rights law unduly bound U.S. hands; the policy solution, according to the United States, was to reinterpret the law itself—and a variety of actors behaved as if these U.S. actions actually had the power to change the rules.[37]

Such behavior is not the preserve of conservative administrations alone. President Barack Obama similarly aimed to chip away at the norms against assassination and extrajudicial execution in justifying a U.S. policy of killing terror suspects without trial in Pakistan, Somalia, and Yemen.[38] The Obama administration popularized new "legal" categories that did not exist (for example, "targeted killing"), applied the laws of war where human rights law should prevail, and stretched concepts like "imminent threat" to their breaking point, in an effort to sanitize and justify what was widely viewed by human rights lawyers as a campaign of extrajudicial execution.[39] Similarly, Donald Trump has aimed to not just restrict refugee flows into the United States, but also to rewrite the very concept of refugee protection, claiming asylum seekers are "illegal" (when asylum seeking is a fundamental human right) and creating a new fictional category in refugee law, calling it "safe third country" status.[40] Clearly, the United States regularly aims to exploit its ideational centrality to the human rights regime to rewrite norms in its own image.[41]

But second, these ploys often do not work. Though powerful states and some human rights organizations believe the behavior of liberal democracies sets the human rights agenda, and act as if it can, evidence is mixed on whether this is actually true. Often, when powerful democracies (or other powerful constituencies)[42] violate, obstruct, or attempt to redefine human rights norms, these behaviors backfire as other actors resist—and that very resistance has the effect of strengthening human rights norms and institutions, and delegitimizing the norm violators or norm spoilers.[43] Instead, as Adam Bowers shows, these normative regimes have been resilient to opposition from powerful states; as Margarita Petrova argues, norms may even have a better shot at life because of powerful state opposition.[44]

For foreign policy under three recent U.S. presidents, the same seems to hold true: norms against torture, assassination, and refugee protection have been strained but resilient in the face of great power contestation. The Bush administration faced condemnation, opposition, and opprobrium for its torture policies; the Supreme Court ruled them unconstitutional, and incoming president Obama renounced the practices.[45] Obama's efforts to create gray areas in international law to legitimatize extrajudicial execution of terror suspects were ultimately rejected by numerous states and international lawyers, most human rights organizations, and major international organizations; senior diplomats, drone pilots, and CIA officers resigned or spoke out in opposition.[46] Trump's refugee policy has provoked an international backlash, with only a single state out of 186 voting to support the United States in a condemnation of UN refugee assistance policy.[47]

Third, one reason that weaponizing ideational interdependence often fails in the human rights and humanitarian law areas is that some of the political consequences of ideational, technological, and institutional interdependence flow in directions that support weaker players—both weaker states and also non-state actors in a system that is designed around Westphalian categories.

In the arena of statecraft, for example, weak states have for much of the post–World War II period used the institutional panopticon of multilateral conferences to undermine the ideational hegemony of the great powers by focusing the spotlight on their intransigence—which has made it harder for great powers to be intransigent. The United States tried very hard to prevent the addition of civilian protection rules in the 1977 Geneva Conventions—but it gave up because it was too embarrassing to be isolated in an open forum by a vast network of newborn, developing countries backed by the Soviet Union.[48]

Interdependence has empowered not just weak states but also individuals and non-state actors vis-à-vis the state system. Ideational interdependence has constituted entire new webs of actors: human rights norms have spawned communities of transnational activists, practitioners and policy networks rooted in territorial states but engaged transnationally in defense of global ideas and identities.[49] There is significant evidence that their presence and efforts constrain state excess, if only at the margins.[50]

Weaker players may also benefit from institutional interdependence. The same multilateral forums that have strengthened the hand of weaker states through institutional interdependence have also created pathways for non-state influence over shared norms and power over outcomes.[51] For example, the successful outcome of the 1998 Rome Conference to form a new International Criminal Court was driven in large part by an NGO coalition that lobbied for progressive provisions, isolated the United States and China during proceedings, and channeled information to the media about state positions by way of pressuring them to go along.[52]

Finally, technological interdependence has created at least the potential for a panopticon effect against state oppression in ways that simply were not possible in the past. Open-source intelligence has revolutionized the ability of private actors to spotlight state abuses.[53] When images and video of human rights violations may be disseminated in real time by YouTube or Facebook without the media as intermediary, this reshapes the network structure of information flows and meaning in ways not always helpful to states.[54]

Ideational, institutional, and technological interdependencies can combine to threaten and weaken state power, not only creating opportunities for states to exploit choke points and panopticon effects, but also empowering weak actors to eradicate informational choke points by using a reverse-panopticon effect.[55] This is what online social bandits like WikiLeaks and Anonymous do, and why the sovereign-state system finds their strategies so threatening.[56] Leaks like the Afghan War Diary and the Panama Papers did more than expose corruption—they frayed the socially constructed boundary between the club of states' discursive traffic and the prying eyes of global citizen audiences, or what Nathalie Marechal calls "state power encountering a technologically enabled counter-power."[57]

More broadly, where states have tried to expand their use of surveillance technology (as with drones), networks of journalists, activists, and ordinary citizens have pushed back with their own kind of panopticon. For example, the Bush administration faced a concerted torrent of whistleblowing episodes, photographic leaks, court filings, human rights reports, and investigative exposes and congressional studies.[58] When the Obama administration aimed to use drones as the ultimate panopticon while hiding evidence of drone deaths, a global network of casualty counters began to record and publicize every death by drone.[59] Under Trump, drones themselves became surveillance tools, used not by the state but against it—taking surveillance footage over detention camps and supplementing the stream of images, words, and data spooled forth by activists, citizen-journalists, and whistleblowers about the disconnect between refugee treatment and refugee law.[60]

Caveats abound: technologies of information (and disinformation) can be and are also deployed by states,[61] used to surveil and control their citizens,[62] exploited to distract or divide foreign societies,[63] and turned by states against their critics.[64] Moreover, as the skilled use of social media by organizations such as ISIS demonstrates, the ability of individuals to amplify their message, and even the language of human rights, using networked technology is as easily available to nefarious actors as it is to those keen to promote a saner world.[65] Nonetheless, structures of interdependence can empower weak pro–human rights actors as well as strong states, and both sides can engage in tactics aimed to exploit and resist one another's own perceived strategies of weaponized interdependence.

Conclusion

I have made three arguments. First, scholars can extrapolate the concept of weaponized interdependence well beyond the issue area of finance or economics to arenas that involve ideas as well as information flows, and productive as well as structural power. Second, it is important to consider not only resistance against weaponizers, but weaponizing itself as a reaction against the concrete vagaries of interdependence—an interdependence the powerful cannot always easily escape. Third, it is vital to think about ways in which the panopticon effect can be used both against and by the powerful—and by networks beyond and within the state.

This suggests a rich research agenda on weaponized interdependence and human rights that stands to enliven and connect with the emerging literature on norm sabotage, contestation, and decay in world politics. Scholars are already theorizing the variation in the extent to which human security norm contestation affects norm robustness. I have argued this is related to the degree of ideational centrality of actors to a regime.[66] This area of study can also expand the understanding of how ideational centrality interacts with material centrality, and how weaker actors leveraging counternetworks can resist, expose, or neutralize weaponization efforts. Such is the warp and weft of a weaponized web.

Notes

I am grateful for the research assistance of Jaeye Baek, Catie Fowler, Arafat Kabir, and Jenna Norosky; Tyler Lovell's analytical insights; and to Dan Drezner, Henry Farrell, Abraham Newman, and the participants in the Fletcher School Workshop on Weaponized Interdependence for feedback.

1. Donald Trump, Twitter post, January 5, 2020, 5:52 p.m. https://twitter.com/realDonaldTrump/status/1213593975732527112?s=20.

2. BBC, "Trump under Fire for Threat to Iranian Cultural Sites," January 6, 2020, www.bbc.com/news/world-middle-east-51014237.

3. Erik Post, "U.S.-Iran Geopolitical Cataclysm Has Weakened International Law," *Katoikos*, January 12, 2020, www.katoikos.eu/analysis/us-iran-geopolitical-cataclysm-has-weakened-international-law-global-governance-and-international-cooperation.html.

4. Mehrnusch Anssari and Benjamin Nußberger, "Compilation of State Reactions to U.S. and Iranian Uses of Force in Iraq in January 2020," January 22, 2020, www.justsecurity.org/68173.

5. Nick Robins-Early, "Trump Walks Back Threat to Commit War Crimes against Iran's Cultural Sites," *Huffington Post*, January 8, 2020, www.huffpost.com/entry/trump-iran-cultural-sites_n_5e14ed9ac5b687c7eb5cda98?ncid=engmodushpmg00000004.

6. I adopt Barnett and Duvall's typology of power in global governance. See Michael Barnett and Raymond Duvall, *Power in Global Governance* (Cambridge University Press, 2005).

7. Antje Weiner, *Contestation and Constitution of Norms in Global International Relations* (Cambridge University Press, 2018); Herald Muller, "Theoretical Approaches in Norm Dynamics," in *Norm Dynamics in Multilateral Arms Control: Interests, Conflicts, and Justice*, edited by Herald Muller and Carmen Wunderlich (University of Georgia Press, 2013), pp. 20–48; Nicole Deitelhoff and Lisbeth Zimmermann, "Things We Lost in the Fire: How Different Types of Contestation Affect the Robustness of International Norms," *International Studies Review* 22 (March 2020), pp. 51–76; Wayne Sandholtz, "Norm Contestation, Robustness, and Replacement," *Journal of Global Security Studies* 4 (February 2019), pp. 139–46; Andrea Schneiker, "Norm Sabotage," *International Studies Perspectives*, March 2020, https://doi.org/10.1093/isp/ekaa003.

8. The cases from which these examples are drawn are elaborated on in Carpenter, Fowler, and Norosky, "Weaponized Interdependence and Human

Security Norms: Ideational Centrality, Norm Contestation, and the Power of the Reverse Panopticon," *Conflict, Violence and Security* working paper (University of Massachusetts-Amherst, June 2020).

9. Amrita Narlikar, "Must the Weak Suffer What They Must? The Global South in a World of Weaponized Interdependence," chapter 16 in this volume.

10. Ibid.

11. John Gerard Ruggie, "What Makes the World Hang Together," *International Organization* 52 (Autumn 1998), pp. 855–85.

12. Audie Klotz, *Norms in International Relations* (Cornell University Press, 1999); Martha Finnemore and Kathryn Sikkink, "International Norm Dynamics and Political Change," *International Organization* 52 (Autumn 1998), pp. 887–917; Richard Price, "How to Detect Ideas and Their Effects," in *The Politics of International Law*, edited by Charles Tilly and Robert E. Goodin (Oxford University Press, 2006), pp. 252–65.

13. Kathryn Sikkink, *The Justice Cascade* (New York: W. W. Norton & Co., 2014); Beth A. Simmons, *Mobilizing for Human Rights* (Cambridge University Press, 2012).

14. Ian Hurd, *How to Do Things with International Law* (Princeton University Press, 2017).

15. Charli Carpenter, *Lost Causes: Agenda Vetting in Global Issues Networks and the Shaping of Human Security* (Cornell University Press, 2014); Wendy H. Wong, *Internal Affairs: How the Structure of NGOs Transforms Human Rights* (Cornell University Press, 2012); Amanda Murdie, "The Ties that Bind: A Network Analysis of Human Rights International Nongovernmental Organizations," *British Journal of Political Science* 44 (January 2014), pp. 1–27.

16. R. J. Rummel, *Death by Government* (New Brunswick, NJ: Transactions Publishers, 1994).

17. Faradj Koliev, "Shaming and Democracy: Explaining Inter-State Shaming in International Organizations," *International Political Science Review* (October 2018), https://journals.sagepub.com/doi/10.1177/01925121 19858660.

18. Emilie M. Hafner-Burton, "Sticks and Stones: Naming and Shaming the Human Rights Enforcement Problem," *International Organization* 62 (October 2008), pp. 689–716.

19. Murdie, "The Ties That Bind"; Wong, *Internal Affairs*.

20. Barnett and Duvall, *Power in Global Governance*, p. 21.

21. James Raymond Vreeland, "Political Institutions and Human Rights: Why Dictatorships Enter into the UN Convention on Torture," *International Organization* 62 (January 2008), pp. 65–101.

22. James Meernik and others, "The Impact of Human Rights Organizations on Naming and Shaming Campaigns," *Journal of Conflict Resolution* 56 (April 2012), pp. 233–56.

23. James Ron and Howard Ramos, "Why Are the United States and Israel at the Top of Human Rights Hit Lists?" *Foreign Policy,* November 3, 2009, www.foreignpolicy.com/2009/11/03/why-are-the-united-states-and-israel-at -the-top-of-human-rights-hit-lists.

24. Cullen S. Hendrix and Wendy H. Wong, "When Is the Pen Truly Mighty? Regime Type and the Efficacy of Naming and Shaming in Curbing Human Rights Abuses," *British Journal of Political Science* 43 (July 2013), pp. 651–72; Cullen S. Hendrix and Wendy H. Wong, "Knowing Your Audience: How the Structure of International Relations and Organizational Choices Affect Amnesty International's Advocacy," *Review of International Organizations* 9 (March 2014), pp. 29–58.

25. James Ron, Howard Ramos, and Kathleen Rodgers, "Transnational Information Politics: NGO Human Rights Reporting, 1986–2000," *International Studies Quarterly* 49 (September 2005), pp. 557–87; Daniel W. Hill Jr., Will H. Moore, and Bumba Mukherjee, "Information Politics Versus Organizational Incentives: When Are Amnesty International's 'Naming and Shaming' Reports Biased?" *International Studies Quarterly* 57 (June 2013), pp. 219–32.

26. Meernik and others, "The Impact of Human Rights Organizations on Naming and Shaming Campaigns."

27. Hendrix and Wong, "When Is the Pen Truly Mighty?"

28. Andrew Moravcsik, "The Paradox of U.S. Human Rights Policy," in *American Exceptionalism and Human Rights*, edited by Michael Ignatieff (Princeton University Press, 2005), pp. 147–97.

29. Colin H. Kahl, "In the Crossfire or the Crosshairs? Norms, Civilian Casualties, and U.S. Conduct in Iraq," *International Security* 32 (June 2007), pp. 7–46; Theo Farrell, *The Norms of War: Cultural Beliefs and Modern Conflict* (Boulder, CO: Lynne Rienner Publishers, 2005).

30. As Vaughn Shannon has argued, even powerful states will attempt to appear to follow norms even if they are motivated to violate them—concealing their actions or carving off exceptions to the rule. See Vaughn Shannon, "Norms Are What States Make of Them," *International Studies Quarterly* 44 (June 2000), pp. 293–316.

31. Nicole Dietelhoff and Lisbeth Zimmerman, "Norms under Challenge: Unpacking the Dynamics of Norm Robustness," *Journal of Global Security Studies* 4 (January 2019), pp. 2–17.

32. Hurd, *How to Do Things with International Law.*

33. Zoltan I. Buzas, "Evading International Law: How Agents Comply with the Letter of the Law but Violate its Purpose," *European Journal of International Relations* 23 (December 2017), pp. 857–83.

34. Diana Panke and Ulrich Petersohn, "Norm Challenges and Norm Death: The Inexplicable?" *Cooperation and Conflict* 51 (March 2016), pp. 3–19.

35. Stephanie Carvin and Machael John Williams, *Law, Science, Liberalism, and the American Way of Warfare: The Quest for Humanity in Conflict* (Cambridge University Press, 2015).

36. Jamal Barnes, "The War on Terror and Battle for the Definition of Torture," *International Relations* 31 (March 2016), pp. 102–24.

37. Shelly McKeown, Haji Shelly, and Neil Ferguson, *Understanding Peace and Conflict Through Social Identity Theory: Contemporary Global Perspective* (New York: Springer Publishing, 2016).

38. Alexandria Nylen, "Frontier Justice: International Law and 'Lawless' Spaces in the 'War on Terror,'" *European Journal of International Relations* (November 2019), https://doi.org/10.1177/1354066119883682.

39. Luca Trenta, "The Obama Administration's Conceptual Change: Imminence and the Legitimation of Targeted Killings," *European Journal of International Security* 3 (February 2018), pp. 69–93; Simon Frankel Pratt, "Norm Transformation and the Institutionalization of Targeted Killing in the US," *European Journal of International Relations* 25 (September 2019), pp. 723–47.

40. Alise Coen, "International Order, the Rule of Law, and U.S. Departures from Refugee Protection," *International Journal of Human Rights* 22, no. 10 (2018), pp. 1269–84.

41. Carpenter, Baek, Fowler, and Norosky, "Weaponized Interdependence and Human Security Norms."

42. Rebecca Sanders, "Norm Spoiling: Undermining the International Women's Rights Agenda," *International Affairs*. 94 (March 2018), pp. 271–92.

43. Dietelhoff and Zimmerman, "Things We Lost in the Fire"; Jeffrey S. Lantis and Carmen Wunderlich, "Resiliency Dynamics of Norm Clusters: Norm Contestation and International Cooperation," *Review of International Studies* 44 (July 2018), pp. 570–93.

44. Adam Bowers, *Norms Without the Great Powers: International Law and Changing Social Standards in World Politics* (Oxford University Press, 2017); Margarita H. Petrova, "Naming and Praising in Humanitarian Norm Development," *World Politics* 71 (July 2019), pp. 586–630.

45. Barnes, "The War on Terror and Battle for the Definition of Torture."

46. Betcy Jose, "How Human Rights Watch Suppressed the Targeted Killing Norm," *Contemporary Security Policy* 38 (August 2017), pp. 237–59; Andris Banka and Adam Quinn, "Killing Norms Softly: U.S. Targeted Killing, Quasi-Secrecy and the Assassination Ban," *Security Studies* 27 (July 2018), p. 700.

47. Carpenter, Baek, Fowler and Norosky, "Weaponized Interdependence and Human Security Norms."

48. Giovanni Mantilla, "Social Pressure and the Making of Wartime Ci-

vilian Protection Rules," *European Journal of International Relations* 26 (August 2019), pp. 317–49. See also Margarita H. Petrova, "Small States in Humanitarian Norm Making," in *Power in a Complex Global System*, edited by Louis W. Pauly and Bruce W. Jentleson (New York: Routledge, 2014), pp. 194–208.

49. Margaret E. Keck and Kathryn Sikkink, *Activists Beyond Borders: Advocacy Networks in International Politics* (Cornell University Press, 1998); Matthew Evangelista and Nina Tannenwald, *Do the Geneva Conventions Matter?* (Oxford University Press, 2017).

50. Matthew Krain, "International Intervention and the Severity of Genocides and Politicides," *International Studies Quarterly* 49 (September 2005), pp. 363–88; Hyeran Jo and Beth A. Simmons, "Can the International Criminal Court Deter Atrocity?" *International Organization* 70 (July 2016), pp. 443–75.

51. Deborah D. Avant, Martha Finnemore, and Susan K. Sell, *Who Governs the Globe?* (Cambridge University Press, 2010); Sarah S. Stroup and Wendy H. Wong, "The Agency and Authority of NGOs," *Perspectives on Politics* 14 (March 2016), pp. 138–44.

52. Johan D. Van Der Vyer, "Civil Society and the International Criminal Court," *Journal of Human Rights* 2 (September 2003), pp. 425–39.

53. For example, it was Bellingcat, an online organization of investigative citizen-journalists, that identified Russia as the culprit in the downing of Malaysia Airlines Flight 17 over Ukraine by analyzing social media traffic of Russian soldiers' wives and mothers. Bellingcat played a similar role in the crash of Ukraine International Airlines Flight 752 over Tehran. See Peter Warren Singer, *Likewar: The Weaponization of Social Media* (Boston: Houghton Mifflin Harcourt, 2018), p. 74.

54. See Singer, *Likewar*.

55. Dawn L. Rothe and Kevin F. Steinmetz, "The Case of Bradley Manning: State Victimization, Realpolitik and WikiLeaks," *Contemporary Justice Review* 16 (June 2013), pp. 290–92.

56. Wendy H. Wong and Peter A. Brown, "E-Bandits in Global Activism: WikiLeaks, Anonymous, and the Politics of No One," *Perspectives on Politics* 11 (December 2013), pp. 1015–33; Nathalie Marechal, "WikiLeaks and the Public Sphere: Dissent and Control in Cyberworld," *International Journal of Technology, Knowledge & Society: Annual Review* 9 (May 2013), pp. 93–106.

57. Marechal, "WikiLeaks and the Public Sphere," p. 93; Henry Farrell and Martha Finemore, "The End of Hypocrisy: American Foreign Policy in the Age of Leaks," *Foreign Affairs*, November/December 2013, www.foreignaffairs.com/articles/united-states/2013-10-15/end-hypocrisy.

58. Spencer Ackerman, "Inside the Fight to Reveal the CIA's Torture

Secrets," *Guardian*, September 9, 2016, www.theguardian.com/us-news/2016/sep/09/cia-insider-daniel-jones-senate-torture-investigation.

59. Susan Breau and Marie Aronsson, "Drone Attacks, International Law, and the Recording of Civilian Casualties of Armed Conflict," *Suffolk Transnational Law Review* 35 (Summer 2012), pp. 255–300; Marc-Antoine Pérouse de Montclos, Elizabeth Minor, and Samrat Sinha, *Violence, Statistics, and the Politics of Accounting for the Dead* (New York: Springer Publishing, 2016).

60. "U.S. Border Patrol Migrant Camp from Above," Reuters, May 16, 2019, www.reuters.com/news/picture/us-border-patrol-migrant-camp-from-above-idUSRTS2HV7C/1387815192; Miriam Jordan, "Whistle-Blowers Say Detaining Migrants Families 'Poses High Risk of Harm,' " *New York Times*, July 18, 2018, www.nytimes.com/2018/07/18/us/migrant-children-family-detention-doctors.html; Nina Hall, "Norm Contestation in the Digital Era: Campaigning for Refugee Rights," *International Affairs* 95 (May 2019), pp. 575–95.

61. Thomas Zeitzoff, "Does Social Media Influence Conflict? Evidence from the 2012 Gaza Conflict," *Journal of Conflict Resolution* 62 (January 2018), pp. 29–63.

62. Zixue Tai, "Casting the Ubiquitous Net of Information Control: Internet Surveillance in China from Golden Shield to Green Dam," *International Journal of Advanced Pervasive and Ubiquitous Computing* 2 (January 2010), pp. 53–70.

63. Renee DiResta and others, *The Tactics and Tropes of the Internet Research Agency* (Washington: U.S. Senate Documents, Congress of the United States, 2018), https://digitalcommons.unl.edu/cgi/viewcontent.cgi?article=1003&context=senatedocs.

64. Evgeny Morozov, *The Net Delusion: The Dark Side of Internet Freedom* (New York: PublicAffairs, 2011).

65. Singer, *Likewar*.

66. Alan Bloomfield, "Norm Antipreneurs and Theorizing Resistance to Normative Change," *Review of International Studies* 42 (April 2016), pp. 310–33; Christopher Kutz, "How Norms Die: Torture and Assassination in American Security Policy," *Ethics & International Affairs* 28 (Winter 2014), pp. 425–49; Sandholtz, "Norm Contestation, Robustness, and Replacement."

16

Must the Weak Suffer What They Must?

The Global South in a World
of Weaponized Interdependence

AMRITA NARLIKAR

Amidst the rich debate that is emerging around the phenomenon of weaponized interdependence (WI), attention has gone first and foremost toward identifying the manifestations of the phenomenon itself, and the mechanisms through which this weapon is wielded.[1] The increased crossfire between the United States and China in the last several years—with detrimental economic consequences not only for each other, but also for the system at large—has meant that considerable academic analysis has gravitated toward these cases. In this chapter, I turn to a different set of actors. I investigate the players that are most likely to get squeezed in great power games and how those players are innovating, responding to, and adapting to the opportunities and constraints posed by WI. The chapter demonstrates that far from being just victims in a redrawn great-power game, seemingly weaker countries also have considerable scope for agency. By covering new empirical ground on the strategies that "the rest" are using, the analysis aims to add to theorizing on WI and also further develop some policy-relevant insights.

WI and "the Rest"

The logic of WI is one that is likely to privilege the already-powerful, rather than weaker, members of the international system—"the rest," which find themselves in the position of rule-takers. Three mechanisms exacerbate preexisting power asymmetries and make it harder for many countries to carve out the bargaining space necessary to achieve their preferred outcomes.

The first mechanism derives directly from the workings of WI itself. Underpinning WI—in contrast to more conventional forms of economic statecraft—is the organization of global production of goods and services via integrated value chains that generate hierarchical economic networks. Henry Farrell and Abraham Newman argue that states holding political authority over network hubs and having domestic institutions that support certain types of strategies are able to weaponize networks of interdependence to their advantage. Some states can do this quite effectively by gathering or restricting information or economic flows through panopticon and choke-point effects. In doing so, they can "discover and exploit vulnerabilities, compel policy change, and deter unwanted actions."[2] The preconditions that states occupy key positions as network hubs and have the necessary political capacity to exploit their positions together suggest that interdependence can be weaponized by only a few major players, such as the United States, China, and possibly some within the European Union (EU). In contrast, for many countries—and especially those in the global south—the chances of controlling these crucial nodes are slight. Long histories of being consigned to the status of colonies in some cases, misguided development policies in others, or a nasty cocktail of these and other tough structural conditions mean that developing countries seldom find themselves located on privileged positions that serve as network hubs. The importance of domestic institutional capacity to successfully implement WI also renders this task difficult for some developing countries, even when they are favored by geographical position or availability of scarce resources. As such, many countries in the global south may find themselves at the receiving end of WI.

Second, the logic of WI suggests that at least in certain key issue areas, the barriers to entry are high. If network externalities under WI are, indeed, so significant that they end up creating natural monopolies,[3] developing countries face a major problem. Not only is it difficult for them to occupy network hubs themselves, but also they are further hamstrung by the lack of alternative suppliers of essential products, infrastructure, and services that a competitive economy might have facilitated. As their Best Alternative to a Negotiated Agreement (BATNA) declines, so does their bargaining power.

Third, WI is not a phenomenon that the international organizations of the post–World War II era were set up to deal with. An important assumption underlying the postwar system was a positive correlation between prosperity and peace;[4] multilateral institutions were therefore premised on the virtues of interdependence. A certain degree of like-mindedness was also assumed among players. Take the example of the world trading system: the Soviet Union and its allies were not a part of the General Agreement on Tariffs and Trade (GATT) in the era of the Cold War.[5] Within the system, increased economic integration was seen as a conduit to both enhanced wealth and greater peace. The European project epitomized this logic, and the end of the Cold War reinforced this assumption. For instance, when the World Trade Organization (WTO) was founded in 1995, a triumphant liberal narrative promoted the idea of progressive convergence. Working with this belief, the WTO welcomed new members such as China and Russia into its fold, and was ill-prepared for two fundamental challenges that were in the offing: (1) states could misuse the deep economic integration, which the international trade regime had been promoting as such a great virtue, for geostrategic gains rather than global peace, and (2) convergence was not an inevitability among all players, and certainly not among "systemic rivals." Caught between trade wars launched by the United States in recent years on the one hand, and the long-standing and persistent violations of WTO law (or at least the spirit of the law) by China on the other (for example, via forced technology transfer requirements, intellectual property rights [IPR] violations, subsidies, and export controls), the WTO failed to keep up with changing realities on the ground. At the time of writing this, neither the substance of the WTO's agreements nor its decision-making processes allow it to deal effectively with these challenges, and all of its three functions (negotiation, dispute settlement, and transparency) are paralyzed.[6]

The WTO provides us with one among several examples of the incapacity of international organizations to contain or adapt to WI. And while this poses a problem for international cooperation at large, the decline of multilateralism is particularly detrimental for weaker players. Albeit to different degrees, international organizations have facilitated the functioning of a rules-based system, transparency, enforceability, and scope for coalition building—all of which helped to strengthen the hand of poor and small countries in international negotiations over the recent decades (and all the more so as developing countries were able to shape and reform the workings of some organizations).[7] A weakening of these multilateral institutions hits the weakest the hardest.

Thus, WI potentially affects the global south via a triple jeopardy: poor and weak states find it hard to occupy key nodes in networks, their BATNAs are reduced, and weakening multilateralism endangers their influence even further. In the next section, I explore how far they can insulate themselves against some of these risks or, indeed, even turn this difficult situation to their own advantage.

Strategic Responses to WI from the Global South

Despite the structural disadvantage that stems from not being in control of a network hub, countries of the global south have at least five promising strategies available to them. I outline these below, with examples. The first four involve working within the system and its constraints; the last engages with the possibility of reshaping the structural processes that Farrell and Newman identify, via the route of narratives and counternarratives.

Lie Low and Make Some Limited Gains

"When elephants fight, the grass gets trampled" need not always be the case.

The U.S.-China trade wars, for all the disruption and uncertainty that they have produced, have also led to a redirection of trade. Although the economic pie has shrunk, it has also been redistributed to the relative benefit of some smaller players. For instance, in its September 2019 report, the Asian Development Bank (ADB) lowered its growth forecasts. But amid overall gloomy projections, it also pointed to some positive developments. Although U.S. imports from China had fallen by 12 percent in the first half of 2019 (compared to the first half of 2018), the ADB also reported, "U.S. imports from the rest of developing Asia rose by about 10%, with notably large increases of 33% for Viet Nam; 20% for Taipei, China, and 13% for Bangladesh. For Viet Nam and Taipei, China, the bulk of the increased exports to the U.S. were electronics and machinery, and for Bangladesh garments."[8] Similarly, when China retaliated against U.S. tariffs by imposing a 25 percent tariff on U.S. soybeans in 2018, other suppliers stood to gain. As the tariff took full effect, Brazil came to supply 77 percent of China's soybean market in 2018–2019; the U.S. share of the Chinese market declined from 30 percent in 2017 to 4 percent in the 2018–2019 market year.[9] When major powers located on network hubs clash, they inadvertently also create space for smaller players to step in. Countries that have nimble production structures, supportive government regulations, and firms that are ready to innovate to new opportunities can fare well when such opportunities arise.

The problem with a "lie low" strategy is that it relies heavily on conducive external conditions to emerge. And gains thus accrued may be transient. Every time a deal to normalize U.S.-China trade relations has been in the offing (or, indeed, when Chinese demand declined due to African swine fever there), newspaper stories have circulated that Brazil's gains will evaporate rapidly. Besides, such opportunism is also open to major powers that already dominate hubs, especially those that are able to move in swiftly to fill new vacuums. For example, even as the European Union grappled with the outbreak of COVID-19 and put up export restrictions on medical equipment while the United States persisted with its "America First" approach, China seized the opportunity to exercise its coronavirus diplomacy with full force. Its campaign involved the exports of masks and other equipment, as well as an aggressive media campaign to promote its own narrative on the origins, spread, and handling of the pandemic.[10] The extent to which this coronavirus diplomacy will be successful remains to be seen. For the purposes of my argument, though, it serves as a useful reminder that opportunism is not a strategy limited to the weak. Chances are that opportunities created, when key players fight, can—and will—be exploited to further enhance the power of the strong by emulating, adapting, and further refining the strategies used by smaller players.

At best, then, to lie and wait for suitable opportunities might serve as a good coping mechanism for a few countries of the global south that have sufficient flexibility in governance and market mechanisms (for instance, those that enable them to respond swiftly and effectively to new possibilities that open up from a redirection of trade). But it is unlikely to work as a long-term, sustainable strategy.

Temporarily Capture Choke Points

At particular points in time, smaller players—states and non-state actors, too—may find that they have greater use of underexploited choke points. This proactive attempt to use WI by weaker players does not easily result in a fundamental alteration of the intrinsic power asymmetry at work. But it can cause considerable disruption to major powers.

For example, Turkey threatened to flood Europe with 3.6 million refugees for the EU's criticism of its attacks on Northern Syria in October 2019.[11] Turkish prime minister Recep Tayyip Erdoğan was able to issue this credible threat due to three crucial factors: the country's strategically vital geographical position, which allowed proximity to Europe; the presence of millions of refugees from the Middle East; and the raw memories of the crisis that had erupted across the EU after German chancellor Angela Merkel's "Wir schaffen das" moment in 2015. European wariness of a repeat of recent events helped in the creation of a choke point controlled by Turkey.

The five-month suspension of airspace for flights to and from India by Pakistan, in retaliation for India's air strike on an alleged terrorist training camp in Balakot in February 2019, is another example. Having to reroute flights around Pakistan caused considerable disruption and financial losses to international airlines (and, especially, Indian airlines). Pakistan was able to take this action due to its location on a key aviation corridor.

India found itself unexpectedly in control of a choke point during the coronavirus pandemic. A study claimed that the antimalarial drug hydroxychloroquine could help lessen the severity of COVID-19 symptoms and progression in patients. As the main producer of the drug (manufacturing 70 percent of the world's supply), India acquired unprecedented power to grant or deny access to (what some believed was) a potentially life-saving medicine. The country's immediate reaction was to impose export controls on sixteen drugs, including hydroxychloroquine and paracetamol, and thereby use the choke point to restrict access. The government subsequently revised its announced policy and agreed that the drug (and other medicines that had initially been placed under the export ban) could be exported to neighboring countries and others severely affected by the pandemic.[12] The fact that Brazil and the United States were receiving these imports suggests that exports of these drugs were also targeted toward strategic partners. India had thus successfully used its control over a new choke point to cultivate allies.

There are also other instances where weaker actors do not have an obvious natural advantage but can nevertheless exploit key vulnerabilities at low costs to themselves. The attack on a Saudi oil facility in September 2019—whether by Iran or Houthi—is one such example of the disruption that smaller players can cause to larger players as well as globally (in this case, via the impact on oil prices).[13]

All of the above examples show ways in which countries that do not enjoy network power may nevertheless be able to create new choke points, or capture existing ones, under special conditions and thereby harness WI to their own ends.

Hedge One's Bets

Even when not located on hubs themselves, smaller players may be able to achieve outcomes in their favor by hedging.

The options for alternative sources of funding and support available to Southeast Asia have expanded amid multipolar competition.

For instance, China has been courting countries in Asia through its Belt and Road Initiative (BRI);[14] Europe has been developing an alternative connectivity initiative;[15] and the United States has been trying to win friends and influence states in the region and thereby balance against China.[16] Rather than simply becoming subjects of a great-power rivalry involving a scramble for spheres of influence, some smaller players have chosen to harness the opportunities to improve their BATNA. This in turn, means enhanced leverage for them.[17]

Japan, caught between a declining U.S. commitment to global order and an increasingly assertive China, has played a hedging game. On the one hand, Japan has coordinated its position with others that share its concerns as part of the Quadrilateral Security Dialogue (comprising Australia, Japan, India, and the United States), as well as the in the Asia-Africa Growth Corridor it has developed in collaboration with India. On the other hand, Japan has also extended conditional support to the BRI and stayed clear of an open challenge to China.[18]

A few players have used a similar strategy of hedging in dealing with the shortages of medical equipment during the coronavirus pandemic. On March 15, 2020, the European Commission (EC) decided to put up emergency export restrictions on hospital supplies to non-EU members. This move threatened devasting consequences for the many countries outside the EU that were also affected by the pandemic (besides potential supply chain disruption on medical equipment for the EU itself).[19] Serbian president Aleksandar Vučić made a classic hedging move in response. He did not mince his words in declaring his disappointment over Europe's decision and announcing that he was turning to China: "European solidarity does not exist. That is a fairy tale on paper. I have sent a special letter to the only ones who can help. That is China."[20] Serbia's hedging strategy was effective. Not only did a planeload of assistance arrive from China, but EU funds also followed (with Serbia getting the greatest proportion of these EU funds), along with an exemption for the Western Balkans on export restrictions.[21]

For smaller players, hedging is a plausible and effective course of action. But it is a strategy that works best in the short run. It is unlikely to be sustainable in the medium to long run, especially if confrontation among the major powers increases and decoupling begins to take place. In such a scenario, small players would have to enter the balance-of-power game and choose sides.

Form New Alignments of Empowerment

External balancing has long been a strategy employed by the weak, be it via formal alliances or informal coalitions. To deal with WI, too, some level of collective bargaining is possible. And while this might involve forming alliances within the global south, coalitions—even with some middle powers—might not be far-reaching enough to acquire influence. Having a key actor on board that already occupies a hub in a network could be a game changer. This could involve bandwagoning with an existing hub (such as the United States or China) or balancing by working with a power that is on the threshold of becoming a hub power. The EU may have the potential to emerge as such a hub for 5G technology or in setting standards on digital governance (for example, in data privacy), especially if it beefs up its connectivity projects with others and takes measures to strengthen its own companies.[22] Whether bandwagoning with one of the existing hubs or balancing collectively with a threshold hub, the global south has the potential to make more of a possible decoupling between the network hubs.

Much of the academic and policy debate on decoupling has focused mainly on the major powers (and especially the United States and China).[23] But this does not mean smaller players are excluded entirely from the game. They can exercise some vital choices in how they engage with competing hubs. Plus, they can indirectly benefit from the decoupling of major players.

Take the example of reactions to the COVID-19 pandemic, which resulted in a heavy disruption of supply chains for many players and also led countries to recognize that high levels of integration in current value chains can result in the weaponization of health policy. Strong reactions ensued. For instance, the European commissioner for competition and EC executive vice president, Margrethe Vestager, stated that European countries should buy stakes in struggling companies amid the risk of Chinese takeovers during the pandemic.[24] Also in response to the devastation wreaked by the pandemic, Japan made the decision to reserve 220 billion yen ($2 billion) from its stimulus package to help its companies move production from China back to Japan, and another 23.5 billion yen ($222 million) to enable Japanese firms to move to other countries.[25] India put up new restrictions that targeted foreign direct investment (FDI) from neighboring countries, to curb "opportunistic takeovers/acquisitions of Indian companies due to the current COVID-19 pandemic."[26] The updated measures, which subjected FDI from neighboring countries to government scrutiny, were seen to be targeting China (given that Pakistan and Bangladesh were already subject to such measures).[27] If this trend of reducing dependence on production hubs continues, new opportunities will arise for smaller players (for instance, via Japanese firms relocating to Southeast Asia) and give them greater leverage. It might further give them opportunities to form new alignments, especially if key powers seek to re-create value chains with like-minded players (countries with which they share fundamental values). So, for example, the EU, Japan, and India could come together, not necessarily as a formal alliance *against* China, but as a coalition for recognizing the linkages between their own trade, investment, and security. Such coalitions could also play a useful role in updating multilateral institutions and enabling them to deal with WI.

Develop Supportive Narratives

Farrell and Newman take into account the role of domestic institutions and norms, which influence the extent to which, and the ways in which, already powerful actors use networks to weaponize interdependence. But, as Daniel Drezner notes in the introduction to this volume, embedded networks had already been around for some time before relevant actors mobilized them for WI. I suggest that the questions of when and why actors decide to use their WI potential may have something to do with narratives.

A narrative, according to Robert Shiller's definition, is "a simple story or easily expressed *explanation* of events that many people want to bring up in conversation or on news or social media because it can be used to *stimulate the concerns or emotions* of others, and/ or because it appears to advance *self-interest*" (emphasis added).[28] Certain narratives can serve as "major vectors of rapid change in culture, in zeitgeist, and ultimately in economic behavior."[29] When and why countries choose to weaponize interdependence may in fact depend a good deal on the (true or false) causal stories the actors tell themselves, as well as their network centrality and the complementary domestic institutions and norms that allows them to exploit it. Indeed, a change in domestic narratives might be the tipping point that leads "centrally located actors" to exploit their strategic positions.

The Trump administration's use of WI via trade is a case in point. Through his "good and easy to win" trade wars, and also his multipronged attacks on the WTO, Trump chose to exploit the long-standing centrality of the United States to trade networks in an unprecedented way. He did this by tapping into and amplifying a causal narrative that attributed growing inequalities, disappearing jobs, weakening infrastructure, and several other problems within the United States to existing trade agreements; the only solution, as per this narrative, was a policy of "Buy American and Hire American."[30] Having developed such a narrative, the administration used the necessary domestic processes to weaponize its foreign economic policy, against not only China but also the EU, Japan, Canada, Mexico, and others, via strategies such as tariffs, export restrictions, sanctions, and blocking the appointment or reappointment of members of the WTO's Appellate Body.[31]

That narratives matter in interesting ways for the effective deployment of WI is important not only for major players—narratives can also serve as a valuable source of agency for members of the global south in weaker structural positions and with weaker governance systems. For instance, China has developed a narrative that claims to stand for the cause of international cooperation and development. This narrative is used to back its BRI[32] within a wider context of declaring the country's commitment to globalization and multilateralism.[33] But even a position of overwhelming control as a hub of connectivity projects does not give China comparable control over narratives. In fact, several counternarratives that are extremely critical of BRI have been developed. Some go so far as to describe it as a "a new version of colonialism";[34] others point to its deleterious consequences for biodiversity and the environment; still others frame BRI in terms of a fundamental security threat. Together, this has resulted in the cancellation of some BRI projects.[35] The confluence of some of these counternarratives of the global south with those of the EU may expand the scope for alliances and the creation of new networks. And smart counternarratives by "the rest" can undermine the effectiveness with which those in control of hubs can deploy WI—thereby reducing the raw structural power that networks offer a few strong players.

Conclusion

My main task in this chapter has been to focus on the scope of re-action and resistance from the global south amid the constraints of WI. Toward this, I have identified five strategies through which "the rest" can exercise agency. But this agency also bears relevance for the powerful states that have jurisdiction over hubs, because it offers them potential allies and friends. The presence of cooperation part-ners from the world regions may be important both for the exercise of panopticon effects and to deter damage caused by the potential capture of choke points. Similarly, narratives that support particular variants of WI can have a greater chance of going viral with the sup-port of network nodes from the global south. How smaller players get empowered or disempowered thus matters for the practice of WI by powerful hub players.

While I have focused primarily on how the global south is adapt-ing to the challenges of WI that come from those occupying hubs in global networks, WI also operates at a regional level, between members of the global south that occupy important nodes.[36] Further, empirical studies might unveil some homegrown uses of WI; others might reveal clear regional learning effects from the practice of WI by hub players or cross-regionally. Low levels of economic integration could provide fertile conditions for classic uses of economic statecraft but less opportunity for WI. Similarly, conflict zones—where eco-nomic exchange might already be curtailed—may be even less likely to show evidence of WI. A future research agenda that incorporates comparative analyses from the global south would enrich the study of WI empirically and theoretically. It could also help to rescue the term from the overuse and misuse that it has been subject to in public and academic debate.

Above all, some of the examples provided in this chapter show that the global south is a site of experimentation and incubation for resistance against WI, as well as innovative uses of it. These experiments naturally generate feedback loops to and from actors occupying privileged hub positions. Studies of the interactions between the hubs and the others in peripheral positions will thus likely serve as a vital step toward building more dynamic models of WI.

Notes

1. Henry Farrell and Abraham L. Newman, "Weaponized Interdependence: How Global Economic Networks Shape State Coercion," *International Security* 44 (Summer 2019), pp. 42–79.

2. Ibid., p. 45.

3. Daniel Drezner, "Weaponized Interdependence in World Politics," workshop discussion, October 10–11, 2019.

4. See, for example, Henry Morgenthau Jr., "Address by the Honorable Henry Morgenthau, Jr., at the Inaugural Plenary Session," speech at International Monetary Conference in Bretton Woods, NH, July 1, 1944, www.cvce.eu/content/publication/2003/12/12/34c4153e-6266-4e84-88d7-f655 abf1395f/publishable_en.pdf.

5. Thomas Wright, "Sifting through Interdependence," *Washington Quarterly* 36 (Fall 2013), pp. 7–23.

6. Amrita Narlikar, "A Grand Bargain to Revive the World Trade Organization," *Modernizing the World Trade Organization: A CIGI Essay Series,* May 11, 2020, www.cigionline.org/articles/grand-bargain-revive-wto.

7. Amrita Narlikar, *Poverty Narratives and Power Paradoxes in International Trade Negotiations and Beyond* (Cambridge University Press, 2020).

8. Asian Development Bank, "Asian Development Outlook 2019 Update: Fostering Growth and Inclusion in Asia's Cities," September 2019, p. 14, www.adb.org/sites/default/files/publication/524596/ado2019-update.pdf; Robin Harding, "Asia's Emerging Economies Are Winning U.S.-China Trade War," *Financial Times,* September 25, 2019, www.ft.com/content/b01d048c-df59 -11e9-9743-db5a370481bc.

9. Fred Gale, Constanza Valdes, and Mark Ash, "Interdependence of China, the United States, and Brazil in Soybean Trade," *Report from the Economic Research Service* OCS-19F-01, United States Department of

Agriculture, June 2019, www.ers.usda.gov/webdocs/publications/93390/ocs -19f-01.pdf?v=4048.3.

10. Jim Waterson and Lily Kuo, "China Steps up Western Media Campaign over Coronavirus Crisis," *Guardian,* April 3, 2020, www.theguardian.com/ world/2020/apr/03/china-steps-up-western-media-campaign-over-corona virus-crisis.

11. Bel Trew, "Erdoğan Threatens to Flood Europe with 3.6 Million Refugees as Syria Offensive Forces Tens of Thousands to Flee," *Independent,* October 19, 2019, www.independent.co.uk/news/world/middle-east/erdogan -syria-turkey-kurds-europe-refugees-invasion-sdf-latest-middle-east -a9150271.html.

12. Elizabeth Roche, "Government Lifts Restrictions on Exports of Key Drugs," Livemint, April 8, 2020, www.livemint.com/news/india/india-allows -limited-exports-of-hydroxychloroquine-used-in-treatment-of-covid-19 -11586236116865.html.

13. Henry Farrell (@henryfarrell), "11. The broader takeaway is: glo-balization has not produced a seamless global market, but lumpy global net-works, with plenty of chokepoints. These create vulnerabilities. And vulnerabilities create strategic opportunities that states and non-state actors are taking up. Finis." Twitter, September 16, 2019, https://twitter.com/henry farrell/status/1173594994864795649); Laila Kearney, "Oil Jumps Nearly 15% Record Trading After Attack on Saudi Facilities," Reuters, September 16, 2019, www.reuters.com/article/us-global-oil/oil-prices-surge-15-after-attack -on-saudi-facilities-hits-global-supply-idUSKBN1W00UG.

14. Thorsten Benner and others, "Authoritarian Advance: Responding to China's Growing Political Influence in Europe," GPPi & MERICS, February 2018, www.merics.org/sites/default/files/2018-02/GPPi_MERICS_Authori tarian_Advance_2018_1.pdf.

15. European External Action Service, "Connecting Europe and Asia: the EU Strategy," September 2019, https://eeas.europa.eu/sites/eeas/files/eu-asian _connectivity_factsheet_september_2019.pdf_final.pdf; High Representative of the European Union for Foreign Affairs and Security Policy & European Commission, "Connecting Europe and Asia—Building Blocks for an EU Strategy," JOIN (2018) 31 final, September 19, 2018, https://eeas.europa.eu/ sites/eeas/files/joint_communication_-_connecting_europe_and_asia_-_ building_blocks_for_an_eu_strategy_2018-09-19.pdf.

16. Mike Pence, for instance, had the following to say: "As we speak, as we're all aware, some are offering infrastructure loans to governments across the Indo-Pacific and the wider world. Yet the terms of those loans are often opaque at best. Projects they support are often unsustainable and of poor quality. And too often, they come with strings attached and lead to staggering debt. . . . Know that the United States offers a better option. We don't drown our partners in a sea of debt. We don't coerce or compromise your indepen-

dence. The United States deals openly, fairly We do not offer a constricting belt or a one-way road. When you partner with us, we partner with you, and we all prosper." See Mike Pence, "Remarks by Vice President Pence at the 2018 APEC CEO Summit," November 16, 2018, www.whitehouse.gov/brief ings-statements/remarks-vice-president-pence-2018-apec-ceo-summit-port -moresby-papua-new-guinea/.

17. See, for example, Gwen Robinson, "Southeast Asia Gains New Leverage as China and U.S. Battle for Influence," *Nikkei Asian Review*, May 29, 2019.

18. Titli Basu, "Geo-economic Contest in Southeast Asia: Great Power Politics through the Prism of Trade, Investments, and Aid," in *The Sage Handbook of Asian Foreign Policy*, edited by Tashika Inoguchi (London: Sage, 2019), pp. 465–500.

19. Chad Bown, "EU Limits on Medical Gear Exports Puts Poor Countries and Europeans at Risk," Peterson Institute for International Economics, March 19, 2020, www.piie.com/blogs/trade-and-investment-policy-watch/eu -limits-medical-gear-exports-put-poor-countries-and.

20. Shaun Walker, "Coronavirus Diplomacy: How Russia, China and EU Vie to Win over Serbia," *Guardian*, April 13, 2020, www.theguardian.com/ world/2020/apr/13/coronavirus-diplomacy-how-russia-china-and-eu-vie-to -win-over-serbia.

21. European Commission, "EU Mobilises Immediate Support for Its West Balkan Partners to Tackle Coronavirus," press release, March 30, 2020, https:// ec.europa.eu/commission/presscorner/detail/en/IP_20_561; European Commission, "Introductory Statement by Commissioner Phil Hogan at Informal Meeting of EU Trade Ministers," April 16, 2020, https://ec.europa.eu/commis sion/commissioners/2019-2024/hogan/announcements/introductory-statement -commissioner-phil-hogan-informal-meeting-eu-trade-ministers_en.

22. The EU began to take some steps in this direction via its EU-China strategic paper, which recognized China as a "systemic rival"; see High Representative of the European Union for Foreign Affairs and Security Policy & European Commission, "EU-China: A Strategic Outlook," JOIN (2019) 5 final, March 12, 2019, https://ec.europa.eu/commission/sites/beta-political/ files/communication-eu-china-a-strategic-outlook.pdf.

23. See Wright, "Sifting through Interdependence"; and Henry Farrell and Abraham L. Newman, "Chained to Globalization: Why It's Too Late to Decouple," *Foreign Affairs* 99 (January/February 2020).

24. Javier Espinoza, "Vestager Urges Stakebuilding to Block Chinese Takeovers," *Financial Times*, April 12, 2020, www.ft.com/content/e14f24c7 -e47a-4c22-8cf3-f629da62b0a7.

25. Isabel Reynolds and Emi Urabe, "Japan to Fund Firms to Shift Production Out of China," Bloomberg, April 8, 2020, www.bloomberg.com/ news/articles/2020-04-08/japan-to-fund-firms-to-shift-production-out-of -china.

26. Government of India, Ministry of Commerce & Industry, "Review of Foreign Direct Investment (FDI) Policy for Curbing Opportunistic Takeovers/ Acquisitions of Indian Companies Due to the Current COVID-19 Pandemic," Department for Promotion of Industry and Internal Trade, FDI Policy Section, press note no. 3 (April 17, 2020), https://dipp. gov.in/sites/default/files/pn3 _2020.pdf.

27. Benjamin Parkin, "India Moves to Curb Chinese Takeovers," *Financial Times,* April 18, 2020, www.ft.com/content/ad3f84b0-fb75-4588-97e8 -4a657ad67883.

28. Robert Shiller, "Narrative Economics," *American Economic Review* 107 (2017), pp. 967–1004.

29. Ibid.

30. See, for example, Donald J. Trump, "The Inaugural Address," January 20, 2017, www.whitehouse.gov/briefings-statements/the-inaugural-address/. On how rich countries have come to use narratives of poverty and victimhood to their own advantage, see Amrita Narlikar, *Poverty Narratives and Power Paradoxes in International Trade Negotiations and Beyond* (Cambridge University Press, 2020).

31. This reconfirms Daniel Drezner's suggestion (see chapter 1 in this volume) that WI is easy to deploy against allies as well as adversaries.

32. See, for example, Xi Jinping, "Work Together to Build the Silk Road Economic Belt and the 21st Century Maritime Silk Road," speech at the opening of the Belt and Road Forum for International Cooperation, May 14, 2017, http://na.china-embassy.org/eng/sgxw/t1461872.htm.

33. See, for example, Xi Jinping, "President Xi's Speech to Davos in Full," World Economic Forum, January 17, 2017, www.weforum.org/agenda /2017/01/full-text-of-xi-jinping-keynote-at-the-world-economic-forum/.

34. President of Malaysia, quoted in Lucy Hornby, "Mahathir Mohamad Warns against 'New Colonialism' During China Visit," *Financial Times*, August 20, 2018, www.ft.com/content/7566599e-a443-11e8-8ecf-a7ae1beff35b.

35. Brahma Chellaney, "Belt and Roadblocks: India's Stance Vindicated as China's Grandiose BRI Plans Run into Resistance," *Times of India* blog, October 29, 2018, https://timesofindia.indiatimes.com/blogs/toi-edit-page/ belt-and-roadblocks-indias-stance-vindicated-as-chinas-grandiose-bri-plans -run-into-resistance/.

36. See, for example, Samuel M. Goodman, Dan Kim, and John VerWey, "The South Korea-Japan Trade Dispute in Context: Semiconductor Manufacturing, Chemicals, and Concentrated Supply Chains," Office of Industries working paper ID-062, U.S. International Trade Commission, October 2019, https://usitc.gov/publications/332/working_papers/the_south _korea-japan_trade_dispute_in_context_semiconductor_manufacturing_ chemicals_and_concentrated_supply_chains.pdf.

17

Weaponized Interdependence and Networked Coercion

A Research Agenda

HENRY FARRELL

ABRAHAM L. NEWMAN

When we initially wrote our article on weaponized interdependence, we hoped that it would help people think more clearly about how economic coercion was changing. We did not anticipate either the reception that the argument has gotten or how dramatically the changes that we wanted to understand would accelerate, thanks to factors including the deterioration of relations between the United States and China, the eagerness of the Donald Trump administration to deploy coercion where it could, and contestation over global supply chains in the wake of the COVID-19 pandemic.

As these unfold, we expect that globalization will become more politicized, and the subject of greater contestation and coercion than it has in recent years. This will inevitably lead to new debates on how globalization and interstate contention are transforming each other.

This volume is an initial down payment on these debates, bringing together an extraordinary group of scholars and experts to think about weaponized interdependence. It is a privilege to have our ideas exposed to this kind of useful, critical engagement. Elaborating on this debate, the conclusion lays out a pathway forward for future research. First, however, we want to clear up what we think weaponized interdependence does and does not do, what its strengths are, and where its limitations lie. Already, the term *weaponized interdependence* is escaping from our original meaning, to refer to a multitude of different forms of what some have called geoeconomics.[1] To avoid conceptual stretching, we want to situate weaponized interdependence more precisely in previous debates and to explain how it differs from, and relates to, other kinds of influence strategies.

When we started thinking about weaponized interdependence, we wanted to characterize more precisely emerging forms of economic coercion based in the network structures that comprise globalization. These included the U.S. Treasury's use of secondary sanctions against Iran, the secret National Security Agency (NSA) programs revealed by Edward Snowden, and the use of the Society for Worldwide Interbank Financial Telecommunications (SWIFT) messaging system to exclude or monitor adversaries. All of these relied on the often-overlooked technical infrastructures of economic exchange—dollar clearing, fiber-optic cables, and messaging systems.

These forms of coercion had been debated by policymakers and policy intellectuals[2] but only fitfully by academics,[3] because they did not fit easily within the frames offered by the scholarly literature. Traditional economic sanctions rested on the denial of access to domestic markets. New forms of sanctioning instead involved the denial of access to the networks that underpinned the global economy. Surveillance, too, was ever less about tailored operations against high-value targets and ever more about bulk surveillance that gathered vast amounts of data from global networks, winnowing it post hoc for useful information. These forms of networked coercion and surveillance were clearly empirically important—but they fit awkwardly with existing international relations perspectives. Many international political economy scholars, in particular, tended to view such networks through the lens of efficiency and market making rather than control. The relevant research, then, was scattered across a number of different debates, making it harder to draw out common themes and organize scholarship.

To explain weaponized interdependence, we have tried to bring three literatures in international relations together into closer conversation with each other. First, much of the existing literature on economic coercion set out to explain when sanctions and related tools were effective. Robert Pape, among others, had claimed that economic sanctions did not work, leading to a vigorous debate in which scholars sought to understand when specific kinds of sanctions might or might not be effective, and how expectations might lead to them having consequences even in cases where they were not actually deployed.[4] A parallel literature on currency regimes examined how dominant states could use currencies to "entrap" other states, with a particular focus on how the post–World War II Western system had entangled monetary and military affairs.[5]

Some of this scholarship looked to broader work on economic interdependence.[6] However, in general, it paid less attention to the technical networks (such as supply chains, the internet, and the dollar clearing system) that facilitated interdependent relations.[7] This literature focused more on the domestic costs of coercion, and the relationship between effective coercion and alliance politics. As global networks started to underpin economic coercion, the result was an increasing disjuncture between the academic and the policy literature.[8]

A second literature set out to understand the relationship between increased economic interdependence and coercion. On the one hand, scholars asked whether increased economic interdependence made war more or less likely.[9] On the other, they investigated how asymmetric interdependence—in which one state was less dependent on another in a bilateral relationship—or trade policy might induce economic dependence.[10] One logic suggested that as states become increasingly economically interpenetrated, war would make less sense, while the other implied that increased interpenetration might make other forms of coercion more attractive.

Again, this literature reached valuable findings. However, it primarily focused on dyadic relations between states and only very gradually has come to consider whether broader network effects might have consequences.[11]

A final literature has been concerned with networks from the beginning. It asked how network structure and topology affected a variety of different phenomena in international relations, including diffusion, international organizations, and humanitarian networks.[12] Building on the sociological scholarship on networks, one group of scholars examined how network nodes that were central, or that played a bridging role across "structural holes," could play an especially important role in networks.[13] Here, the focus was very often on mapping out the key nodes in a given network and understanding influence relations. Another group—most prominently, Thomas Oatley and his colleagues—built on a different network literature derived from statistical scholarship on the topology of large-scale networks, and the origins and consequences of networks with highly skewed distribution of degree.[14] Here, the impetus of scholarship was to understand how these networks arose in the first place, how they propagated shocks, and how robust they were. The primary focus was on how networks acted to channel influence, persuasive power, shocks, and resources, rather than to examine how they might reshape coercion.

Thus, our goal in writing about weaponized interdependence is twofold: to explain an important new empirical phenomenon, and to bring together valuable insights from these different debates. Coercion is both important and increasingly difficult to understand without paying attention to the networks that often enable it. Interdependence affects the power of states not simply through bilateral ties and relationships, but through the larger network structures that it entails. The obverse is true as well—understanding network power today means not just paying attention to diffusion, but also examining how networks have restructured interdependence (so that states depend on each other in ways that would have been inconceivable a few decades ago) and how this enables different forms of coercion. Weaponized interdependence explores how some states have used their privileged position in the networks that underpin global interdependence to achieve coercive outcomes, whether by seizing strategically valuable information that would otherwise be unavailable, or by denying other states access to the network.

Weaponized Interdependence as Network-Based State Coercion

The above reflects our own understanding of weaponized interdependence. As often happens with new concepts, it has quickly been adapted and stretched as scholars apply it to new empirical puzzles and theoretical questions. It is rare that a concept takes off without such stretching; the street finds its own uses for things, regardless of the intentions of those things' originators. This is healthy up to a point, but it can also lead to confusion.

To understand weaponized interdependence, it is useful to distinguish between enabling conditions and the actions that are enabled. Weaponized interdependence is not a historic universal. It depends on a specific structural condition—the presence of essential globalized networks that create high levels of interdependence among states. Looking for previous instances of weaponized interdependence, the most plausible parallels are from the last great era of globalized markets and communications at the beginning of the twentieth century.[15] This suggests an important future research agenda—better understanding how the ebb and flow of global connectivity are related to state coercion strategies, causing them to change and perhaps sometimes changing in response to the threat of coercion.

More specifically, these parallels suggest that we need to pay attention to the structural geography of the world order, mapping the topologies of the networks that shape it. The image of globalization as global competition, an increasingly flat world in which everyone plays on the same level playing field, is seductive but dangerously misleading. Networks have their own geographies, which are the consequence of physical geography, investment decisions, and the strategic deployment of state power. Initially contingent decisions about railroad networks gave Chicago a self-reinforcing advantage in the nineteenth-century economy, for example.[16] The topology of globalized networks has advantaged the United States in the twenty-first century, but in far more political ways. The conditions for weaponized interdependence are satisfied when economic networks are heavily asymmetric, so that they are effectively dominated by hubs (that is, highly connected nodes), and when state actors with coercive power have the appropriate institutional capacities to seize upon these hubs.

The actions enabled by weaponized interdependence involve a quite specific kind of economic coercion. To state our definition more succinctly, weaponized interdependence is states' use of global economic networks to achieve geostrategic objectives. This distinguishes it from the other forms of economic coercion that states employ.

The distinction can readily be seen if we organize the different forms of economic coercion available to states along two dimensions—the target of coercion and the channel through which pressure is applied. We can reasonably distinguish between two targets of coercion— political actors (states, terrorists, or other political adversaries) and economic actors. Equally, we can distinguish between coercion that rests on influence over global networks and coercion based on bilateral pressure. This allows us to construct a 2x2 table that provides a simple heuristic for distinguishing different forms of coercion from each other (although, as with all such heuristics, there will inevitably be borderline and hybrid cases that are difficult to categorize) (figure 17-1).

The top-left quadrant involves state action against other states or geopolitical adversaries through bilateral channels. Such action is possible because of bilateral dependence: the targeted state or adversary in some way depends on access to the targeting state's economy, making it vulnerable to a variety of forms of economic coercion,

FIGURE 17-1

Varieties of Economic Coercion:
What Weaponized Interdependence Is and Is Not

		Target	
		States/Adversaries	Economic Actors
Channel	Bilateral	*Asymmetric interdependence (Traditional sanctions)*	*Market power (Market access restriction)*
	Network	*Weaponized interdependence (Choke point/Panopticon)*	*Points of control (Payment system restrictions)*

which we label asymmetric interdependence. The classic study of this form of coercion in the academic literature on interdependence is Albert Hirschman's early examination of how Nazi Germany deployed asymmetric economic relations in Eastern Europe to assert its dominance.[17] Robert Keohane and Joseph Nye argue that asymmetric bilateral relations play a crucial role in the politics of complex interdependence.[18] Such asymmetric interdependence is what enables forms of economic coercion such as National Security Tariffs and traditional sanctions.

The top-right quadrant, which we label market power, involves the bilateral use of economic interdependence for economic rather than political ends, targeting economic actors such as firms. States with large markets often condition access to their markets on compliance with rules or standards. This, in turn, may reshape the behavior of foreign businesses, perhaps with broader consequences for the global economy, as David Vogel argues.[19] Both the United States and the European Union (EU) have done this to externalize their domestic regulations.[20]

We label the bottom-right quadrant as involving points of control, building on a broad literature in technology studies (see also Natasha Tusikov's chapter in this volume). This quadrant includes networked rather than bilateral actions against firms. States can restrict businesses' or private actors' access to global economic networks. The U.S. government, for example, has employed its influence over payment systems, like credit card providers Visa and Mastercard, to suppress unwanted economic activity in third-party jurisdictions. It has used these means to suppress internet gambling and generic drug sales. In other words, states use choke points in global networks to shape business activity.[21]

The final quadrant is where weaponized interdependence is situated. Like asymmetric interdependence, weaponized interdependence involves the targeting of states and geostrategic adversaries. Like points of control, it involves the use of networks rather than market access. Equally, it differs from asymmetric interdependence in that weaponized interdependence involves the use of networks rather than bilateral market access, and from points of control in that its final targets are political rather than commercial actors.

As we discussed in our original article, powerful states can limit access to global networks through choke-point strategies, thereby dramatically raising the cost that targets would have to bear for noncompliance. So, for instance, states do not simply limit domestic market access but access to the entire network. Alternatively, powerful states can tap into the information flowing through key economic hubs as part of panopticon strategies, monitoring the activity of their adversaries. Such coercion couples private economic network reach with state strategies.

This allows us to understand both what weaponized interdependence is and what it is not. This typology also captures some important nuances in the new politics of economic coercion. For example, one of the key features of economic contention between the United States and China is that the United States is capable of deploying weaponized interdependence because of its control of the key networks of globalization, while China (which was not fully integrated into the global economy when these networks were created) is not. Instead, China often relies on asymmetric interdependence or market power as it deals with U.S. coercion. This typology, then, helps to explain the strategies and tactics of both sides. It allows us to think about the relative trade-offs of the two strategies. Are there conditions, for example, under which bilateral interdependent relations may be more inelastic than networked relations, so it is more difficult for a state to escape particular relations with a country on which it depends than to escape relations that depend on global networks? Plausibly, the answer to this question will be different depending on the relative importance of bilateral exchange vis-à-vis global networks, which has varied significantly over recent history.

Advancing Research on Weaponized Interdependence

As should be clear from the above, we wrote our initial article to set out some core claims as to how states behave in the context of particular economic network structures. We also wrote it in the hope that it might get people thinking, arguing, and disagreeing in new ways. We are extraordinarily grateful for the pushback as well as the praise. Our article was limited in what it could cover, both by word length and by our own limitations. Now that others have had the chance to point out the limitations of our initial research, we can begin to start thinking more systematically about the future research agenda. Building on the contributions to this edited volume, below are our ideas as to what this agenda might involve.

From Static Model to Dynamic Model

Our original article described a specific period in time, explaining the structural conditions of globalization in the 2000s and how they allowed some powerful states to undertake actions that had previously been hard. While we do discuss possible counterstrategies against weaponized interdependence at the end of the article, Bruce Jentleson is right to say that the article's presentation of weaponized interdependence is largely static and not interactive enough. Moving to a broader agenda will necessarily involve building a more dynamic model. We suggested in the article that the network structures that allow weaponized interdependence can change over the longer term. Now, we need to start thinking about the likely mechanisms through which they could change.

More specifically, we need to explore how network structures might be changed or undermined by actors who are disadvantaged by current forms of weaponized interdependence. These actors might be states. Stacie Goddard provides a comprehensive brief account of how revisionist states may look to turn existing networks to their own uses. Harold James also explains how powers can covertly use the international monetary system for their own advantage in times of ferment or when the system is so complex as to be poorly understood. Thomas Cavanna's description of China's Belt and Road strategy, not as a form of weaponized interdependence in itself but as an effort to mitigate the risks of U.S. action, offers a concrete example of what resistance strategies might involve. Adam Segal provides a detailed account of how China has sought to encourage its own technology industry to insulate itself against U.S. measures designed to deprive it of access to sophisticated semiconductors.

The European Union, too, is trying to insulate itself against U.S. financial dominance. Across the chapters, a range of response strategies are presented, from insulating against future aggression by creating alternative arrangements such as the Instrument for Supporting Trade Exchanges (INSTEX), described in Oatley's chapter, to possible bandwagoning with powerful states, as in Amrita Narlikar's description of strategies by the global south. Each of these examples not only tells us how states may respond to specific instances of weaponization, but also suggest mechanisms through which the network may evolve over time.

It is also possible that other states might themselves seek to build competitor hubs to weaponize interdependence or, alternatively, to exploit asymmetric interdependence, by themselves using choke points or selectively denying access to their home markets. The EU, for example, would like to make the euro into an internationally dominant currency, although Europe would have to radically transform itself to do this. China, which has little ability to use weaponized interdependence, frequently employs asymmetric interdependence against other states, threatening to deny market access to their firms if they take political decisions that the Chinese government does not like. As Tusikov notes, it also employs market power against foreign firms.

However, these strategies may run into difficulties. Mikhail Krutikhin describes the problems that Russia has encountered in trying to use Europe's dependence on Russian gas, while Narlikar's example of India temporarily leveraging control over hydroxychloroquine supplies suggests the limits of such strategies.

More broadly, we can reasonably speculate that weaponized interdependence will only be successful in the medium term where network structures are robust and self-reinforcing, regardless of what states do in response. At one end, the dominance of the U.S. dollar appears to rely on robust networks that are difficult for adversaries to displace or defect from, however much they want to. Events like domestic protests in Hong Kong and the Brexit decision underscore how a state's ability to construct competitor hubs may be thwarted by internal domestic political complications. We can guess that it will be hard (though not impossible) for China, in the middle of the spectrum of difficulty, to build a truly independent technology industry, which is why the United States has been tempted to try to hamper the rise of Huawei and a state it sees as an adversary. Such efforts will be further complicated by the blurring of the relationship between the state and firms within the Chinese political economy, where foreign firms and governments might both be wary of relying on networks that have close ties to the state. However, it would not be difficult for pharmaceutical companies in many countries to start producing hydroxychloroquine or for other businesses to produce many other basic components in supply chains, in the event that these products are essential and that other states try to choke off access. In other words, the ease with which states can substitute key economic hubs will influence the long-term viability of weaponized interdependence strategies.

The other important actors are firms. Our original theory did not provide any real independent agency to businesses, treating them as the passive transmitters of state policy. As weaponized interdependence becomes a broader research agenda, it will be critical to think about what happens when this assumption is relaxed. As Jentleson says, U.S. businesses often act in ways that undercut U.S. foreign policy. Sarah Bauerle Danzman rightly notes that this imposes limits on the ability to weaponize interdependence: if the United States goes too far, firms are likely to push back. This was most certainly the case after the United States put Huawei on the entity list, as U.S. semiconductor firms feared that they would lose a major customer. As Michael Mastanduno notes, the Trump administration has often deployed the tools of weaponized interdependence in crude and over-reaching ways. This is likely to provoke pushback among firms and efforts by businesses to limit their exposure to U.S. jurisdiction so as to mitigate risks. In particular, we expect that the legitimacy of targeting particular adversaries will affect firm decisions. Targeting terrorists after 9/11, firms had few options but to cooperate with U.S. government requests for data. A decade later, Apple and Google have rolled out encryption systems that make it much more difficult for the companies to comply with government surveillance requests. They were able to do this, in part, because consumer beliefs about threats had changed. At this point, we have only anecdotal evidence about the creative ways in which businesses respond to compliance, but we know enough to be sure that these firm strategies are important.

Networks Vary and Interact

A second key challenge is mapping out the relevant networks and understanding how they interact with each other. Globalization does not have one uniform structure but is comprised of many subnetworks, which differ in terms of their relative levels of concentration and asymmetry. James points to how such variations in the complexity of networks is likely to influence contention. The current fight between the United States and China over 5G communications networks reflects U.S. fears that the Chinese telecommunications giant Huawei might give the Chinese government an unprecedented level of influence over global internet communications as wireless connections become increasingly ubiquitous. As Segal notes, the United States is using weaponized interdependence to prevent China from weaponizing interdependence, limiting Huawei's access to sophisticated semiconductors.

This battle is a particularly interesting one. China faces challenges in persuading other countries to use Huawei technology, not only because of American pressure and China's government, but also because countries may be less willing than before to depend on networks that may later be used against them. It will be interesting to see how the clash plays out between commercial logic (industry sources agree that Huawei equipment is generally cheaper and better than its competitors) and the logic of security (Huawei's murky relationship with a Chinese government that has enthusiastically used economic coercion for political purposes in the past).

Yet, really understanding this and other disputes requires understanding how the relevant networks operate. At the moment, there is some data available on global financial relationships, albeit there is far less research on networks such as SWIFT and the network mechanics underlying the dollar clearing system than their importance would justify.[22] The lack of such data makes it hard to understand crucial relationships. Oatley notes both the centrality of the United States in the global financial system, and the possibility that states will turn to alternative payment systems if the United States abuses its centrality too much. Really assessing these possibilities would require a detailed level of information on payment networks that is not currently available. There is even less information on the workings of many critical global supply chains. Of course, as James points out, information asymmetries about how networks actually operate are at the heart of the covert advantages they give to some states and not to others.[23]

Equally important is the need to better understand how different networks intersect with each other, driving new strategies of contention and economic coercion. Goddard points out that economic networks may interact with other political networks, while Emily Meierding explains how there are distinct networks for products and finance within the energy domain. Again, we know that these interaction effects are crucially important. When states get them right, they can achieve unexpected effects, and when they get them wrong, their actions can have serious repercussion, as was visible when U.S. efforts to sanction the Russian aluminum giant Rusal gravely affected Western European car manufacturing. Yet, the data on network interactions is at best sporadic, and at worst impressionistic.

Weaponized Interdependence Poses Policy Challenges

All of this is important to policymakers as well as scholars. The debate in the United States is straightforward: When should weaponized interdependence be deployed? There are increasing worries that weaponized interdependence is being overused in ways that undermine the economic dominance on which it depends. Mastanduno's chapter provides a masterly discussion of the relationship between hegemony and fear, highlighting how weaponized interdependence can damage relations with allies. Bauerle Danzman explains how the process of the Committee on Foreign Investment in the United States (CFIUS) is relatively restrained because the United States relies on global investment. Florian Bodamer and Kaija Schilde illustrate how weaponizing arms production networks can both hurt supplies to the United States and antagonize allies. And Segal illustrates how crude forms of weaponized interdependence may spur adversaries to develop their own independent technology infrastructures.

Of course, the United States is not the only actor that matters. Narlikar's chapter provides a valuable corrective to U.S.-centric accounts, explaining how countries in the global south are responding to weaponized interdependence. Cavanna and Segal, too, look at how other states are responding, while Oatley explains why the structural characteristics of global finance render some forms of opposition improbable. Krutikhin demonstrates how the European Union has counteracted Russian attempts at weaponized interdependence. Charli Carpenter reveals how global civil society can use "reverse panopticon" effects on key nodal actors.

Governments across the world will have to invest in new bureaucratic resources to understand how global economic networks function and integrate those efforts into national security structures.[24] The networks of globalization are complex and opaque. Using weaponized interdependence without a map risks miscalculations and errors. Governments will then have to figure out how to conduct the necessary analysis, building up and coordinating specialized agencies.

Yet, many of the problems of weaponized interdependence cannot be solved by national policies in isolation from each other. As argued elsewhere, this is a historical moment that in some ways resembles the beginning of the Cold War.[25] States have suddenly realized that they are far more vulnerable to each other than they were before, and they are now trying to figure out what to do next. As Mastanduno suggests, this may easily lead to offense-defense spirals. Businesses, too, have come to realize that political risk does not simply come from kleptocracies that might seize their assets, but from core countries in the global system pressing them into conflict as unwilling proxies.[26] Citizens and individuals are liable to be the casualties in a world where, as Rosa Brooks describes it, war has become everything, so that everyday commercial and technical systems are the subject of international contention.[27] And all this is happening in a world where external changes—global warming, coronavirus, and other threats that are only beginning to emerge—may act as potential fuel to conflict.

It is easy to fear that we are accelerating into one of the dystopian futures described by science-fiction writers such as William Gibson, where external accelerants and political dysfunction feed upon each other.[28] Yet, it is also possible to see how some of the threats of weaponized interdependence can be mitigated by arriving at common rules of the road. For example, the risk of offense-defense spirals identified by Mastanduno could be mitigated if central states such as the United States recognize that it will sometimes be legitimate for other states to insulate themselves against U.S. power or to build their own networks for defensive purposes.[29]

Weaponized interdependence, then, should be seen as a tool to achieve an objective rather than an end in and of itself. Policymakers face many of the same kinds of trade-offs as they have with other forms of economic coercion. What are the risks of retaliation? What is proportional use? When should coercion end? Haphazard pressure with no clear strategy will generate the types of fear that Mastanduno warns us of. One could imagine a set of objectives—mitigating climate change or preventing tax evasion—that could generate broad coalitions in support of using weaponized interdependence. Equally, deploying weaponized interdependence against other great powers is likely to be very dangerous. While weaponized interdependence is ultimately a unilateral tool of coercion, the more that states can build multilateral support and legitimacy for its use, the better they will be able to maintain pressure and achieve their goals.

Building shared understandings—let alone common rules—presents some extraordinary challenges. Yet, it is far less risky than the two alternatives: assuming weaponized interdependence can continue as before or the problems of weaponized interdependence can be mitigated purely through self-help. The first alternative is a recipe for overreach, as Mastanduno, Oatley, and others in this volume recognize, and for a continued deterioration in economic relations. The second implies a large-scale unraveling of interdependent relations at a time when global problems loom larger than they ever have before.

Perhaps the greatest challenge, then, is not in understanding weaponized interdependence on its own terms, how it fits with other forms of economic coercion, or how it will affect power relations among states. It is fitting it together with the other aspects of interdependence that we have to live with in a world where our fates are increasingly intertwined. Environmental interdependence, energy interdependence, interdependence in dealing with pandemics and other health threats: all of these are important and all, in one way or another, can be weaponized. Our challenge is figuring out how best to close, mitigate, or live with vulnerabilities while continuing to cooperate in those many areas where cooperation is essential.

Notes

We are grateful to the contributors to this volume, and owe a particular debt of gratitude to Dan Drezner for the idea of bringing together a group of scholars and practitioners to think about weaponized interdependence at a meeting in the Fletcher School on October 10–11, 2019, which ultimately led to this edited book.

1. Mark Leonard, "Geo-economics: Seven challenges to globalization," in *World Economic Forum* (2015), pp. 1–16; Anthea Roberts, Henrique Choer Moraes, and Victor Ferguson. "Toward a Geoeconomic Order in International Trade and Investment," *Journal of International Economic Law* 22 (2019), pp. 655–76.

2. Stewart Baker, *Skating on Stilts: Why We Aren't Stopping Tomorrow's Terrorism* (Stanford: Hoover Institution Press, 2010); Juan Zarate, *Treasury's War: The Unleashing of a New Era of Financial Warfare* (London: Hachette UK, 2013); Peter Harrell and Elizabeth Rosenberg, *Economic Dominance, Financial Technology, and the Future of U.S. Economic Coercion* (Washington: Center for New American Security, 2019).

3. For an important early intervention, see Thomas Wright, *All Measures Short of War: The Contest for the Twenty-First Century and the Future of American Power* (Yale University Press, 2017).

4. See, for example, Lisa L. Martin, *Coercive Cooperation: Explaining Multilateral Sanctions* (Princeton University Press, 1992); Robert A. Pape, "Why Economic Sanctions Do Not Work," *International Security* 22 (1997), pp. 90–136; Daniel W. Drezner, *The Sanctions Paradox* (Cambridge University Press, 1999); Nicholas L. Miller, "The Secret Success of Nonproliferation Sanctions," *International Organization* 68 (2014), pp. 913–44. As with the other literatures we briefly describe, we offer only a small sample of a few particularly influential works in a very extensive debate.

5. Francis J. Gavin, *Gold, Dollars and Power: The Politics of International Monetary Relations, 1958-1971* (The University of North Carolina Press, 2004); Jonathan Kirshner, *Currency and Coercion: The Political Economy of International Monetary Power* (Princeton University Press, 1995); Carla Norrlof, "Dollar Hegemony: A Power Analysis," *Review of International Political Economy* 21 (September 2014), pp. 1042–70.

6. Bruce W. Jentleson, *Pipeline Politics: The Complex Political Economy of East-West Energy Trade* (Cornell University Press, 1986).

7. For a recent exception, see Bryan R. Early and Keith A. Preble, "Going Fishing Versus Hunting Whales: Explaining Changes in How the U.S. Enforces Economic Sanctions," *Security Studies* 29 (2020), pp. 231–67.

8. Elizabeth Rosenberg and others, *The New Tools of Economic Warfare: Effects and Effectiveness of Contemporary U.S. Financial Sanctions* (Washington: Center for a New American Security, 2016).

9. Katherine Barbieri, "Economic Interdependence: A Path to Peace or a Source of Interstate Conflict," *Journal of Peace Research* 33 (February 1996), pp. 29–49; Erik Gartzke, Quan Li, and Charles Boehmer, "Investing in the Peace: Economic Interdependence and International Conflict," *International Organization* 55 (2001), pp. 391–438; Dale C. Copeland, "Economic Interdependence and War: A Theory of Trade Expectations," *International Security* 20 (1996), pp. 5–41.

10. Robert O. Keohane and Joseph S. Nye Jr., *Power and Interdependence: World Politics in Transition* (New York: Little, Brown, 1977); Albert O. Hirschman, *National Power and the Structure of Foreign Trade* (University of California Press, 1945); Lloyd Gruber, *Ruling the World: Power Politics and the Rise of Supranational Institutions* (Princeton University Press, 2000).

11. Han Dorussen, Erik A. Gartzke, and Oliver Westerwinter, "Networked International Politics: Complex Interdependence and the Diffusion of Conflict and Peace," *Journal of Peace Research* 53 (2016), pp. 283–91.

12. Frank Dobbin, Beth Simmons, and Geoffrey Garrett, "The Global Diffusion of Public Policies: Social Construction, Coercion, Competition, or Learning?" *Annual Review of Sociology* 33 (2007), pp. 449–72; Charli Carpenter and others, "Explaining the Advocacy Agenda: Insights from the Human Security Network," *International Organization* 449 (2014), pp. 449–70; Paul Ingram, Jeffrey Robinson, and Marc Busch, "The Intergovernmental Network of World Trade: IGO Connectedness, Governance and Embeddedness," *American Journal of Sociology* 11 (2005), pp. 824–58.

13. Emilie M. Hafner-Burton, Miles Kahler, and Alexander H. Montgomery, "Network Analysis for International Relations," *International Organization* 63 (2009), pp. 559–92.

14. Thomas Oatley and others, "The Political Economy of Global Finance: A Network Model," *Perspectives on Politics* 11 (2013), pp. 133–53.

15. Nicholas A. Lambert, *Planning Armageddon* (Harvard University Press, 2012).

16. William Cronon, *Nature's Metropolis: Chicago and the Great West* (New York: W.W. Norton, 1992).

17. Albert O. Hirschman, *National Power and the Structure of Foreign Trade* (University of California Press, 1980).

18. Keohane and Nye Jr., *Power and Interdependence.*

19. David Vogel, *Trading Up: Consumer and Environmental Regulation in a Global Economy* (Harvard University Press, 2009).

20. Beth A. Simmons, "The International Politics of Harmonization: The Case of Capital Market Regulation," *International Organization* 55 (2001), pp. 589–620; David Bach and Abraham L. Newman, "The European Regulatory State and Global Public Policy: Micro-Institutions, Macro-Influence," *Journal of European Public Policy* 14 (2007), pp. 827–46; Daniel W. Drezner, *All Politics is Global: Explaining International Regulatory Regimes* (Princeton University Press, 2007); Nikhil Kalyanpur and Abraham L. Newman, "Mobilizing Market Power: Jurisdictional Expansion as Economic Statecraft," *International Organization* 73 (2019), pp. 1–34.

21. Henry Farrell, "Regulating Information Flows: States, Private Actors, and E-Commerce," *Annual Review of Political Science* 9 (2006), pp. 353–74; Kathryn Judge, "Intermediary Influence," *University of Chicago Law Review* 82 (2015), p. 573; Natasha Tusikov, *Chokepoints: Global Private Regulation on the Internet* (University of California Press, 2016).

22. Jennifer A. Jeffs, "The Politics of Financial Plumbing: Harmonization and Interests in the Construction of the International Payment System," *Review of International Political Economy* 15 (2008), pp. 259–88; Nick Bernards and Malcolm Campbell-Verduyn, "Understanding Technological Change in Global Finance Through Infrastructures" *Review of International Political Economy* 26 (2019), pp. 773–89.

23. Henry Farrell and Abraham L. Newman, "The Folly of Decoupling from China," *Foreign Affairs*, June 3, 2020.

24. Ibid.

25. Henry Farrell and Abraham L. Newman, "Chained to Globalization: Why It's Too Late to Decouple," *Foreign Affairs* 99 (2020), p. 70.

26. Henry Farrell and Abraham L. Newman, "Choke Points: Countries Are Turning Economic Infrastructure into Political Weapons, and That Poses a Major Risk to Business," *Harvard Business Review* 98 (1), 124–31.

27. Rosa Brooks, *How Everything Became War and the Military Became Everything: Tales from the Pentagon*, (New York: Simon & Schuster, 2016).

28. William Gibson, *The Peripheral* (New York: G.P. Putnam's Sons, 2014).

29. Farrell and Newman, "Chained to Globalization," p. 70.

Contributors

FLORIAN DAVID BODAMER is a PhD student at Boston University's Department of Political Science, focusing on international relations and comparative politics. His main research interests are at the intersection of political economy and security in defense industries, primarily in advanced industrialized economies. Taking a comparative political economy approach, he studies state interactions with business and industry interest groups, variation in industrial policies, arms exports, defense industry globalization, and domestic procurement patterns and defense spending, as well as how alliances shape these developments.

CHARLI CARPENTER is professor in the Department of Political Science and Legal Studies at the University of Massachusetts-Amherst, specializing in international law and human security. She is the author of three books and numerous articles on human rights and the laws of war, and has consulted for the UN, State Department, Department of Defense, and human rights NGOs. Her writings appear in the *New York Times, Washington Post, Foreign Affairs, Foreign Policy, World Politics Review,* and *The American Prospect.*

THOMAS P. CAVANNA is an assistant research professor at the Fletcher School of Law and Diplomacy at Tufts University. He has published in the *Texas National Security Review*, the *Journal of Strategic Studies*, and the *Oxford Research Encyclopedias*, among other publications. He is writing a book on China's rise and U.S. grand strategy. He holds a French "agregation," an MA and PhD in history from Sciences Po, and an MA from Audencia Business School. He was also a Fox Fellow at Yale University.

SARAH BAUERLE DANZMAN is an assistant professor of international studies at the Hamilton Lugar School of Global and International Studies at Indiana University Bloomington. Her research examines the politics of global investment and multinational production, the nexus of national security and foreign investment policy, and how global business accrues and uses political power. She is the author of *Merging Interests: When Domestic Firms Shape FDI Policy* (2019), and her research has appeared in various outlets, including *International Studies Quarterly*, *Perspectives of Politics*, and *Business and Politics*. In 2019–2020, she was an international affairs fellow at the Council on Foreign Relations, working in the U.S. State Department's Office of Investment Affairs on matters related to investment screening and security.

DANIEL W. DREZNER is professor of international politics at the Fletcher School of Law and Diplomacy at Tufts University, a nonresident senior fellow at the Brookings Institution, and a regular contributor to the *Washington Post*. Prior to Fletcher, he taught at the University of Chicago and the University of Colorado at Boulder. He has previously held positions with Civic Education Project, the RAND Corporation, and the U.S. Department of the Treasury. He has written seven books, including *All Politics Is Global*, and edited two others, including *Avoiding Trivia*. He has published articles in numerous scholarly journals as well as in the *New York Times*, *Wall Street Journal*, and *Foreign Affairs,* and has been a contributing editor for *Foreign Policy* and *The National Interest*. He received his BA in political economy from Williams College and an MA in economics and PhD in political science from Stanford University.

HENRY FARRELL is SNF Agora Institute Professor of International Affairs at the Johns Hopkins School of Advanced International Studies, 2019 winner of the Friedrich Schiedel Prize for Politics and Technology, and editor in chief of the *Monkey Cage* blog at the *Washington Post*. His first book, *The Political Economy of Trust: Interests, Institutions, and Inter-Firm Cooperation*, was published in 2009. His second book (with Abraham Newman), *Of Privacy and Power: The Transatlantic Fight over Freedom and Security*, published in 2019 and was awarded the 2019 Chicago-Kent College of Law/Roy C. Palmer Civil Liberties Prize, the ISA-ICOMM Best Book Award, and a Foreign Affairs Best Book of 2019. In addition, he has authored or co-authored thirty-four academic articles, as well as numerous nonacademic publications. He is a member of the Council on Foreign Relations.

STACIE E. GODDARD is the Mildred Lane Kemper Professor of Political Science and Paula Phillips Bernstein Director of the Madeleine K. Albright Institute at Wellesley College. Her work engages with issues of legitimacy and how they affect power politics. She is the author of *When Right Makes Might: Rising Powers and World Order* (2018) and *Indivisible Territory and the Politics of Legitimacy: Jerusalem and Northern Ireland* (2010).

HAROLD JAMES is the Claude and Lore Kelly Professor in European Studies, director of the Program in Contemporary European Politics and Society, and professor of history and international affairs at the Woodrow Wilson School *of Public and International Affairs* at Princeton University. He writes a monthly column for Project Syndicate. His books include a study of the interwar depression in Germany, *The German Slump* (1986), *International Monetary Cooperation Since Bretton Woods* (1996), and *The End of Globalization* (2001). His most recent books include *Making the European Monetary Union* (2012), *The Euro and the Battle of Economic Ideas* (with Markus K. Brunnermeier and Jean-Pierre Landau) (2016), and *Making a Modern Central Bank: The Bank of England 1979–2003* (2020). He is also the official historian of the International Monetary Fund.

BRUCE W. JENTLESON is William Preston Few Professor of Public Policy and professor of political science at Duke University. He is also a global fellow at the Woodrow Wilson International Center for Scholars, and nonresident senior fellow at the Chicago Council on Global Affairs. In 2015–2016, he was the Henry A. Kissinger Chair in Foreign Policy and International Relations at the John W. Kluge Center, Library of Congress. He received the 2018 American Political Science Association International Security Section Joseph J. Kruzel Award for Distinguished Public Service. His most recent book is *The Peacemakers: Leadership Lessons from Twentieth-Century Statesmanship* (2018). His most recent article is "Refocusing U.S. Grand Strategy on Pandemic and Environmental Mass Destruction," *The Washington Quarterly* (Fall 2020). He has served in a number of policy positions, including senior advisor to the U.S. State Department policy planning director (2009–2011).

MIKHAIL KRUTIKHIN is a co-founder and leading analyst of RusEnergy, an independent consulting agency based in Moscow, Russia. A graduate of the Institute of Oriental Languages at the Moscow Lomonosov State University, he majored in Iranian philology and a PhD in modern history. Between 1972 and 1992, he worked at the TASS news agency on missions to Egypt, Syria, Lebanon, and Iran. Since 1993, he has been analyzing opportunities and specifics of investments in the energy industry in the former USSR, first with the US-based Russian Petroleum Investor, Inc., and then with RusEnergy. His current occupation includes academic lecturing and participation in think tanks, both inside Russia and internationally.

MICHAEL MASTANDUNO is the Nelson A. Rockefeller Professor of Government at Dartmouth and served as Dean of the Arts and Sciences faculty from 2010 through 2017. His articles have appeared in *World Politics, International Organization, International Security, International Studies Quarterly,* and *Security Studies,* among others. He is author of *Economic Containment,* co-author of *International Relations: Perspectives, Connections, and Enduring Questions,* and co-editor of numerous books on international relations theory. He has been a guest faculty member at the University of Tokyo, the Graduate

School of Economics and International Relations at Milan, and the Geneva Center for Security Policy. During the fall term of 2017, he was the inaugural Susan Strange Professor of International Relations at the London School of Economics.

EMILY MEIERDING is an assistant professor of National Security Affairs at the Naval Postgraduate School. Her research examines conflict and cooperation over energy and environmental resources. Her book, *The Oil Wars Myth: Petroleum and the Causes of International Conflict* (2020) finds that competition over oil and natural gas resources is a far less common cause of international aggression than most people assume. She has published articles in *Security Studies*, *International Studies Review, Energy Research & Social Science*, and *Foreign Policy*.

AMRITA NARLIKAR is president of the German Institute for Global and Area Studies (GIGA), professor at Hamburg University, and nonresident senior fellow at the Observer Research Foundation. Prior to moving to Hamburg, she held the position of Reader in International Political Economy at the University of Cambridge and a fellowship at Darwin College. She was also senior research associate at the Centre for International Studies at the University of Oxford from 2003 to 2014. She is the author or co-author of several books, including *Poverty Narratives and Power Paradoxes in International Trade Negotiations and Beyond* and *Bargaining with a Rising India: Lessons from the Mahabharata.*

ABRAHAM L. NEWMAN is professor in the Edmund A. Walsh School of Foreign Service and the Government Department at Georgetown University. He is the director of the Mortara Center for International Studies. His research focuses on the politics generated by globalization and is the co-author *Of Privacy and Power: The Transatlantic Struggle over Freedom and Security* (2019), which was the winner of the 2019 Chicago-Kent College of Law/Roy C. Palmer Civil Liberties Prize, the 2020 International Studies Association ICOMM Best Book Award, and a Foreign Affairs Best Books of 2019; co-author of *Voluntary Disruptions: International Soft Law, Finance, and*

Power (2018); and author of *Protectors of Privacy: Regulating Personal Data in the Global Economy* (2008). His work has appeared in a range of journals, including *Comparative Political Studies, International Organization, International Security, Science,* and *World Politics.*

THOMAS OATLEY holds the Corasaniti-Zondorak Chair of International Politics at Tulane University. He has authored articles and books that focus on the politics of global finance, American power, and international economic and financial institutions. His current research focuses on the development and operation of socioeconomic and political complexity with a particular focus on the role of information and energy in these processes. He is working on a book that examines the relationship between energy regimes and domestic and international political order. Before moving to New Orleans, he spent more than twenty years at the University of North Carolina at Chapel Hill and held visiting appointments at Harvard University, George Washington University, and the Norwegian University of Science and Technology.

KAIJA E. SCHILDE is an associate professor at the Boston University Pardee School of Global Studies. Her current book manuscript addresses why states outsource the economic "public good" of security to firms and industries. Her first book, *The Political Economy of European Security* (2017), theorizes EU-interest group state-society relations, identifying the political development of security and defense institutions as an outcome of industry interest and mobilization. Her research spans multiple dimensions of comparative national security institutions along the public-private divide. She has published articles in the *Journal of Common Market Studies, Journal of Global Security Studies, Security Studies, European Security,* and the *Journal of Peace Research.* She has a policy background in defense and transatlantic security institutions.

ADAM SEGAL is the Ira A. Lipman Chair in Emerging Technologies and National Security and director of the Digital and Cyberspace Policy program at the Council on Foreign Relations (CFR). An expert on security issues, technology development, and Chinese domestic and foreign policy, he was the project director for the CFR-sponsored Independent Task Force reports "Innovation and National Security: Keeping Our Edge" and "Defending an Open, Global, Secure, and Resilient Internet." His book *The Hacked World Order: How Nations Fight, Trade, Maneuver, and Manipulate in the Digital Age* (2016) describes the increasingly contentious geopolitics of cyberspace. His work has appeared in the *Financial Times, New York Times, Foreign Policy, Wall Street Journal*, and *Foreign Affairs*, among others.

NATASHA TUSIKOV is an assistant professor of criminology at York University in Toronto, a visiting fellow with the School of Regulation and Global Governance (RegNet) at the Australian National University, and a senior fellow at the Center for Global Cooperation Research at the University of Duisburg-Essen, Germany. Her research examines intersections among crime, technology, and regulation. She is the author of *Chokepoints: Global Private Regulation on the Internet* (2017), and the co-editor of *Information, Technology and Control in a Changing World: Understanding Power Structures in the 21st Century* (2019). Prior to her work in academia, she was a strategic criminal intelligence analyst with the Royal Canadian Mounted Police in Ottawa, Canada.

Index

Figures and tables are indicated by *f* and *t* following the page number.